Perspectives on Social Welfare Applications' Optimization and Enhanced Computer Applications

Ponnusamy Sivaram
Department of Artificial Intelligence, G.H. Raisoni College of Engineering, Nagpur, India

S. Senthilkumar
University College of Engineering, BIT Campus, Anna University, Tiruchirappalli, India

Lipika Gupta
Department of Electronics and Communication Engineering, Chitkara University Institute of Engineering and Technology, Chitkara University, India

Nelligere S. Lokesh
Department of CSE–AIML, AMC Engineering College, Bengaluru, India

A volume in the Advances in Web Technologies and Engineering (AWTE) Book Series

Published in the United States of America by
    IGI Global
    Engineering Science Reference (an imprint of IGI Global)
    701 E. Chocolate Avenue
    Hershey PA, USA 17033
    Tel: 717-533-8845
    Fax: 717-533-8661
    E-mail: cust@igi-global.com
    Web site: http://www.igi-global.com

Library of Congress Cataloging-in-Publication Data

Names: Sivaram, Ponnusamy, 1981- editor. | Senthilkumar, S., 1973- editor.
  | Gupta, Lipika, 1980- editor. | Lokesh, Nelligere S., 1983- editor.
Title: Perspectives on social welfare applications' optimization and
  enhanced computer applications / edited by: Ponnusamy Sivaram, S.
  Senthilkumar, Lipika Gupta, and Nelligere S. Lokesh.
Description: Hershey PA : Engineering Science Reference, [2023] | Includes
  bibliographical references. | Summary: "Perspectives on Social Welfare
  Applications' Optimization and Enhanced Computer Applications discusses
  new computer applications and analyzes the existing ones to introduce a
  subsystem of the current system to make the social interactions towards
  digital world initiatives. This book provides a platform for scholars,
  researchers, scientists, and working professionals to exchange and share
  their computer application creation experiences and research results
  about all aspects of application software system development within
  computer science with emerging and advanced technologies. Covering
  topics such as applied computing, data science, and mobile computing,
  this premier reference source is ideal for industry professionals,
  computer scientists, academicians, engineers, researchers, scholars,
  practitioners, librarians, instructors, and students"-- Provided by
  publisher.
Identifiers: LCCN 2022061142 (print) | LCCN 2022061143 (ebook) | ISBN
  9781668483060 (hardcover) | ISBN 9781668483077 (paperback) | ISBN
  9781668483084 (ebook)
Subjects: LCSH: Medicine--Data processing. | Health risk assessment--Data
  processing. | Public health--Data processing.
Classification: LCC R858.A3 P47 2023 (print) | LCC R858.A3 (ebook) | DDC
  610.285--dc23/eng/20230228
LC record available at https://lccn.loc.gov/2022061142
LC ebook record available at https://lccn.loc.gov/2022061143

This book is published in the IGI Global book series Advances in Web Technologies and Engineering (AWTE) (ISSN: 2328-2762; eISSN: 2328-2754)

Advances in Web Technologies and Engineering (AWTE) Book Series

Ghazi I. Alkhatib
The Hashemite University, Jordan
David C. Rine
George Mason University, USA

ISSN:2328-2762
EISSN:2328-2754

MISSION

The **Advances in Web Technologies and Engineering (AWTE) Book Series** aims to provide a platform for research in the area of Information Technology (IT) concepts, tools, methodologies, and ethnography, in the contexts of global communication systems and Web engineered applications. Organizations are continuously overwhelmed by a variety of new information technologies, many are Web based. These new technologies are capitalizing on the widespread use of network and communication technologies for seamless integration of various issues in information and knowledge sharing within and among organizations. This emphasis on integrated approaches is unique to this book series and dictates cross platform and multidisciplinary strategy to research and practice.

The **Advances in Web Technologies and Engineering (AWTE) Book Series** seeks to create a stage where comprehensive publications are distributed for the objective of bettering and expanding the field of web systems, knowledge capture, and communication technologies. The series will provide researchers and practitioners with solutions for improving how technology is utilized for the purpose of a growing awareness of the importance of web applications and engineering.

COVERAGE

- Data and knowledge capture and quality issues
- IT readiness and technology transfer studies
- Web systems performance engineering studies
- Software agent-based applications
- Integrated user profile, provisioning, and context-based processing
- Information filtering and display adaptation techniques for wireless devices
- Quality of service and service level agreement issues among integrated systems
- Web systems engineering design
- Case studies validating Web-based IT solutions
- Data and knowledge validation and verification

IGI Global is currently accepting manuscripts for publication within this series. To submit a proposal for a volume in this series, please contact our Acquisition Editors at Acquisitions@igi-global.com or visit: http://www.igi-global.com/publish/.

Titles in this Series

For a list of additional titles in this series, please visit: www.igi-global.com/book-series

Internet of Behaviors Implementation in Organizationa Contexts

Luísa Cagica Carvalho (Instituto Politécnico de Setúbal, Portugal) Clara Silveira (Polytechnic Institute of Guarda, Portugal) Leonilde Reis (Instituto Politecnico de Setubal, Portugal) and Nelson Russo (Universidade Aberta, Portugal)
Engineering Science Reference • © 2023 • 320pp • H/C (ISBN: 9781668490396) • US $270.00

Advancements in the New World of Web 3 A Look Toward the Decentralized Future

Jane Thomason (UCL London Blockchain Centre, UK) and Elizabeth Ivwurie (British Blockchain and Frontier Technology Association, UK)
Engineering Science Reference • © 2023 • 323pp • H/C (ISBN: 9781668466582) • US $240.00

Supporting Technologies and the Impact of Blockchain on Organizations and Society

Luís Ferreira (Polytechnic Institute of Cávado and Ave, Portugal) Miguel Rosado Cruz (Polytechnic Institute of Viana do Castelo, Portugal) Estrela Ferreira Cruz (Polytechnic Institute of Viana do Castelo, Portugal) Helder Quintela (Polytechnic Institute of Cavado and Ave, Portugal) and Manuela Cruz Cunha (Polytechnic Institute of Cavado and Ave, Portugal)
Engineering Science Reference • © 2023 • 310pp • H/C (ISBN: 9781668457474) • US $270.00

Architectural Framework for Web Development and Micro Distributed Applications

Guillermo Rodriguez (QuantiLogic, USA)
Engineering Science Reference • © 2023 • 268pp • H/C (ISBN: 9781668448496) • US $250.00

Trends, Applications, and Challenges of Chatbot Technology

Mohammad Amin Kuhail (Zayed University, UAE) Bayan Abu Shawar (Al-Ain University, UAE) and Rawad Hammad (University of East London, UK)
Engineering Science Reference • © 2023 • 373pp • H/C (ISBN: 9781668462348) • US $270.00

Strategies and Opportunities for Technology in the Metaverse World

P.C. Lai (University of Malaya, Malaysia)
Engineering Science Reference • © 2023 • 390pp • H/C (ISBN: 9781668457320) • US $270.00

3D Modeling Using Autodesk 3ds Max With Rendering View

Debabrata Samanta (CHRIST University, India)
Engineering Science Reference • © 2022 • 291pp • H/C (ISBN: 9781668441398) • US $270.00

701 East Chocolate Avenue, Hershey, PA 17033, USA
Tel: 717-533-8845 x100 • Fax: 717-533-8661
E-Mail: cust@igi-global.com • www.igi-global.com

To the Almighty, who has supported us with steadfast love and support, our parents, family members, loved ones, mentors, instructors, and moral supporters. For all of you, we dedicate this. Your unwavering affection, acceptance of our promises, and faith in our talents have motivated our efforts.

Editorial Advisory Board

Table of Contents

Chapter 1
R. Srinivasan, Department of Computing Technologies, School of Computing, College of
Engineering and Technology, SRM Institute of Science and Technology, India
Rajeswari D., Department of Data Science and Business Systems, School of Computing,
College of Engineering and Technology, SRM Institute of Science and Technology, India

Chapter 2
Jayavadivel Ravi, Department of Computer Science and Engineering, Alliance University,
Bangalore, India

Chapter 3
Senthilkumar Subramanian, University College of Engineering, BIT Campus, Anna
University, Tiruchirappalli, India
Nithya Venkatachalam, University College of Engineering, Villupuram, Anna University,
India
Regan Rajendran, University College of Engineering, Villupuram, Anna University, India

Chapter 4
Jenifer Mahilraj, Depatment of AI and DS, NPR College of Engineering and Technology,
Natham, India
Josephine Sahaya Vergin, Alagappa University, India
Vidhyavathi Ramasamy, Alagappa University, India
Nooriya Begam, Alagappa University, India
Joseph Sahayarayan, Alagappa University, India

University Institute of Engineering and Technology, Chitkara University, India
Tripti Sharma, Chandigarh University, Punjab, India
Shilpi Birla, Department of Electronics and Communication Engineering, Manipal University, Jaipur, India
Neeraj Kumar, Electrical Engineering Department, College of Engineering, King Khalid University, Abha, Saudi Arabia

Detailed Table of Contents

Chapter 1
A Framework for Classifying Imbalanced Tweets Using Machine Learning Techniques 1
    R. Srinivasan, Department of Computing Technologies, School of Computing, College of
        Engineering and Technology, SRM Institute of Science and Technology, India
    Rajeswari D., Department of Data Science and Business Systems, School of Computing,
        College of Engineering and Technology, SRM Institute of Science and Technology, India

The research work presented focuses on utilizing social media platforms as a source of data to diagnose depression-related issues. The popularity of social platforms such as LinkedIn, Instagram, Twitter, YouTube, and Facebook, gave researchers an opportunity to analyse user experiences and gain insights into depression. Depression is a significant problem that affects individuals' lives, disrupts normal functioning, and impacts their perspectives. The primary objective of this research is to employ machine learning (ML) approaches for classifying tweets. Additionally, the research addresses the issue of data imbalance by using sampling techniques. This research work utilizes a sampling technique to normalize the dataset. The study explores four techniques that helps to extract meaningful information from the tweets. The research work conducts an empirical study to evaluate the performance of various ML techniques. Based on the experimental results, it is found that the AdaBoost classifier with the BoW feature extraction technique achieves the best results among all the classifiers tested.

Chapter 2
A Novel Approach for Predicting COVID-19 Using Machine Learning-Based Logistic Regression
Classification MODEL 18
    Jayavadivel Ravi, Department of Computer Science and Engineering, Alliance University,
        Bangalore, India

Recently, several studies have stated that mild weather can perhaps halt the global epidemic, which has already afflicted over 1.6 million people globally. Clarification of such correlations in the worst affected country, the US, can be extremely valuable to understand the function of weather in transmission of the disease in the highly populated countries, such as India. The authors developed a machine-learning approach as logistic regression classification models that used data from several sources to determine whether a patient is at risk of COVID-19 using one of the classification models with the greatest accuracy. They are working on a model that uses simple features available through basic clinical inquiries to detect COVID-19 patients. When testing resources are tight, their approach can be used to prioritize testing for COVID-19, among other things.

Chapter 3
    Senthilkumar Subramanian, University College of Engineering, BIT Campus, Anna University, Tiruchirappalli, India
    Nithya Venkatachalam, University College of Engineering, Villupuram, Anna University, India
    Regan Rajendran, University College of Engineering, Villupuram, Anna University, India

As the web and applications for knowledge technology developed, many attacks and security problems started to emerge. The last couple of years have seen a significant development in 6G wireless networking. It is challenging to create a secure wireless network. In phishing attacks on wireless networks, attackers create phishing websites that allow users to enter personal information such as usernames, passwords, security numbers, and credit card details. Phishing emails that contain links to websites that are used to spread malware. This project suggests a real time phishing detection plug-in for the web browser which uses a random forest classifier to identify and notify users. As a result, the consumer can get an alert right away. The suggested systems specify wireless phishing attack detection in the current context and produce superior results. The authors proposed 18 traits in order to cover every aspect of phish behavior. With the help of an accepted dataset, the suggested phishing detection system was trained.

Chapter 4
    Jenifer Mahilraj, Depatment of AI and DS, NPR College of Engineering and Technology, Natham, India
    Josephine Sahaya Vergin, Alagappa University, India
    Vidhyavathi Ramasamy, Alagappa University, India
    Nooriya Begam, Alagappa University, India
    Joseph Sahayarayan, Alagappa University, India
    Sivaram Ponnusamy, Department of Artificial Intelligence, G.H. Raisoni College of Engineering, Nagpur, India

Over the past few years India has a significant rise in mobile applications. The development of apps for remote work, education, and healthcare has dramatically increased. Applications for cloud meetings, food delivery, gaming, business, social media, healthcare, and fitness are being downloaded by more users. The prevalence of smart phones, increased internet usage, and the incorporation of artificial intelligence and machine learning into mobile applications all suggest that demand for mobile will continue to increase in the future (apps). The importance of AI and ML in application development will rise over time. The aforementioned software is moreover generally acquired from app store websites like the Google Play Store and the App Store for any mobile OS. This chapter provides mobile intelligent applications (MOB-I App) are used to developing based on a model of AI for the human needs to their day-to-day life of their situation. A brief overview of some of the intelligent applications employed in the fields of medical and agriculture.

Chapter 5

Kswaminathan Kalyanaraman, Department of Electronics and Communication, University
College of Engineering, Pattukkottai, India

In WSN, sensor nodes will be distributed heterogeneity concerning their basic requirements such as location, power backup, and the distance between the nodes. With these metrics, research is carried on energy conservation, media-based problems, packet aggregation, effective routing, quality of link, etc. But the energy consumption and data processing system in WSN makes a scenario for not using an artificial intelligence (AI)-based system in network structure. In this chapter, a heuristic packet routing (HPR) strategy for effective path identification on the packet transmission between the nodes is given. The proposed methodology also improvises the routing process on diffusion and energy management methodology defined in previous research work. A comprehensive study was done with the help of a network simulator. Based on the result, the work is compared with various research work defined previously.

Chapter 6

Sunil Sharma, National Institute of Technology, Kurukshetra, India
Minakshi Sharma, National Institute of Technology, Kurukshetra, India

The high-tech world we live in today is dominated by multimedia. Multimedia is being created at a rapid rate in the current technological era. Consumption and the exchange of the same between users happen quickly. Choosing whatever form of content or multimedia to consume next depending on interests and preferences is a conundrum while consuming this content. Nowadays, all online streaming sites utilize multimedia recommender systems. These are utilized to anticipate the following collection of multimedia that users can enjoy based on their prior usage patterns. By identifying the points of commonality between the user and the goods, preexisting models can forecast this utilizing the collaborative field. By treating this as a sequence prediction problem, the proposed model in this chapter increases the predicted accuracy using collaborative filtering (CF), ripple nets, deep learning, and recurrent neural networks (RNNs).

Chapter 7

Anisha Kumari, National Institute of Technology, Rourkela, India
Manoj Kumar Patra, National Institute of Technology, Rourkela, India
Bibhudatta Sahoo, National Institute of Technology, Rourkela, India

Cloud computing has been the most demanding technology in the last decade, which several organizations have widely adopted. Most enterprise applications and data are migrated to the public or hybrid cloud due to the ease of access and infrastructure facilities provided by the cloud provider. One significant issue in the cloud environment is the security and data controlling mechanism, which needs to be focused on for better service quality. Users usually hesitate to use public cloud services due to privacy and security concerns about the personal data they want to process online. Unlike standard cloud computing notions, serverless computing does not expose the infrastructure or platforms on which the services operate to the end-user. Clients only have to worry about the application's business logic, and the service provider usually takes care of everything, including configuration, infrastructure provision, servers, etc. In this chapter, the authors have discussed several cloud computing issues regarding data security and data controlling mechanisms.

Chapter 8

Jenifer Mahilraj, Department of AI and DS, NPR College of Engineering and Technology, Natham, India

T. Avudaiappan, Department of AI and DS, K. Ramakrishnan college of Technology, Trichy, India

Sivaram Ponnusamy, Department of Artificial Intelligence, G.H. Raisoni College of Engineering, Nagpur, India

In the past two decades, the use of various materials for various structural and mechanical aspects has become increasingly important. Scientists in today's high-tech world have a vested interest in exotic materials with novel features. Composite material utilisation has increased dramatically during the past two decades to satisfy the needs of the aerospace, nuclear, and aeronautics industries. Fibre reinforced polymer matrix composites are increasingly being used in place of traditional metallic materials due to their superior performance in a number of areas, including fatigue, damage tolerance, and greater resistance to oxidation. In this investigation, the authors set out to develop and characterise a polymer-based composite packed with nano-micro particles for use in aerospace. In this chapter, the authors employ a hybrid of the FAHP and FTOPSIS to assign an overall rating to various dental composites. The research results presented here enhance the development of effective and precise damage detection techniques for composite materials.

Chapter 9

D. Rajeswari, Department of Data Science and Business Systems, School of Computing, College of Engineering and Technology, SRM institute of Science and Technology, Kattankulathur, India

Athish Venkatachalam Parthiban, Department of Data Science and Business Systems, School of Computing, College of Engineering and Technology, SRM Institute of Science and Technology, Kattankulathur, India

S. S. Sree Nandha, Department of Data Science and Business Systems, School of Computing, College of Engineering and Technology, SRM Institute of Science and Technology, Kattankulathur, India

Self-care has acquired relevance, especially in light of the COVID-19 scenario. For anyone to diagnose underlying disorders without a doctor's involvement, improved remote healthcare equipment was required. Due to recent technical breakthroughs, this mission is no longer insurmountable. The objective is to develop an interactive application that can identify potential reasons for a person's discomfort. The primary objective is to carry out a trustworthy machine learning technique that can accurately predict a person's status depending on their symptoms. The collection includes 5000 individual cases and 133 distinctive symptom types. On the same dataset, three alternative models (support vector classification, random forest and Naive Bayes) were instructed to achieve maximum accuracy. The second part involves developing a web application and integrating the model with it. The primary aim of the project is to implement a machine learning based web application that is user-friendly and easy to understand, so that patients can detect their problems before visiting a doctor.

    G. Krishnakanth, SASTRA University, India
    M. Malini Deepika, Sathyabama University, Chennai, India
    M. Yuvaraja, SASTRA University, India

The major problem while treating the tumor is that each responds differently to drug therapies. 3D printing is an aid to solve the difficulty faced in radiation therapy that enables personalized treatment by creating mimic models with micro information to facilitate complex therapies like implanting and tumor structural analysis. The data from modern imaging modalities are combined to construct the 3D structure. In the chapter, 3D construction is done with MIMICS software, and the printing is done with Ultimaker 3 ext to produce the vitro implant model as a reference for pre-operative planning and allows the creation of patient-specific models.

    Madhumita Choudhury, St. Xavier's College, Kolkata, India
    Durba Paul, St. Xavier's College, Kolkata, India
    Anal Acharya, St. Xavier's College, Kolkata, India
    Nisha Banerjee, St. Xavier's College, Kolkata, India
    Debabrata Datta, St. Xavier's College, Kolkata, India

With the recent outbreak and rapid transmission of the COVID-19 pandemic, the need for the people to follow social distancing and wear masks in public is only increasing. So, the main objective of this chapter is to build a machine learning model based on TensorFlow object detection API and YOLO Objection Detection that will determine a green and red rectangle around the face if the person detected in the camera wears or does not wear a mask, along with an email alert being sent to the authority in charge informing about a person's violation of face mask policy and will return a green or red bounding box accordingly if social distancing is maintained between two people and at the same time alert others by a beep alarm. The accuracy of the model is nearly 97% so it can be used by governments to alert people if the situation turns serious.

Chapter 12

   *N. Prabakaran, School of Computer Science and Engineering, Vellore Institute of
      Technology, Vellore, India*

   *Aditya Deepak Joshi, School of Computer Science and Engineering, Vellore Institute of
      Technology, Vellore, India*

   *Rajarshi Bhattacharyay, School of Computer Science and Engineering, Vellore Institute of
      Technology, Vellore, India*

   *R. Kannadasan, School of Computer Science and Engineering, Vellore Institute of
      Technology, Vellore, India*

   A. S. Anakath, Depatment of CSE, Saveetha School of Engineering, Chennai, India

In recent years, deep learning and its subtopics have found a near gold-rush stature in the industry. This booming response has not been restricted to niche applications, but rather to titanic domains such as healthcare, self-driving cars, cybersecurity, and more. This "rise" has consequently led to a large influx of practitioners and users to this domain. One such subdomain is generative adversarial networks (GANs), an application of deep learning centered on image segmentation. The researchers aim to study the trajectory of and attempt to extrapolate the future of this subdomain in an attempt to discern if the meteoric rise of this technique is based on concrete positive results or a trend deemed to ebb. This study aims to first gather the most salient aspects and recent advancements of GANs. Specifically, the study emphasizes the importance of GANs and presents differing types utilized in various domains. Finally, the researchers present the current research gaps and the difficulties that could potentially be faced in the attainment of the aforementioned trajectory of this field.

Chapter 13

   Sumathi Rajyam, SASTRA University, India

   N. R. Raajan, SASTRA University, India

   G. Samyuktha, SASTRA University, India

   V. Priyadharshini, SASTRA University, India

   M. Sindhujaa, SASTRA University, India

The cutting-edge technologies cloud computing and IoT are taking an upper hand in every domain. A huge and wide variety of data is being handled and processed by clouds. The cloud federation technique further adds up to this. In the coming years, quantum computers will replace the conventional computers. Pulling out particular data from the gigantic data set processed by clouds in a conventional computer would take a considerable amount of time. In the chapter, Grover's algorithm, a search algorithm, is implemented on traditional computers on IBM quantum simulator and also on QUIRK quantum simulator. Three qubit data is considered in the proposed scheme. The objective of this chapter is to compare the execution time taken to run the Grover's algorithm on IBM and Quirk quantum simulators and on classical computers. The work carried out proves that quantum computer execution speed is high compared to the classical counterpart. This could be effectively used in the future in searching for specific data from a mammoth data set using quantum simulators.

Chapter 14

A photovoltaic (PV) system uses the maximum power point tracking (MPPT) controller used in a photovoltaic (PV) system to get the maximum power operating point at different temperatures and irradiance conditions. Several optimization methods from conventional to soft computing methods have been applied to software and hardware platforms to generate duty cycles and optimize fuzzy membership functions. The PV system with partial shading condition is also considered for better tracking of power peaks. Merits and demerits of different MPPT optimization methods have been discussed to conclude better. The results obtained by recently developed algorithms in the MPPT controller have been compared to show better performance and effectiveness of the algorithm. This chapter references undertaking research work to optimize MPPT controllers in PV systems under partial shading conditions.

With the overwhelming success of three-dimensional (3D) modeling technology of patient anatomy, surgeons are able to intuitively understand the most complex morphologies. In this work, the tractography model is constructed by focusing on the sub-voxel asymmetry and fiber consistency to enhance cortical tractography with strongly bent axonal trajectories which help to identify the fiber track by using the diffusion tensor imagining (DTI) method. The DTI algorithm is compared with the other tracking algorithms and the track parameters for different patients are compared. It is proven that the DTI method provides higher accuracy of 96.76% in tracking the cross fibers. The Y-axis dispersion for the different regions of interest from the tract center is measured. The tract amplitudes at this separation are decreased by 75% from the peak value. The 3D model is printed using an ultimate 3D printing machine at a diameter of about 0.025 mm at a low cost with high accuracy.

Chapter 16

Shaminder Kaur, Chitkara University Institute of Engineering and Technology, Chitkara University, India

Lipika Gupta, Department of Electronics and Communication Engineering, Chitkara University Institute of Engineering and Technology, Chitkara University, India

Tripti Sharma, Chandigarh University, Punjab, India

Shilpi Birla, Department of Electronics and Communication Engineering, Manipal University, Jaipur, India

Neeraj Kumar, Electrical Engineering Department, College of Engineering, King Khalid University, Abha, Saudi Arabia

The burden on agricultural productivity is growing as the global population continues to increase at a rapid rate. Due to the growth of metro areas, agricultural land is being lost daily, which could result in a shortage of arable land. Vertical farming (VF) is the answer to this issue. IoT system can be utilized to monitor and control these vertical farming systems. By using the latest technology such as IoT, it becomes very easy for the farmers to monitor the growth of their plants. It becomes easy for them to monitor plants in terms of what action is needed and how much care is required at appropriate time. It is important for determining the optimum growth of plants.

Foreword

Optimization and enhanced computer applications in social welfare have become paramount in today's rapidly evolving world. The intersection of technology and social welfare offers immense opportunities to address complex societal challenges and improve the lives of individuals and communities. Within this dynamic context, *Perspectives on Social Welfare Applications' Optimization and Enhanced Computer Applications* emerges as a valuable contribution to the field.

This book is a comprehensive exploration of the diverse perspectives and innovative approaches to optimizing social welfare applications through the power of computer technology. It brings together leading experts, practitioners, and researchers who share a common goal: to harness the potential of technology to create more efficient, effective, and equitable social welfare systems.

The chapters within this book traverse a wide range of themes and domains, encompassing areas such as healthcare, education, poverty alleviation, social justice, and community development. The authors delve into the intricate details of optimization techniques, data analysis, artificial intelligence, machine learning, and other cutting-edge technologies that can revolutionize addressing social challenges.

What sets this book apart is its multidisciplinary approach, combining insights from computer science, social sciences, economics, and policy analysis. The book fosters a holistic understanding of the intricate relationship between technology and social welfare by weaving together these diverse perspectives. It invites readers to explore the potential synergies, ethical considerations, and socio-economic implications that arise when these fields converge.

The authors present theoretical frameworks and conceptual models and share practical examples, case studies, and real-world applications that demonstrate the transformative power of technology in social welfare. By showcasing success stories and lessons learned, they inspire readers to think creatively and critically about how technological advancements can be harnessed to build more inclusive, sustainable, and compassionate societies.

I hope this book will provide inspiration, knowledge, and reflection for researchers, practitioners, policymakers, and students in various fields. The insights contained within these pages have the potential to shape the future of social welfare, informing policy decisions, guiding the development of innovative solutions, and ultimately improving the lives of individuals and communities around the world.

I thank the authors for their invaluable contribution and commitment to advancing the discourse on social welfare optimization through enhanced computer applications. I also thank the editors and the team behind this publication for their dedication and hard work in bringing this important volume to fruition.

May this book ignite curiosity, spark collaborations, and pave the way for a future where technology is a powerful tool in pursuing social justice and human flourishing.

Sachin Untawale
G. H. Raisoni College of Engineering, Nagpur, India

Preface

As editors, we are delighted to present this edited reference book *Perspectives on Social Welfare Applications' Optimization and Enhanced Computer Applications*. This book explores the intersection of computer science and social welfare, focusing on the advancements and applications of various cutting-edge technologies.

In today's digital era, integrating advanced technologies into social welfare applications has the potential to revolutionize how we interact with our society. The chapters in this book provide a comprehensive platform for scholars, researchers, scientists, and working professionals worldwide to exchange their experiences and research findings in application software system development within computer science.

The topics covered in this book encompass a wide range of emerging and advanced technologies, including Artificial Intelligence, the Internet of Things, Data Science, Cloud Technology, Blockchain Technology, Virtual Reality, and many more. By leveraging these technologies, we can enhance existing social welfare applications or create new ones to address critical societal challenges.

The book also aims to foster collaboration and professional relationships among experts in computer application development worldwide. We hope this collaboration will lead to innovative solutions and further advancements in digital social interactions across various domains such as agriculture, business, healthcare management, insurance, and finance.

We encourage professionals, industrialists, researchers, engineers, students, and scientists to contribute their work to this book. By sharing your expertise and research results, you will contribute to the collective knowledge in the field of social welfare applications and inspire others to explore new avenues in their respective areas of interest.

The intended audience of this book is not limited to any particular domain or specialization within computer science. Instead, it is open to anyone interested in leveraging technology to improve society. Whether you are involved in community organizing, progressive management, policy change, social action and activism, advocacy and coalition work, or project and program development, this book offers insights into how computer applications can support and enhance these initiatives.

We also extend a special invitation to final-year undergraduate, postgraduate, and PhD scholars in engineering and arts to submit the details of their academic projects as chapters and their research/project supervisors as co-authors. This opportunity allows young researchers to showcase their work and contribute to the growing body of knowledge in computer science.

This book's diverse chapters encompass various topics, ranging from computational engineering to information security, data science, and software engineering. Each chapter offers a unique perspective and contributes to understanding how technology can transform social welfare applications.

CHAPTER OVERVIEW

Chapter 1 focuses on the use of social media platforms as a data source for diagnosing depression-related issues. The research employs machine learning approaches to classify tweets and addresses the issue of data imbalance through sampling techniques. The study evaluates the performance of various machine learning techniques and identifies the most effective classifier for depression classification.

Chapter 2 presents a machine-learning approach for assessing the risk of COVID-19 using logistic regression classification models. The research utilizes data from multiple sources to determine if a patient is at risk of COVID-19. The aim is to prioritize testing resources and provide accurate predictions using simple features obtained through basic clinical inquiries.

Chapter 3 proposes a real-time phishing detection plugin for web browsers. The system utilizes a random forest classifier to identify and notify users about potential phishing websites. The system's effectiveness is evaluated, and the proposed method shows superior results in detecting wireless phishing attacks.

Chapter 4 explores the rise of mobile applications in India and their increasing importance in various domains such as healthcare and agriculture. The paper highlights the incorporation of artificial intelligence and machine learning into mobile applications and their impact on future developments. It provides an overview of intelligent applications used in medical and agricultural fields.

Chapter 5 discusses a heuristic packet routing strategy for effective path identification in wireless sensor networks. The proposed methodology improves the routing process by incorporating energy management and diffusion methodologies. The research includes a comprehensive study comparing the proposed work with previous research.

Chapter 6 focuses on enhancing multimedia recommender systems using collaborative filtering, ripple nets, deep learning, and recurrent neural networks. The study explores the prediction accuracy of preexisting models by treating the recommendation problem as a sequence prediction problem. The proposed model increases the accuracy of predictions for multimedia recommendations.

Chapter 7 addresses data security and control mechanisms in cloud computing. It discusses the challenges associated with data privacy and security concerns in public cloud services. The chapter explores serverless computing as an alternative solution and highlights the advantages of not exposing infrastructure and platforms to end-users.

Chapter 8 focuses on developing damage detection techniques for polymer-based composite materials. The research aims to enhance the effectiveness and precision of damage detection using a hybrid of the FAHP and FTOPSIS methods. The presented results contribute to advancing effective damage detection techniques for composite materials.

Chapter 9 presents the development of a machine learning-based web application for self-diagnosis. The application aims to predict a person's health status based on symptoms accurately. The chapter includes collecting and analyzing a dataset, training three alternative models, and developing a user-friendly web application for self-diagnosis.

Chapter 10 focuses on using 3D printing for pre-operative planning in dentistry. The research aims to develop and characterize a polymer-based composite model for dental applications. The chapter discusses constructing a 3D model using software and the printing process, facilitating effective pre-operative planning.

Chapter 11 introduces a computer vision-based system for monitoring face mask usage and social distancing. The system utilizes machine learning models and object detection techniques to detect and alert authorities about violations. The chapter emphasizes the accuracy and potential applications of the developed model in enforcing safety measures.

Chapter 12 overviews generative adversarial networks (GANs) and their advancements, applications, and challenges. The research examines the importance of GANs in various domains and presents different types of GANs used in different applications. The chapter discusses current research gaps and potential challenges in the field.

Chapter 13 explores quantum computing and its potential for efficient data retrieval. The research compares the execution time of Grover's algorithm on IBM and Quirk quantum simulators and classical computers. The results highlight the faster execution speed of quantum computers and their potential impact on data retrieval.

Chapter 14 discusses the optimization of maximum power point tracking (MPPT) controllers in photovoltaic (PV) systems. The research explores different optimization methods and algorithms to improve the efficiency and performance of MPPT controllers. The chapter provides a comparative analysis of recently developed algorithms and their effectiveness.

Chapter 15 focuses on enhancing cortical tractography using diffusion tensor imaging (DTI). The research aims to improve the accuracy of fiber track identification by considering sub-voxel asymmetry and fiber consistency. The chapter discusses the construction of tractography models, compares DTI with other tracking algorithms, and presents the results obtained.

Chapter 16 explores the utilization of the Internet of Things (IoT) in vertical farming. The research highlights the role of IoT systems in monitoring and controlling vertical farming systems. The chapter emphasizes the benefits of IoT technology in improving agricultural productivity and discusses the future potential of IoT in farming.

These chapter overviews provide a glimpse into the diverse topics covered in the book, ranging from machine learning in healthcare and social media analysis to quantum computing, composite materials, and IoT applications. Each chapter offers valuable insights and contributes to the overall understanding of optimized computer applications in social welfare domains.

In conclusion, we would like to express our gratitude to all the authors who have contributed to this book. Their dedication and expertise have made this compilation possible. We hope that this book will serve as a valuable resource for researchers, practitioners, and enthusiasts in the field of computer science, inspiring them to explore new frontiers in social welfare applications' optimization and enhanced computer applications.

Ponnusamy Sivaram
Department of Artificial Intelligence, G.H. Raisoni College of Engineering, Nagpur, India

S. Senthilkumar
Department of CSE, University College of Engineering, BIT Campus, Anna University, Tiruchirappalli, India

Lipika Gupta
Department of Electronics and Communication Engineering, Chitkara University Institute of Engineering and Technology, Chitkara University, India

Nelligere S. Lokesh
Department of CSE-AIML, AMC Engineering College, Bengaluru, India

Acknowledgment

Many people need support, direction, and participation in the collaborative process of writing a book. As we complete our work on *Perspectives on Social Welfare Applications' Optimization and Enhanced Computer Applications*, we sincerely thank everyone who helped make this endeavour possible.

We want to begin by thanking the Almighty God, Parents and Family Members for their unending love, support, and guidance during every step of our lives. We are grateful to our cherished family members for supporting us throughout our careers and helping us progress by editing this book. Your unwavering support, confidence in our talents, and unwavering love have been the pillars that have kept us going during this process.

We want to express our sincere gratitude to every author for contributing their insightful opinions, vast experience, and thorough research to this book. Your enthusiasm for social welfare applications and eagerness to impart knowledge has greatly aided in developing a comprehensive and informative resource. It was determined that every chapter in the book was necessary; otherwise, it wouldn't have been complete.

We also appreciate the careful work and valuable time that each member of our editorial board and chapter reviewers put into the book to assist us in raising the standard of the information presented therein. Our gratitude to the reviewers who carefully examined the chapters offered helpful criticism, and contributed to raising the calibre of the data. Your knowledge and critical analysis have significantly contributed to the quality of this book's scholarship.

We want to thank the IGI Global editorial and production teams for their hard work in making this book a reality. Your dedication to excellence, professionalism, and attention to detail have benefitted the entire publishing process.

We appreciate our coworkers' and peers' support as we prepared this book. Your support, conversations, and experiences with us have shaped our viewpoints and improved the information in our work.

We want to express our sincere gratitude to everyone who helped write this book, whether they were directly involved or not. *Perspectives on Social Welfare Applications' Optimization and Enhanced Computer Applications* is the result of our collaborative efforts, and we anticipate that it will be a valuable tool for those working in social welfare applications and computer technology.

Chapter 1
A Framework for Classifying Imbalanced Tweets Using Machine Learning Techniques

R. Srinivasan

Department of Computing Technologies, School of Computing, College of Engineering and Technology, SRM Institute of Science and Technology, India

Rajeswari D.

(iD) https://orcid.org/0000-0002-2677-4296

Department of Data Science and Business Systems, School of Computing, College of Engineering and Technology, SRM Institute of Science and Technology, India

ABSTRACT

The research work presented focuses on utilizing social media platforms as a source of data to diagnose depression-related issues. The popularity of social platforms such as LinkedIn, Instagram, Twitter, YouTube, and Facebook, gave researchers an opportunity to analyse user experiences and gain insights into depression. Depression is a significant problem that affects individuals' lives, disrupts normal functioning, and impacts their perspectives. The primary objective of this research is to employ machine learning (ML) approaches for classifying tweets. Additionally, the research addresses the issue of data imbalance by using sampling techniques. This research work utilizes a sampling technique to normalize the dataset. The study explores four techniques that helps to extract meaningful information from the tweets. The research work conducts an empirical study to evaluate the performance of various ML techniques. Based on the experimental results, it is found that the AdaBoost classifier with the BoW feature extraction technique achieves the best results among all the classifiers tested.

DOI: 10.4018/978-1-6684-8306-0.ch001

INTRODUCTION

Depression is cause of disability in every region of the country (Dewa CS et al., 2010). Clinical depression is a lethal medical issue that is associated with a person's mental health (G. Geetha et al., 2020). United Nation (UN) health agency estimates approximately thirty crore people are affected by it, with the highest rates among women, young people, and the elderly (D. M. Shukla et al., 2020). Depression analysis evaluates depression based on social media textual activity, a Natural Language Processing (NLP) domain problem, affecting individuals with symptoms like melancholy, low self-esteem, and poor sleep habits (P. Arora & P. Arora, 2019). The severity of the depression is determined by the symptoms, but it is not applicable to everyone.

The best way to diagnose depression is to consult with a specialist in the field. Many people will wait until their symptoms become severe. The reason for the people become severe is unaware of the symptoms whether they are having depression or not. As a result, modern users use social media platforms to express their opinions, ideas, thoughts, and emotions, allowing them to empathize with their counterparts. The reason for using social media platforms is to express emotions in their native language (S., Soumya & K.V., Pramod, 2020).

The study focuses on utilizing information from social networking sites to evaluate an individual's mental well-being. Previous research suggests that social media platforms predominantly consist of human emotions and thoughts expressed through words like 'happy,' 'sad,' 'excited,' 'nervous,' 'depressed,' and others. These platforms also include self-disclosed phrases indicating mental disorders, lack of confidence, bipolarity, and depression (Islam et al., 2018). By analyzing tweets and short messages from social media, the researchers extract patterns to construct an effective classification model. Previous studies have employed various techniques for text classification, yielding satisfactory outcomes.

The present work offers a comprehensive exploration of different machine learning methods for classifying depression-related tweets. Twitter data, consisting of 80 percent non-depressive tweets, is utilized in this study. The principal conclusions drawn from this research indicates.

1) Incorporation of various approaches to preprocess the data extracted from twitter
2) Identifying the optimal feature from the dataset
3) Smote Techniques are applied to normalize the tweet imbalance problem
4) Predict the best Ml model to classify this tweets

LITERATURE REVIEW

Many researchers have investigated various approaches to classifying tweets. Recent Studies have proved that depression can be predicted from speech using Machine Learning Techniques. From human speech, the author developed a depression dataset. The author obtained the data from Northwest Normal University (NNU) and used the self-reference effect (SRE) as a conventional paradigm (D. Shi et al., 2021). The author produced an achievable result of 65% using Support Vector Machine (SVM). Shubam et al had recognized the depression from the low level audio, visual and textual process (Dham et al., 2017). The results are obtained from the baseline features for audio, visual (head pose) and textual process. The author proved that notable results are obtained by applying the SVM techniques.

S. Sangamnerkar proposed the ensembled model for fake news detection using ML approaches (S. Sangamnerkar et al., 2020). Using ensemble approaches, the author experimented with fake news identification and help to deliver the real news to the user. The evaluation was carried out on the "National Health and Nutrition Examination Survey (NHANES)" benchmark datasets (Tao et al., 2021). The author used ensemble approaches to improve the classifier's performance and achieved a 97.6% f1 - score. Ensemble approaches outperform all other baseline methods for the NHANES dataset.

The researchers are able to detect the depression from their native language tweets. For English dataset, several standard feature extraction process are available to extract the sentiments. Jayakrishnan et al had annotate the sentiments from the Malayam novels (Jayakrishnan et al., 2018). Every language has some unique feature to convey the meaning. Most of the Indic languages are partially free word order. To extract sentiments from native language is very difficult. The author obtained the good results from Malayam sentences from the novels to extract the different emotions. The author used different syntactic features or better classification. The first study used a Deep Neural Network (DNN) classifier to analyze four types of depression indicators, achieving a high 96.1% F1-score. Song and their team established an attention network or extracting feature to detect depressed sentences from social media platorms (Song and Hoyun, 2018). The FAN method showed good results compared to other approaches, except for CNN.

Kannampallil et al. used ML techniques, specifically Support Vector Machines (SVM), to predict depression in patients undergoing Problem Solving Therapy (PST) and achieved 72% accuracy (Kannampallil et al., 2022). This study intends to use ML techniques to predict depression remission in participants who undergo a 6-month active treatment involving problem-solving therapy. Additionally, the study aims to generate model-agnostic explanations to identify the factors that contribute to remission. Hopman and their team employed ML techniques to predict clinical response in patients undergoing Transcranial Magnetic Stimulation (rTMS) (Hopman HJ et al., 2021). The study aims to validate the predictive value of specific brain connectivity patterns, explore alternative biomarkers, assess the impact of pre-processing methods, and investigate the potential use of these biomarkers for personalized treatment decisions using ML. Although the sample size and identified features were limited, the research achieved good test accuracy.

The goal of the study is to achieve state-of-the-art results in early detection of depression. The researchers highlight the importance of early detection, given the significant impact of depression on global disability and its association with suicide. The performance values were 0.39 and 0.80, respectively for both problem, which underperformed compared to other classifiers. Additionally, they used a CNN approach with different word embedding techniques to predict depression, producing cutting-edge results when combined with a linguistic metadata-based LR model. (Trotzek et al., 2018).

Data augmentation can help improve the generalization and robustness of ML models by providing more varied training instances. The author investigated a text augmentation methods to address class imbalance in minor datasets, improving the performance of ML approaches. They applied augmentation techniques to three different datasets and demonstrated improved performance. (Marivate, V & Sefara, T, 2020).

Oduwa Edo Osagie et al. reviewed the usage of Twitter in public health research. They identified six categories of Twitter applications for public health and learned about domain-specific methods, algorithms, and the examination of various conditions and diseases over time (Oduwa Edo-Osagie et al., 2020). Shaghayegh Jabalameli and their team showed a study on public attitudes during COVID-19 in Twitter. They utilized NLP and Linear Discriminant Analysis (LDA) to identify subjects and sub-topics in the data. The study revealed insights about public responses and reactions to the pandemic, including geographic patterns and sensitivity to news and government responses (Shaghayegh Jabalameli et al., 2022).

The author developed a strategy to understand optimistic and pessimistic attitudes in Twitter discussions during Covid time. They employed transformer embeddings and various network architectures, achieving good identification models for optimism and pessimism during different phases of the pandemic (Guillermo Blanco et al., 2022). Srinivasan and Subalalitha developed a ML framework for identifying sentiments using ML approaches. This research work works well on the code-mixed sentences that is extracted from the youtube comments. This research work performs well on Multilabel classification and addresses different feature extraction techniques based on the domain of the dataset.

Shailesh Hinduja et al. (2022) monitored mental health using Twitter data and proposed a general architecture for active mental health surveillance. They applied data cleansing, tweet pre-processing, and sentiment analysis, with LSTM (Long Short-Term Memory) for forecasting. The proposed technique showed improved accuracy in mental health prediction. Overall, these studies highlight the use of various ML algorithms, deep learning methods, and preprocessing techniques to analyze social media data, particularly Twitter, for mental health classification and surveillance.

PROPOSED SYSTEM

Figure 1 is not provided in the text you shared, but based on the information provided, it seems that the proposed work focuses on analyzing a dataset extracted directly from social media platforms, specifically Twitter. The dataset consists of 13,874 tweets, containing depressed and non-depressed tweets. The research work mentioned that approximately 24% of the tweets are non-depressed, while the rest are depressed tweets, indicating a class imbalance issue. To address this, the proposed work employs various approaches to solve noisy data present in the dataset.

Figure 1. Architecture diagram of depressed tweets identification

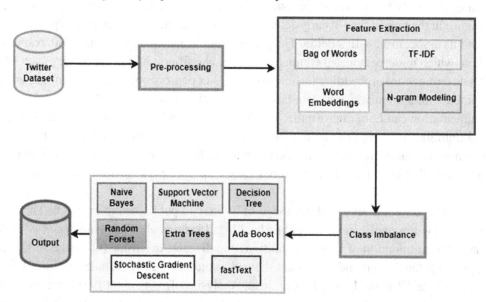

After preprocessing, the work involves several steps, including feature extraction and classification techniques. The dataset obtained from kaggle and the link is shared as (https://drive.google.com/drive/u/0/folders/1bpbE4_ibxwsKhjpalzq-sJcg4MOxfGMm). Overall, the proposed work seeks to leverage the dataset of tweets, preprocess the data, extract relevant features, and apply classification techniques to classify the tweets into depressed and non-depressed categories. The architecture of the proposed work, as described in Figure 1 likely illustrates the flow and components of the proposed approach.

Data Preprocessing

In text classification for NLP tasks, data pre-processing plays a crucial role in improving the performance of ML models. It involves several techniques to clean and normalize the text data, making it suitable for analysis. . Pre-processing techniques can be applied to address the challenges posed by social media data in order to improve the quality and usefulness of the text for analysis. To eliminate URLs, emoticons, and special symbols, you can use the Scikit-learn library along with other NLP libraries like NLTK (Natural Language Toolkit) or spaCy.

1) Expanding Word Contraction: Expanding these contractions can be useful in formal writing or when clarity is needed in communication. This step is very important in propose work that implies expanding contractions can provide a more formal tone, contractions are widely accepted and used in everyday conversation and informal writing.
   Example: You've -> You have

2) Eliminating URLs, Emoticons, and Special Symbols: It's important to consider the context and purpose of the text when deciding how to handle URLs, emoticons, or special symbols. In some cases, they may need to be retained or appropriately replaced to ensure the meaning and clarity of the text. The proposed work comprises of three things, eliminate URL, eliminate emoticons, and eliminate special symbols. To eliminate URLs, you can simply remove them or replace them with a generic placeholder like "[URL]". Emoticons are often used to convey emotions or expressions in text. To eliminate them, you can replace them with a descriptive term or remove them altogether. Special symbols like currency symbols, mathematical symbols, or other non-alphanumeric characters can be eliminated or substituted with plain text alternatives.
   Examples:
   Original text: "I'm so happy!:-)"
   Text without emoticon: "I'm so happy!"
   Original text: "The product costs $100."
   Text without currency symbol: "The product costs 100 dollars."

3) Splitting Joint Words: Splitting joint words, also known as compound words, can be done to separate the individual words that make up the compound. This can be useful for various reasons, such as improving readability or analyzing the components of the compound. The important note that not all compound words should be split, as they are often written as a single unit for a specific reason. This proposed work addresses various compound words like Noun-Noun, Adjective – Noun, Hyphenated Compounds, etc (Hucka, M., 2018 & https://github.com/casics/spiral).

4) Lemmatization: Lemmatization is often preferred over stemming, another technique used to reduce words to their base forms. Stemming uses simpler rules to chop off word endings, lemmatization

relies on linguistic knowledge and uses a more comprehensive approach. Consequently, lemmatization tends to produce more accurate and meaningful results.

Example: "ran", "running", "runs" –> "run"

Feature Extraction

BoW

The BoW model performs independent matching and counting of each element in a text in order to create a vector representation of the document. However, this method ignores a significant amount of information on correlations between words (D. Yan et al., 2020). This proposed work uses 1000 words at the maximum limit to process the BoW approach.

TF-IDF

The TF-IDF score for a term within a document is obtained by multiplying its TF value with its IDF value. The resulting score provides a measure of how relevant or important a term is to a specific document in the context of the entire collection of documents. Higher TF-IDF scores indicate greater importance or relevance (Shetty et al., 2020).

N-Gram

In the context of NLP, these items are typically words or characters. N-grams are widely used in various language modelling tasks, including text prediction, machine translation, and speech recognition. The "N" in N-gram represents the number of items in the sequence (I. Kaibi et al., 2019). N-grams capture the local context and statistical properties of a language, enabling models to make predictions based on the patterns observed in the training data. N-gram models are built by counting the occurrences of N-grams in a given corpus of text and calculating the probabilities of the next item in the sequence given the preceding N-1 items. These probabilities can be used to generate new text or predict the likelihood of a particular sequence occurring in the language.

Word2Vec

The main idea behind Word2Vec is to capture the semantic and syntactic relationships between words by representing them as dense vectors in a continuous vector space. The algorithm learns these vector representations by training a shallow NN on a large corpus of text. The network predicts the context words surrounding a target word or vice versa, given a window of words as input.

Classification Techniques

Naïve Bayes (NB), Support Vector Machine, Decision Tree

NB is a simple yet effective classification algorithm based on Bayes' theorem with an assumption of independence among the features. It is widely used for text classification tasks, spam filtering, sentiment analysis, and various other machine learning applications (Chatterjee et al., 2021). Naive Bayes classifiers come in different variants, such as Gaussian Naive Bayes for continuous features assuming a Gaussian distribution or Multinomial Naive Bayes for discrete features. The choice of variant depends on the nature of the data being classified.

SVM is a one of the popular ML technique that is commonly used to solve classification tasks (Yu, J et al., 2016). The main objective of SVM is to find an optimal hyperplane in a high-dimensional feature space that separates the data points of different classes with the largest possible margin. The hyperplane is defined by a subset of training data points called support vectors, which are the closest points to the decision boundary. The key points present in the SVM are hyperplane, margin, kernel tricks, support vectors, etc. SVM can be used for various applications, such as text categorization, image classification, bioinformatics, and more. The Radial Bias Function (RBF) is calculated from,

$$f\left(x_1, x_2\right) = \exp\left(-\frac{\|x_1 - x_2\|}{2\sigma^2}\right)^2 \tag{1}$$

where, $\|x_1 - x_2\|$ represents Euclidean distance, " σ " is hyper parameter or variance, x_1, x_2 are the two different words that helps to find the similarity among the words

A DT is a supervised ML algorithm used for both classification and regression tasks. It is a tree-like model where each internal node represents a feature or attribute, each branch represents a decision rule, and each leaf node represents the outcome or predicted class label. The DT algorithm recursively partitions the data based on the values of different features. The goal is to create a tree that can effectively classify or predict the target variable. The decision tree builds the tree structure based on a set of rules derived from the training data (Le Yang et al., 2016).

Ensemble Methods

Ensemble approach combines the one or more baseline techniques like Naïve Bayes, SVM, and Logistic Regression etc. The proposed work make use of the ensemble methods named as "Extra Tree (ET)", "Random Forest (RF)" and "AdaBoost".

ET, short for Extremely Randomized Trees, is an ensemble learning method that is closely related to DT. It is an extension of the random forest algorithm and shares many similarities with it. Like DT, ET builds an ensemble of trees to make predictions. However, there are a few key differences between ET and traditional DT are Random Feature Selection, Aggregation, and Randomized Threshold's. Extra Trees is commonly used in machine learning tasks, especially when working with high-dimensional data, noisy datasets, or when computational efficiency is important. It can be applied to both classification and regression problems.

RF is an ensemble learning method that combines multiple DT to create a robust and accurate predictive model. It is widely used for both classification and regression tasks in ML. (Lal, Sangeeta et al., 2020). Random Forest can be computationally expensive, especially when dealing with a large number of trees or high-dimensional datasets. RF can provide feature importance measures, the interpretability of the overall model may be limited compared to individual DT.

AdaBoost, short for Adaptive Boosting, is an ensemble learning algorithm that combines multiple weak classifiers to create a strong classifier. It is particularly effective for binary classification tasks but can be extended to multi-class problems as well. AdaBoost is a popular and powerful algorithm that has been widely applied in various domains, including face detection, object recognition, and bioinformatics. Its ability to leverage multiple weak classifiers to create a strong classifier makes it an effective tool in machine learning.

SGB refers to Stochastic Gradient Boosting, which is an extension of the gradient boosting algorithm. It is a powerful ensemble learning method that combines multiple weak learners to create a strong predictive model. The key idea behind SGB is to introduce randomness during the training process by using random subsets of the training data.

This randomization helps to improve both the generalization and computational efficiency of the algorithm. A key hyper parameters to consider include the number of boosting rounds, learning rate, maximum depth of weak learners, and subsampling ratios. SGB has been successfully used in various domains, including web search ranking, recommendation systems, and Kaggle competitions. It provides a powerful tool for building accurate predictive models by combining the strengths of gradient boosting with the benefits of randomization.

FastText

In recent, Facebook invented a popular classifier called FastText. FastText representation can be applied in supervised and unsupervised approaches. FastText representation is similar kind of pretrained model like word2vec and glove representation. The vector representation of words is applied to the sentence and some of the words are combined together. The pretrained model assigns a zero value, if the word is not occurred in the dictionary. But FastText helps to divide the combined words into an n-gram character and assigns a value instead of zero. FastText helps to reduce the complexity and solves imbalance issue occurred in the dataset (Khasanah, Isnaini. 2021, Choi, Jaekeol & Lee, Sang & Woong 2020). This research investigates the recent approach called fastText on the Twitter dataset.

Class Imbalance

The class imbalance problem is a common issue in machine learning where the classes in the target variable are not represented equally. In other words, there is an unequal distribution of classes, with one or more classes having significantly fewer instances compared to the others. This imbalance can occur in binary classification problems (two classes) or multi-class classification problems (more than two classes).

Class imbalance can pose challenges for machine learning algorithms because they often have a bias towards the majority class, leading to poor performance on the minority classes (P. Babu & E. Parthasarathy 2021). The algorithms tend to optimize their predictions based on the overall accuracy, which can be misleading when the data is imbalanced. The major finding to solve problem in proposed work is Synthetic Minority Oversampling technique (SMOTE) (Adams et al., 2020).

RESULTS AND DISCUSSION

Several feature extraction strategies namely, FastText, BoW, FastText+bigram, N-gram modelling and Tf-Idf are tested in a series of experiments. The experiment setup discuss the tweets are classified into different classes, and the dataset suffers from a class imbalance problem. Due to class imbalance problem, the proposed work chosen the F1-score as the performance metric.

Splitting the dataset into an 80:20 ratio is standard rule to evaluate the performance in ML process. It allows you to train the model on a substantial amount of data while still reserving a separate set for unbiased evaluation. It's important to note that other metrics, such as accuracy, may not be appropriate in the case of imbalanced datasets because they can be misleading due to the disproportionate class distribution. The F1-score provides a more reliable assessment of the model's performance in such scenarios. The experiments are carried out using cross validation method (5 fold). After applying the cross validation the average values is depicted in figure 2 to 8.

Figure 2. Performance of Naïve Bayes, support vector machine, decision tree, random forest, extra tree, AdaBoost, stochastic gradient Boost using BoW

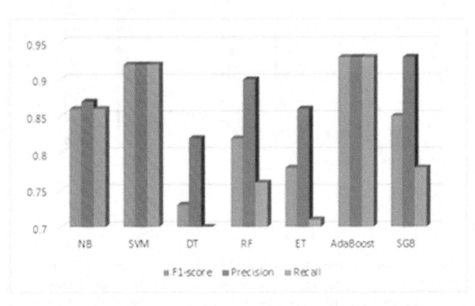

It appears that you have provided the performance of different techniques called BoW approach is depicted in figure 2. According to Figure 2, the AdaBoost classifier achieved the highest F1-score of 0.93, indicating good overall performance. The Support Vector Machine (SVM) approach follows closely with an F1-score of 0.92. These results suggest that both AdaBoost and SVM are effective in classifying the tweets in your dataset. The F1-score, being a combination of precision and recall, provides a balanced assessment of the model's performance in handling the class imbalance problem. It's important to note that these results are specific to the BoW approach and the particular dataset used in your experiment. The performance of different techniques can vary depending on the characteristics of the dataset, the choice of features, hyper parameter settings, and other factors.

Additionally, it would be beneficial to compare these results with the performance of other techniques and consider statistical significance tests to determine if the differences in F1-scores are statistically significant. It's also worth exploring other performance metrics, such as precision, recall, and accuracy, to gain a more comprehensive understanding of the models' performance across different evaluation measures. Overall, based on the information provided, the AdaBoost classifier and SVM demonstrate strong performance in classifying tweets using the BoW approach, with AdaBoost achieving the highest F1-score. BoW approach treat every single word as an independent feature that helps to avoid the correlation among words. The interpretation of the BoW feature extraction is thoroughly examined in the Figure 2.

Figure 3. Performance of Naïve Bayes, support vector machine, decision tree, random forest, extra tree, AdaBoost, stochastic gradient boost using TF-IDF

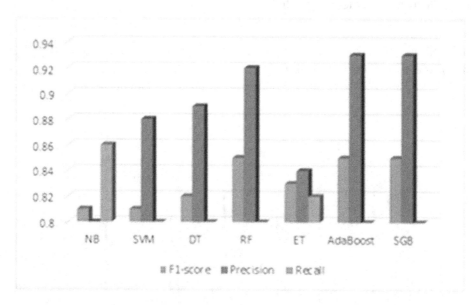

It seems like you are summarizing the results and findings from several figures related to different techniques and approaches used in text classification, specifically on the Twitter dataset. Figure 2 discuss the AdaBoost classifier performs the best among all the techniques using the TF-IDF method. SGB follows AdaBoost with an F1 score of 0.85. Figure 3 suggests that the Bag-of-Words (BoW) approach yields better F1 scores compared to TF-IDF. The lower F1 scores obtained with TF-IDF are attributed to the rarity of words, as TF-IDF assigns weightage to both frequently occurring and rarely occurring words. SVM achieves the highest F1 score of 83.8% in figure 4 among the different ML approaches discussed.

Figure 4. Performance of Naïve Bayes, support vector machine, decision tree, random forest, extra tree, AdaBoost, stochastic gradient boost using Word2Vec

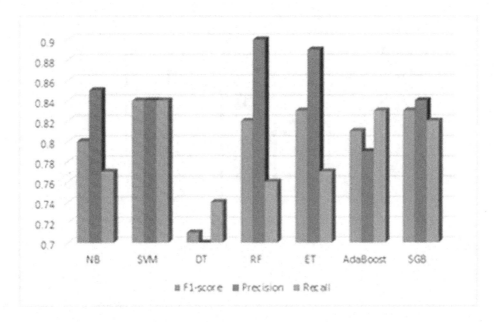

Comparing Figure 2 to Figure 4, it is observed that Word2Vec does not perform as well. Word2Vec struggles with words that are not part of its vocabulary, which is common in the Twitter dataset. Word-2Vec is generally more effective for larger datasets compared to smaller ones. Figure 5 to 7 discuss various feature extraction methods (Unigram, Bigram, and Trigram) combined with different ML algorithms. Unigram approach produces good results, although not the best. The nature of tweets, including the use of abbreviations and short forms, makes it challenging to find consistent patterns in expressing emotions. Figure 8 explains FastText, a recent method, shows promising results in many classification tasks. FastText combines with the Bigram approach is used to evaluate the classification performance.

Figure 5. Performance of Naïve Bayes, Support vector machine, decision tree, random forest, extra tree, AdaBoost, stochastic gradient boost using unigram

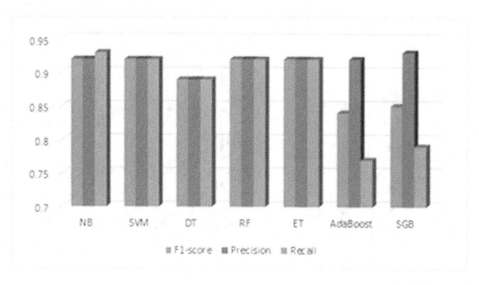

Figure 6. Performance of Naïve Bayes, support vector machine, decision tree, random forest, extra tree, AdaBoost, stochastic gradient boost using Bigram

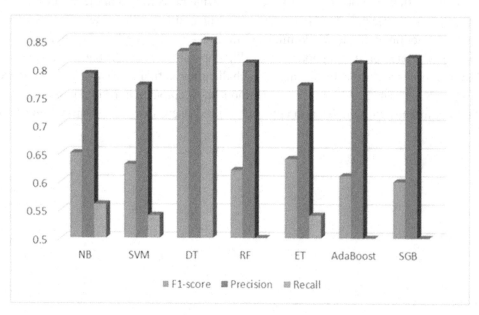

Figure 7. Performance of Naïve Bayes, support vector machine, decision tree, random forest, extra tree, AdaBoost, stochastic gradient boost using N-gram

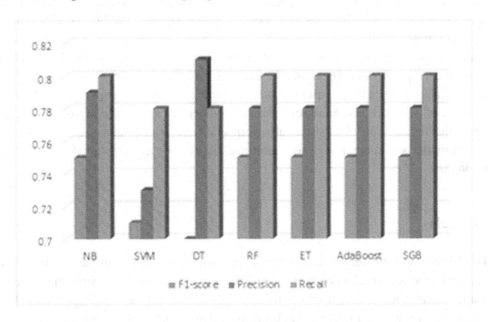

Figure 8. Performance of FastText

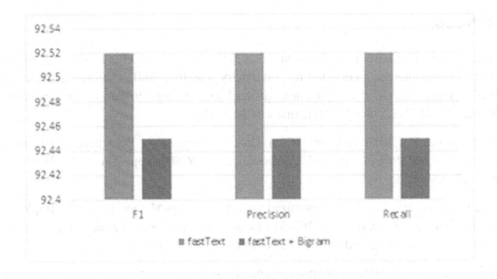

Overall, the figures provide insights into the performance of different techniques and approaches for text classification on the Twitter dataset. AdaBoost and SGB with TF-IDF perform well, while SVM achieves the highest F1 score among the ML approaches. Word2Vec struggles with out-of-vocabulary words, and FastText shows promising results, particularly when combined with the Bigram approach. Unigram extraction produces good but not optimal results due to the unique characteristics of tweets. From figure 2 to 6, sampling techniques are necessary before applying the ML techniques to solve imbalance problem in the dataset.

FastText classifier does not necessary to apply the sampling techniques. FastText classifier itself solves the imbalance problem in the dataset. FastText classifier got good f1-score but not the best one. There is a marginal difference occur FastText compared with an ensembling approaches. After analyzing the performance of ML methods, AdaBoost Classifier outperforms all other approaches. This research helps to prove that the AdaBoost Classifier outperforms the best result in all aspects of feature extraction techniques. In twitter sentimental analysis, AdaBoost algorithms performs good result for the binary classification task.

CONCLUSION

The goal of this project is to create a technique for detecting depression from skewed Twitter data. Ada Boost with BoW feature extraction outperforms all other models in terms of performance. Because the dataset is imbalanced, the f1-score would be the appropriate metric for evaluating the models. To avoid the class imbalance problem, this dataset has been augmented using SMOTE approaches. The proposed work is also tested against the FastText classifier to compare the performance metrics. Though the proposed work achieves good performance to the twitter dataset, still there is a gap due to high dimensional data. The new discovery will be used to solve dimensional data issues in large datasets in the future.

REFERENCES

Adams, M., Massey, F., Chastko, K., & Cupini, C. (2020). Spatial modelling of particulate matter air pollution sensor measurements collected by community scientists while cycling, land use regression with spatial cross-validation, and applications of machine learning for data correction. *Atmospheric Environment, 230*, 117479. doi:10.1016/j.atmosenv.2020.117479

Arora, P., & Arora, P. (2019). Mining Twitter Data for Depression Detection. *2019 International Conference on Signal Processing and Communication (ICSC)*, (pp. 186-189). IEEE. 10.1109/ICSC45622.2019.8938353

Babu, P., & Parthasarathy, E. (2021). Optimized Object Detection Method for FPGA Implementation. *2021 Sixth International Conference on Wireless Communications, Signal Processing and Networking (WiSPNET)*, (pp. 72-74). IEEE. 10.1109/WiSPNET51692.2021.9419407

Blanco, G. & Lourenço, A. (2022). Optimism and pessimism analysis using deep learning on COVID-19 related twitter conversations. *Information Processing & Management, 59*(3), 102918. . doi:10.1016/j.ipm.2022.102918

Chatterjee, R., Gupta, R., & Gupta, B. (2021). Depression Detection from Social Media Posts Using Multinomial Naive Theorem. *IOP Conference Series. Materials Science and Engineering, 1022*(1), 012095. doi:10.1088/1757-899X/1022/1/012095

Choi, J., & Lee, S.-W. (2020). Improving FastText with inverse document frequency of subwords. *Pattern Recognition Letters*, *133*, 165–172. doi:10.1016/j.patrec.2020.03.003

Dewa, C. S., Chau, N., & Dermer, S. (2010, July). Examining the comparative incidence and costs of physical and mental health-related disabilities in an employed population. *Journal of Occupational and Environmental Medicine*, *52*(7), 758–762. doi:10.1097/JOM.0b013e3181e8cfb5 PMID:20595909

Dham, S., Sharma, A., & Dhall, A. (2017). *Depression Scale Recognition from Audio*. Visual and Text Analysis.

Edo-Osagie, O., De La Iglesia, B., Lake, I., & Edeghere, O. (2020). A scoping review of the use of Twitter for public health research. *Computers in Biology and Medicine*, *122*, 103770. doi:10.1016/j.compbiomed.2020.103770 PMID:32502758

Expand work contractions: https://pypi.org/project/pycontractions/

Geetha, G., Saranya, G., Chakrapani, K., Ponsam, J. G., Safa, M., & Karpagaselvi, S. (2020). Early Detection of Depression from Social Media Data Using Machine Learning Algorithms. *2020 International Conference on Power, Energy, Control and Transmission Systems (ICPECTS)*, (pp. 1-6). IEEE. 10.1109/ICPECTS49113.2020.9336974

Hinduja, S., Afrin, M., Mistry, S., & Krishna, A. (2022). Machine learning-based proactive social-sensor service for mental health monitoring using twitter data. *International Journal of Information Management Data Insights*, *2*(2), 100–113. doi:10.1016/j.jjimei.2022.100113

Hopman, H. J., Chan, S. M. S., Chu, W. C. W., Lu, H., Tse, C. Y., Chau, S. W. H., Lam, L. C. W., Mak, A. D. P., & Neggers, S. F. W. (2021). Personalized prediction of transcranial magnetic stimulation clinical response in patients with treatment-refractory depression using neuroimaging biomarkers and machine learning. *Journal of Affective Disorders*, *1*(290), 261–271. https://drive.google.com/drive/u/0/folders/1bpbE4_ibxwsKhjpalzq-sJcg4MOxfGMm. doi:10.1016/j.jad.2021.04.081 PMID:34010751

Hucka, M. (2018). Spiral: Splitters for identifiers in source code files. *Journal of Open Source Software*, *3*(24), 653. doi:10.21105/joss.00653

Islam, M. R., Kabir, A., Ahmed, A., Kamal, A. R. M., Wang, H., & Ulhaq, A. (2018). Depression detection from social network data using machine learning techniques. *Health Information Science and Systems*, *6*(1), 8. doi:10.100713755-018-0046-0 PMID:30186594

Jabalameli, S., Xu, Y., & Shetty, S. (2022). Spatial and sentiment analysis of public opinion toward COVID-19 pandemic using twitter data: At the early stage of vaccination. *International Journal of Disaster Risk Reduction*, *80*, 103204. doi:10.1016/j.ijdrr.2022.103204 PMID:35935613

Jayakrishnan, R. (2018). Multi-Class Emotion Detection and Annotation in Malayalam Novels. *2018 International Conference on Computer Communication and Informatics (ICCCI)*, (pp. 1-5). IEEE. 10.1109/ICCCI.2018.8441492

Kaibi, I., Nfaoui, E. H., & Satori, H. (2019). A Comparative Evaluation of Word Embeddings Techniques for Twitter Sentiment Analysis. *2019 International Conference on Wireless Technologies, Embedded and Intelligent Systems (WITS)*, (pp. 1-4). IEEE. 10.1109/WITS.2019.8723864

Kannampallil, T., Dai, R., Lv, N., Xiao, L., Lu, C., Ajilore, O. A., Snowden, M. B., Venditti, E. M., Williams, L. M., Kringle, E. A., & Ma, J. (2022). Cross-trial prediction of depression remission using problem-solving therapy: A machine learning approach. *Journal of Affective Disorders*, *308*, 89–97. doi:10.1016/j.jad.2022.04.015 PMID:35398399

Khasanah, I. (2021). Sentiment Classification Using fastText Embedding and Deep Learning Model. *Procedia Computer Science*, *189*, 343–350. doi:10.1016/j.procs.2021.05.103

Le Yang, D. J., He, L., Pei, E., Oveneke, M. C., & Sahli, H. (2016). Decision Tree Based Depression Classification from Audio Video and Language Information. In *Proceedings of the 6th International Workshop on Audio/Visual Emotion Challenge (AVEC '16)*. Association for Computing Machinery. 10.1145/2988257.2988269

Marivate, V., & Sefara, T. (2020). Improving Short Text Classification through Global Augmentation Methods. In A. Holzinger, P. Kieseberg, A. Tjoa, & E. Weippl (Eds.), Lecture Notes in Computer Science: Vol. 12279. *Machine Learning and Knowledge Extraction. CD-MAKE 2020*. doi:10.1007/978-3-030-57321-8_21

Sangamnerkar, S., Srinivasan, R., Christhuraj, M. R., & Sukumaran, R. (2020). An Ensemble Technique to Detect Fabricated News Article Using Machine Learning and Natural Language Processing Techniques. *2020 International Conference for Emerging Technology (INCET)*, (pp. 1-7). IEEE. 10.1109/INCET49848.2020.9154053

Sangeeta, L., Lipika, T., Ravi, R., Verma, A., Sardana, N., & Mourya, R. (2020). Analysis and Classification of Crime Tweets. *Procedia Computer Science*, *167*, 1911–1919. doi:10.1016/j.procs.2020.03.211

Shetty, N., Muniyal, B., Anand, A., Kumar, S., & Prabhu, S. (2020). Predicting depression using deep learning and ensemble algorithms on raw twitter data. [IJECE]. *Iranian Journal of Electrical and Computer Engineering*, *10*(4), 3751. doi:10.11591/ijece.v10i4.pp3751-3756

Shi, D., Lu, X., Liu, Y., Yuan, J., Pan, T., & Li, Y. (2021). Research on Depression Recognition Using Machine Learning from Speech. *2021 International Conference on Asian Language Processing (IALP)*, (pp. 52-56). IEEE. 10.1109/IALP54817.2021.9675271

Shukla, D. M., Sharma, K., & Gupta, S. (2020). Identifying Depression in a Person Using Speech Signals by Extracting Energy and Statistical Features. *2020 IEEE International Students' Conference on Electrical, Electronics and Computer Science (SCEECS)*, (pp. 1-4). IEEE. 10.1109/SCEECS48394.2020.60

Song, H., You, J., Chung, J., & Park, J. (2018). *Feature Attention Network: Interpretable Depression Detection from Social Media*. PACLIC.

Soumya, S., & Pramod, K. V. (2020). Sentiment analysis of malayalam tweets using machine learning techniques. *ICT Express.*, *6*. doi:10.1016/j.icte.2020.04.003

Srinivasan, R., & Subalalitha, C. N. (2023). Sentimental analysis from imbalanced code-mixed data using machine learning approaches. *Distributed and Parallel Databases*, *41*, 37–52. doi:10.100710619-021-07331-4 PMID:33776212

Tao, X., Chi, O., Delaney, P. J., Li, L., & Huang, J. (2021). Detecting depression using an ensemble classifier based on Quality of Life scales. *Brain Informatics*, *8*(1), 2. doi:10.118640708-021-00125-5 PMID:33590388

Trotzek, M., Koitka, S., & Friedrich, C. (2018). Utilizing Neural Networks and Linguistic Metadata for Early Detection of Depression Indications in Text Sequences. *IEEE Transactions on Knowledge and Data Engineering*, *32*(3), 588–601. doi:10.1109/TKDE.2018.2885515

Yan, D., Li, K., Gu, S., & Yang, L. (2020). Network-Based Bag-of-Words Model for Text Classification. *IEEE Access : Practical Innovations, Open Solutions*, *8*, 82641–82652. doi:10.1109/ACCESS.2020.2991074

Yu, J., Xue, A., Redei, E., & Bagheri, N. (2016). A support vector machine model provides an accurate transcript-level-based diagnostic for major depressive disorder. *Translational Psychiatry*, *6*(10), e931. doi:10.1038/tp.2016.198 PMID:27779627

Chapter 2
A Novel Approach for Predicting COVID–19 Using Machine Learning– Based Logistic Regression Classification MODEL

Jayavadivel Ravi

Department of Computer Science and Engineering, Alliance University, Bangalore, India

ABSTRACT

Recently, several studies have stated that mild weather can perhaps halt the global epidemic, which has already afflicted over 1.6 million people globally. Clarification of such correlations in the worst affected country, the US, can be extremely valuable to understand the function of weather in transmission of the disease in the highly populated countries, such as India. The authors developed a machine-learning approach as logistic regression classification models that used data from several sources to determine whether a patient is at risk of COVID-19 using one of the classification models with the greatest accuracy. They are working on a model that uses simple features available through basic clinical inquiries to detect COVID-19 patients. When testing resources are tight, their approach can be used to prioritize testing for COVID-19, among other things.

1. INTRODUCTION

The coronavirus disease epidemic of 2019 (COVID-19) is still a public health issue on a global scale. Many viral infections of humans have a well-known seasonality. It's still unclear how environmental influences, particularly those that affect the spread of infectious diseases, affect the spread of sickness from person to person.

The COVID-19 has a noteworthy impact on the adoption of UCaaS. A mixed research technique will be used to collect data on the aspects that may have contributed to an increase in UCaaS sales during

DOI: 10.4018/978-1-6684-8306-0.ch002

the pandemic by using both "Primary and Secondary" forms of data collecting to get the most accurate results. It will focus on obtaining primary data and information from significant Indian corporations. Because of this, it will be simpler to understand and analyse the impact of UCaaS sales on large Indian enterprises, both before and after the pandemic (Lythgoe & Middleton, 2020).

COVID-19 is the phenomena of the analytical study of the features and reasons for using the services to enhance employee participation. The third chapter has presented the methodological approach of the study along with identifying the research design, approach, and philosophy that can help in improving the entire part of the development services regarding the lower costs of the situation of Covid-19 (Sabino et al., 2020). For example, positivism philosophy is the most important part of the study that has helped in maintaining the relation of the entire study along with the approaches towards collecting data (Bailey & Breslin, 2021).

Secondary and primary data collection are the most essential aspect in the procedure of managing the different aspects in the form of the contributions and results for the anticipated approaches when it comes to following the sample and the analysis approaches through the results (Boiral et al., 2021). Both the primary and secondary techniques of data collection are the most crucial part in managing the predictions regarding the growth and analysis of the data. For example, tools that have helped in collecting data from primary sources include online survey, interview, and questionnaire.

SARS-COV2 (COVID-19) erupted in Wuhan City in China in late 2019 andsubsequently evolved as a global pandemic. The COVID-19 pandemic extends to morethan 220 nations and territories globally and has altogether influenced each part of ourday-to-day lives. The quantities of contaminated cases passing despite everythingincrement essentially and do not indicate a very much controlled circumstance; as of 22ⁿᵈJanuary, 2022, a total aggregate of 34,64,64,304 (55,85,224) contaminated (deceased)COVID-19 cases were accounted all over the worldOn the other hand, secondary data collection has come with tools such as conference appearances and magazines that have helped in collecting data on the process of using UCaaS. On the other hand, the understanding of the productivity approaches has also been identified from the data sources (Kuščer et al., 2022).

India is considered as the leader in the IT services industry for the world. We have a huge population of engineers in the country and every year India produces 1.5Million Engineers. India is considered Tech Hub of the world and has been providing IT outsourcing and application development services to the world at much lower costs that the developed countries. This calls for a huge requirement of knowledge workers in India.

As the organizations are geographically dispersed and so are the employees, the need for solutions to collaborate and work in teams to deliver projects globally has been growing by each day. Team collaboration became need of the hour for all organizations having knowledge workers like the IT Services, Research organizations or Consulting organizations etc (Lotfi et al., 2020).

Compared to SARS-CoV-1, this new coronavirus has a longer incubation period and has a higher pathogenicity, which we discuss. To supplement respiratory droplet transmission, these unique coronavirus molecular features likely allow it to use aerosols in totalling to respiratory droplet spread as indirect means of transmission.

A public health strategy of this aggressive character is designed to reduce the exponential rise in disease transmission rates. Using social distancing to keep infections from spreading within a three- to six-foot radius through respiratory droplets is proven to be effective. Persons in a community must choose activities that increase the gap between themselves and others in order to participate in this practise (infected, asymptomatic carriers, or non-infected). Distancing oneself socially or physically helps to decrease the spread of respiratory droplets containing SARS-CoV-2 and reduces the likelihood of viral exposures. It also shows how crucial the public health system and policies are to ensuring that the medical and healthcare systems operate as intended. Preventative measures can help reduce the number of severely ill patients who need medical attention at the same time by acting quickly and mobilising precautionary actions.

COVID-19's most feared complication, i.e., severe bilateral pneumonia, is reduced as a result of this reduction in the load on the healthcare system (4). As a result of this notion, critically sick patients are given the best chance of survival by receiving life-saving supportive therapy in hospitals (Ndaïrou et al., 2020). As a result, the overall mortality rate is reduced dramatically (1).

Many more individuals would die as a result of a lack of access to life-saving treatment if the number of critically sick patients exceeds the capacity of hospitals. SARS-CoV-2 could spread outside of respiratory droplets, according to specific epidemiological observations. Ten cases of COVID-19 were found on a Diamond Princess Cruise ship.

The ship was quarantined for 14 days off the coast of Japan as a result of this. Despite the use of droplet precautions and social distance rules during the ship's quarantine, a total of 634 people were found to have tested positive for COVID-19 (7). Public health professionals now admit that this was not the greatest way to contain COVID-19 in the first place. California was also treated differently by public health officials because of suspicions that interconnected central ventilation between cabins on board the ship may have worsened the dramatically widespread transmission of COVID-19 aerosols. Public health officials removed all passengers who were either vulnerable or uninfected from this cruise ship in order to decrease the number of COVID-19 infections. In healthcare, machine learning offers a lot of potential. It may be beneficial to use a new model in the future to improve the precision of the task. Multiple sensors and features can be integrated into single AI-based software to help find and diagnose diseases (Samui et al., 2020).

2. LITERATURE REVIEW

Huntington's disease (HD) individuals with reduced reaction times can be predicted using a computerised behavioural model. Fuzzy logic and neural networks were used to develop a mobile app for assessing how healthy people and HD patients react to stimuli. Backpropagation of the neural network with a fuzzy logic yielded the best results (Lauraitis et al., 2018).

To forecast cholera, a fuzzy logic model was also constructed. Chloroform was studied with the help of this model's variables. It also produced a prediction model to help environmental health workers educate people about the likelihood of cholera disease, and it helped environmental health workers make better decisions (Aroyehun et al., 2018).

Figure 1. Perception of the COVID-19 virion

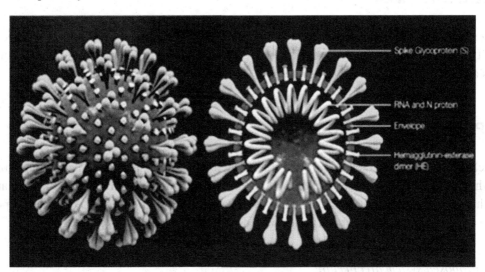

It has been used to identify human diseases using fuzzy logic systems. Even a web-based clinical application developed to increase the excellence of health data interchange among health care professionals and patients showed promising outcomes (Hasan et al. (2010).

In addition, a system of fuzzy logic has been developed for the early detection of Ebola Virus Disease (EVD). In order to evaluate the probability of EVD, this system collects replies from persons who are exhibiting symptoms such as fever, vomiting, bleeding, diarrhoea, and muscle discomfort. The data are then processed using a fuzzy classification. An advantage of this method is that it responds more quickly than slower manual laboratory testing approaches, which reduces the risk of quarantining an uninfected person (Emokhare, 2015).

The Temporally Deformable Alignment Network, proposed by Tian et al. (), solves the issue of video frame temporal alignment by employing deformable convolutions rather than optical flow computations to achieve this goal. As a means of displaying motion, the researchers Xue et al. (2019) used a flow image to represent the task-oriented flow.

As Su and colleagues (n.d.) explain, video de-blurringcan be achieved without requiring precise temporal alignment by merging neighbouring frames together. A Single Stage Headless (SSH) face detector with context layers has been proposed by Najibi et al. (2017) to increase mean average accuracy. Real-time is crucial when using detectors in real-world systems.

Algorithms based on artificial intelligence could be used to prevent the spread of the COVID-19 virus and other ailments by limiting physical interactions between people, according to Hassan et al. (2020). They use bipartite graph and Hopcroft-Karp network algorithms to estimate the public locations using simulated and collected data. In the beginning, the collected and simulated data are graphed, and the graph nodes and links are identified. In the Hopcroft-Karp approach, the bipartite graph is reconstructed. Driver nodes are found in large numbers in matching sets. Finally, the data can be used to make decisions concerning potentially hazardous networks and driver nodes for public safety drives. Conclusions it has been demonstrated through testing that implementing network events reduces public transmission of the COVID-19 virus by 67%

PROBLEM STATEMENT

Curtail the mortality rate caused by COVID-19 by increasing the accuracy of both early detection and the severity levels of the corona virus-contaminated individuals by developing an effective contactless diagnosis and decision support system employing Applied Intelligence.

3. PROPOSED METHODOLOGY

In this section, the proposed methodology is to use machine learning and web development abilities to predict whether or not a person has COVID-19. The forecast is made based on clinical facts about the patients that they are aware of, such as headaches, breathing difficulties, and so on. The purpose is to determine whether or not a patient can be identified with COVID-19.

Figure 2. Proposed system architecture

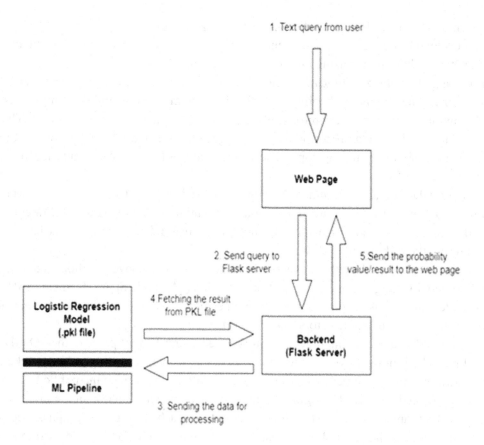

So, our system architecture lies of few modules, where the user is going to provide inputs in html, which are basically x sets or clinical variables. So firstly, we have to setup the flask environment, once the environment is ready then we have to run the project. Once the project is started a local host will be created in the system, then enter the local host (URL) in the browser.

3.1 Dataset

The Israeli Ministry of Health made a RT-PCR test on a nasopharyngeal swab obtained from persons who were suspected of having SARS-CoV-2 public. All COVID-19 diagnostic laboratory tests were performed in accordance with Israeli Ministry of Health protocols during the early months of the COVID-19 epidemic in Israel. An evaluation was conducted based on parameters such as clinical symptoms, likely exposure to COVID-19-infected people in certain geographic areas, and risk of long-term complications. A very small number of persons were tested as part of a poll of healthcare professionals, but everyone else showed indicators that they should be checked. That's why this study's dataset contained so few people who showed any sign of referral prejudice, a finding that contrasts sharply with previous research that found referral biases to be problematic.

RT-PCR was also used to confirm all COVID-19 cases in this dataset that were either negative or positive. In the model build (training) phase, a classification algorithm finds relationships between the values of the predictors and the values of the target. Different classification algorithms employ different strategies for finding relationships. These associations are summarised in a model, which may later be applied to a different data set in which the class assignments are unknown.I n most cases, the training set contains more data than the test set. Models are trained using this data.

The purpose of this data set is to test the model's capacity to generalise. Therefore, the data set is randomly divided into training and test data sets that each contains 80% and 20% of the data from each class, respectively.

3.2 The Logistic Regression Model

Analysis or measurement of the relationship among variables and the independent variables is known as regression. An equation expressing this relationship as an equation with parametric coefficients allows one to predict future values of the dependent variable (Paul. There are two primary kinds of regression: linear and logistic. When using linear regression, the dependent variable must be either a continuous variable or a categorical variable. Once the discrete variable has been turned into a continuous value that is dependent on the probability of the event occurring, logistic regression can be utilised.

$$J\left(\theta\right) = 1m \sum cost(h\theta\left(xi\right), mi = 1\left(yi\right)$$

$$Logp\left(x\right)1 - p\left(x\right) = {}^{2}0 + {}^{2}1\left(x\right)$$

Regression is used for three main purposes: (1) description Logistic regression (LR) assigns each predictor a coefficient that measures its independent contribution to the fluctuation of the dependent variable. If the answer is "Yes," the dependent variable Y is set to 1, and if the answer is "No," it is set to 0. The most likely collection of parameters to explain the given data is found via maximum likelihood estimation. An independent variable and its associated outcome are shown to be highly associated by their regression coefficients (R2). Each coefficient reflects the change in the response variable that would be expected if the predictor variable changed by one unit. The best model to accurately forecast the category of outcome for each given case. For this, a model with all predictor factors relevant for predicting the response variable is developed. The likelihood of success is compared to the likelihood of failure. The study's findings are presented as an odds ratio.

Figure 3. Linear and logistic regression model

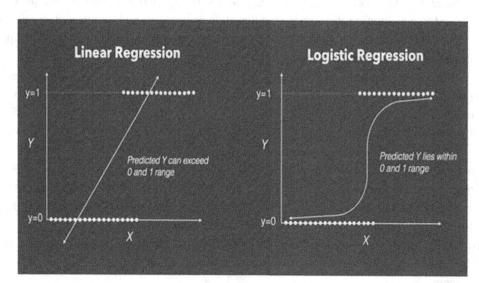

An explanatory variable x1 is used to explain the link between a dichotomous response variable (Y) coded to take one of two values, either success or failure: 1 or 0. There are two types of explanatory variables: quantitative and indicator variables. It has a Bernoulli distribution (BD) with $p = P (Y=1)$, which means that p is the probability of success for given values of the explanatory variables x1, x2,. $E[Y] = P (Y = 1) = p$ for a Bernoulli variable. Following is a definition of the logistic regression model: So, let pi represent Yi's average, which is $E [Yi] = P$ (since Yi is 1), and assume that each of these Bernoulli variables is an independent Bernoulli variable. Explanatory variables xi,1 and xi,2 can be used to express the mean value pi.

Using the sklearn library's Breast cancer dataset. An easy dataset for classifying objects into one of two categories. The sklearn datasets module contains a link to the data collection you want to use. Next, you may use the built-in function to extract X and Y from the dataset, as shown below. It is common to be able to classify a result event as either occurring or not occurring, depending on the circumstances. A heart attack or not; or a caesarean section or not, are examples of events that may simply be categorised as either occurring or not. Once this classification has been established, it will be possible to look at the factors that influence this outcome. A cutoff criterion has been created and the data has been transformed from continuous to categorical at the cutoff point. In other circumstances, the outcome may be considered dichotomous, but in reality, it is the result of censoring continuous data. Choosing the result variable can be more difficult in some situations. A dichotomous event can be formed from continuous results in specific cases. There are a lot of situations where well-defined cutoff points for the presence of an event are at issue. High blood pressure, which is defined as a systolic pressure more than or equal to 140 mm/Hg, is one such example. One thing to keep in mind is that many continuous or multi-category variables can be reduced to binary alternatives. A seven-category scale, from "totally healthy" to "terminal condition," could be simplified to two categories, such as "healthy" and "unhealthy," for example, if a patient's health status is expressed.

3.3 Advantages and Disadvantages of Logistic Regression

In comparison to discriminant analysis, logistic regression provides various advantages: Independent variables do not have to be regularly distributed or equal in variance within each group, making this method more robust. Nonlinear relationships between independent and dependent variables are not assumed.

- A non-linear impact may be handled by this software.
- Power and interaction terms can be explicitly stated.
- It is not necessary that the dependent variables have a normal distribution.
- There is no assumption of homogeneity of variance.
- It is not assumed that the error terms are normally distributed.
- No independent variables are required to be interval or unbounded.

3.4 Effect Size

Logistic regression is a bit like regression; therefore individuals who are familiar with regression ask "what's the R value?" R (or R squared) provides an indication of the equation's predictive power for the variable of interest in conventional regression. R close to 1 suggests a strong relationship, whereas R close to zero indicates a poor relationship. There is no direct equivalent of R for logistic regression. However, to keep those happy who insist on a R value, statisticians have come up with various R-like measures for logistic regression. Logistic regression does not make use of R at all.

3.5 Characteristics of COVID-19

While the profoundly pathogenic infection predominantly influences individuals through respiratory droplets, disseminated via ecological contact Unlike the various respiratory infections, other studies recommended that theSARS-CoV-2 communicated through the oral-fecal course. An ongoing investigation was done in ref. (Lauraitis, 2018) on stool specimens of seventy-one individuals with COVID-19, 39individuals +ve for fecal COVID-19 RNA, which supports the speculation that fecal-oral contamination could be an extra course for the extent of the infection. Generally, COVID-19 manifestations are cough, fever, as well as fatigue. Various gastrointestinal indications showed in contaminated individuals like diarrhea, nausea, as well as deficiency of appetite (Tian et al., ; Xue et al., 2019). It is also important to note that the infection contamination could happen with no manifestation; asymptomatic people are a possible wellspring of infection transmission.

4. RESULT AND DISCUSSION

OpenCV was used in a Python context for this project. Covid 19's range would be reduced by this model. Health officials in Israel made public the results of nasopharyngeal swabs tested for SARS-CoV-2 using the RT-PCR method. Table 1 shows the total number of cases and deaths of COVID-19 affected by the top ten nations.

Table 1. Statistics of the total number of cases and deceased cases due to COVID-19 affected by top ten countries as of 22nd January, 2022

Location	Total Cases	Deaths
India	3,89,03,731	4,88,884
Germany	86,35,461	1,16,668
United States	7,01,30,650	8,64,182

4.1 Performance Measures

There are four parametric measures used to evaluate the proposed model presentation, which are labelled as follows as,

Sensitivity: It defines the proportion of positives measured as such is defined by using the Equation (1);

$$Sensitivity = \frac{TP}{TP + FN} \tag{1}$$

Specificity: It defines the proportion of real negatives that are correctly recognized by using the Equation (2);

$$Specificity = \frac{TN}{TN + FP} \tag{2}$$

Accuracy: It is the proportion of true outcomes (both TP and TN) in the population is definedby using the Equation (3);

$$Accuracy = \frac{TP + TN}{TP + TN + FP + FN} \tag{3}$$

F-score:When calculating the model's sensitivity and specificity, you'll use the F-score, which is also known as the harmonic mean of those two values.

Table 2. Performance analysis of the proposed scheme under different training sizes and diverse measures

Test and Training Size	Accuracy (%)	Sensitivity (%)	Specificity (%)	F-Score (%)
10%-20%	81.62	78.65	85.72	72.12
60%-40%	86.35	83.96	87.48	72.64
40%-60%	89.99	86.64	88.35	84.25
80%-20%	92.95	90.01	91.20	89.47
Average	**87.71**	**85.01**	**88.25**	**79.62**

Figure 4. Graphical representation of performance measure

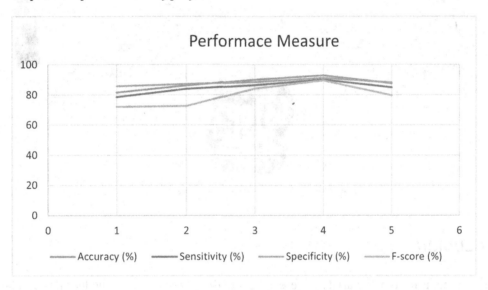

Figure 5. Testing user input model

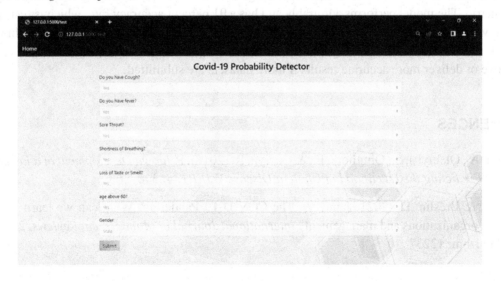

$$F - score = 2 \cdot \frac{Sensitivity \cdot Specificity}{Sensitivity + Specificity} \tag{4}$$

Figure 6. User output model

5. CONCLUSION

This study can be utilized by a variety of researchers to discover how machine learning can be used to foresee not only this but also other scenarios. Our approach uses a logistic regression model to calculate a likelihood percentage value for the presence or absence of covid-19. The chosen algorithm was honed using the clinical data of the patient. The trained algorithms were evaluated using the accuracy performance metric. The model performs admirably and has a 91 percent accuracy rate, which is respectable; however, various models can be used to improve the accuracy and produce even better results. In various countries, COVID-19 has killed a significant number of people. The model's performance is expected to improve or deliver more accurate results if more datasets are submitted.

REFERENCES

Aroyehun, A., Olabiyisi, S., Omidiora, E., & Ganiyu, R. (2018). P. *Idowu Development of a Fuzzy Logic Model for Predicting the Likelihood of Cholera Disease WJERT, 4*, 340–363.

Bailey, K., & Breslin, D. (2021, January). The COVID-19 Pandemic: What can we learn from past research in organizations and management? *International Journal of Management Reviews, 23*(1), 3–6. doi:10.1111/ijmr.12237

Boiral, O., Brotherton, M. C., Rivaud, L., & Guillaumie, L. (2021, January). Organizations' management of the COVID-19 pandemic: A scoping review of business articles. *Sustainability (Basel)*, *13*(7), 3993. doi:10.3390u13073993

Emokhare, B. & Igbape, B. (2015). Fuzzy Logic Based Approach to Early Diagnosis of Ebola Hemorrhagic Fever. *Proceedings of the World Congress on Engineering and Computer Science, 2*, 1-6.

Hasan, M. A., & Sher-E, K. M. (2010). -Alam, A.R. *Chowdhury Human Disease Diagnosis Using a Fuzzy Expert System Journal of Computing*, *2*, 66–70.

Hassan, M., & Hasson, S. T. (2020). *A controllability algorithm to minimize the spreading chance of COVID-19 in individual networks.* In Proc. 4th Int. Conf. I-SMAC, Palladam, India. 10.1109/I-SMAC49090.2020.9243481

Kuščer, K., Eichelberger, S., & Peters, M. (2022). Tourism organizations' responses to the COVID-19 pandemic: An investigation of the lockdown period. *Current Issues in Tourism*, *25*(2), 247–260. doi:10.1080/13683500.2021.1928010

Lauraitis, R. & Maskeliūnas, R. (2018). Damaševičius ANN and Fuzzy Logic Based Model to Evaluate Huntington Disease Symptoms. *J HealthcEng*, *2018*, 1–10.

Lotfi, M., Hamblin, M. R., & Rezaei, N. (2020). COVID-19: Transmission, prevention, and potential therapeutic opportunities. *Clinica Chimica Acta*, *508*, 254–266. doi:10.1016/j.cca.2020.05.044 PMID:32474009

Lythgoe, M. P., & Middleton, P. (2020, June 1). Ongoing clinical trials for the management of the COVID-19 pandemic. *Trends in Pharmacological Sciences*, *41*(6), 363–382. doi:10.1016/j.tips.2020.03.006 PMID:32291112

Najibi, M., Samangouei, P., Chellappa, R., & Davis, L. S. (2017). Ssh: Single stage headless face detector. *Proceedings of the IEEE International Conference on Computer Vision (ICCV)*. IEEE. 10.1109/ICCV.2017.522

Ndaïrou, F., Area, I., Nieto, J. J., & Torres, D. F. (2020, June 1). Mathematical modeling of COVID-19 transmission dynamics with a case study of Wuhan. *Chaos, Solitons, and Fractals*, *135*, 109846. doi:10.1016/j.chaos.2020.109846 PMID:32341628

Sabino, C. P., Ball, A. R., Baptista, M. S., Dai, T., Hamblin, M. R., Ribeiro, M. S., Santos, A. L., Sellera, F. P., Tegos, G. P., & Wainwright, M. (2020, November 1). Light-based technologies for management of COVID-19 pandemic crisis. *Journal of Photochemistry and Photobiology. B, Biology*, *212*, 111999. doi:10.1016/j.jphotobiol.2020.111999 PMID:32855026

Samui, P., Mondal, J., & Khajanchi, S. (2020, November 1). A mathematical model for COVID-19 transmission dynamics with a case study of India. *Chaos, Solitons, and Fractals*, *140*, 110173. doi:10.1016/j.chaos.2020.110173 PMID:32834653

Su, S., Delbracio, M., Wang, J., Sapiro, G., Heidrich, W., & Wang, O. (2017). Deep video deblurring for hand-held cameras. *Proceedings of the IEEE Conference on Computer Vision and Pattern Recognition (CVPR)*, (pp. 1279–1288). IEEE.

Tian, Y., Zhang, Y., Fu, Y., & Xu, C. (2020). Tdan: Temporally-deformable alignment network for video super-resolution. *Proceedings of the IEEE/CVF Conference on Computer Vision and Pattern Recognition (CVPR)*. IEEE. 10.1109/CVPR42600.2020.00342

Xue, T., Chen, B., Wu, J., Wei, D., & Freeman, W. T. (2019). Video enhance- ment with task-oriented flow. *International Journal of Computer Vision, 127*(8), 1106–1125. doi:10.100711263-018-01144-2

Chapter 3
A Novel Phishing Attack Prediction Model With Crowdsouring in Wireless Networks

Senthilkumar Subramanian

University College of Engineering, BIT Campus, Anna University, Tiruchirappalli, India

Nithya Venkatachalam

University College of Engineering, Villupuram, Anna University, India

Regan Rajendran

University College of Engineering, Villupuram, Anna University, India

ABSTRACT

As the web and applications for knowledge technology developed, many attacks and security problems started to emerge. The last couple of years have seen a significant development in 6G wireless networking. It is challenging to create a secure wireless network. In phishing attacks on wireless networks, attackers create phishing websites that allow users to enter personal information such as usernames, passwords, security numbers, and credit card details. Phishing emails that contain links to websites that are used to spread malware. This project suggests a real time phishing detection plug-in for the web browser which uses a random forest classifier to identify and notify users. As a result, the consumer can get an alert right away. The suggested systems specify wireless phishing attack detection in the current context and produce superior results. The authors proposed 18 traits in order to cover every aspect of phish behavior. With the help of an accepted dataset, the suggested phishing detection system was trained.

DOI: 10.4018/978-1-6684-8306-0.ch003

INTRODUCTION

Network users gain from developing and using the Internet in various ways. Security is becoming crucial due to the widespread use of networks, yet, Wireless devices, computers, networks, data, applications, etc., are all strongly tied to wireless security. Wireless networks can easily access, modify, and disrupt those systems because there are more and more web connection in schools, e-markets, hospitals, banks, and the armed forces. Smartphone have become the go-to electronic devices for most people because of their low cost, ease of use, small size, and battery life. As the use of mobile phone has grown, so too have the security risks associated with them. Attackers now frequently target wireless gadgets. Attackers solicit the user's private information by sending SMS links to phishing Web Pages. The privacy of user data on networks has emerged as one of the most important research concerns because wireless networks make a vast amount of data readily available. The usage of mobile phishing assaults results in numerous incidences of privacy infringement. It is challenging to protect wireless networks from phishing and other assaults since they provide open access. When using a Wi-Fi to Wi-Fi connection, regular consumers must be aware of security precautions and are more susceptible to phishing scams(Goel, D., & Jain, A. K. 2018). In this phishing attack, the "No Internet Connection" web page is displayed in the victim's browser to trick him into thinking he does not have an internet connection. The victim may notice Google Chrome with the message "Unable to Connect to the Internet" if they use that particular browser. The victim is operating Windows; therefore, the same header allows us to display a web-based mimic of Windows network manager.

In the review "Phishing Insights 2021" by Sophos, researcher insecurity claims that phishing attempts against enterprises increased significantly during the pandemic as millions of employees working from home became a primary target for hackers. According to 60% of IT teams, the number of phishing emails aimed at employees grew in 2020. It was possible to identify which phishing URLs were related to each issue by analyzing them globally between January 2020 and February 2021, COVID-related topics, keywords created and applying to match. We discovered that between December 2020 and February 2021, phishing attempts about and targeting pharmacies and hospitals increased by 189%, while vaccine-related phishing assaults increased by 530%. Software as a Service (Saas), webmail, and phishing attacks reached 22.2% in a quarter, according to Comparitech Security Company's study on attack data for 2019–2021. As a result, financial institutions now represent the majority of targets (22.5%). As shown in figure 1 below, assaults against payment and e-commerce platforms have increased by a small percentage.

Figure 1. Most targeted industries 2020

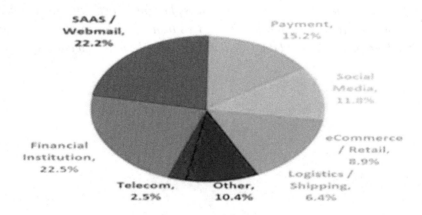

BACKGROUND

List of Phishing in Wireless Medium

1. Phishing attacks use search engines to guide users to online retailers selling goods and services cheaply. The website stores the MasterCard data when the user attempts to purchase the item. While the website below is false and was made by the hacker to collect personal data, the search engine is authentic.
2. When mobile devices are connected with Bluetooth, the attacker's device can connect to Bluetooth with the victim's device and send malicious data to it using the default credentials. Contacts, messages, and files are accessible by the attacker after he has gained access to the device over Bluetooth.
3. Host file poisoning is changing a website's entries to drive users to a fraudulent website where their l data is stolen.
4. Wi-Fi access points for an attacker. In most cases, users don't verify the access point they're using, and the attacker can crash between 6G
5. User submitting credentials for session hijacking is authenticated by the application server using cookie values that contain the session id. A user's SID can be obtained by an attacker, who can then use it to hack the user's account and get access.
   5. A potential attacker hunts down weak web servers and compromises them. Backdoors with password protection are deployed, and an attacker can access the server using an encrypted backdoor. Download websites with phishing that have already been established and advertised bogus websites.
   6. MiTM stands for "Man in The Middle Attack, where victim is put between the attacker and the website."
   7. To ensure that users' transactions are unaffected, the attacker keeps sending the data to a trustworthy website.

Security Concerns of Wireless Devices

The many security issues and risks relating to smartphones are covered in this section. Wireless resources are assets that motivate hackers to launch assaults against Smartphone devices. Assets include things like data, software, and the actual gadget. Smartphones should consider security concerns like availability, confidentiality, and integrity. Smartphone flaws allowed the attacker to take control of the device.

Assets

Due to the assets, which include information, hardware, and applications in smartphones, hackers target wireless devices. The 6G mobile devices' information is one of their assets. Both the data kept on the device and the data sent by the smartphone are included for instance, call history, contacts, SMS, location data, login information, etc. The device itself is useful. An attacker may utilize a stolen phone to carry out a variety of destructive actions. Applications are another plus. Applications come in two varieties: those that are free to use and those that are commercial and need payment. Users save their

ID and password on programmers to save typing-in login information again. So applications are closely connected with data.

Security Objectives

Confidentiality, integrity, and availability are among the security goals of wireless devices. Attackers compromise these security goals by hacking the equipment. Security goals for building secure support between client and server include confidentiality. It creates permission for the right person to access corresponding information. Only authorized persons are allowed to alter the resources and must do it legally; it is integrity. Information integrity refers to safeguarding it against unauthorized alteration. The users must always have access to the resources, which means they must immediately satisfy their needs.

Reasons for Vulnerabilities in Wireless Devices

Even though researchers continuously study wireless devices' security, they must analyze the device's numerous security dangers. Identification of smartphone vulnerabilities is necessary to establish secure wireless commutation. Here, provided a brief overview of the various causes of smartphone vulnerabilities (Goel, D., & Jain, A. K. 2018). A mobile device's web Brower open in less screen .It is challenging to check the page's integrity on mobile browsers due to small size and lack of complete URL display. The bulk of information comes in second to the mobile device. Smartphones have a lot of personal data stored on them. This information is essential because most users use their smartphones to conduct financial transactions like online buying or banking. Attackers may benefit financially significantly from this knowledge. Open-source platforms come in third. The majority of smartphones run on open-source platforms like Android. Because the kernel for Android is open source, malware developers may easily learn about the 6G mobile platform, encouraging them to create and distribute dangerous programs. The risk of introducing malware into smartphones rises as a result of user downloads and installations of programmers. Fourth is a straightforward login screen. The typical login experience of 6G mobile apps makes it easier for attackers to create a phishing app or website. Fifth, users are not aware of Smartphone security because of ignorance or negligence. The sixth point is to download software from an independent app store. Hackers propagate dangerous software using third-party application stores. Users of smartphones can download and install downloadable applications freely. Sometimes attackers create fake apps and post in Play store to trick users. They then release an update that changes the software to include the malicious code.

Threats to Wireless Devices

Wireless devices may be threatened by users or by outside intruders. Malware threats from attackers can disclose or change personal information saved on smartphones, disrupt the accessibility of services, and impair the device's functionality. Wireless hackers use techniques such as listening in, tampering and monitoring to corrupt, manipulate, and interruption information transmitted via wireless networks. Another concern is a denial of service (DoS) attack, which threatens the user's ability to use their mobile phone and its features. The threat of a break-in is when an attacker can take partial or whole control of the device by injecting code, exploiting coding faults, or utilizing logical flaws. Malfunctioning, phishing, device loss, and platform manipulation are threats from consumers' ignorance. Some apps may not perform properly due to improper user settings. Another issue resulting from user negligence is phishing, where hackers obtain users' personal information by deceiving them. Another risk arises from losing the device since criminals can grab it and use it maliciously.

Phishing Through Online Social Networks

Social networking websites are used by millions of individuals worldwide for both personal and professional contact, and they have grown to be a significant component of the Internet. Users of social networking sites can communicate with one another and exchange ideas. These networking sites are a new target for assaults because they attract many users. Hackers abuse users' confidence in social networking platforms for personal gain. The following discussion covers various techniques attackers can employ to trick people on social networking sites.

1. *Impersonation*: On social networking sites, users like and follow well-known people and join organizations that interest them. However, no process exists to determine whether a social network profile is real. Hackers will take advantage of this by impersonating a well-known individual and posting links to sales, gifts or coupon links, and when clicked, request personal information or download malware.
2. Promoting malicious URLs: hackers employ malicious URLs to send users to a fake website they control on an external network. Dummy accounts might have posted the links. Nearly 90% of clicks on malicious URLs posted by the attacker occur within 24 hours of the posting. When the link appears to be a promising link, social engineering can be used to divert users. Due to the difficulty in determining whether a social engineering attack is legitimate, social media providers struggle to prevent them. The website to which you were redirected can contain misleading information, such as fraudulent login pages, applications, or adverts for bogus products.
3. *Fake profiles:* hackers may approach users by sending friend requests and posing as an old acquaintance. Once attackers connect to the user's friend list, they can access the user's sensitive information shared with friends, family, and coworkers. An attacker may email the user and request a phone number or email inbox for additional information.
4. *Fake Groups:* The attacker may form a phoney communities in the name of a recognized organization and include select persons linked with that organization. They issue group requests to other workers, who accept them when they see that their coworkers are already in the group. After eavesdropping on their private chats, the attacker applies his knowledge to himself.
5. *Content spoofing*: To trick the user and lead him away from the authentic website where he is solicited for personal information, the phisher updates a portion of the text of the reputable website. For instance, malicious code could be injected into the system to capture user data and send it to the hacker's server.

RELATED WORK

Attacks can be characterized as attempts to get beyond the system's security measures, making information simpler to access, edit, or completely delete. Due to the openness of wireless channels, vulnerabilities to network security have increased along with the development of wireless communication systems. In this part, we will look at similar work to identify phishing attacks in wireless networks because privacy and security are vulnerable on the open wireless Internet. (Amritsar et al. 2017)suggested the browser extension kAYO, distinguishing between good and bad mobile web pages. It distinguishes between malicious and desktop websites. In order to identify fraudulent mobile websites, kAYO examines static properties of web pages. In order to protect internet users from being targeted by phishing attacks, using formal concept analysis, and rough set analysis (D.P. Aharajya, P.S. Ahmed, N.S. 2017), it is proposed that users assess whether the web addressi s correct and semantically compatible with the site content. Bottazzi et al. (2015) suggested an MP-Shied Architecture for Phishing Attempts on Mobile Webpages. This Android app is a proxy service that makes use of the TCP/IP stack. It attempts to analyses the structure of Internet Protocol packets originating from and passing to mobile apps by removing the Hypertext Transfer Protocol get operations from a packet. The packets are examined using a virtual private network (VPN) service, and a watchdog engine is utilized to determine whether or not the URL is blacklisted. (Tianjun Chen et al. 2021) Develop Android-based phishing by researching and identifying phishing attacks. The proposed study assesses wireless network risk using the TMM and HDT algorithms. The popular procedures that (Martinovic, Ivan, et al.2007) suggested for web-based authentication are used to illustrate two distinct attacks on it. One assault hijacks wireless clients by making use of operational flaws in low- and middle-priced devices, while the other takes advantage of a wired network weakness that is already well known.

Authentication technique by (Munivel, E., &Kannammal,2019) A. was made in order to secure mobile services. The user and service provider will be verified using the zero_knowledge evidence-based authentication protocol without revealing the password. According to(Musthyala, Harish et al. 2021), wireless networks are the most vulnerable without a physical connection to the network. Python makes hacking simple and requires little technical expertise because of its benefits. Avoid choosing. "Automatically Connect "while connecting to a Wi-FiWi-Fi network to prevent this attack. A visual cryptography-based anti-phishing strategy is offered by (V. and R. Kumar. 2015). This method calls for the user to create two copies of an image using the (2, 2) visual cryptography scheme. "MobiFish" was offered by Wu et al.2014 as a small-scale phishing prevention solution for smartphones and tablets to protect users from phishing attacks on mobile pages, apps, and personal accounts.. In this model, phishing issues occur whenever there is a discrepancy between an instance's real identity and the identity that it claims to be. The user's displayed screen returns the claimed identification.

Current Issues and Challenges

Researchers have proposed several ways to identify and stop mobile phishing assaults; however, the now available solutions do not work for all sorts of attacks. We have covered a few unresolved issues in this area that require attention. Updates to the Blacklist and White List are required often. These lists' effectiveness could be improved by the time and effort needed to update them. Phishing attempts that exploit vulnerabilities the day they are discovered are known as zero-day attacks. There is currently no technology that can accurately identify zero-day phishing assaults. In machine learning-based defense approaches, choosing the right classifier might be difficult. A good classifier has high detection accuracy and requires little training time. Phishing websites resemble their related genuine websites almost exactly. In order to compare the two occurrences' levels of resemblance, a threshold value is calculated. In order to present correct results, it is crucial to choose the right threshold value. Another critical issue is phishing attacks on user knowledge. Non technical users, for the most part, do not want to learn, and if they do, the majority of them will quickly need to recall what they've learned. In order to collect features and evaluate them in real-time, machine learning approaches are currently employed frequently to find phishing attacks in desktop computers and 6G mobile phones. Therefore, these methods needed to be enhanced.

OVERVIEW OF THE PROPOSED SYSTEM

Social networks have emerged as one of the most often-used venues for user interaction. In a In a web-based phishing effort, a hacker creates fake websites that seem like significant websites, such as online social platforms, in order to trick visitors into entering personal information, such as login credentials, Security numbers, payment card details, and so on. The resemblance between websites may be a crucial statistic for identifying phishing because the appearance of websites is one of the most important variables in misleading users. In order to address this issue, we offer Phishing-Alarm, a workaround that leverages attributes that are challenging for attackers to evade to spot phishing attempts. We compare the predictive performance of various machine learning methods, including Logistic Regression (LR), Classification and Regression Trees (CART), Bayesian Additive Regression Trees (BART), Support Vector Machines (SVM), Random Forests (RF), and Neural Networks, in order to predict phishing websites (NNet).

System Architecture

Using Python's Scikit-Learn, a Random Forest classifier is trained using data from phishing sites. The learned classifier is extracted to JSON since a random forest classifier representation has been developed. An implemented browser uses the JSON model format to categorize the web page loading in the current browser tab. The system's goal is to alert the user if phishing occurs. The Random Forest classifier evaluates 18 aspects of a website to determine whether it is a real or site of spoofing. The The Python Arff Library loads the dataset's arff file and chooses 18 of the 30 available features. The features chosen are picked with the understanding that they will be retrieved off-line and separated from any online service or third party. Training and testing groups are generated from the features-rich dataset. The Random Forest is then exported in the above-mentioned JSON format. A URL serves as the host for the JSON file. The client-side web browser plug-in is set up to execute a script coding that extracts and encodes your selected features immediately after a page loads. After the features have been decoded, the plug-in checks to see if the exported model JSON is cached before downloading it again. Figure 2 contains the whole system's schematic diagram.

Figure 2. Architecture for phishing alarm

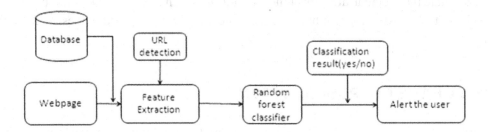

The script can use the feature and the JSON for classification. If the phishing website is detected, the user will be shown a warning. The whole system is made from lightweight materials to reduce detection time.

UI Design

A user-friendly interface for the plug-in has been created using HTML and CSS. A sizable circle in the user interface (UI) shows the legitimate proportion of the web page in the active tab. Additionally, the circle's color varies according to the classification outcome (Green for legitimate websites and Light Red for phishing). The results of the analysis, including the recovered features, are displayed below the circle in the following color scheme

Green – Legitimate request
Yellow – Suspicious request
Light Red – Phishing request

To prevent users from transmitting confidential information to the website, the plug-in also shows a phishing warning. Test results are shown on a separate screen, including precision, recall, and accuracy. In Figure 3, the UI is displayed.

Figure 3. UI Design

Pre-Processing

A numpy array is filled with the dataset retrieved from the UCI repository. The dataset, which has thirty characteristics, must be reduced for the browser to retrieve it. Each feature is tested on the browser to guarantee that it can be used without the aid of a third party or other external web services. Based on the investigations, 18 features were chosen out of thirty with low loss in test data accuracy. More features improve accuracy, but because feature extraction takes time, they also slow down the capacity to detect quickly. In order to balance the tradeoff, a subset of features is chosen.

Table 1. Web-page features

IP address	Degree of subdomain	Anchor tag href domain
Length of URL	Hypertext Transfer Protocol Secure	Link and script domains
URL shortened	domain favicon	Empty Form Handler
@ Symbol in URL	TCP port number	mailto link in HTML
// Redirection	domain name HTTPS	<iframe> tag
Domain '-'	Cross-domain request	<a> anchor tag

The collection dataset is then split in two phase, with the testing dataset making up 35% of the training dataset. Both testing and training data is stored on a disk.

Training

The pre-processing module's training dataset is imported from the disk. In data mining approach classification used to train dataset using the science-kit-learn. Random Forest employs 10 decision tree estimators in its ensemble learning method. All decision trees use CART to minimize gini impurity.

$$gini(D) = 1 - \sum pj^2 \tag{1}$$

Where pj is the probability of class. The cross validation is calculated from the dataset. F1 is calculated from the test data. The trainable model is converted to JSON in the module below.

Exporting Model

Each machine learning algorithm learns its parameters values in the training process. Each decision tree in Random Forest is an independent learner that learns class probabilities and node threshold values from the leaf nodes. In order to express the Random Forest in JSON, a format must be developed. The key number of estimators, number of classes, and others make up the total JSON structure.

Figure 4. Random forest JSON structure

```
{
    "n_features": 17,
    "n_classes": 2,
    "classes": [-1, 1],
    "n_outputs": 1,
    "n_estimators": 10,
    "estimators":[{
        "type": "split",
        "threshold": "<float>",
        "left": {},
        "right": {}
    },
    {
        "type": "leaf",
        "value": ["<float>", "<float>"]
    }]
}
```

Plug-in Feature Extraction

Each web page must have the 18 properties above extracted and encoded in real-time as the page loads. It uses a content script to access the web page's DOM. Each page automatically contains the content script as it loads. The features must be gathered by the content script and sent to the plug-in. The primary goal of this effort is to avoid utilizing any external online services, and the features must be independent of network latency and quick to extract. All of these are taken into account while creating feature extraction techniques. Depending on the following notation, a feature is encoded into the numbers "-1, 0, 1" after extracting it.

0 - Suspicious 1 – Legitimate 1: Phishing

The content script sends the feature vector with 18 encoded values to the plug-in.

Classification Phishing Attack

The data in the code sends the feature vector-based to Random Forest for classification. The JSON for the random forest settings is then downloaded and saved to the hard disc. When the cache fails, the script attempts to load the random forest JSON from disc and re-cavities it. Using JSON, a structure based on

JavaScript is constructed to mimic the random forest's behaviour. It computes the binary classification by comparing the feature vector to the node threshold. The binary model classification produces results depending on the values of the leaf nodes. If a web page is discovered to be a phishing site, the user is alerted.

Random Forest Classifier

Using bagging, Random Forests can be constructed alongside random attribute selection. Random Forests use a divide-and-conquer performance improvement method known as the ensemble approach to learning. The input or test is introduced at the top of a straightforward decision tree and travels down the tree, arriving at smaller subsets. The ensemble mechanism in a random forest mixes several random subsets of trees. All of the trees are explored by the input/test. In contrast, categorical data is the result of a majority vote rather than an average with weighting of every participant's outcomes. The strength of each classifier and the degree of classifier reliance determine the accuracy of a random forest, which also solves the issue of decision trees' overfitting.

System Development

Overall, the system is divided into a backend and a plug-in. Dataset pre-processing and training modules make up the backend. The plug-frontend comprises JavaScript files for background and content scripts, including the Random Forest script. The plug-in also has files for the user interface's mark up and styles. The system analyses the web page while also extracting its properties. A random forest classifier was used to extract the features. Therefore, the choice was made based on the web page utilizing 18 criteria for URL detection.

Figure 5. Module split up

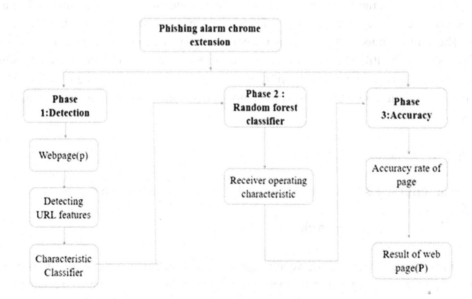

Algorithm

Let *P* web page;
    Using a Random forest classifier
    Phase I: Detection
    Function Detect ()is

1.   *input*: a Web-page *P*
2.   *output*: URL extraction
3.   *Compute*: Compute web page (P) characteristics by using the classifier.

    Phase II: Random forest classifier.
    Function compare web-page (p) characteristic,

1.   *input*: characteristic of webpage(p),
2.   *output*: Classifier of webpage(p),
3.   *compute* Receiver operating characteristic
4.   *compute* the precision score of (P),
5.   *Compute* Recall score of (*P*).

    Phase III: Accuracy

1.   *input*: precision of (P), recall of (P);
2.   *output*: the Accuracy rate of *P*,
3.   the web pages (P) is in value 1, then;
4.   Display ``warning'' and the Accuracy rate of (*P*).

Deployment Details

The Classifier JSON and Test set are delivered through HTTP protocol, and Python 3 is needed for the backend. The plug-in is distributed as a single file and functions for the Chrome browser. The following features consider to detect the phishing attack sites.

1.Domain Name in IP Address.
    2.   length of URL
    3.   URL Shorter
4.URL having @ symbol
    5.   Redirect URL
    6.   prefixes and suffixes added to domain name
    7.   Number of sub domain
    8.   Not Trusted website using HTTPS
    9.   External domain favicon website loaded
    10. opening the ports
    11. "HTTPS" token to a URL's domain portion

12. URL Request
13. URL Request with <a> tag
14. <script> and links
15. URL with abnormal request
16. Mailto tag in HTML
17. iframe tag in HTML
18. Form Handler for the Server

STUDIED METHODS FOR PHISHING

Logistic Regression

Logistic regression, is the most commonly used statistical model to evaluate binary response. It is widely used due to its ease of use and high level of interpretability. Logit function is often used as part of generalized linear models. For example, if b is a binary variable, and p predictors can be vectors of p, x can be used as a parameter of p regression (x=(x1, x2,...xp)). Logistics regression works best when variables have a close-to-neither-neither relationship. On the other hand, it may perform better if variables have more complex non-neither-nor relationships. Logistics models also require additional statistical assumptions prior to use compared to the other methods. The accuracy of the predictions is evaluated for missing data in a dataset.

Classification Regression Trees

CART, which stands or Classification and Regression Trees, can be used to model the conditional probability distribution of b given a. The model is made up of a tree with I terminal nodes and parameters connected to the i-th terminal node. Models for discrete answers (y) are often referred to as classification trees, whereas models for continuous responses (x) are referred to as regression trees. As a binary tree recursively divides the predictor space into discrete homogenous parts, the terminal nodes of the distinct regions serve as the tree's nodes. The binary tree structure can be used to approximate non-standard relationships. The internal nodes of the binary tree's related splitting criterion also determine the division. If the shape is invalid, the split node's left and right are assigned correspondingly. If the splitting variable is discrete, the shape is dropped, and the proper and subsequent left of the splitting node, respectively, are given a splitting rule. CART is flexible and can easily irregular relationships. It is the capacity to comprehend the interplay between predictor interactions. Its binary form also makes it simple to interpret. CART, however, has to make improvements in a number of areas, including its propensity to over-inform. Furthermore, since only one giant sequoia is grown, it is difficult to consider additions.

Support Vector Machines

In recent years, Support Vector Machines (SVM) have emerged to be one of the top successful classifiers. By increasing the distance between their closest points, the optimal separation hyperplane between the two classes can be discovered. Assume we have a discriminating function with +1 and -1 desired values. and two classes that can be linearly separated. A discriminating hyperplane will boost the margin of separation by meeting the support vectors, or the border points. The best-separating hyperplane is therefore located in the middle of the margin. SVMs have a lot of shortcomings despite the fact that they are highly effective and frequently used in classification. The necessary and significant computations are used to teach the knowledge. They additionally risk overfitting because they are sensitive to noisy data.

Neural Networks

It is constructed from connected, identical components (neurons). The synapses commonly transmit signals from one neuron to its opposite. The linkages also feature weights to improve neuronal delivery. Despite their inherent weakness, neurons can perform complex calculations when connected to other neurons. Because the constraints on the connections change as the network is being trained, major connections become more crucial during the testing phase. Because connections do not chain back or pass over other neurons, the network is called feed-forward. The nonlinear nature of hidden neurons contributes to the strength of neural networks. Nonlinearity must be added into the network before it can learn complex mappings. In neural network research, a sigmoid equation is commonly used.

Bayesian and Regression Trees

The method for discovering the undiscovered relationship between an infinite output (B) and a p-dimensional vector of inputs (BART) is known as Bayesian and Regression Trees. The fundamental idea behind BART is to estimate or model f(A) via a set of regression trees, that only fully explains a small fraction of the input-output relationship. This idea was influenced by ensemble methods in general and boosting algorithms in specific. Other additive models can find it challenging to account for high-order interactions between input variables whereas BART makes this task straightforward. Additionally, BART does not require the selection of variables because the trees are automatically built. Due to the nature of the Bayesian technique, computation times are frequently long. Prior to estimation, the model's parameters must be determined, and thereafter, the posterior probability must be calculated. Markov chain Monte Carlo (MCMC) simulation is typically used to approx. the posterior conclusion process (Wu, Yirui et al. 2020).

Sample Screenshot During Testing

The plug-output in's when a user visits a phishing website, as captured by Phish Tank. Visual studio code is used to implement the application. In this case, the goal is to identify the phishing page using a Chrome extension. The plug-in output while visiting a phishing site was taken from Phish Tank. This is the plug-in of the chrome extension.

Figure 6. Phishtor home page

Phishtor Detection With Safe Site

Figure 7. Phishtor safe sites
Note: Figure 7 shows the site's safety and accuracy rate.

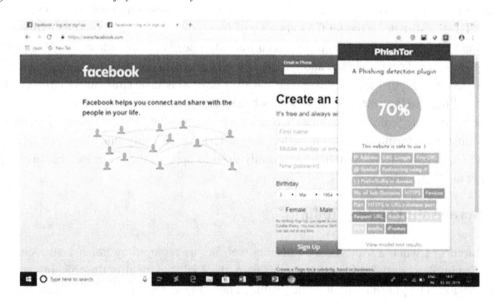

Phishing Detection for Phish Site

Figure 8. Phishing site
Note: Figure 8 shows whether the site is phishing and its accuracy rate.

Phishtor With Alert Box

Figure 9. Phishtor alarm
Note: Figure 9 shows detecting phishing sites to show an alert box.

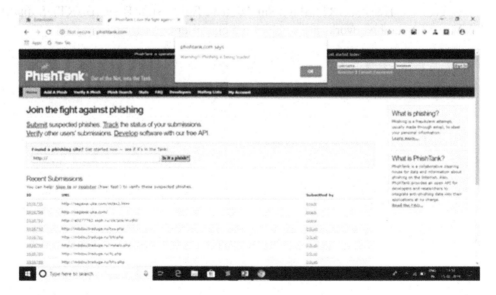

Analysis Dimensions

Accuracy parameter serves as a safeguard by enabling detection with fewer false positive and false negative results. Precision = tp / (tp + fn)

Recall = tn/ (fp+ tn)

true positive (tp): raises an alert when a phishing request is made.

true negative (tn): an event that is not a phishing attack and does not raise an alert.

false positive (fp): an event that raises an alert, although it is not a phishingattack.

false negative (fn): an event that, although a phishing attack, does not raise an alert.

The entire system's performance is evaluated using the standard parameters described below.

Table 2. Comparison of proposed work with existing classifiers

Techniques	Precision	Recall	F1 Measure
LR	95.11%	82.96%	88.59%
CART	92.32%	87.07%	89.59%
SVM	92.08%	82.74%	87.07%
Nnet	94.15%	78.28%	85.07%
Bart	94.18%	81.08%	87.09%
Proposed work (RF)	91.71%	88.88%	90.24%

Classification and Regression Trees (CART), Random forests (RF), Logistic Regression (LR), Classification and Regression Trees (CART), Bayesian Additive Regression Trees (BART), Support vector machines (SVM) and Neural Networks are some of the classifiers.

Accuracy Graph

Figure 10. ROC classifier
Note: The test set's F1 score was calculated to be 0.904. Here, it achieves excellent accuracy than other existing systems

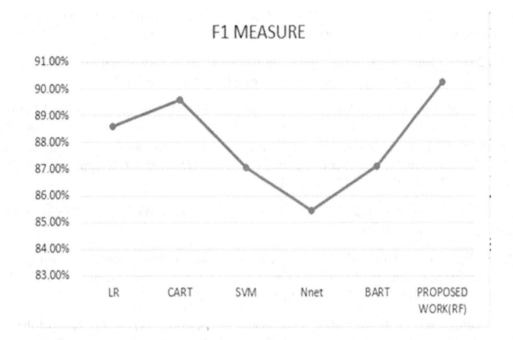

CONCLUSION

More people are utilizing smartphones every year. Global Smartphone usage is expected to increase from the current 6.4 billion users to 8 billion users by 2023. Attackers are now concentrating more on users of 6G Core mobile devices than on users of desktop computers because they are well aware of this development. Mobile application, emails, web pages, SMS and are just a few of the ways that phishers attack users on mobile devices. As a result, our phishing detection technology focuses on client-side deployment and fast detection to keep users safe from phishing attempts. The main implementation of the random forest classifier is in JavaScript. Identification depends on similar efforts as they often use web page features that are difficult to extract from client side. Before the page has fully loaded, the plug-in can already identify phishing. The test set's F1 score was calculated to be 0.904. The core implementation of the project will be the random forest method in this instance. Here, it achieves excellent accuracy, and our project's false-negative and true-positive rates were met. The classifier has trained 18 features to recognize phishing websites thus far. However, more than removing the phishing web page functionality is required. Therefore, there are many opportunities for upgrades and enhancements, and this approach offers a more useful solution for phishing detection.

REFERENCES

Ahmed, N. S. S., Acharjya, D. P., & Sanyal, S. (2017). A framework for phishing attack identification using rough set and formal concept analysis. *International Journal of Communication Networks and Distributed Systems*, *18*(2), 186–212. doi:10.1504/IJCNDS.2017.082105

Amrutkar, C., Kim, Y. S., & Traynor, P. (2017). Detecting malicious mobile web pages in real-time. *IEEE Transactions on Mobile Computing*, *16*(8), 2184–2197. doi:10.1109/TMC.2016.2575828

Azeez, N. (2020). Identifying phishing attacks in communication networks using URL consistency features. *International Journal of Electronic Security and Digital Forensics 12*(2), 200–213.

Bottazzi, G., Casalicchio, E., Cingolani, D., Marturana, F., & Piu, M. (2015). MP-Shield: A Framework for Phishing Detection in Mobile Devices. *IEEE International Conference on Computer and Information Technology; Ubiquitous Computing and Communications; Dependable, Autonomic and Secure Computing; Pervasive Intelligence and Computing (CIT/IUCC/DASC/PICOM)*, pp. 1977-1983. IEEE (2015) 10.1109/CIT/IUCC/DASC/PICOM.2015.293

Chen, T. (2021). Development and Implementation of Anti Phishing Wi-Fi and Information Security Protection APP based on Android. *J. Phys*.

Singh, S., Sarje, A. K., & Misra, M. (2012). Client-side counter phishing application using adaptive neuro-fuzzy inference system. In *2012 Fourth International Conference on Computational Intelligence and Communication Networks* (pp. 788–792). IEEE

Goel, D., & Jain, A. K. (2018). Mobile phishing attacks and defense mechanisms: State of the art and open research challenges. *Computers & Security*, *73*, 519–544. doi:10.1016/j.cose.2017.12.006

Gupta, B. B., Tewari, A., Jain, A. K., & Agrawal, D. P. (2017). Fighting against phishing attacks: State of the art and future challenges. *Neural Computing & Applications*, *28*(12), 3629–3654. doi:10.100700521-016-2275-y

Kumar, V., & Kumar, R. (2015). Detection of a phishing attack using visual cryptography in ad hoc network. *2015 International Conference on Communications and Signal Processing (ICCSP)*, (pp. 1021–1025). IEEE. 10.1109/ICCSP.2015.7322654

Martinovic, I. (2007). Phishing in the Wireless: Implementation and analysis. *IFIP International Information Security Conference*. Springer. 10.1007/978-0-387-72367-9_13

Munivel, E., & Kannammal, A. (2019). New authentication scheme to secure against phishing attacks in mobile cloud computing. *Security and Communication Networks*, 2019.

Musthyala, H., & Nagarjuna Reddy, P. (2021). Hacking wireless network credentials by performing phishing attack using Python Scripting. *2021 5th International Conference on Intelligent Computing and Control Systems (ICICCS)*. IEEE. 10.1109/ICICCS51141.2021.9432155

Wu, L., Du, X., & Wu, J. (2014, August). MobiFish: A lightweight anti-phishing scheme for mobile phones. In *Computer Communication and Networks (ICCCN), 2014 23rd International Conference on* (pp. 1-8). IEEE. 10.1109/ICCCN.2014.6911743

Wu, Y., Wei, D., & Feng, J. (2020). Network attacks detection methods based on deep learning techniques: A survey. *Security and Communication Networks*, *2020*, 1–17. doi:10.1155/2020/8872923

ADDITIONAL READING

Basit, A., Zafar, M., Liu, X., Javed, A. R., Jalil, Z., & Kifayat, K. (2021). A comprehensive survey of AI-enabled phishing attack detection techniques. *Telecommunication Systems*, *76*(1), 139–154. doi:10.100711235-020-00733-2 PMID:33110340

Bhavsar, V., Kadlak, A., & Sharma, S. (2018). Study on phishing attacks. *Int. J. Comput. Appl*, *182*, 27–29.

Goodman, J. T., Rehfuss, P. S., Rounthwaite, R. L., Mishra, M., Hulten, G. J., Richards, K. G., Deyo, R. C. (2012). U.S. Patent No. 8,291,065. Washington, DC: U.S. Patent and Trademark Office.

Irimie, A., Bartlett, W., & Austin, D. (2018). U.S. Patent No. 9,894,092. Washington, DC: U.S. Patent and Trademark Office.

Rehfuss, P., Goodman, J., Rounthwaite, R., Mishra, M., Hulten, G., Richards, K., & Deyo, R. (2006). U.S. Patent Application No. 11/129,665.

Chapter 4
Advanced Method of MOB–I App Used for Medical and Agriculture

Jenifer Mahilraj

https://orcid.org/0000-0002-6257-9682

Depatment of AI and DS, NPR College of Engineering and Technology, Natham, India

Josephine Sahaya Vergin

Alagappa University, India

Vidhyavathi Ramasamy

Alagappa University, India

Nooriya Begam

Alagappa University, India

Joseph Sahayarayan

Alagappa University, India

Sivaram Ponnusamy

https://orcid.org/0000-0001-5746-0268

Department of Artificial Intelligence, G.H. Raisoni College of Engineering, Nagpur, India

ABSTRACT

Over the past few years India has a significant rise in mobile applications. The development of apps for remote work, education, and healthcare has dramatically increased. Applications for cloud meetings, food delivery, gaming, business, social media, healthcare, and fitness are being downloaded by more users. The prevalence of smart phones, increased internet usage, and the incorporation of artificial intelligence and machine learning into mobile applications all suggest that demand for mobile will continue to increase in the future (apps). The importance of AI and ML in application development will rise over time. The aforementioned software is moreover generally acquired from app store websites like the Google Play Store and the App Store for any mobile OS. This chapter provides mobile intelligent applications (MOB-I App) are used to developing based on a model of AI for the human needs to their day-to-day life of their situation. A brief overview of some of the intelligent applications employed in the fields of medical and agriculture.

DOI: 10.4018/978-1-6684-8306-0.ch004

INTRODUCTION

In recent years, the usage of mobile applications has spread to a wide range of industries, influencing ones like agriculture, health care, and education for the better. Mobile apps using artificial intelligence can streamline our job. The arduous process of creating a mobile app can be greatly accelerated by incorporating AI and machine learning. We may advance things by applying artificial intelligence in mobile app development, which makes use of the knowledge and information we gather and save in our databases. Applications must continually adjust to the dynamically evolving nature of AI and IoT technology. There has been a significant shift in technology trends that favours intelligent apps. I-Apps, or intelligent applications, help you to fully utilise the capabilities of your smart devices and simplify routine activities.

The farming sector is seeing a rise in demand for greater efficiency as a result of technological advancement. These days, agricultural mobile devices rely on cutting-edge technologies like artificial intelligence, the internet of things, and machine learning. As a result, they can enhance transaction processing, data analysis, field monitoring, and more. Seeding, watering, harvesting, managing animals, and supply chain management are all entirely or at least partially automated thanks to creative technologies. But none of that would be feasible without smart phone apps that provide farmers the ability to monitor and manage what actually occurs on the farm. The idea of "smart farming" is gaining popularity and becoming easier to implement. The major objective of cutting-edge agriculture apps is to maximise crop productivity while lowering the amount of effort required from humans. Using smart agriculture applications, we may keep track of the goods that are kept in a warehouse or follow the path of the supply chain at every stage.

Mobile healthcare apps powered by AI are a great method to support health management. It can recommend routines and treatment strategies using data from wearable devices. AI can assist clinicians in making precise diagnosis, identifying high-risk profiles, and scheduling important tasks. When computers and other machines mimic human cognition and are able to learn, understand, and make decisions or take actions, this is referred to as artificial intelligence (AI). It can assist doctors and other healthcare professionals in providing more precise diagnoses and treatment recommendations by using patient data and other information. The use of ML and other cognitive disciplines for medical diagnosis is an important use of AI in healthcare. By analysing large data to create better preventive care suggestions for patients, AI can also assist in making healthcare more proactive and predictive.

LITERATURE REVIEW

Primary preventive strategies, such as vaccination, are receiving more and more attention due to the increased use of digital technology in healthcare. This review aimed to describe and evaluate existing digital health initiatives that encourage HPV vaccination among adolescents and their parents and to provide recommendations for how such programs could be improved. Factors including HPV-related information, talks about immunization, and vaccination intentions all improved due to the treatments (Choi et al., 2023). Smart homes, which include sensors for detecting motion, contact, light, temperature, and humidity; external memory aids, which combine activity learning through an intelligent home with mobile apps; and hybrid technologies, which combine multiple technologies such as devices installed at patients' homes and telemedicine, make up the intervention above technologies. Using intelligent houses in the community might have several advantages for continuity of care since it would let local and hospital health services constantly monitor the health of the elderly (Facchinetti et al., 2023). Mobile eHealth applications are rapidly gaining prominence in the healthcare management toolkit with the ability to provide information and assistance anytime. There is significant potential for pre-and post-operative patient assistance thanks to the author's creation of a unique digital health information technology (Görtz et al., 2023) that facilitates tailored support for doctor-nurse-patient dialogue.

Improve remote patient care and facilitate the spread of intelligent homes by integrating AI methods into the current Internet of Medical Things (IoMT) infrastructure. Integrating IoT medical sensors' data, analysis, and deep learning algorithms' complexity into a mobile AI engine's implementation on an AI-based cloud infrastructure presents a formidable programming challenge when working with real-time settings of AI technologies (Elbagoury et al., 2023). Rehabilitation treatments, such as anorectal biofeedback, are resource- and labour-intensive but may be delivered successfully and affordably via home-based healthcare. There was a case study done using biofeedback training methods. Clinical gold standard high-definition anorectal manometry was used to evaluate IoMT data. By presenting anorectal pressure profiles comparable to clinical manometry, we showed that our suggested IoMT is feasible and might be utilized for anorectal biofeedback treatment in the comfort of a patient's home (Zhou et al., 2022). The proliferation of mobile network data over the last several years has opened the door to fine-grained urban function identification by permitting the extraction of actionable insights about urban functions. The data from these cellular towers exhibit similarities while displaying differences for the same metropolitan functional zone. Three typical supervised learning models are used to test our system and chosen features; all three obtain above-average classification accuracy (Deng & Hu, 2022).

Among the younger elderly, behavioural attitude, subjective norms, and perceived behavioural control play a crucial role in determining their propensity to utilize applications designed for ageing. The emotional happiness of the young and old is significantly affected by the habit of using age-appropriate apps. The younger elderly's selective usage of age-appropriate applications is a good sign that they are actively adapting to and accepting new technology, boosting their happiness and quality of life (Liu & Tang, 2022). Finally, the authors present their system, which aggregates user categorization data to produce spatiotemporal analytics concerning regional and seasonal disease patterns, and makes these analytics available to all system users to raise awareness of global agricultural trends (Reda et al., 2022). This article aims to investigate the impact of a continuous nutrition management intervention based on a mobile medical APP on the health and growth of preterm newborns. Premature babies' nutritional health, growth and development, and quality of life may all benefit from an intervention plan centred on ongoing nutrition management delivered by mobile medical apps after they are discharged from the hospital (Zhang & Huo, 2022).

A usability study may be conducted before launching a smartphone-based SmartMed app (application) designed to encourage patient self-management, medication adherence, and data gathering for patients on anticoagulant treatment to guarantee the value of OAC app creation and adoption. The SmartMed app's perceived effect on frequent OAC use was measured using the System Usability Scale (SUS) and the app-specific domain of the Mobile App Rating Scale (MARS) (Wang et al., 2022). The usability test results validate that the app is suitable for use by citrus growers. The study's use of Greek as its only language and the relatively small size of its assessment sample are also caveats. To better serve farmers in the field, researchers want to create crop-specific mobile applications that integrate location-based services, warnings, and cloud data storage (Karetsos et al., 2022). The widespread availability of smartphones provides hope that mobile health apps may be able to reach and motivate people living with type

2 diabetes to manage their condition via increased self-care better. The authors interviewed 29 people with type 2 diabetes using a semi-structured format. Patients were selected using a purposeful sample method from the diabetes and metabolism clinic in Singapore. The results may guide the development of an AI-powered mobile health app intervention to enhance diabetic self-care (Yoon et al., 2022).

CATEGORIES OF AI IN MOBILE

These are the categories:

- Speech recognition: In intelligent mobile applications, speech recognition is utilised to convert the user's voice to text.
- Image recognition is frequently used in mobile applications to locate a person or car involved in a collision.
- Voice recognition: People can talk to their mobile devices without using a keyboard by using voice recognition in mobile applications.
- Text to speech: this technology can be used to create mobile applications that read or speak text to users.
- Object recognition: Text in photographs can be recognised and read using object recognition.
- Speech synthesis: A mobile application can converse with consumers about how a person speaks via speech synthesis.

BENEFITS OF AI IN MOBILE APP DEVELOPMENT

Figure 1. AI

Authentication Power of Application

The app will be able to stay informed about irregularities and anomalies in user behaviour with the use of AI integration on mobile devices. AI will have a bigger impact on user authentication and app security. This is due to the fact that hackers and cybercriminals are also utilising new technology. Block chain and other cutting-edge technologies like machine learning and AI might lessen vulnerabilities and danger perceptions. As a result, the authentication procedure and user experience are made possible.

Possible Automated Reply Features

This function is already present in Google's Gmail programme. It is seen as a shrewd response. Google's auto-reply tool s read messages, receives and proposes responses based on what it learns. We can include auto-reply capabilities in mobile app development by utilising artificial intelligence. We can do this to make it possible for the user and the device to communicate.

Real-Time Language Translation is Made Possible

People may interact with others worldwide more easily thanks to mobile devices with AI-enabled translators. As machine learning is made possible by artificial intelligence, these apps may learn several dialects of the same language and translate them. Numerous translation apps are available. Most of them, however, do not function offline. AI also enables the translation to be latency-adjusted. Thus, the user can control how long it takes for a spoken word to be translated. AI technology incorporate the translators with AI capabilities into mobile apps. This is where translators with AI capabilities excel. Smartphone might be able to translate between several languages almost immediately and in real time without an internet connection.

Facial Recognition Enhanced by Security

A face recognition algorithm powered by AI is used. Light sensitivity was one problem with facial recognition, and it also had trouble recognising people when their appearance changed, such as when they put on eyeglasses. It now offers more functionality and features. Therefore, even if a user changes their appearance, they may now effortlessly unlock their mobile phones. Its ability to scan a patient's face, recognise his symptoms, and provide a diagnosis is another benefit.

Emotion Reading

Reading human emotions is a benefit that emotion recognition AI offers. Voice intonation, delicate verbal cues, and technologies for recognising changes in face expressions are used to record human senses. Businesses employ this technology to complement the already-existing apps since it enhances the performance of mobile apps.

Automated Reasoning

Mobile apps may now employ logical and analytical reasoning to resolve problems, such as proving theorems and resolving puzzles, thanks to AI. At board games like Chess and professional tasks like stock market trading, AI-powered robots outperform humans. It analyses and processes trillions of pieces of data using logical reasoning. The user will benefit from a smoother and more comfortable experience thanks to this functionality.

Understanding Behavior Patterns

Apps with AI capabilities can learn from a user's usage patterns and apply that information to the subsequent session to make it more fluid and intuitive. It combines Natural Language Processing (NLP) and Machine Learning (ML) to create dialogues with users that sound natural and are tailored to their preferences.

ARTIFICIAL INTELLIGENCE IN MEDICAL

Figure 2. AI in medical

When computers and other machines mimic human cognition and are able to learn, understand, and make decisions or take actions, this is referred to as artificial intelligence (AI). Therefore, AI in healthcare refers to the application of machines to analyse and take action on medical data, frequently with the aim of forecasting a specific outcome. The use of ML and other cognitive disciplines for medical diagnosis is an important use of AI in healthcare. AI can assist doctors and other healthcare professionals in providing more precise diagnoses and treatment recommendations by using patient data and other information. By analysing large data to create better preventive care suggestions for patients, AI can also assist in making healthcare more proactive and predictive.

How Artificial Intelligence Is Used in Medical (Healthcare)

Figure 3. AI in healthcare

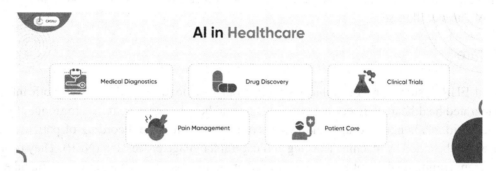

Medical Diagnostics

By enabling healthcare professionals to more swiftly choose the best course of therapy for their patients, AI in diagnostics has the potential to increase access to and the cost-effectiveness of high-quality healthcare. It might possibly revolutionise the back office by handling otherwise time-consuming and onerous administrative duties, freeing up workers to concentrate on things that provide value, reducing inefficiencies, and making better use of available resources. A recent study that examined the use of AI to identify COVID-19 positive patients emphasised the potential of the technology to aid in the early diagnosis of diseases.

Drug Discovery

Large data sets are being used by businesses to swiftly detect patient response markers and create more effective and cost-effective drug targets thanks to AI. Because the design is in line with the chemical environment of the target protein location, it can help in structure-based drug discovery by anticipating the 3D protein structure. Its use in drug discovery has been extended to a variety of applications, including robotics control, image analysis, and logistics.

Clinical Trials

AI has a wide range of possible near- and long-term uses. Clinical trial advancements made feasible by AI technology include the seamless integration of phases I and II, the creation of unique patient-centered endpoints, and the collection and analysis of Real World Data.

Pain Management

With its ability to provide high-quality treatment plans in only a few minutes, the AI planning system significantly decreases the time and associated expenses needed to develop radiation treatments. Artificial intelligence is now used to create radiation treatments. Roughly 40% of cancer cases require radiation therapy. The delivery of radiation to the tumour must be carefully balanced with limiting the dose received by surrounding healthy organs in each patient undergoing radiation therapy. It can be used to identify acute abnormalities, flag key discoveries in medical imaging, help radiologists prioritise life-threatening situations, identify cardiac arrhythmias, forecast the results of strokes, and support the treatment of chronic illnesses.

Patient Care

AI-powered EHR systems provide solutions with a range of features and allow smooth integration. Large, integrated healthcare delivery networks' electronic health record systems are frequently seen as monolithic, rigid, challenging to use, and expensive to configure. The recording of patients' medical experiences can be aided by machine learning and natural language processing (NLP). They nearly usually come from commercial suppliers, and their implementation, support, and optimization take a lot of time, money, and consulting help.

Advantages of AI Mobile Apps in Healthcare

Healthcare apps with AI-enabled tracking capabilities send alarms at an early stage before they are paid. Additionally, it guards against online fraud and theft of patient data. By predicting the treatment plan, the AI-enabled clinical judgement raises the prognosis for a particular medical condition. In order to take serious precautions, AI evaluates the danger of specific diseases. Based on the patient's medical history, it offers a customised online consultation experience. Data on doctors, treatments, medical histories, and other healthcare records are now simple to retrieve. By early disease diagnosis and increased operational effectiveness of healthcare management systems, the applications enhance healthcare systems.

Some of the Healthcare Applications

Geofencing

Geofencing is a virtually-constructed radius used by mobile marketers to promote certain ads to potential customers within a specified geographic area. It uses technologies such as GPS, radio-frequency identification (RFID), WiFi, or cellular data to build a 'virtual fence' or geofence around the specified location.

Youper

Youper is a chatbot-based mental health software that bills itself as a "emotional health helper." Youper is one of a rising number of apps that use chatbots powered by AI to assist users in bettering their emotional well-being. The chatbot for youper encourages users to concentrate on their thoughts and choose from a list of adjectives that best describe their feelings. Then, using a scale from "somewhat" to "very," they can rate the intensity of that emotion. They can track their mood and narrow down what is producing those feelings with the use of additional questions. For those who were concerned about the stigma associated with seeing a professional, Youper offers a far lower access hurdle.

Sense.ly

Sensely intelligently connects insurance and health plan participants with advice and services through natural user interfaces. The platforms powered by Sensely's avatar and chatbot technology provide patients and members of insurance plans with the insurance services and healthcare resources they require, when they need them. On their cellphones, users of the Sense.ly app are asked to do five-minute "check ins" with a nurse avatar to provide updates on their wellbeing. Patients don't need to type; they can just speak to the app. The information people submit during check-ins is combined into a medical record that can only be accessed by licenced healthcare professionals. In addition, the reports incorporate information that Sensely gathers from a variety of wearables, medical devices, and other internet-connected technology that patients use on a daily basis.

Zephyr Health

Data can be structured or formatted in any way, or it can be completely unstructured, and the Zephyr platform, a cloud-based data management software solution, uses that data to create distinctive, "non-obvious" interpretations of client data. Information about clients is safeguarded by a variety of security elements used by Zephyr health data management. These consist of redundant databases, data encryption, and accounting procedures that have been approved by the American Institute of Certified Professional Accountants.

CareSkore

With the help of individualised, in-the-moment interventions from a variety of patient demographics, CareSkore offers a health management solution that employs predictive analytics to enhance clinical and financial outcomes. Based on their electronic medical record and claims data, it enables users to assess the clinical and financial risk associated with hospital patients. This enables the hospitals to concentrate on the patients who require the most attention and management during their stay and after they are discharged. As a direct reaction to the Affordable Treatment Act, which makes healthcare organisations responsible for the standard of the care they deliver.

ADA

The most downloaded symptom checker app worldwide is called Ada. Clinical research demonstrates that Ada is the best reliable symptom checker software for anonymizing personal and health information. It is ours to possess and govern.

ARTIFICIAL INTELLIGENCE IN AGRICULTURE

Figure 4. AI in agriculture

The traditional methods that are used by the farmers are not sufficient to fulfil the need at the current stage. In the agriculture sector, it is playing a very crucial role, and it is transforming the agriculture industry. AI saves the agriculture sector from different factors such as climate change, population growth, employment issues in this field, and food safety. Different hi-tech computer-based systems are designed to determine various important parameters such as weed detection, yield detection, crop quality, and many more.

Advantages of AI Mobile Apps in Agriculture

AI can simplify crop selection and help farmers identify what produce will be most profitable. It can be used for forecasting and predictive analytics to reduce errors and minimize the risk of crop failures. AI can help produce crops that are less prone to disease and better adapted to weather conditions. It can conduct chemical soil analyses and provide accurate estimates of missing nutrients. It monitor the state of plants to spot and even predict diseases, identify and remove weeds, and recommend effective treatment of pests. AI is useful for identifying optimal irrigation patterns and nutrient application times and predicting the optimal mix of agronomic products. With the help of AI, it's possible to automate harvesting and even predict the best time for it.

How Artificial Intelligence Is Used in Agriculture

Figure 5. How to use AI in agriculture

Crop Prediction

AI is beneficial for determining the best irrigation schedules, when to apply nutrients, and how to blend agronomic goods together. It can quickly determine which plants grow the quickest in a specific region, which genes support plant growth there, and which plants, when crossed, generate the best gene combination for a given place, choosing features that increase yield and fend off the effects of a changing climate.

Intelligent Spraying

A smart sprayer reduces the need for insecticides. A smart sprayer typically has a targeted detection system and spraying system, where the precision spraying management is built around the targeted sensor. A smart sprayer's sensing system is utilised to gather data in target locations and make spraying decisions. The farmer benefits indirectly from these increases in pesticide application efficiency, which also lowers labour and gas costs due to fewer sprayer fill-ups, reduces water use for sprayer fill-ups, and lessens the environmental effect of the chemicals used.

Predictive Insights

Artificial intelligence (AI) has a significant role to play in the effective and successful management of crop pests. It can keep an eye on the health of plants to detect and even predict diseases, spot and get rid of weeds, and suggest effective pest control measures.

Agriculture Robots

AI technology aids in the detection of pests, plant diseases, and undernutrition in farms. Artificial intelligence (AI) sensors can identify and target weeds before deciding which herbicide to use in the area. This lowers the need for herbicides and lowers costs.

Crop and Soil Monitoring

Machine learning (ML) and artificial intelligence (AI) technologies use various agricultural analysis algorithms to keep track of the fertility and quality of the soil. Farmers can identify potential nutrient deficits in soil quality using artificial intelligence technology, particularly electronic applications for deep learning.

Disease Diagnosis

The color of the leaves and the presence of spots can be used to manually diagnose illness. Computer vision systems, however, have taken use of it to segment these afflicted leaf sections and categorise them as being connected to a disease or not. Businesses like SkySquirrel Technologies use aerial photography captured by drones to monitor farm health and advise farmers on when and where to apply pest treatments.

Some of the Agriculture Applications

Plantix

Plantix offers matching treatment options for plant diseases, pest damage, and nutritional deficits impacting crops. Users are given access to soil restoration methods, Software algorithms analyse data by correlating specific foliage patterns with specific soil imperfections, plant pests, and plant illnesses. The Plantix app finds potential flaws and nutrient shortages in soil. To find plant illnesses, the app uses photos. The smartphone camera's photos can be used by the image recognition programme to spot any flaws. The farmers can interact with other farmers in the online community to talk about problems with plant health and get access to local weather forecasts.

Tumaini

It aids banana growers in inspecting plants for symptoms of five serious illnesses and one widespread insect. The programme allows farmers to upload a snapshot of a crop that is infected, and image recognition software scans the image for signs of pests and illnesses using a library of more than 50,000 photographs. The information is gathered by Tumaini and entered into the database, along with the location of the data. The software then offers a diagnosis and suggests treatments for the condition.

Vence Corp

It is an app for remote animal control and virtual fence. To maximise the land's yield, use the artificial intelligence technologies in the app. Farmers can use a smartphone to monitor and control the grazing and movement of their animals. It also has other features, like the ability to draw virtual fence lines anywhere on the property or by using specialised sensors that the cattle wear to assess animal well-being.

Meteum

Meteum offers precise hyperlocal weather forecasts, notifications, and live, interactive weather radar data. With information from radars and satellites, thousands of automated weather stations are present worldwide.

Agro.Club

Agro Club is a company that creates an online agricultural marketplace to link crop buyers, suppliers, and growers. It creates a mobile application that links crop growers, suppliers, and buyers. Users can utilise it to locate the greatest deals on things like CP, seeds, fertiliser, and more. Additionally, it provides services including quality assurance, quality analysis, and farmers' profit programmes.

CONCLUSION

By 2050, we can expect the world population to grow up to 10 billion people and knowing that there is no denying that global food production will have to increase accordingly. To prevent global famine, it will need to rise by 70%. Another obstacle concerns labor shortage, increasing production costs, food waste, and transparency in the farm management and food supply chain.

Clearly, the agriculture and healthcare industry of the 21st-century faces some grave challenges, and technology is the answer. As we could see, among a variety of applications, there are many ready-made software solutions. However, if you can't find your perfect choice or want to get your own app designed, do not hesitate to contact us, and we will estimate the project for us.

Smart-assistant features and functionality on smart phones must support fast—yet precise decisions from the flows of data. Slow storage and memory means slow AI training performance, creating longer standby time and a fast-draining battery. The good news is that memory and storage innovations are delivering faster I/O operations and near-real-time AI calculation, feeding the growing data needs of these AI engines to create a powerful user experience.

A promising area of development is the application of artificial intelligence in clinical practise. There are numerous AI techniques that can be used to address a wide range of therapeutic issues. The clinicians' attitude about the use of technology in the decision-making process is one explanation for this. There is strong evidence that medical AI can help clinicians provide healthcare effectively in the twenty-first century. There is little question that these methods will help to improve and supplement the future clinician's "medical intelligence."

REFERENCES

Choi, J., Tamí-Maury, I., Cuccaro, P., Kim, S., & Markham, C. (2023). Digital Health Interventions to Improve Adolescent HPV Vaccination: A Systematic Review. *Vaccines*, *11*(2), 249. doi:10.3390/vaccines11020249 PMID:36851127

Deng, L., & Hu, H. (2022). Fine-Grained Urban Functional Region Identification via Mobile App Usage Data. *Mobile Information Systems*, *2022*, 1–17. Advance online publication. doi:10.1155/2022/6434598

Elbagoury, B. M., Vladareanu, L., Vlădăreanu, V., Salem, A. B., Travediu, A. M., & Roushdy, M. I. (2023). A Hybrid Stacked CNN and Residual Feedback GMDH-LSTM Deep Learning Model for Stroke Prediction Applied on Mobile AI Smart Hospital Platform. *Sensors, 23*(7), 3500. doi:10.3390/S23073500

Facchinetti, G., Petrucci, G., Albanesi, B., De Marinis, M. G., & Piredda, M. (2023). Can Smart Home Technologies Help Older Adults Manage Their Chronic Condition? A Systematic Literature Review. *International Journal of Environmental Research and Public Health*, *20*(2), 1205. doi:10.3390/ijerph20021205 PMID:36673957

Görtz, M., Wendeborn, A., Müller, M., & Hohenfellner, M. (2023). The Mobile Patient Information Assistant (PIA) App during the Inpatient Surgical Hospital Stay: Evaluation of Usability and Patient Approval. *Healthcare (Switzerland)*, *11*(5), 682. doi:10.3390/healthcare11050682 PMID:36900686

Karetsos, S., Costopoulou, C., Gourdomichali, N., & Ntaliani, M. (2022). A Mobile App for Supporting Citrus Fruit Growers in Greece. *Electronics, 11*(20), 3342. doi:10.3390/ELECTRONICS11203342

Liu, W., & Tang, W. (2022). Effects of Age-Appropriate Mobile APP Use Behavior on Subjective Well-being of Young Elderly. *Security and Communication Networks*, *2022*, 1–12. Advance online publication. doi:10.1155/2022/3209804

Reda, M., Suwwan, R., Alkafri, S., Rashed, Y., & Shanableh, T. (2022). AgroAId: A Mobile App System for Visual Classification of Plant Species and Diseases Using Deep Learning and TensorFlow Lite. *Informatics, 9*(3), 55. doi:10.3390/INFORMATICS9030055

Wang, S. W., Chiou, C. C., Su, C. H., Wu, C. C., Tsai, S. C., Lin, T. K., & Hsu, C. N. (2022). Measuring Mobile Phone Application Usability for Anticoagulation from the Perspective of Patients, Caregivers, and Healthcare Professionals. *International Journal of Environmental Research and Public Health*, *19*(16), 10136. doi:10.3390/IJERPH191610136

Yoon, S., Kwan, Y. H., Phang, J. K., Tan, W. B., & Low, L. L. (2022). Personal Goals, Barriers to Self-Management and Desired mHealth Application Features to Improve Self-Care in Multi-Ethnic Asian Patients with Type 2 Diabetes: A Qualitative Study. *International Journal of Environmental Research and Public Health*, *19*(22), 15415. doi:10.3390/ijerph192215415 PMID:36430134

Zhang, Q., & Huo, Z. (2022). Effect of Continuous Nutrition Management Intervention on Nutritional Status and Development of Premature Infants Based on Mobile Medical APP. *Computational and Mathematical Methods in Medicine*, *2022*, 1–8. Advance online publication. doi:10.1155/2022/8586355 PMID:35979052

Zhou, J., Ho, V., & Javadi, B. (2022). New Internet of Medical Things for Home-Based Treatment of Anorectal Disorders. *Sensors, 22*(2), 625. doi:10.3390/S22020625

Chapter 5
An Artificial Intelligence Model for Effective Routing in WSN

Kswaminathan Kalyanaraman

(iD) https://orcid.org/0000-0002-8116-057X

Department of Electronics and Communication, University College of Engineering, Pattukkottai, India

ABSTRACT

In WSN, sensor nodes will be distributed heterogeneity concerning their basic requirements such as location, power backup, and the distance between the nodes. With these metrics, research is carried on energy conservation, media-based problems, packet aggregation, effective routing, quality of link, etc. But the energy consumption and data processing system in WSN makes a scenario for not using an artificial intelligence (AI)-based system in network structure. In this chapter, a heuristic packet routing (HPR) strategy for effective path identification on the packet transmission between the nodes is given. The proposed methodology also improvises the routing process on diffusion and energy management methodology defined in previous research work. A comprehensive study was done with the help of a network simulator. Based on the result, the work is compared with various research work defined previously.

1. INTRODUCTION

In WSN, sensor nodes have an extensive development in their physical and power management processes with smaller in size and less expensive. Sensor nodes will be deployed in a challengeable environment for measuring some parameters of the application-defined with thousands of nodes in the network density. With some basic needs such as minimum energy consumption, effective routing, erroneous data transmission is a challenging task. In (E et al., 2005) energy management, data reliability, data security is important metrics in designing of a network. Hence, it is a important for consideration of collision on data transmission, intrusion attacks.

Also (Akyildiz et al., 2002; Karl & Willig, 2003) states an effective routing methodology in packet transmission with effective multi hopping in data path. The path establishment was effectively carried out. But data path establishment was done on expensive energy usage which leads to minimize nodes'

DOI: 10.4018/978-1-6684-8306-0.ch005

power backup. As the power of a node is not rechargeable, usage of explainable Artificial Intelligence is introduced on the network designing and data packet transmission cycles. With this enhancement, we can monitor the network working strategy and efficiency of packet transmission. Here we proposed an artificial intelligence bases data routing method for improving network lifetime with efficient usage of energy for making a successful data transmission.

A multi-hopping protocol in Wireless Sensor Networks (WSNs) is a routing protocol that enables communication between sensor nodes that are beyond the direct wireless transmission range of each other. In multi-hopping, data is relayed through intermediate nodes to reach a destination node that is located far away. The main objective of multi-hopping protocols is to extend the network coverage area and overcome the limitations of individual node transmission range. By utilizing intermediate nodes as relays, data can be transmitted over multiple hops to reach a destination node that is out of range for direct communication.

1. ***Ad-Hoc On-Demand Distance Vector (AODV):*** AODV is a reactive routing protocol that establishes routes on-demand. When a node wants to send data to a destination node, it initiates a route discovery process by broadcasting a route request packet. Intermediate nodes receiving the request packet can forward it or reply with a route reply packet if they have a valid route to the destination. A route is established by accumulating replies from multiple nodes.

2. ***Dynamic Source Routing (DSR):*** DSR is also a reactive protocol that discovers routes when needed. It utilizes source routing, where the source node includes the entire route in the packet header. Intermediate nodes store the routes and forward the packets based on the source routing information. DSR allows for flexibility in route selection and can handle topology changes dynamically.

3. ***Destination-Sequenced Distance Vector (DSDV):*** DSDV is a proactive routing protocol that maintains routing tables at each node. It uses sequence numbers to differentiate between new and old routes and to avoid routing loops. The protocol updates the routing tables periodically or when a topology change occurs. Nodes exchange routing table updates to ensure consistent and up-to-date routing information.

4. ***Routing Protocol for Low-Power and Lossy Networks (RPL):*** RPL is a routing protocol specifically designed for WSNs with resource-constrained nodes. It supports both proactive and reactive routing approaches. RPL organizes nodes in a hierarchical structure, where nodes are assigned specific roles such as root, parent, and child. It enables efficient routing by leveraging the hierarchical topology. A multi-hopping protocol in WSN is designed to enable efficient communication between sensor nodes by allowing packets to be relayed through intermediate nodes. Here's a high-level description of the flow for a multi-hopping protocol:

   1. ***Initialization:*** The protocol begins by initializing the network and sensor nodes. Each node is assigned a unique identifier and initial parameters.
   2. ***Data Collection:*** Sensor nodes in the network start sensing the environment and collecting data. They periodically sample the environment and generate data packets.
   3. ***Packet Transmission:*** When a sensor node generates a data packet, it first checks if it is the final destination node. If it is, the packet is sent directly to the sink node or the base station. Otherwise, the node looks for the next hop neighbor node to relay the packet.
   4. ***Next Hop Selection:*** The node evaluates its neighboring nodes to determine the best next hop for packet transmission. This selection is typically based on factors such as signal strength, energy level, distance, or routing metrics.

5. *Packet Forwarding:* Once the next hop neighbor is identified, the current node forwards the data packet to that node. The packet is then passed through a series of intermediate nodes, each relaying it to the next hop, until it reaches the destination node.

6. *Routing Table Maintenance:* Each node maintains a routing table that stores information about the network topology, including the next hop neighbors and their corresponding metrics. This table is periodically updated to reflect changes in the network, such as node failures or topology changes.

7. *Error Handling and Retransmission:* In case of transmission errors or packet loss, the protocol may incorporate error detection and recovery mechanisms. These mechanisms can include error checking codes, acknowledgment messages, or retransmission strategies to ensure reliable packet delivery.

8. *Sink Node Reception:* Once the packet reaches the sink node or base station, it processes the data and performs any required analysis or storage. It may also send acknowledgments back to the source nodes to confirm successful reception.

Figure 1. Flow diagram of multi-hopping protocol in a wireless sensor network

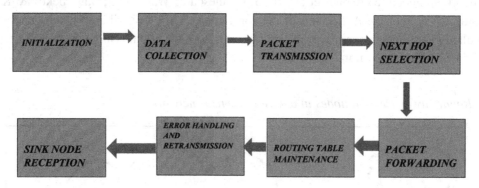

This flow diagram in Figure 1 provides a general overview of the multi-hopping protocol in a WSN. The actual implementation and specific details may vary depending on the protocol being used and the network requirements.

In Section 2, we defined important aspects in data routing of networks with some predefined network routing protocols. A neural network-based data path identification is introduced for enhancing the quality in link establishment with neighboring nodes in Section 3. The proposed system performance comparison is given in Section 4 with a conclusion and social welfare represented by Sections 7 and 8.

2. DESIGNING OF NETWORK MODEL

Here the network topology used was designed with some predefined metrics. While designing network architecture, quality of the data path, data redundant, integration of sensor nodes in data hopping, data packets aggregation, intra communication between various network structures, etc. should take into consideration.

The protocol characterized in the research work is based on the OSI layer architecture for the successful data hopping processes. In the OSI model, we can use any of the IEEE 802.11 based methodology or protocol defined by Arachane (Barbancho et al.,). In the upper layer, we may use clock-based protocol, data ping methods, packet aggregation methods, or our proposed HPR structure. In any application, if the sensed data are given sensor nodes used to be aggregated for deciding the results. We may define a priority on a collection of sense data for making all the nodes take part in the data aggregate processes. This will increase nodes' lifetime, network efficiency.

As the path selection of data transmission impacts network lifetime, power management we have to decide on the routing in conjunction with the scheduling of nodes in the network design. This may be carried by routing the data packets with possible combinations of nodes which makes all nodes in the network take part in the data processing system.

Many research works (Al-Karaki & Kamal, 2004; Royer & Toh, 1999) were carried out on the above problem. Here we standardized the situation of all nodes to take part in the data forwarding processes. In section 3 proposed HPR protocol for effective routing with all possible nodes in the network processing.

Generally, nodes in a network structure have a specified range of coverage in the geographical location. In previous years, Extensive work has been carried on making the connectivity between nodes in the network architecture (Aspnes et al., 2003; Calinescu & Wan, 2003; Saginbekov & Korpeoglu, 2005; Stratil, 2005). For the Adhoc sensor network, nodes will be distributed heterogeneous manner which resulted in arising of coverage problems between the node points. Here we assume a randomized distribution of nodes as shown in Figure 2.

Figure 2. Randomly distributed nodes in a wireless sensor network

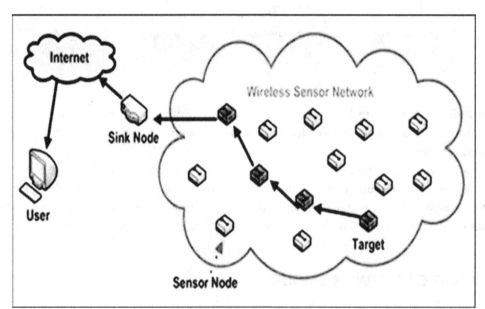

From the above diagram, we may see the nodes are distributed randomly with each node having a separate transmission module with specified transmitting power. This allows the specific range of coverage areas. For solving the coverage metrics issues two different types of the procedure will be followed

1)   Direct link-based protocol
2)   Intermediate multi hopping protocol

2.1 Direct Link-Based Protocol

Here nodes will be distributed randomly to cover all geographical areas of the network. Using this protocol, all the nodes must have a direct data path to the sink or base station. For any node to transmit data packets, using the direct link to the base station data transmission will be finished. As each node has a separate path to BS increase the network structure to complex and also increased more power to be consumed on each data transmission.

2.2 Intermediate Multi-Hopping Protocol

In this protocol, nodes are implemented in all the locations with reference to the position of sensor nodes. Here, the data transmission has been furnished with the help of the intermediate nodes between the source node and sink node. This results that all intermediate nodes will act as a router. As the router is the point to forward data packets towards any destination point. The problem is to select the intermediate path for utilizing the minimum power of a nodes.

For effective routing, depending on the way of identification of data path as an *equal assigned task, Priority-based routing, geographical location-based routing.* Among these techniques, we use the equal assigned task method as it assigns equal work to all nodes in the network structure. In the routing technique, the proposed system considers *direct data diffusion* and *power-aware* methods to compute the impact of the usage of artificial intelligence (AI).

In *direct data diffusion* (Shah & Rabaey, 2002), each node will maintain the frequency of data transfer, hopping count, the remaining power of all its neighbor nodes. For data transfer, the sink will send startup messages to all nodes. The node which is ready to transfer data will send its interest to the sink node. In this way, data will be transmitted to destinations from the source point.

In *power-aware* methods (Sheu et al., 2005), the supervisor node will maintain a probability of path discovered for earlier data transmission cycles. Depending on the frequency of the path in the probability list it will be used for future data transmission.

3. INITIATING NEURONS IN NETWORKS STRUCTURE

The establishment of the data path between nodes is the main motto of routing protocols. As WSN is used for deployment in a heterogeneous application, nodes connectivity is chosen by focusing on the network parameters like minimum data hopping, maximum data packet rate, minimum retransmission rate, etc. This criterion is focused because using the decided path data transmission will be carried over the network architecture. The hardness of discovering a path usage of the minimal network resource is solved by describing a *network routing formation*.

The proposed methodology introduces artificial Intelligence in the discovery of data path which enhance network efficiency. Although many of the researchers worked on introducing Artificial Intelligence in WSN for making a experts WSN network (Jin et al., 2003; Sheu et al., 2005; Talekder et al., 2005). The AI system were working on the path decision with some restrictions but the proposed system implement the AI inside the working of Sensor nodes in a network architecture. For having a best results we may have a constraint on the network to be *Self Grouping network* used in the proposed module.

3.1 Network Routing Formation

Routing formation is formulated with the help of mathematical based *graph theory*. A graph is omni directional path between the vertices.

A graph g is said to have a vertices v represented as g=(v, a), in which a is the weighted edges between the nodes in sensor network known as *directed sensor network.*

In our network, it is assumed networks to have nodes with symmetry path between them. For example, the cost required to reach from node x and node y is same. This implies that the network resources need to move from x to y and y to x us same. This result that our network to be *undirected sensor network.*

We proposed a modified network structure having nodes with a data path. The data path will be formed by focusing on the minimum usage of network resources. The path r from the base station to every node in the network. This is named HPR. Every link between the node Vx and Vy has a cost as Wxy with the assumption as Wxy = Wyx. The distance between the sink node or base station to a node Vx is given as d(Vx). The neighboring nodes for a node Vx are represented as £(Vy)={Vy € V}. The path from the base station to a nice is denoted as £p(j).

Initially every node is assigned with minimum cost of every path to neighboring nodes. In the following data transmission cost is updated to every nodes. Algorithm for network routing formation is as follows

Algorithm for Network Routing Formation

Step 1: Initiate path to be zero as £p(j) = 0
Step 2: The cost for link establishment happens to be
            d(Vi) = Wij, if Vi *belongs to* £p(i),
             d(Vi) = 0, if Vi *not belongs to* £p(i).
Step 3: After the cost of the data path is assigned, root variable **r** as,
            £p(i) = r, if Vi *belongs to* £p(i)
            £p(i) = 0, if Vi *not belong to* £p(i)
Step 4: Calculate *minimum distance* using the minimum cost for a data path as,
        d(Vi) = { min[d(Vi) = Wij] }
Step 5: compute Ti using the weight of the link between the sink and the source node
            Ti = d(Vi) + Wij, when Vi *belongs to* £p(i)
Step 6: if the value Ti has a real number go to **Step 2**
Step 7: Stop the routing process.

3.2 Quality Analysis of Service in WSN Module

As the routing process is computed, data transmission may be started by initiating a startup message from the sink node and the cost of the link *Wij*. The quality of the service on data transmission by focusing on the environment of the node located

3.2.1 Sensing node in Noise Free Location

The Geographic Region of a sensing node agrees on the quality of the data transmission. This also makes a truthful link between the sink and the source node. With this, we conclude the root variable as *r*

3.2.2 Sensing Nodes in a Noisy Environment

If the nodes are in any challenging environment, sensing data may lose its originality. This may occur due to the collision occurring in the sensed data. This may also make an error data to be sent to the sink node.

This situation is handled by alternative root *r* from the source node to sink node as *r'*. The path will not be updated in the sink as it is a temporary path. The traditional way on analysis of the quality of the data path focused on end-to-end data delay, data loss, throughput, and efficiency of the network. Many research work has been carried in this strategy (Aurrecoechea et al., 1998; Sabata et al., 1997).

But other than this network reliability, availability link, data security, the robustness of the data is often avoided in the quality of the network. They also state the optimum number of nodes to be live for the errorless data transmission with a concern total number of nodes deployed in the network architecture (Kay & Frolik, 2004; Perillo & Heinzelman, 2003; Rakocevic et al., 2004). Hence, the analysis on quality also focused on the density of the sensor on the network, node energy conservation, maintenance of data quality up to end of data processing.

Finally, we define three paradigms for quality analysis as timeliness of data, data precision between nodes, data accuracy. As the network in this research work is a distributed type with nodes are in the random quality analysis is also spreader manner.

Each sensor node sends a *startup* message to all neighbor nodes to make a note of the basic network metrics such as latency of the network, data error rate, network throughput. With these metrics, the proposed system decides the quality of the data link. After this distance between the neighbor nodes is computed as,

$$d(V_x) = d(V_y).Q_{qos} \tag{1}$$

For a node X distance from the root node through a node Y is computed. The qos is a real number given as the output of an artificial neural network explained in Section 4. Using the above expression data transmission carried through the path having minimum cost, avoiding collision in the data path.

3.2.3 Self-Grouping Network

This type of network is a self decision capacity networks without supervisor node. They will have in directional link between the nodes with two layers as shown in Figure 2.

Figure 3. Arrangements of self-grouped network

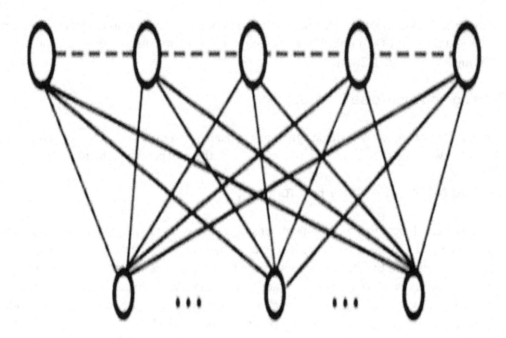

First layer is a buffer zone for input sequence given to the network. Second one us rectangular arranged layer of m x n size. The input sequence is stochastic sequence varying on time t it represented as x(t). Each node us represented by mXn dimension with coat if the link is stated as $W'_{ij} = \{W'_{ij1}, W'_{ij2}, \ldots W_{ij}m\}$ where *m* is the dimension of input data sequence.

From figure 2, we may see that each node in output side is connected to all other in input side for making the efficient data path. Here, the working of this module is broadly classified into

1) Learning phase
2) Mapping phase

In the first stage, nodes are arranged with a centralized data center in the network architecture. This is done before the data transmission takes place in the network. Hence it us also known as *offline mode*. On other hand, the mapping is done on the basis of input sequence given to the network which tells about the density of nodes to be alive. This phase is termed as *online mode*.

3.2.3.1 Learning Phase

For our convenience, we may term each sensor node as *neuron*. The neurons in second later is connected to each and every neuron in first layer for making better connection. Depending on the input sequence specific set if neurons will be active. This is computed by comparing the neurons vectors stored in buffer layer (first layer). The neurons whose vector data is exactly or approximately fitted with input sequence will be selected. The cost and weight of the corresponding neurons represented as,

$$d(W_s) = \min\{d(W_{mn}, X\}$$ (2)

In the mean time cost neighbor neurons are updated for the path recovery. This is given as *robust learning phase.*

3.2.3.2 Mapping Phase

After the active neurons are selected which matches the input sequence. It is formed as a selected neurons as group $s=\{s1,s2\}$. The cost of data link is represented as Ws marches the input data sequence. This implementation is shown as coding and it is formed as clustered network. The output of self grouping network is given as Q_{qos}. The value of this returned by a function ϵ to the routing module.

4. SIMULATION ANALYSIS OF PROPOSED SYSTEM

As to desire to compute performance of *HPR* methodology, simulations carried out in three different wireless scenarios. Each node(neuron) implemented with *self grouping* strategy as explained in following algorithm 2.

Algorithm 2: Organizing of Self Grouping Network

```
 int Winning Neuron(float *x)
{
float D2 = 0; % distance ^
2
float b[12];
% distance between input and
every neuron weight
for (int c = 0; c < 12; c++)
b[c] = 0;
for (int i=0; i < 12; i++)
{
D2 = 0;
for (int j = 0; j < 4; j++)
{
float sgn= WI[i][j]-x[j];
% WI[i][j] is the input weights matrix,
% obtained in the learning phase
D2 += sgn*sgn;
}
b[i] = sqrt(D2);
}
float sgn = b[0];
```

```
int neurn = 1;
for (int u = 0; u < 12; u++)
{
if (sgn > b[u])
{
sgn = b[u];
neurn = n+1;
}
}
return neurn;
}
```

Table 1. Simulation parameter

Simulation Parameter	Value
Simulator	NS-2
Simulation time	150 s
Number of nodes	100
Simulation area	$1500 \times 1500 \text{ m}^2$
Mac Protocol	IEEE 802.11
Data rate	12 Mbps
Radio range	100m
Mobility model	Random way point model
Antenna	Omni directional antenna

The simulation parameters used for the system is stated in Table 1. Also as shown in Figure 1, assume nodes are distributed as random manner. This implies distance between any two nodes will be random. The density of the nodes used for the evaluation is 100.

5. CREATION OF SELF GROUPING NETWORK

As we known that the self-grouping structure has two layers of neurons in first layer to receive input data sequence which is followed by layer of neurons to process the received neurons to destination point or sink node

5.1. Learning Phase

The sensor nodes are arranged in two dimensional manner with the help of input parameters i(t) => { data latency(t), network throughout(t), data error rate(t), network duty cycle(t)}. Using this training sequence quality of the link between nodes will be established. The stability of the link and for trustful data transmission, system is simulated with different range of noisy levels and various range of data traffic with density of nodes as 100. The steps to follow the quality of the link is as follows,

1) Initially neurons in first layer close to input vector is selected
2) The selected node(neuron) e.g Vx, Vy. Vx will send a startup message to its neighbor for measuring basic network metrics
3) The neighbor nodes will send a ACK as response to the corresponding node
4) With this, noise level between a node (eg.Vx) to all of the neighbor node
5) This gives a knowledge of noises in link and the root metrics *r* can be decided

In the way node Vx receives this ACK determines a specific quality environment, expressed on the four metrics selected: network latency (s),network throughput (bits/s), data error rate (%) and network duty cycle (%). For eg., for a noise power density of n= -90 dBm/Hz and a distance of between node Vx and node Vy of 90 meters the quality measured in node Vx and conveyed in the parameters defined is [0.78, 1200,12.2,50]. It will be repeated 90 times with different noise level *n*.

On the basis of noise level received, *self grouping network* is shaped using neural network simulation tool MATLAB. The network is trained with its learning phase input in *offline mode* without implementation of wireless sensor network architecture.

The above steps will be followed to form a cluster base mapping with specific cost matrix $Wij = \{$ *Wij1,Wij2....Wijm}*. This will result in a specific connection between input and output neurons groups.

5.2 Mapping Phase

After the grouping of neurons were finished in the *learning phase,* each sensor node will measure the quality of the link on a regular basis by sending *startup* messages to all the neighbor node.

On comparison with input data sequence, if any particular neurons are selected for data transmission. It will execute the quality evaluation relation equation(1). This execution is carried out in wireless network architecture. Hence it is given as *Online mode.*

6. SIMULATION RESULTS

As a study of impacts on AI in routing protocols, the simulation has been carried out in three different scenarios as 1) No node failure 2) 30% node failure.

6.1. No Node Failure

Here, we assume there us no node failure which tells that all sensor node have enough energy backup, no delay, enough data rate, no data link failure. This shows all nodes have link with identical data link quality.

Average power dissipation: It shows how much energy needed for ACK a startup message to the sink node. With this, sink will analyze energy backup and other network parameters of a node. This will gives lifespan of a node.

The energy needs to transmit for a source node and to receive a message for destination is computed by,

$$E_{tr} = (E_{electr} * K) + (E_{am} * K * d^2)$$ (3)

$$Erec = (E\ electr * K)$$ (4)

Where E electr represent the energy for a transmitter or recover to transmit and receive data's respectively, K shows number of data bits, d is the distance between the nodes.

Figure 4. Power dissipation model of a WSN

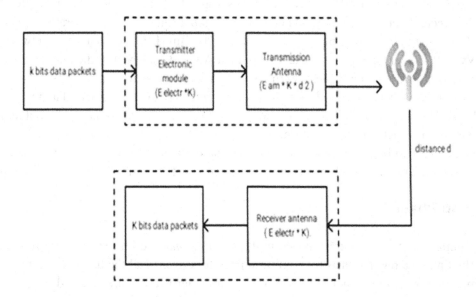

In the proposed system link are identical, the power need to receive a message is lesser than message to transmit a message. This is because nodes will transmit the message more than it receive a message from sink node. The average delay and power dissipation is shown in Figure 4 and 5 respectively.

Event delay: Thus is delay in occurrence of a event to transmitting a data from a sensor node to sink and the same is received in sink node side. A comparison of proposed and conventional routing systems in table format as shown in Table 2.

Table 2. Comparison of proposed and conventional protocol

Network Metrics	Traditional WSN Protocol	Latest Protocol
Energy Efficiency	Moderate	High
Scalability	Limited	High
Network Lifetime	Short	Extended
Throughput	Moderate	High
Delay	Moderate	Low
Reliability	Limited	High
Data Security	Basic	Advanced
Overhead	Moderate	Low
Self-Organization	Limited	High
Adaptability	Limited	High
Quality of Service (QoS)	Basic	Enhanced
Mobility Support	Limited	High
Robustness to Node Failure	Limited	High
Data Aggregation Efficiency	Moderate	High
Ease of Deployment	Moderate	High

Figure 5. Comparison average delay of various methods (no node failure)

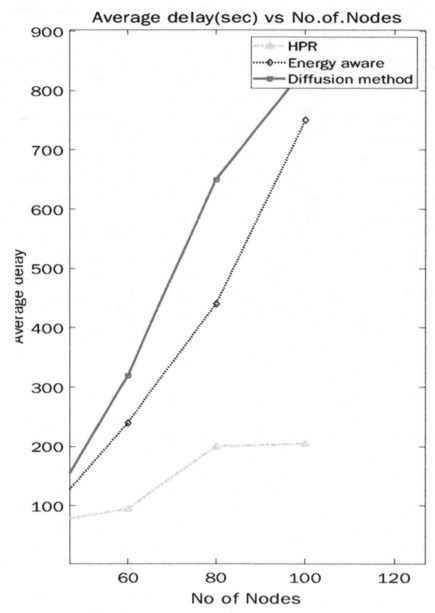

Figure 6. Average power dissipation in data processing (no node failure)

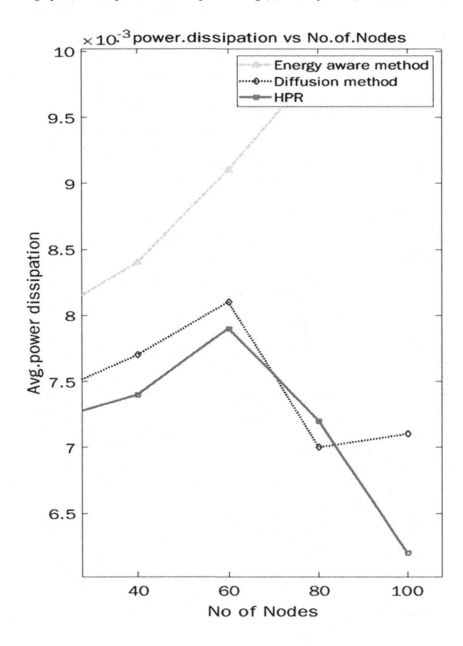

6.2 Simulation on 30% Node Failure

In this scenario, 30% of node is inactive mode. This happens due to noises in the environment, data collision, low quality data link between the nodes.

Signal to noise ratio: This metrics tells about how the nose is prone to noises in the link. When the noise increases nodes power backup will decreased for neglecting noises in the link. This will also result to minimize its neighbor node also.

With this 30% of node losses in the network, average delay and power dissipation is shown in Figure 6 and Figure 7.

Figure 7. Average delay on 30% of nodes failure

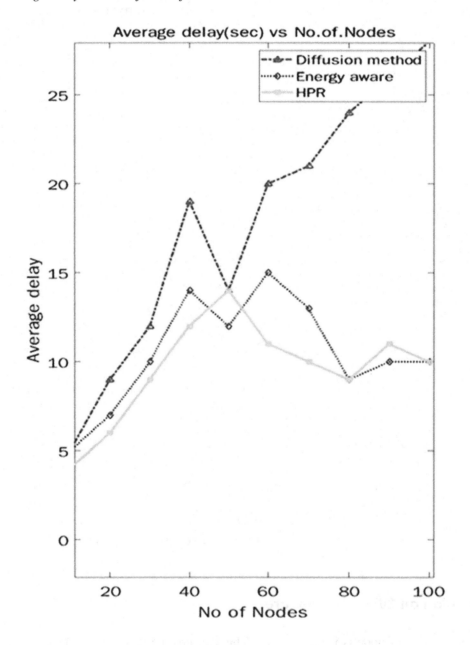

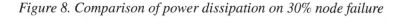

Figure 8. Comparison of power dissipation on 30% node failure

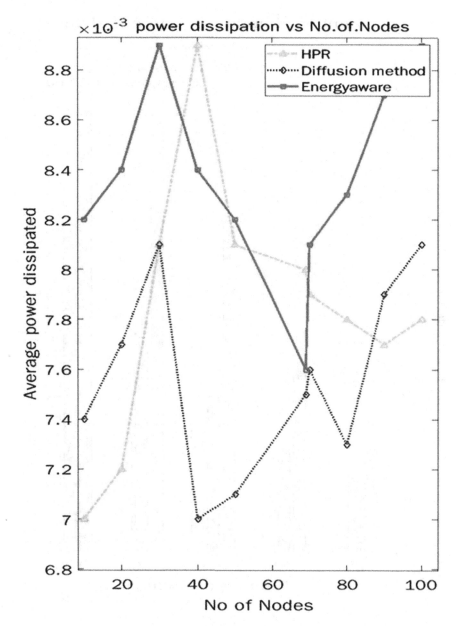

In the data transmission end-to-end delay, packet delivery ratio is important metrics. This is because as delivered ratio is high which implies that error occurrences will be low, delay metrics tells about the time span of data packet processing between source and sink node. Proposed methodology have appreciated performance when compared to other methods as shown in Figures 8 and 9.

Figure 9. Comparison of packet delivery ratio

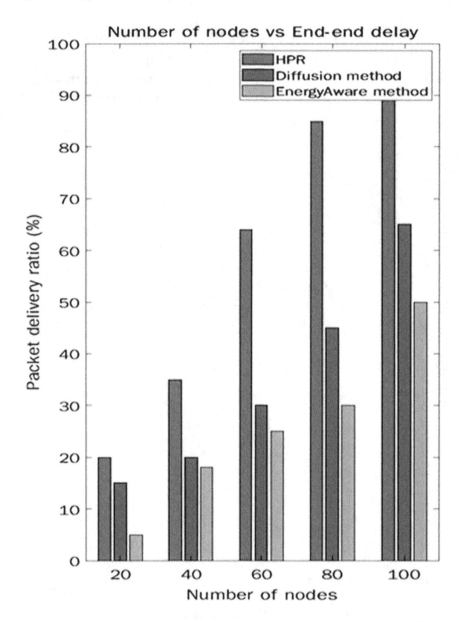

Figure 10. Various methods end to end delay comparison

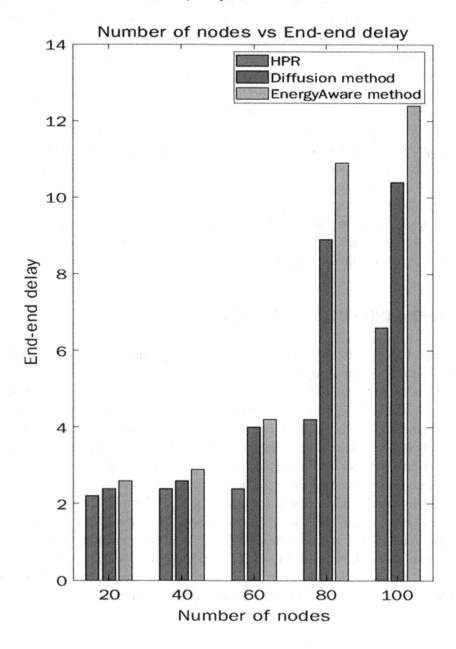

7. SOCIAL WELFARE OF THIS PROJECT

The field of wireless sensor networks (WSNs) has the potential to bring numerous social welfare benefits to people. Here are some ways in which WSNs contribute to the well-being of individuals and communities:

In the Environmental Monitoring strategy, WSNs can be deployed to monitor environmental factors such as air quality, water quality, temperature, humidity, and pollution levels. This data can help in identifying and addressing environmental risks, ensuring the health and safety of individuals and communities. In some disaster management part, WSNs play a crucial role by providing real-time information about natural disasters like earthquakes, floods, and wildfires. This data enables early warning systems, facilitates effective evacuation plans, and supports timely response and rescue operations, ultimately saving lives and minimizing damage.

Also in Healthcare and Medical Application, sensors are utilized in healthcare settings for remote patient monitoring, tracking vital signs, and detecting anomalies. They enable telemedicine services, facilitate the monitoring of chronic diseases, and enhance the overall efficiency and effectiveness of healthcare delivery. Finally, WSNs contribute to the development of smart cities by monitoring and managing various aspects of urban life, including traffic flow, energy consumption, waste management, and public safety. These systems optimize resource utilization, reduce environmental impact, and enhance the overall quality of life for city residents.

Overall, the social welfare benefits of WSNs encompass a wide range of domains, including environmental monitoring, disaster management, healthcare, smart cities, agriculture, wildlife conservation, and industrial applications. By enabling efficient data collection, analysis, and decision-making, WSNs contribute to improved quality of life, enhanced safety, resource conservation, and sustainable development.

8. CONCLUSION AND FUTURE EXTENSION

In the comparison of simulation results, it becomes evident that the introduction of Artificial Intelligence (AI) has a positive impact on improving the network lifetime and efficiency of node and data transmission. In both diffusion-based and energy-aware methods, the average delay and power dissipation increase as the node density increases. However, the AI-based HPR method demonstrates stable performance. The reason for the degradation in other methods lies in the fact that they select intermediate nodes based on standard protocols without considering the analysis of noise in the link periodically. On the other hand, HPR selects intermediate nodes by running a quality analysis function at regular intervals, making the data path less prone to environmental noise compared to other methods.

Furthermore, the results indicate that as the number of node failures increases, the other methods experience degradation in their power dissipation and delay. In contrast, HPR maintains stability by running a quality function and selecting alternate data links in noisy environments. The HPR routing protocol proposed in this study, which is AI-based, can be adopted for IEEE standard 802.15, Bluetooth technology, and SCAMS technologies. When compared to other AI-based methods, HPR is an efficient approach. This is attributed to the effort taken to incorporate AI techniques within the sensor nodes themselves.

REFERENCES

Abielmona, R., Groza, V., & Pretiu, W. (2003). Evolutionary neural network network-based sensor self-calibration scheme using IEEE1451 and wireless sensor networks. *International Symposium on Computational Intelligence for Masurement Systems and applications, CIMSA 2003*, Lugano, Switzerland. 10.1109/CIMSA.2003.1227198

Akyildiz, I., Su, Y., Sankarasubramaniam, W., & Cayirci, E. (2002). Wireless sensor networks: A survey. *Computer Networks, 38*(4), 393–422. doi:10.1016/S1389-1286(01)00302-4

Al-Karaki, J., & Kamal, A. (2004). Routing techniques in wireless sensor networks: A survey, Wireless Sensor Networks. *IEEE Wireless Communications, 4*(6), 6–28. doi:10.1109/MWC.2004.1368893

Aspnes, K., Goldenberg, D., & Yang, Y. (2003). On the computational complexity of sensor network location. *Lecture Notes in Computer Science, 3121*, 235–246.

Aurrecoechea, C., Campbell, A., & Hauw, L. (1998). A survey of QoS architectures. *Multimedia Systems, 6*(3), 138–151. doi:10.1007005300050083

Barbancho, J., Leo'n, C., Molina, F., & Barbancho, A. (2006). SIR: A new wireless sensor network routing protocol based on artificial intelligence. *Lecture Notes in Computer Science, 3842*, 271–275. doi:10.1007/11610496_35

Barbancho, J., Molina, F., Leo'n, D., Ropero, J., & Barbancho, A. OLIMPO, an ad-hoc wireless sensor network simulator for public utilities applications. In *Proceedings of the Second European Workshop on Wireless Sensor Networks* (pp. 419–424). IEEE. 10.1109/EWSN.2005.1462037

Calinescu, G., & Wan, P. (2003). Range assignment for high connectivity in wireless ad hoc networks. *Lecture Notes in Computer Science, 2865*, 235–246. doi:10.1007/978-3-540-39611-6_21

E., C., Ayirci, T. C, Plu, & Emiroglu. (2005). Power aware many to many routing in wireless sensor and actuator networks. In *Proceedings of the Second European Workshop on Wireless Sensor Networks* (pp. 236–245). IEEE.

Intanagonwiwat, C., Govindan, R., & Estrin, D. (2004). Directed diffusion: a scalable and robust communication paradigm for sensor networks. In *Proceedings of ACM Mobicom 2000* (pp. 56–67). ACM. 10.1145/345910.345920

Iyer, R., & Kleinrock, L. (2003). QoS control for sensor networks. *IEEE International Conference on Communications, ICC'03, 1*, 517–521. 10.1109/ICC.2003.1204230

Jin, S., Zhou, M., & Wu, A. S. (2003). Sensor network optimization using a genetic algorithm. *7th World Multiconference on Systemics, Cybernetics, and Informatics*, Orlando, FL.

Karl, H. & Willig, A. (2003). *A short survey of wireless sensor networks, TKN*. Technical Report Series.

Kay, J., & Frolik, J. (2004). Quality of service analysis and control for wireless sensor networks. In *2004 IEEE International Conference on Mobile Ad-hoc and Sensor Systems*, (pp. 359–368). IEEE. 10.1109/MAHSS.2004.1392175

Molina, F., Barbancho, J., & Luque, J. (2003). Automated meter reading and SCADA application. *Lecture Notes in Computer Science, 2865*, 223–234. doi:10.1007/978-3-540-39611-6_20

Perillo, M., & Heinzelman, W. (2003). Sensor management policies to provide application QoS. *Ad Hoc Networks, 1*(2-3), 235–246. doi:10.1016/S1570-8705(03)00004-0

Rakocevic, V., Rajarajan, M., McCalla, K., & Boumitri, C. (2004). QoS constraints in bluetooth-based wireless sensor networks. *Lecture Notes in Computer Science, 3266,* 214–223. doi:10.1007/978-3-540-30193-6_22

Royer, E., & Toh, C. K. (1999). A review of current routing protocols for ad-hoc mobile wireless networks. *IEEE Personal Communications, 4*(2), 46–55.

Sabata, B., Chatterjee, S., Davis, M., Sydir, J., & Lawrence, T. (1997). Taxonom for QoS specifications. In *Proceedings of the third International Work- shop on Object-Oriented Real-Time Dependable Systems.* IEEE.

Saginbekov, S., & Korpeoglu, I. (2005). An energy efficient scatternet formation algorithm for bluetooth-based sensor networks. In *Proceedings of the Second European Workshop on Wireless Sensor Networks.* IEEE. 10.1109/EWSN.2005.1462012

Shah, R., & Rabaey, J. (2002). Energy aware routing for low energy ad hoc sensor networks. In *Proceedings of IEEE WCNC,* (pp. 17–21). IEEE. 10.1109/WCNC.2002.993520

Sheu, P., Chien, S., Hu, C., & Li, Y. (2005). An efficient genetic algorithm for the power-based qos many-to-one routing problem for wireless sensor networks. In *International Conference on Information Networking, ICOIN 2005,* (pp. 275–282). IEEE. 10.1007/978-3-540-30582-8_29

Stratil, H. (2005). Distributed construction of an underlay in wireless networks. In *Proceedings of the Second European Workshop on Wireless Sensor Networks.* IEEE. 10.1109/EWSN.2005.1462009

Talekder, A., Bhatt, R., Chandramouli, S., Ali, L., Pidva, R., & Monacos, S. (2005). Autonomous resource management and control algorithms for distributed wireless sensor networks. In *The 3rd ACS/ IEEE International Conference on Computer Systems and Applications* (pp. 19–26). ACM.

Chapter 6
Applications of Deep Learning–Based Product Recommendation Systems

Sunil Sharma

National Institute of Technology, Kurukshetra, India

Minakshi Sharma

National Institute of Technology, Kurukshetra, India

ABSTRACT

The high-tech world we live in today is dominated by multimedia. Multimedia is being created at a rapid rate in the current technological era. Consumption and the exchange of the same between users happen quickly. Choosing whatever form of content or multimedia to consume next depending on interests and preferences is a conundrum while consuming this content. Nowadays, all online streaming sites utilize multimedia recommender systems. These are utilized to anticipate the following collection of multimedia that users can enjoy based on their prior usage patterns. By identifying the points of commonality between the user and the goods, preexisting models can forecast this utilizing the collaborative field. By treating this as a sequence prediction problem, the proposed model in this chapter increases the predicted accuracy using collaborative filtering (CF), ripple nets, deep learning, and recurrent neural networks (RNNs).

1. INTRODUCTION

A customised computerised recommendation system known as a "multimedia recommender system" (MRS) makes recommendations based on the inherent characteristics of multimedia objects, historical user behaviour, and the collective user community's behaviour (Yang et al., 2021; Kim et al.,2019) To address the issue of information overload, it is used to filter, prioritise, and effectively provide pertinent and tailored information. The multimedia recommender system uses a variety of media to recommend different material. It can alternatively be explained as a system that uses information filtering to present

DOI: 10.4018/978-1-6684-8306-0.ch006

users with information that may be relevant to their everyday lives. The field of movies, music, games, books, and other media can all be predicted using this recommender system (Yang et al., 2021; Greff et al.,2015; Lavanya et al., 2021)The recommendation is challenging, though, and there have been various methods put forth over the years. Most of the methods encounter certain difficulties. The Cold Start problem, which arises when there is insufficient data for a product (due to a new release or low popularity), is one of the most frequent problems encountered. In this study, the model's accuracy has been improved by addressing the shortcomings of the many current models, merging them to provide more accurate results, and providing the user with more exact suggestions.

2. MOTIVATION

With a lot of content available online to consume, time being limited, and a large amount of knowledge to be ingested, there is a possible difficulty of information overload which impacts the quick and timely access to the items of interest (Rendle et al., 2010; Mikolov et al., 2013; Cho et al., 2014; Ruihui et al., 2018). The issue brought about by the enormous growth of the media market is that it is now difficult to decide what kind and how much of it should be consumed in order for it to be best and in line with user preferences (Yang et al., 2021; Brafman et al., 2000; Ruihui et al., 2018; Kim et al., 2019]. As a result, the recommender system provides the user with a very tiny, usable dataset that is well suited to the description after being provided with a big amount of data and the description they are looking for. By retrieving the information the user wants based on preferences, interests, and observed behaviours, recommender systems assist in resolving the issue of information overload. Users in complex information contexts can use it to make great decisions. As a result, there is a great need for effective and precise recommendation strategies within the system that offers users reliable and pertinent recommendations (Lavanya et al., 2021).

3. RELATED WORK

The previous research in this area as well as the competing models are explained in this section.

3.1 Existing Popular Approaches

Due to the advent of data-driven architectures, which attempt to analyse user behaviours and preferences to recommend goods, multimedia recommendation has suddenly grown to be a very hot topic. Machine learning models have been developed using this data-driven methodology, with variable degrees of success. However, recommendation is a highly challenging topic, thus there has always been a global effort to improve models each year. For instance, both the Image Classification Challenge for dog breeds and the Netflix Challenge for creating a model for movie and television show suggestions attracted a lot of interest. To attain the same goal, other models have been suggested. The most widely used models are Collaborative Filtering versions, such as User-to-User CF, Item-to-Item CF, and Hybrid CF (Brafman et al., 2000). The fact that RNN-based (Robin et al., 2017) models can encode sequence data contributes to their popularity. Graph-Based (Yang et al., 2021; Wang et al., 2018), Knowledge-Based(Mikolov et al., 2010), CNN (Hidasi et al., 2015), (Qian, 1999; Zeiler et al., 2012) models, and many others.

However, a hybrid model, which borrows concepts from a variety of previous models and mixes them to create a superior one, always produces the best outcomes. The St RippleNet (Shown in Figure 1), a Graph Knowledge-based model, is explored in this research as a state-of-the-art implementation (Yang et al., 2021).

Figure 1. St_RippleNet's model overview

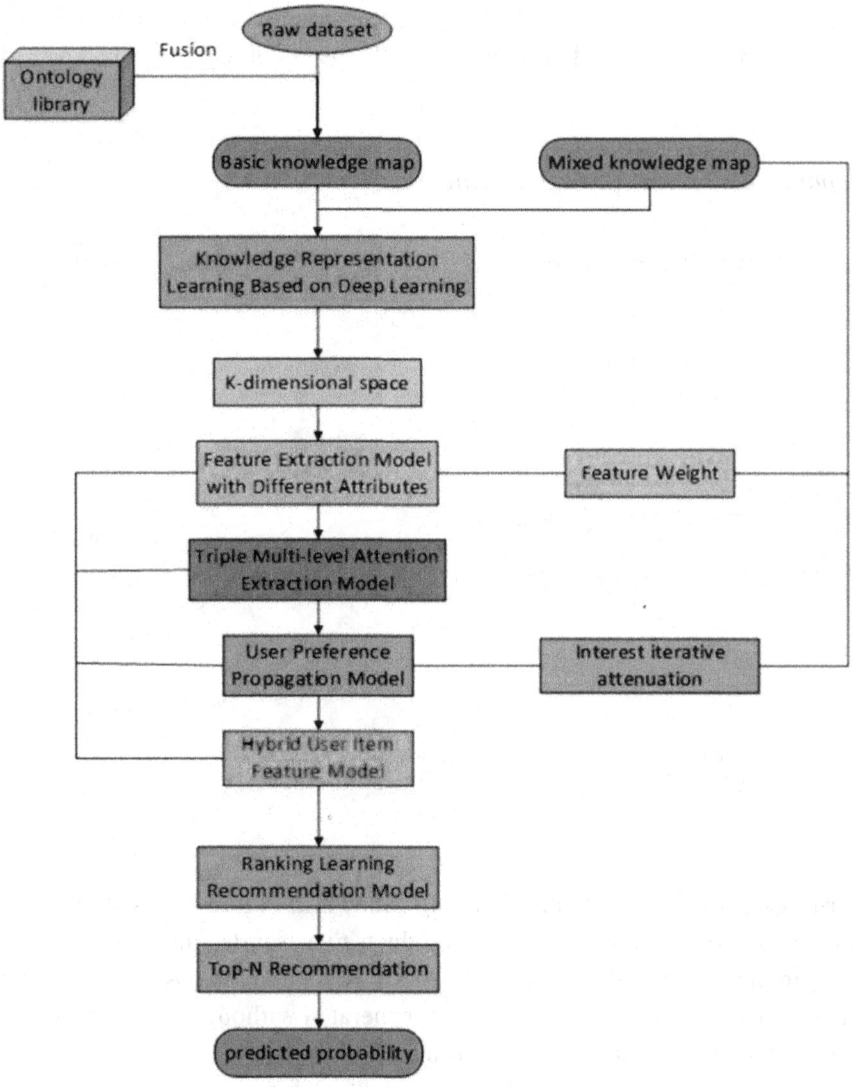

3.2 Competing Models

Several of the competing models have been described in this section:

The distribution of user click preferences for past items and the implementation of a triple-based multi-layer attention mechanism, Zhisheng and Jinyong attempted to connect the knowledge graph with deep learning and update the models underlying the RippleNet (Yang et al., 2021).They assert that their findings are far superior than those of current models. Here is an overview of their model:

In order to track a user's changing viewing patterns and make movie recommendations based on them, Devooght and Bersini investigated how to incorporate sequence data of movie watching for a user into an RNN (Robin et al., 2017). The authors' goal in this case was to increase the k-SPS, which is a metric where the top K things are chosen and the next item in the sequence receives a score of 1 or 0 if it matches any one of the top K items. With the one-hot encoding of movies and some of its features, they employed a unidirectional LSTM (Hochreiter et al.,1997) del and a Dense layer at the end with softmax activation.

Figure 2. Collaborative VS content-based filtering

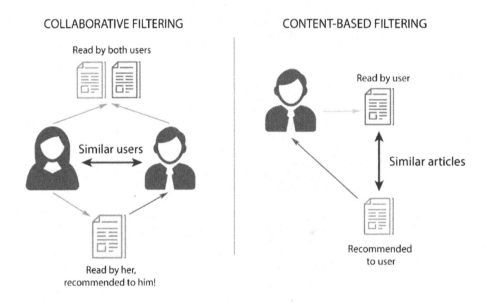

Generic user-to-user based collaborative filtering (Shown in Figure 2)was studied by Brafman and others. The major goal in this case was to suggest products to a user depending on how similar that user was to other users in the database (Brafman et al., 2000). KNN and the cosine similarity measure were used to determine user similarities. Predictions were generated without consulting the goods that these other individuals who share similarities have consumed.

User similarity criteria used in this model were altered by Kingma and Adam (Kingma et al., 2014). Better methods for locating comparable users were supposed to result in more accurate forecasts for the user.

4. THE PROPOSED WORK

This section explains the suggested strategy and a few key concepts for a clearer understanding.

4.1 Problem Formulation

Predicting the top K items for a user who would have the highest click-through rate (CTR) for the stated user is the major objective of the proposed approach. The top K items with the highest likelihood of being consumed by that user are essentially predicted (P(C)). For this, data on user interests and behaviours over time is needed, as well as information on how items relate to one another and how similar they are based on intrinsic qualities such as the composer of the music or the director of the movie, among other things, rather than just how other users rated and liked them.

Let $U = \{u_1, u_2, \dots \}$ be the set of all users. Let $V = \{v_1, v_2, \dots \}$ and an interaction matrix $Y = \{ y_{uv} \mid u \in U, v \in V \}$. Where

$y_{uv} = 1$, if interaction (u, v) is detected.
$y_{uv} = 0$, if interaction (u, v) is not observed.

We want to present a list $R = \{v_i, v_{i+1}, \dots \}$, based on the aforementioned information, where v_i is the item with the greatest P(C), followed by v_{i+1} and so on.

4.2 Sequence Information for Habit Detection and RNN Prediction

Information regarding the development of the user's interests as well as the interests of the user as a whole can be found in the habits, history, and sequence of the user's media consumption. For instance, after watching Toy Story 1, Toy Story 2, and Toy Story 3 in that order, it's more probable that a user will want to watch Toy Story 4. This sequence information is not used in any way in the majority of top-N recommendation algorithms.

Formally speaking, we wish to predict S_i^{t-} as a function of S_i^t given a sequence S_i^t for user i at time t, S_i^{t-} being the history of products the user ingested before time t, and S_i^{t+} being the goods the user will consume after time including time t. RNN are especially useful in this situation because of how well they can be used to identify patterns in sequence data. RNN is chosen over CNN because the order matters and the sequence itself cannot be jumbled (Sutskever et al., 2014; Józefowicz et al., 2015; Chen et al., 2015).

Instead of using a long-term prediction score to assess the model's efficacy, Devooght and Bersini describe the necessity for a short-term prediction score (Robin et al., 2017).An informal evidence that SPS is more than sufficient for training a better model than LPs is presented in a thought experiment, where SPS itself can train the model so that long-term predictions may also be made. At the conclusion, the outcomes are also confirmed.

4.3 Knowledge Graphs

Due to the lack of user-item, user-user, user, and item data, the majority of standard recommender systems struggle with cold start. These restrictions prevent the aforementioned models from providing more accurate advice. This introduces the idea of a Knowledge Graph (KG), which keeps track of information about the similarities between objects. Movie A and Movie B, for instance, may share a common director, while Music A and Music B may share a common performer, release year, etc. This particular kind of graph has the data necessary to establish a causal connection between two objects.

Improved encodings for two things in the item space, which require that similar items in the item space have a smaller distance between them than unrelated items do, will result in better predictions, according to Zhisheng and Jinyong (Yang et al., 2021). By thoroughly identifying commonalities between the two items, KG accomplishes the same for us (Shown in Figure 3).

Figure 3. Knowledge graph

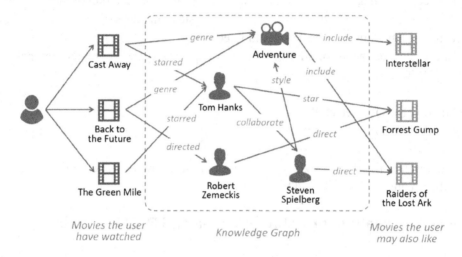

4.4 Hybrid Approach

The aim is to combine a cutting-edge recommendation algorithm known as RippleNet (Wang et al., 2018), a very novel RNN (Robin et al., 2017) based sequencing model, and one of the most well-liked recommendation strategies known as user-to-user based collaborative filtering (Brafman et al., 2000). There are implementations for each of the combined models, each of which has increased its own accuracy. The primary objective of the combined model is to overcome each of the aforementioned models' shortcomings by leveraging those of the others. The models were selected to complement one another, and this produced some incredibly favourable outcomes.

To build sets of (user, item) tuples for the user for whom we want to provide predictions, the Person-Based CF Brafman et al., 2000) is used to find a group of users who are highly similar to the user for whom we want to offer predictions. The "item" in the tuple is chosen from a list of films by the RNN. A subset of movies from the extensive library are chosen by the RNN-based model based on the user's preferences. This subset is chosen in order to raise the RippleNet's prediction score.

5. DATA FLOW DIAGRAMS

The data flow diagrams in this section show how each application section interacts with one another and transfers data.

Figure 4. Level 0: DFD

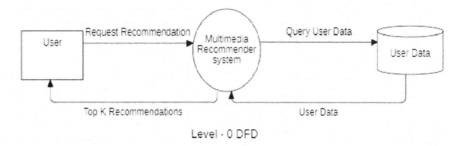

This level 0 DFD (Shown in Figure 4) designates a system where the user asks the recommender system a question. Currently, the recommender system is a "black box" that performs some processing after querying certain user data and then provides the users with the top K predictions.

The UI, the Backend, and the Database are the three main components of the program, according to the DFDs. In addition, the Hybrid Model has three sub-models, as shown in Fig. 5 and Fig. 6. The entirety of the user's information is contained in the User Data database. Additionally, user interactions with catalogue items are documented in the User Behavior Database. Firebase has been used for authentication, and it takes care of everything for the application. The Django server uses Prediction Controller as its entry point to run the whole ML model and obtain predictions depending on the data entered by the front-end server.

6. IMPLEMENTATION

This part provides a detailed explanation of the model's implementation from the previous section.

Figure 5. Level 1: DFD

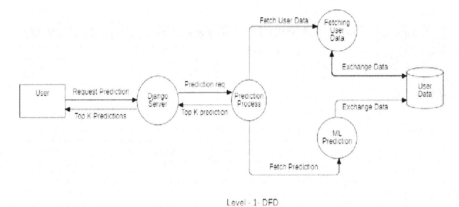

6.1 Framework

Figure 5 depicts the hybrid model's framework (DFD-2). It calculates the possibility that user u would click on item v after receiving user u and item v as inputs. It is also known as the click-through probability. For prediction, the historical information about each user and their viewing pattern is taken into account. When there are no server requests, the RNN and RippleNet models are saved to disc. Which are subsequently loaded as needed. All relevant functions must be called and data passed around by the ML Controller.

Figure 6. Level 2: DFD

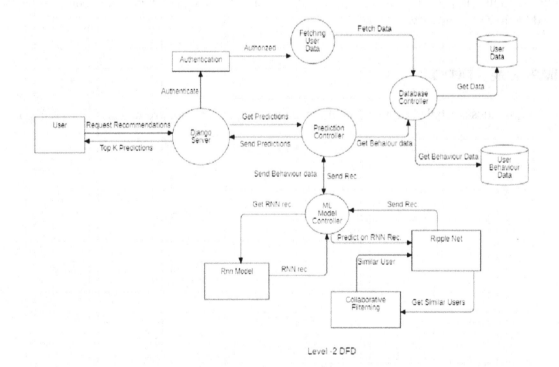

6.2 Metrics

Use the click-through measure for RippleNet, as in the original study (Yang et al., 2021), and compare RNN models based on k-SPS, as in the original paper (Robin et al., 2017). On the metrics that they were supposed to be the best at, the suggested model performs better than those models.

- SPS stands for Short Term Prediction Score and measures how well a model can forecast what will come next in a sequence. It's a 1 or 0 if the predicted item appears in the sequence.
- K - SPS: Short Term Prediction @ K, which compares the predicted item to the subsequent K items in the sequence and returns 1 if the predicted item is present or 0 otherwise.
- The likelihood that a user will click on the item that is offered to him is known as CTP (P(C)). Here, a chance of larger than 50% is treated as a 1 or 0. It can then be changed to a binary accuracy in this manner.

6.3 Dataset

Finding a reasonable dataset with all the data provided and one that was sizable enough to provide variety in training and prediction was the key challenge with dataset selection. The MovieLens-1M was utilised for that. Over 3706 movies, 1 million ratings, and 6040 users are present. The sex, age, and profession of the user, as well as the year and the movie's genre, are all included in this dataset. The knowledge graph for the dataset is created using Microsoft Satori in our case it was already created in the base version of RippleNet.

6.4 Components and Working

This hybrid model consists of three parts. Each component is there to address some other component's problems, as was previously stated. The parts are described in detail as follows:

6.4.1 Recurrent Neural Networks

When the word order contains some innate meaning, RNNs are typically employed to train NLP (Graves et al., 2013) models. Multimedia in this instance is stored as words, and the user's history is recorded as a sentence containing those words. The RNN model aims to foretell the subsequent word in the string. In other words, it tries to foretell what media will come after it in the succession of media. The complete number of each type of media in the database that can be taken into account is represented by the dictionary of terms. The model's input is a one-hot encoding of the current item, and its output is a softmax layer with a neuron for each word in the dictionary. The k items that the RNN model is going to forecast are the ones whose neurons are most active. We go ahead and employ the "gated" RNN LSTM (Bernhardsson, 2014) for the first layer. The categorical cross-entropy is reduced, and SPS is increased, by training the model. In the one-hot encoding of the input to the LSTM, rating and genre information are encoded. The final layer is a thick layer with softmax activation. The LSTM layer has a dropout of 0.2 and 128 neurons. Adam is used as the model's optimizer and has a learning rate of 10^{-4} and a decay rate of 10^{-6} (Kingma et al., 2014).

6.4.2 User-Based CF

One of the most common techniques for discovering individuals with similar interests so that movies from their watchlists that the current user hasn't seen can be recommended is user-based CF. We use KNN to identify the users who are nearest to one another in the userspace, which makes the method itself relatively simple. We apply the cosine formula to measure similarity. The following step in the RippleNet process, which will be covered in the next subsection, can leverage these groups of users for final processing.

6.4.3 RippleNet

A ripple set, or a group of nodes that are k distances from the seed node, is a concept that is used in the ripple network, or *Vu*. The interaction between these sets and the item embeddings of the softmax layer is then utilised to determine the CTR for each item. In order to provide a better prediction because there are fewer options, we aim to restrict the number of movies on which the softmax is being performed in our model. We run the entire collection of RNN items in order to determine the optimal subset of movies, and then we create K1 items on which the RippleNet runs.

We now need a number of users who are comparable to the user for whom we are attempting to anticipate after we get the goods. To do this, we searched for similar users using User-Based CF of User-Based KNN. For our prediction calculation, we matched every user with every other item and assigned them a "interact it" value of 1. For the best outcomes, the model was trained using the whole dataset. To shorten the time needed to generate a prediction and to boost the P(C) for the smaller selection, a subset of items was selected for prediction. Figure 7 and 8 illustrate the structure of RippleNet and the aforementioned Ripple Sets.

Figure 7. Ripple net architecture

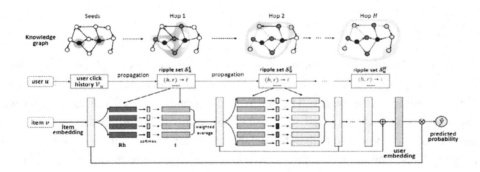

Figure 8. Ripple net e.g. k - hop ripple set

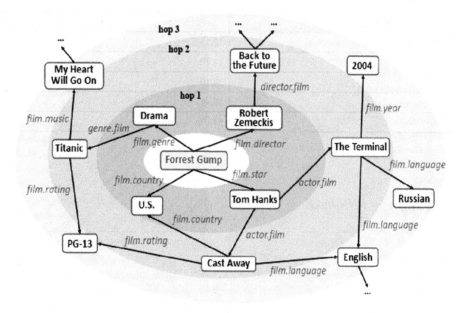

6.5 Model Compatibility

As we've already indicated, the models are picked so that they work well together. For instance, the RNN model struggles with its lack of item knowledge and attempts to base its predictions purely on a user's prior interactions with the system and a basic measure of item similarity. This issue is resolved by using RippleNet, which strongly relies on the relationships between items to assess the RNN-selected subset of items more accurately. But to produce that data, we'll need a group of users who are similar to one another in order to create the prediction dataset. To achieve this, we employ a portion of the user-to-user CF to create a user set that is sufficiently similar to one another to enable accurate prediction.

7. RESULTS

This section will examine the findings from our comparison of our models to those of other models using the MovieLens 1M dataset, as previously reported.

7.1 RNN Model

The authors of the original research (Robin et al., 2017) attempted to include every movie in the model but neglected to account for movie popularity metrics to cut down on the amount of redundant movies in the prediction. Even with the identical user base for which the projections were created, we implemented those modifications and saw noticeably better outcomes as shown in Table 1as well as in Figure 9.

Table 1. Methods

Method	10-SPS (%)
BPR-MF	12.18
User KNN	14.40
MC	29.20
RNN	33.69
RNN-mod	**54.65**

Figure 9. k - SPS graph for RNN-mod

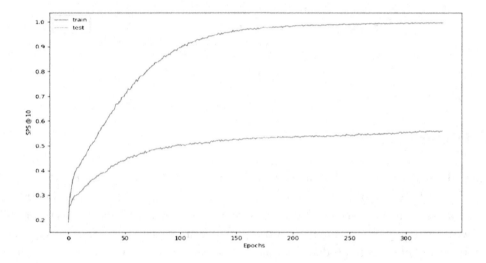

7.2 RippleNet

In the original paper (Wang et al., 2018), RippleNet was utilised alone; however, in our situation, we combined it with additional models to get a more accurate prediction (Shown in Table 2 and in Figure 10) by addressing RippleNet's overall shortcomings.

Table 2. Models

Models	ACC over MovieLens - 1M
CKE	73.9%
LibFM	81.2%
DKN	58.9%
SHINE	73.2%
PER	66.7%
Wide&Deep	82.2%
RippleNet	84.4%
ST_RippleNet	85.2%
Hybrid RippleNet	**87.7%**

Figure 10. Accuracy graph for hybrid RippleNet

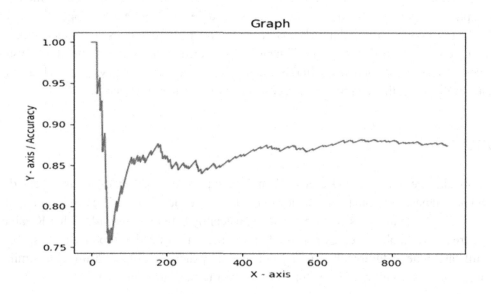

8. OBSERVATIONS

We will go over a few of the observations that were made when these models were being developed in this part.

- The St RippleNet model is actually a more advanced iteration of the already well-liked RippleNet with some extra capabilities. For all intents and purposes, however, our model performed better when combined with RippleNet than when combined with St RippleNet, probably because St RippleNet was slightly more overfitting than RippleNet implementations. Using our own version of the RippleNet, the results showed that our model outperformed St RippleNet.

- Exploiting better item encoding and reducing the size of the item dictionary by using item popularity, the RNN-based recommendation system's SPS @ 10 model was greatly improved.
- Changing the top K values for our RNN models allows us to reach extremely high accuracies, but doing so incurs processing costs.
- Testing revealed that a shorter maximum sequence length limits the model SPS because the sequence data actually carries valuable information about the items.
- The choice of neurons in the first layer of the RNN models was challenging because we experimented with a number of different numbers with variable degrees of success and failure. If the learning rate is either low or too high, the data will over fit . The number of features that would be used to solve the same issue using matrix factorization is actually the first benefit. We specifically selected 128 neurons for our situation. However, 100 would have been acceptable.

9. PROPOSED WORKS' SOCIAL WELFARE

Over the past few years, usage of online social networks has grown significantly. Social media networks in particular enable people to interact, share, comment on, and view many forms of multimedia material. Due to this phenomenon's quick pace of change, vast volume, and inherent heterogeneity, a significant amount of data is produced that exhibits Big Data characteristics. To help users navigate these data collections and identify "what they truly need" inside this informational sea, recommender systems have been developed over the past ten years. In this chapter, new recommending system has been introduced for big data applications that can provide suggestions based on user interactions.

10. CONCLUSION

When multimedia objects were encoded as words and the sequences as sentences, we investigated the usage of recurrent neural networks and their efficacy in predicting sequence data. The experiments shown that LSTM generates excellent results, and we obtain significantly better results with higher K values. In our situation, a greater K number is easily permissible because it is utilized to produce a subset of products from the full catalogue. Additionally, RippleNet adds many more tools to measure item similarity on a much wider scale. It is a cutting-edge solution to the recommendation problem.

REFERENCES

Adadelta, M. D. (2012). *An adaptive learning rate method*. arXiv preprint arXiv:1212.5701.

Bernhardsson. E. (2014). *Recurrent neural networks for collaborative filtering*. arXiv preprint.

Brafman, R. I., Heckerman, D., & Shani, G. (2000). Recommendation as a stochastic sequential decision problem. In ICAPS, 164–173.

Chen, X., Liu, X., Gales, M. J., & Woodland, P. C. (2015). Recurrent neural network language model training with noise contrastive estimation for speech recognition. In ICASSP. IEEE. doi:10.1109/ICASSP.2015.7179005

Cho, K., Merrienboer, B. V., Bahdanau, D., & Bengio, Y. (2014). On the properties of neural machine translation: Encoder-decoder approaches. In *Proceedings of SSST@EMNLP 2014, Eighth Workshop on Syntax, Semantics and Structure in Statistical Translation*. IEEE..

Graves, A., Mohamed, A. R., & Hinton, G. (2013). Speech recognition with deep recurrent neural networks. In *Acoustics, Speech and Signal Processing (ICASSP), IEEE International Conference*, (pp. 6645–6649). IEEE. 10.1109/ICASSP.2013.6638947

Greff, K., Srivastava, R. K., Koutník, J., Steunebrink, B. R., & Schmidhuber, J. (2015). LSTM: A search space odyssey. arXiv preprint arXiv:1503.04069.

Hidasi, B., Karatzoglou, A., Baltrunas, L.,& Tikk. D. (2015). *Session-based recommendations with convolutional neural networks*. CoRR.

Hochreiter, S., & Schmidhuber, J. (1997). Long short-term memory. *Neural Computation, 9*(8), 1735–1780. doi:10.1162/neco.1997.9.8.1735 PMID:9377276

Józefowicz, R., Zaremba, W.,& Sutzkever. I. (2015). *An empirical exploration of recurrent network*. arXiv.

Kim, M., Jeon, S., Shin, H., Choi, W., Chung, H., & Nah, Y. (2019). Movie Recommendation based on User Similarity of Consumption Pattern Change. In *IEEE Second International Conference on Artificial Intelligence and Knowledge Engineering (AIKE)*, (pp. 317-319). IEEE. 10.1109/AIKE.2019.00064

Kingma. D., & Adam. J. Ba. (2014). *A method for stochastic optimization*. arXiv preprint arXiv:1412.6980.

Lavanya, R., et al. (2021).Comparison Study on Improved Movie Recommender Systems. *Special Issue on Computing Technology and Information management.*

Mikolov, T., Chen, K., Corrado, G., & Dean, J. (2013). Efficient estimation of word in vector space. arXiv preprint arXiv:1301.3781.

Mikolov, T., Karafiát, M., Burget, L., Cernock'y, J., & Khudanpur, S. (2010). Recurrent neural network-based language model. In INTERSPEECH, 2, 3.

Qian, N. (1999). On the momentum term in gradient descent learning algorithms. *Neural Networks, 12*(1), 145–151. doi:10.1016/S0893-6080(98)00116-6 PMID:12662723

Rendle, S., & Freudenthaler, C., & Thieme. L. Schmidt. (2010). Factorizing personalized Markov chains for a next-basket recommendation. *In Proceedings of the 19th international conference on the world wide web*, (pp. 811–820). ACM. 10.1145/1772690.1772773

RobinD.HuguesB. (2017). *Collaborative Filtering with Recurrent Neural Networks*. arXiv:1608.07400 [cs.IR].

Ruihui, M., Xiaoqin, Z., & Lixin, H. (2018). A Survey of Recommender Systems Based on Deep Learning. *IEEE Access : Practical Innovations, Open Solutions, 6*, 1–1. doi:10.1109/ACCESS.2018.2880197

Sutskever, I., Vinyals, O., & Le, Q. V. (2014). Sequence to sequence learning with neural networks. In Advances in neural information processing systems, 3104–3112.

Wang, H., Zhang, F., Wang, J., Zhao, M., Li, W., Xie, X., & Guo, M. (2018). RippleNet: Propagating User Preferences on the Knowledge Graph for Recommender Systems. *International Conference on Information and Knowledge Management,* (pp. 417-426). ACM. 10.1145/3269206.3271739

Yang. Z., & Cheng, J. (2021). Recommendation Algorithm Based on Knowledge Graph to Propagate User Preference. *International Journal of Computational Intelligence Systems.*. doi:10.2991/ijcis.d.210503.001

Chapter 7
Data Controlling and Security Issues in Cloud:
A Step Towards Serverless

Anisha Kumari

National Institute of Technology, Rourkela, India

Manoj Kumar Patra

National Institute of Technology, Rourkela, India

Bibhudatta Sahoo

National Institute of Technology, Rourkela, India

ABSTRACT

Cloud computing has been the most demanding technology in the last decade, which several organizations have widely adopted. Most enterprise applications and data are migrated to the public or hybrid cloud due to the ease of access and infrastructure facilities provided by the cloud provider. One significant issue in the cloud environment is the security and data controlling mechanism, which needs to be focused on for better service quality. Users usually hesitate to use public cloud services due to privacy and security concerns about the personal data they want to process online. Unlike standard cloud computing notions, serverless computing does not expose the infrastructure or platforms on which the services operate to the end-user. Clients only have to worry about the application's business logic, and the service provider usually takes care of everything, including configuration, infrastructure provision, servers, etc. In this chapter, the authors have discussed several cloud computing issues regarding data security and data controlling mechanisms.

INTRODUCTION

Computer hardware and software advancements have made cloud computing a major topic in business and academia. Several factors have led to cloud computing, including conventional computer technol-

DOI: 10.4018/978-1-6684-8306-0.ch007

ogy, communication technologies, and business practices (Hashizume, Rosado, Fernandez-Medina, & Fernandez, 2013). It is built on the network and features a consumer-oriented service structure. Scalability and dependability are critical characteristics of a cloud computing system (Gong, Liu, Zhang, Chen, & Gong, 2010; Stieninger & Nedbal, 2014). The location of the computing resource in the cloud computing system is hidden from both the developer and the end user. In a cloud computing system, the customers are allowed to access the application, and their data from any location in the world (Rashid & Chaturvedi, n.d.). Many customers may utilize cloud computing resources at the same time. When the workload increases, the cloud system's capacity may be raised by adding additional hardware to manage it. As a service, cloud resources are made available on a pay-per-use basis. Significantly large quantity of commodity-grade servers are often used to create highly scalable and dependable on-demand services in the cloud systems (Y. C. Lee & Zomaya, 2012). It is possible to raise or reduce the number of resources available to users in a cloud system depending on their needs. The resource can be computing, storage, and other specification services. It has been observed by several information technology sector organizations that cloud computing has a significant influence on the social benefits of IT advancements in the near future (Kuiper, Van Dam, Reiter, & Janssen, 2014). Data centers constructed on servers using various levels of virtualization technology presently make up the vast majority of cloud computing infrastructure (Kumari, Sahoo, Behera, Misra, & Sharma, 2021). It's possible to use the services from anywhere globally, and the cloud serves as a central hub for all of your computing requirements. Using cloud computing has revolutionized the way software is developed. It's possible to store data in the cloud, making it accessible to the user at any time and from any location. Most of the data is saved on a personal computer or similar device. Cloud computing may provide data security without requiring the user to take further steps to safeguard their information. The safety of data kept in the cloud is thus a prerequisite for the use of cloud computing (Deshpande, Sharma, & Peddoju, 2019; Wang, 2011). Cloud computing platforms including Google, IBM, Microsoft, Amazon, VMware, and EMC are offered by a wide range of enterprises (Dikaiakos, Katsaros, Mehra, Pallis, & Vakali, 2009). The user's private data is at risk in the cloud computing system; thus, the data must not be deleted or stolen. When hackers know that the user's information is stored on a cloud system, they may pay greater attention to accessing it. When a hacker knows that the user's data is stored on a cloud system, they may pay greater attention to accessing it. Protecting this new system requires a higher level of attention than previously required. The data is kept in the cloud by the business. Those who are not employees of the firm may access the data. The organization must have assurance in cloud computing to keep confidential information in the cloud. Regardless of whether a firewall protects the cloud system, governance and security are essential to cloud computing (Krutz & Vines, 2010). As cloud computing progresses, securing the system is a major concern. Conventional security measures cannot fully protect the cloud system. Cloud computing may rise to a wide range of new security issues with no limits and mobility. These include data privacy, user data security protection, cloud platform reliability, and management of cloud computing.

Serverless computing frees application developers from the burden of maintaining infrastructure (Baldini et al., 2017). The cloud service provider provisioned, scaled, and managed the infrastructure to execute the code using serverless applications. There are several benefits of serverless computing over conventional server-based, or cloud-based technology (Li, Lin, Wang, Ye, & Xu, 2022; Shafiei, Khonsari, & Mousavi, 2019). Serverless architectures appeal to many developers because of their lower costs, increased scalability, and increased adaptability (Castro, Ishakian, Muthusamy, & Slominski, 2019). Developers do not have to worry about procuring, deploying, or maintaining back-end servers with serverless architectures. On the other hand, serverless computing isn't a one-size-fits-all solution for every web application developer. Serverless computing may be beneficial for software developers who wish to reduce the time it takes to get a product to market and create a lightweight. These extensible applications can be easily updated (McGrath & Brenner, 2017; Sewak & Singh, 2018). Many serverless providers now provide Function-as-a-Service (FaaS) platforms (Lynn, Rosati, Lejeune, & Emeakaroha, 2017), such as AWS Lambda (Sbarski & Kroonen-burg, 2017), Google Cloud Functions (Kim & Lee, 2019), and Microsoft Azure Functions (H. Lee, Satyam, & Fox, 2018), and database and storage capabilities.

The rest of the chapter is arranged in the following ways. Section-2 presents the motivation for this study. Section-3 presents different aspects of cloud computing. In Section-4, presents the concept of the data flow mechanism in the cloud and multiple components of the data classification model in the cloud. Section-5 discusses Various security issues and challenges in the cloud along with the existing approaches used to protect the data. Section-6 talks about the serverless architecture and its characteristics. Function as a Service (FaaS) in serverless architecture has been discussed in Section-6.2. In Section-7, we have mentioned serverless solutions for data management and security in the cloud. Section-8 summarizes the conclusion of the chapter.

MOTIVATION AND RESEARCH QUESTIONS

Because the cloud system is connected to the internet, any security issues that arise on the internet also affect it. There are no major differences between a cloud-based system and a typical PC system when it comes to security. Cloud computing technology poses a number of issues and challenges with respect to safety and privacy (Jansen, 2011; Takabi, Joshi, & Ahn, 2010). The cloud system may also be threatened by traditional security issues, such as security holes, malware, and assaults from outside parties (Sen, 2015). Due to the inherent properties of cloud computing, they may appear in greater levels of vulnerability. It's possible for hostile actors to get unauthorized access to cloud services and gain unauthorized access. The cloud system must protect business and data applications that are housed in the cloud.

The amount of data in cloud environment is increasing very rapidly and some of which may include personally identifiable information (PII). The hacker might pay greater attention to stealing data from the cloud system if the information stored there is critical to the user. Security for this system must be tighter than the conventional system. The data is kept in the cloud by the enterprise. The data may be accessed by persons who the firm does not employ. The organization must have faith in the technology if it intends to keep sensitive data in the cloud. Whether or not a firewall protects the cloud system, security and governance are essential for cloud computing. Standard security mechanisms cannot completely protect the cloud system.

Research Questions

The following research questions may be posed in data management and security aspect in the cloud:

- RQ1: In what aspect do the cloud deployment models differ from one other?
- RQ2: How do various cloud service models effects the data controlling mechanism in the cloud?
- RQ3: What are the major security concerns in the cloud?
- RQ4: What data protection mechanisms are available for traditional cloud technology?
- RQ1: How the serverless architecture differs from conventional cloud architecture?

- RQ6: What are the different essential features of serverless computing?
- RQ7: What are the data management layers in serverless architecture?
- RQ8: How is the data handled in the era of big data, especially in the batch processing layer?
- RQ9: What is Data Lake? How can it be used to manage the storage in serverless architecture?
- RQ10: What could be the data analytics solution in a serverless platform?

CLOUD COMPUTING ARCHITECTURE

Computers with massive data centers are managed, configured, and provisioned to provide services in an extensible way via cloud computing, a new form of network-based computing. Using the cloud symbol, we can identify the boundaries of a cloud computing environment. Virtual servers, physical servers, software, storage devices, network devices, and services (Cloud) may all be provided in a specified environment through a cloud that has a defined boundary (Kumari, Behera, Sahoo, & Sahoo, 2022). There are five essential qualities, five deployment models, and three cloud computing service models.

Characteristics of Cloud Computing

Some of the fundamental features of cloud computing are as follows;

- **On-Demand Capabilities:** In the cloud, the necessary computing services are given by the service provider without the intervention of any individuals whatsoever AWS, IBM, Google, and Salesforce.com are some of the cloud services companies that provide on-demand self-services to their users.
- **Ubiquitous Network access:** Standard techniques are used to make cloud computing services accessible via a network. These methods may serve a variety of client platforms, including laptops, smartphones, and workstations.
- **Flexibility:** Any number of nodes may be added or deleted from the cloud architecture at any moment, depending on the organization's needs.
- **Location Independent Resource Pooling:** IT resources such as virtual computers, storage, networks, and e-mail services may be shared across several users due to the multiple-tenant approach. The dynamic assignment and reallocation of both physical and virtual resources takes place in response to changes in user requirement.
- **Measured Services:** Cloud computing services are offered to customers on a ``pay per use" basis, meaning that the more you use them, the more you'll pay.

Deployment Model in Cloud

The cloud deployment model describes where and how it will be utilized (Patra, Sahoo, Sahoo, & Turuk, 2019). These four deployment types' differences may be seen in the Table 1. In terms of deployment models, there are four basic options;

- **Private Cloud:** There are just a few organizations can access private clouds. Depending on the organization's needs, private clouds may be on-premise or off-premise. Maximum security and privacy are the primary goals of the private cloud.
- **Public Cloud:** Cloud infrastructure that may be used by the public and maintained by an institute or a third-party cloud service provider is public cloud infrastructure. In terms of shared resources, the public cloud is the most effective, but it also lacks the protection and control of private clouds.
- **Community Cloud:** Hybrid clouds are combinations of public, private, and community cloud architectures that provide consistent access to applications and data. Even though they are all part of the same group, they all have their own individual personalities.

Table 1. Essential factors of four cloud deployment models

Parameter	Public	Private	Community	Hybrid
Configuration	Easy	IT experts are needed for this.	IT experts are needed for this.	IT experts are needed for this.
Data Protection	Low	High	Very High	High
Flexible scaling	High	High	Fixed need	High
Cost efficiency	More affordable	More expensive	Members share the burden of the costs	Cheaper than private cloud but more expensive than public cloud
Reliability	Low	High	Higher	High

Cloud Service Model

In cloud computing, there are three different service models that, which are explained in the Figure. 1 and a detailed description is given in Table 2.

- **Infrastructure as a Service (IaaS):** There is a layer of infrastructure as a service at the bottom of the cloud's pyramid that includes virtual storage, network virtualization (e.g., VMware), and virtual machines (such as hypervisors) (Manvi & Shyam, 2014). IaaS is only the infrastructure, not the application or database.
- **Platform as a Service (PaaS):** This service model is a method of developing and deploying applications online. This service model uses the application, middleware, and operating system stacks to deliver essentially the same thing as a development environment in the cloud (Keller & Rexford, 2010). The user does not need to know the inner workings of the cloud infrastructure but must understand how to use middleware data integration tools to install cloud applications (Patra, Patel, Sahoo, & Turuk, 2020).
- **Software as a Service(SaaS):** SaaS is a composed entirely operating system that distributes software services and applications to end-users through a web browser on cloud infrastructure (Sun, Zhang, Chen, Zhang, & Liang, 2007). Organizing cloud infrastructures such as technology, storage, and networks is no longer necessary with SaaS.

Figure 1. Cloud service models

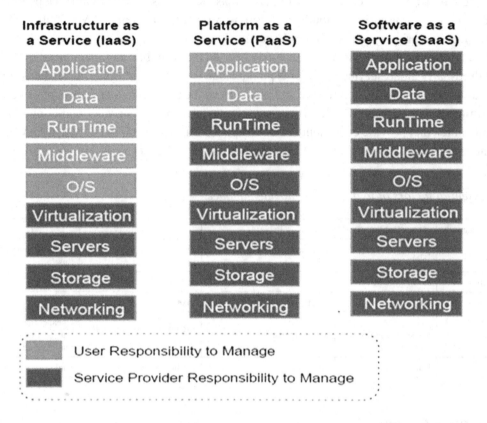

Table 2. Essential factors of three cloud service models

	IaaS	PaaS	SaaS
Benefits	• One of the most adaptable and dynamic frameworks. • Affordable because of its pay-as-you-go structure. • Because the hardware is deployed automatically, it's very user-friendly.	• Highly scalable, available and multitenant. • Development process is quickened and simplified. • Simplifies transitioning to a hybrid cloud environment.	• No hardware cost. • No initial set-up. • Automated upgrades.
Limitations	• Problems with data integrity stemming from the multitenant design. • When a provider experiences an outage, its clients lose access to their data for an extended time. • The necessity of educating a employee to operate the new infrastructure.	• Problems with the safety of sensitive information. • Functionality of current infrastructure. • Dependency on vendors speed, reliability and support.	• Loss of control. • Few options for fixing the problem. • The ability to communicate is crucial.

Figure 2. Schematic drawing of data flow in cloud-based storage and delivery services

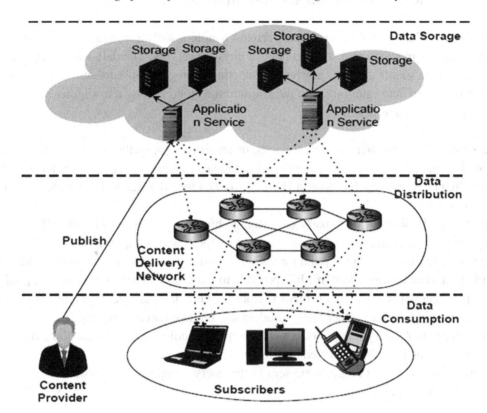

DATA CONTROLLING MECHANISM IN CLOUD

Data Flow in Cloud-Based Storage and Delivery Services

An example of a typical three-tier architecture for public cloud-based content storage and distribution system is shown in Figure. 2, a cloud oriented storage service, a content delivery network (or service), and subscribers with various devices (content consumers or clients). Storage and content distribution are the two main functions of a cloud provider. Content providers use these two functions to store, share, and distribute their material to many customers. Access to the material is provided through a cloud-based application software service, which reads and manages the data stored in a storage service using APIs (Behera, Rath, Misra, Leon, & Adewumi, 2019). The content provider or any third-party application service may be implemented in the cloud. To deploy the application software, data or content storage, and content distribution service, the content provider may employ numerous services based in the cloud are provided by a variety of cloud service providers. Netflix, for example, makes use of Amazon EC2 and S3 for content processing and storage, as well as Limelight, Level 3, and Akamai for content delivery.

Various Components of Data Classification Model

Data storage brokers, data management systems, request handlers, and query mappers are all components of the cloud, which is made up of a large number of physical servers. The data storage broker receives the data from the data source and uses a privacy protection strategy to obscure sensitive information in the data. A privacy and data categorization paradigm in the cloud is shown in Figure. 3. Each of these components are discussed as below:

- **Data Provider:** Infrastructure, web services, or enterprise applications offered in the cloud are provided by data providers. Businesses and individuals may use cloud services located in a data center. Clients are paying for using a shared infrastructure that the data provider uses to serve numerous clients.
- **Data Storage Broker:** A third-party data storage broker works as an intermediate between the cloud computing service provider and the user of the cloud computing service. Data Storage Broker is a central management point for various cloud services for commercial or technical use.
- **Cloud Data Management System:** It is possible to manage data across many cloud platforms in the cloud, either with or without on-premise storage. It is a database management system for cloud data delivered as a service rather than a product and offers cloud computing.
- **Query Mapper:** A query mapper matches the request handler's query to the cloud data management system to acquire the requested information.
- **Request Handler:** Client requests are sent to the query mapper by the system known as the request handler that controls them.

Figure 3. Privacy protection and data classification model in the cloud

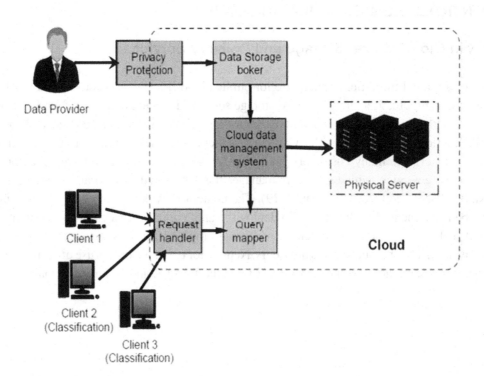

SECURITY ISSUES AND CHALLENGES IN CLOUD

Cloud computing is advancing quickly and has a lot of commitments for the future. Many aspects of information management and service delivery may be impacted by cloud computing. Data security in the cloud computing environment is more critical than in conventional networks since the data is heavily reliant on the web and server. The data privacy and security of cloud computing consumers is a major concern for many customers who do not want to send their data to the remote cloud platform. The progress of cloud computing has been hampered by several issues, the most important of which is security.

Major Security Concern in Cloud

While the benefits of cloud computing are undeniable, there are several security concerns to be aware of. Some of the cloud computing security concerns are listed below (Bisong, Rahman, et al., 2011; Kaur & Kaushal, 2011; Khalil, Khreishah, Bouktif, & Ahmad, 2013):

- **Data Loss:** In Cloud Computing, data loss or leakage is a problem. We don't have total control over the database, and our critical information is in someone else's hands. As a result, if cloud services are breached, hackers may be able to gain access to our private information.
- **Interference of Hackers and Insecure API's:** We are, of course, referring to the Internet when we discuss the cloud and its associated services. Additionally, we know that API is the quickest and most efficient method of interacting with the cloud. As a result, securing the APIs and interfaces that an external user interacts with is critical. However, only a limited number of cloud computing services are open to the ordinary people. Since it's conceivable that unauthorized individuals may get access to these services, the cloud is at risk from this weakness. As a result, hackers may be able to quickly access our data if they use one of these services.
- **User Account Hijacking:** It is one of the most serious security problems of cloud. A hacker somehow takes in charge of a user's or account of a company. Hackers have the power to carry out unauthorized activities if they are given full control.
- **Changing Service Provider:** Vendor lock-in is a critical security and privacy issue in cloud. When changing vendors, many firms may run across a variety of issues. For example, a company is looking to switch from AWS Cloud Services to google cloud services. Moving all of the data is only one of several challenges. It's also worth noting that each cloud service has its own unique set of issues. It is also likely that the costs for AWS, Google Cloud, etc., may vary from one to the other.
- **Lack of Skill:** The most common issues that arise in an IT company with understaffed technical support departments are having to switch to a different service provider, wanting more features, and not knowing how to utilize them. Therefore, using cloud computing effectively necessitates the expertise of an expert.
- **Denial of Service (DoS) attack:** When the system is overloaded, an attack of this kind may take place. DoS assaults are more common against major institutions like banks and governments. Data is lost due to denial-of-service attacks. As a result, data recovery is a costly and time-consuming endeavor.

Data Protection Techniques in Cloud

Theft and unauthorized modification of cloud-based data is a real possibility. Before it is saved in the cloud, the data might be encrypted. However, more time and computational resources will be required if the data set is huge. Those outside of the firm will be able to read the secret information. In the cloud, users' personal data may be safeguarded to some extent using traditional methods. Some of the tools available are encryption, security identification, and procedures for restricting who has access. Here, we'll go through some of the most often used cloud data security strategies.

- **Encryption:** Data encryption is the act of encrypting or altering data before moving it to a cloud storage location. The clients of cloud providers often have access to various encryption options. With the right platform, companies may use encryption to meet their security goals while saving money and gaining more control over their encryption keys. Data at rest in the cloud must be protected by secure encryption, particularly for data that has a longer life period. Before uploading data to your cloud service, ensure that it is encrypted. Once you've completed modifying a file, you should encrypt and password-protect it. Companies and organizations must adopt a data-centric strategy to secure their confidential information in today's mobility environments, complex virtualization, cloud services, etc., to defend against sophisticated attacks.

- **Security authentication:** In order to authenticate, you need information that you can only obtain. Personal information includes things like a person's full name, DoB, SSN i.e., social security number, or even the number plate on their car. A badge, fingerprint, or face recognition system are all examples of standard physical identification systems. Even while single-factor authentication might be a good place to start, it is always better to use two-factor authentication if feasible. Typically, a password is combined with a one-time passcode (OTP) SMS in a multi-factor authentication system. In today's remote environment, several firms have implemented Single Sign On (SSO) for their staff (Mainka, Mladenov, Schwenk, & Wich, 2017). Using SSO, a user may sign in to various apps with a single point of identity. When working with several cloud service providers, relying on conventional identification methods may be problematic. Annual third-party audits should be performed, and they should be able to provide you with proof of their completion.

- **Access control policy:** For the purpose of verifying that the actual users have the required access to firm content, the usage of access control is necessary. Access control is a form of selective restriction that regulates who has access to specific pieces of information at a granular level. Daniel Crowley, chief of research for IBM's X-Force Red, which focuses on data security, explains that authentication and authorization are the two major components (Sharma, Shakya, & Mishra, 2022). Companies must ensure that their access and authentication management solutions are maintained evenly across their cloud and apps to shift to virtual environments like private clouds. When dealing with several levels of the stack, access control is essential. Organizations must choose the best access control approach based on the type and sensitivity of the information they handle. Some traditional access control methods include DACs and MACs or mandatory access controls. Attribute-based access control has recently supplanted role-based access control as the most popular option (ABAC).

SERVERLESS COMPUTING: A NEW EDGE OF CLOUD

Developers may build and deploy application software on different cloud platforms without worrying about the underlying implementation and infrastructure, such as distribution of load evenly, increasing and decreasing of resources i.e., auto-scaling, and monitoring of several operation. Serverless computing is the new cloud computing paradigm. Serverless computing has been a prevalent issue in academia and business. Due to its enormous benefits, its market growth is predicted to approach 8 billion dollars per year by 2024. A collection of interdependent functions (called "serverless functions") is assembled to prototype an application driven by several events by making use of serverless computing.

Serverless Architecture

On the other hand, serverless platforms assume all operational and computational duties, such as resource management, scalability, function deployment, and monitoring, by abstracting the administration of underlying infrastructure. For developers, functions' business logic might precede the development process. Figure. 4, depicts the serverless computing paradigm of execution. Serverless systems' small-granularity scalability and billing might potentially significantly lower costs. However, although serverless architecture makes it easier to manage resources and reduces costs, several issues prevent it from being widely adopted by potential users, including the absence of cost models and performance metrics and a comparison of serverless applications' costs and performance. To ensure that serverless applications meet their service level agreement (SLA) cost-effectively, modeling of cost, evaluation of performance, and optimization are essential steps that must be taken.

Figure 4. Serverless computing architecture

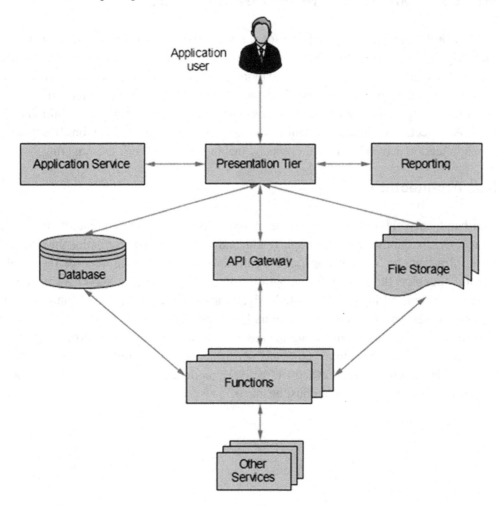

Figure. 4, illustrates the concept of serverless computing architecture. There is no one typical back end in a serverless system. An API gateway directly connects the application's front end to the database, computation functions, or other services. Several backends compute service functions will be hidden, allowing for enhanced protection and validation.

Function as a Service Model

With serverless computing, customers don't have to bother regarding maintaining servers while running cloud applications; FaaS, on the other hand, is at the core of the serverless computing concept. The function is a piece of program code that hides a portion of an application's internal business logic under the FaaS paradigm. Functional programming and object-oriented programming use concepts are known as "methods" or "functions" to describe concepts that FaaS uses to describe a stateless process that performs a single job. An isolated environment is supplied by lightweight virtualization technologies like Docker containers, Unikernels, or even processes, which package and execute the function's source code and dependencies together.

Essential Features of Serverless Computing

Because the infrastructure and platforms through which resources function are invisible to clients, a Serverless computing idea varies from typical cloud computing (we term it serverful in this chapter). If the service provider takes care of everything else, consumers are just worried about their application's intended performance. They are choosing a platform requires engineers to be aware of these structural considerations. The following paragraphs provide an overview of serverless computing's key characteristics.

- **Cost:** When serverless functions are being executed, consumption is often estimated, and consumers only pay for the time based on the resources consumed. In a serverless system, this is one of the most important advantages. Services and resources based on metal, such as memory and CPU, and pricing models, such as lower-priced discounts, differ from CSP to CSP.
- **Auto-scaling:** Instant, automated, and on-demand scalability of resources is anticipated from a cloud platform. With serverless models, thousands of events may be sent in seconds with little initial latency. To maintain an inactive application's execution, operational conditions must be zero in the absence of request flow.
- **Deployment:** The goal of frameworks is to make deploying their components as easy as possible. Typically, the function's source code is all that is required from the developer or user. Aside from that, there are numerous ways to package the code, such as a Docker image with binary code and an archive with several files. Translation or group resources are also helpful, although they're few.
- **Security and Accounting:** Suppose there are numerous tenants in a serverless architecture. In that case, it's essential to segregate performance jobs across them and alert consumers of thorough accounting so that customers know how much they'll be charged.
- **Performance and Limits:** Many restrictions are imposed on business logic's resource needs during runtime in serverless computing, that includes maximum number of simultaneous requests and the high storage and processing resources available. Some constraints, such as a one-time application limit, may be increased as user demand grows, while others, such as a huge memory capacity, are inherent in the base.
- **Programming Languages:** Java, Javascript, Swift, Go, and Python is some of the programming languages supported by serverless services. A large number of forums support several programming languages. Specific serverless frameworks support program written in any programming language if it is incorporated into a Docker image that supports an application programming interface.

Figure 5. Data management layers in serverless architecture

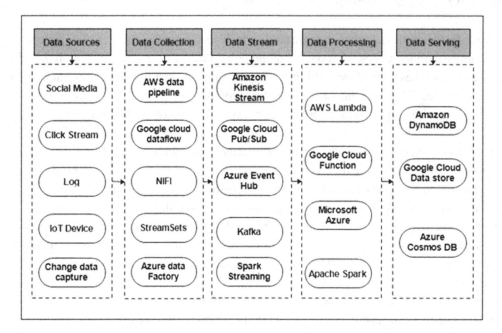

SERVERLESS SOLUTIONS FOR DATA MANAGEMENT AND SECURITY

Serverless Architecture for Data Management and Real-time Analytics

Serverless architecture can be set up for different data management layers, which can be defined as:

- **Data Collection Layer:** The data collection layer is the first layer of data management in a serverless platform where the data source is explicitly defined in the system. The data collected from these sources can be transformed into a real-time data stream. After the translation process, the data stream can be fed into the data processing module of the data management system. Some potential data sources like Twitter Streaming, IoT Analytics, and so on constantly push data. Serverless architecture can play a vital role in loading the streaming data from Twitter API streaming (Trupthi, Pabboju, & Narasimha, 2017) and other social media streaming. Some of the open-source serverless platforms like AWS Cloud DataFlow, Google Cloud DataFlow (Krishnan & Gonzalez, 2015), Azure DataFactory (Klein, 2017), and Apache Nifi (Klein, 2017) can be adopted for the collection of streaming data for further processing.
- **Data Streaming Layer:** It's impossible to predict how much data producers can write at a particular point. That is why it is necessary to have real-time storage that can scale up and down in response to the pace of incoming data (Behera, Das, Jena, Rath, & Sahoo, 2017). Amazon Web Services (AWS) offers Kinesis and DynamoDB streaming for serverless real-time stream. PUB/SUB is a service provided by Google. Event and IoT hubs are available from Azure.
- **Data Processing Layer:** Data pre-processing, filtering, validation, data manipulation, etc., are all common activities at this layer. Using a temporal frame of the past five or ten minutes, we also do real-time analytics on receiving data streams at this tier. The next step is the data processing layer,

where the huge collection of data can be processed seamlessly with better throughput and quality of service. The real-time data can be ingested from the streaming layer, and the result of the data analysis layer can be fed into the serving layer. In the AWS serverless platform, the DynamoDB component can be integrated with the Lambda function to process and publish it through other components of AWS serverless. This can also be achieved by using other serverless frameworks like Google CloudFunction (Kim & Lee, 2019), Spark engine, and Google's publish-subscriber model. The Microsoft platform uses similar components, including EventHub (Kettner & Geisler, 2022) and Azure serverless function. Google Cloud Serverless computing enables infinite server scalability without administering the server's resources.

- **Data Serving Layer:** This layer is accountable for delivering to end-users the data processed by our Information Processing Layer. Real-time Visualization requires this layer to scale dynamically to serve millions of customers. Serving layers may be divided into two categories.
- **Streams:** On Amazon Web Services (AWS), the Data Processing Layer may post results to DynamoDB Streams, and a WebSocket server consumes DynamoDB's results, and WebSocket-based Dashboard Clients can see the data in real-time. You may use Azure Event Hub and Google PUB/SUB as a streaming serving layer.
- **NoSQL Datastore:** For our Serving layer, we may utilize DynamoDB NoSQL Datastore and REST API, and Dashboard will leverage REST API to view the real-time results. Additionally, Google Cloud Datastore and Azure Cosmos DB are also viable options.

Serverless Batch Processing

The serverless framework can efficiently handle batch processing in big data. Batch Processing of Data may be used in a variety of situations. An ETL job has to retrieve data from an OLTP database like Amazon RDS, perform transformations, and then store the data in a serverless storage service called DataLake. Some potential serverless tools that act as the storage service are Amazon's S3, Google cloud storage, and Microsoft Azure storage. The data warehouse service provided by the serverless platforms is Azure SQL. BigTable, Redshift, etc. Data from the DataLake can be extracted by defining an ETL (Pogiatzis & Samakovitis, 2020) job and perform transformations on it, and then transferring it to a Data Warehouse, among other things. Batch Data Processing is the underlying technology in all of these scenarios. Data must be extracted and collected from the data sources at a regular interval such as once a day for RDBMS or once an hour for Data Lake. As it is pretty difficult to predict the amount of data that will be extracted in the next batch, batch processing is found to be very challenging. The serverless architecture for big data is very cost-effective as it can be auto-scalable as per the demand of resources. Unlike Hadoop and Spark clustering setup, the serverless component of ETL can be scaled up and scaled-down based on the resource need.

Serverless Databases

Serverless architecture is a new architectural paradigm. Databases are embracing big data as well. Amazon has introduced Aurora serverless database (Mete & Yomralioglu, 2021), which reshapes the way the interaction is carried out with the databases. Databases have been optimized in several ways, including using cache frequent requests to speed up reads and compressing data to speed up storage. On the other hand, the Serverless architecture big data approach emphasizes distributing the storage and the computing nodes. Additionally, pricing should be determined by consumption, similar to how Amazon Aurora prices its services on a per-second basis. Therefore, it indicates that you do not always have to pay for database server infrastructure. Customers will only be charged for the period of time during which the database was in a dormant condition.

Serverless Data Lake

A serverless data lake can store massive amounts of any form of data, making it suitable for use in place of almost any other kind of work. The term data lake refers to the storage location in a serverless architecture, where the data is kept in its original form (Miloslavskaya & Tolstoy, 2016). The following is a description of the steps required in constructing Data Lake:

- **Data Ingestion:** With the ability to accept data from many data sources (both streaming and batch), it should be scalable to accommodate any volume of data. The only expenses should be those incurred during the execution of data migration operations. Kinesis Streams and Firehose with AWS Lambda are examples of streaming and batch sources, respectively (Singh, Hoque, & Tarkoma, 2016).
- **Data Storage:** There should be no restrictions on file type, and the system should be scalable enough to store data for many years at a minimal cost. Examples include Azure Storage, Google Cloud Storage, AWS S3, etc.
- **Data Catalogue:** The Catalog Service is constantly being updated as new data is added to our Data Lake. Only a Data Catalog with regularly updated information about the Data Lake may be used to allow Data Discovery. For example, consider the Azure Data Catalog, the AWS Glue Data Catalogue Service, and Apache Atlas.
- **Data Discovery/Searching:** To explore the Data Lake, a serverless querying engine is needed. This engine should be scalable to thousands of searches and only charge when a query is run. There are two ways to migrate data from our operating systems to a Data Lake/Warehouse.
  ○ ETL (Extract, Transform and Load)
  ○ ELT (Extract, Load, and Transform)
- **ETL vs ELT:** In the ETL approach, data is typically retrieved from the data source, converted, and fed into the data warehouse utilizing a data processing platform such as Spark. Data is retrieved from a source and immediately deposited into the Data Lake, where Data Transformation Jobs changes it. It's well-known that in the Big Data world, there are many different sorts of data sources, such as REST APIs and databases, as well as many types of data formats such as JSON, Avro, and Binary Files (EBCDIC), and Parquet. So, in certain circumstances, we may wish to put data in our Data Lake as it is since we can later design transformations on particular data alone. To summarize, this means that the ELT strategy is preferable to the ETL technique, which involves loading data into Data Lake in its raw form, allowing data scientists to explore the data, and then specifying the changes to be applied.

Using Azure Serverless Computing, a user may construct a serverless application and concentrate on the business objectives of their project. For further information, refer Azure Serverless Computing.

Building a Serverless Analytics Solution

Here is an example of a Big Data Analytics solution built using Serverless Architecture that we can use to establish a Data Lake. There are a variety of uses for Big Data Analytics:

- The data included in the Data Lake needs to be investigated by Data Scientists.
- It is necessary for the company's management team to examine its operations from the perspective of the Data Lake.
- Offline data from Data Lake is also used to train Deep Learning and Machine Learning models.

As a result, some considerations must be made while developing a Serverless Analytics Solution.

- Should be able to use a Data Discovery Service that only charges us for the time it takes to run our queries.
- Multiple users should be able to access the Data Lake simultaneously using a scalable query engine.

CONCLUSION AND FUTURE POSSIBILITIES

Deployment model examples are provided in this chapter, and three service-oriented architectures (SOAs) are also discussed. Some of the cloud's security issues are also presented in this chapter. Fast-moving cloud computing offers enormous promise and a lot of future promises. Cloud computing has a wide range of applications in administering and delivering information and services. Because the data in the cloud computing environment is so reliant on the network and server, the problem of data privacy is magnified. Many customers view the security and privacy of cloud computing consumers with suspicion, and they are reluctant to shift their information to the cloud platform from their corporate or private system. Several issues have hampered cloud computing, with security being the most serious. The cloud computing provider must use a variety of security procedures to address these issues adequately. Cloud-based serverless computing has emerged as a possible method of sustaining data management and privacy at cheap costs and quick response times. Depending on the customer's needs, a serverless provider may provide on-demand, on-reserve, or instance data storage services.

REFERENCES

Ajamie, L. (2018). *Flood Control: Using Apache NiFi to Streamline Data Integration*. University of Notre Dame.

Baldini, I., Castro, P., Chang, K., Cheng, P., Fink, S., Ishakian, V., & Suter, P. (2017). Serverless computing: Current trends and open problems. *Research advances in cloud computing*, 1-20.

Behera, R. K., Das, S., Jena, M., Rath, S. K., & Sahoo, B. (2017). A comparative study of distributed tools for analyzing streaming data. In *2017 International Conference on Information Technology (ICIT)* (pp. 79-84). IEEE. 10.1109/ICIT.2017.32

Behera, R. K., Rath, S. K., Misra, S., Leon, M., & Adewumi, A. (2019). Machine learning approach for reliability assessment of open source software. In Computational Science and Its Applications–ICCSA 2019: 19th International Conference. Springer International Publishing.

Bisong, A., & Rahman, M. (2011). An overview of the security concerns in enterprise cloud computing. *arXiv preprint arXiv:1101.5613.*

Castro, P., Ishakian, V., Muthusamy, V., & Slominski, A. (2019). The rise of serverless computing. *Communications of the ACM, 62*(12), 44–54. doi:10.1145/3368454

Deshpande, P. S., Sharma, S. C., & Peddoju, S. K. (2019). *Security and Data Storage Aspect in Cloud Computing* (Vol. 52). Springer. doi:10.1007/978-981-13-6089-3

Dikaiakos, M. D., Katsaros, D., Mehra, P., Pallis, G., & Vakali, A. (2009). Cloud computing: Distributed internet computing for IT and scientific research. *IEEE Internet Computing, 13*(5), 10–13. doi:10.1109/MIC.2009.103

Gong, C., Liu, J., Zhang, Q., Chen, H., & Gong, Z. (2010, September). The characteristics of cloud computing. In *2010 39th International Conference on Parallel Processing Workshops* (pp. 275-279). IEEE. 10.1109/ICPPW.2010.45

Hashizume, K., Rosado, D. G., Fernández-Medina, E., & Fernandez, E. B. (2013). An analysis of security issues for cloud computing. *Journal of Internet Services and Applications, 4*(1), 1–13. doi:10.1186/1869-0238-4-5

Jansen, W. A. (2011, January). Cloud hooks: Security and privacy issues in cloud computing. In *2011 44th Hawaii International Conference on System Sciences* (pp. 1-10). IEEE.

Kaur, P. J., & Kaushal, S. (2011). Security concerns in cloud computing. In *High Performance Architecture and Grid Computing: International Conference, HPAGC 2011,* (pp. 103-112). Springer Berlin Heidelberg.

Keller, E., & Rexford, J. (2010). The" Platform as a Service" Model for Networking. *INM/WREN, 10,* 95-108.

Kettner, B., & Geisler, F. (2022). IoT Hub, Event Hub, and Streaming Data. In *Pro Serverless Data Handling with Microsoft Azure: Architecting ETL and Data-Driven Applications in the Cloud* (pp. 153–168). Apress. doi:10.1007/978-1-4842-8067-6_8

Khalil, I. M., Khreishah, A., Bouktif, S., & Ahmad, A. (2013, April). Security concerns in cloud computing. In *2013 10th International Conference on Information Technology: New Generations* (pp. 411-416). IEEE. 10.1109/ITNG.2013.127

Kim, J., & Lee, K. (2019, July). Functionbench: A suite of workloads for serverless cloud function service. In *2019 IEEE 12th International Conference on Cloud Computing (CLOUD)* (pp. 502-504). IEEE. 10.1109/CLOUD.2019.00091

Klein, S., & Klein, S. (2017). Azure data factory. *IoT Solutions in Microsoft's Azure IoT Suite: Data Acquisition and Analysis in the Real World,* (pp. 105-122). Springer.

Krishnan, S. P. T., & Gonzalez, J. L. U. (2015). *Building your next big thing with google cloud platform: A guide for developers and enterprise architects*. Apress. doi:10.1007/978-1-4842-1004-8

Krutz, R. L., Krutz, R. L., & Russell Dean Vines, R. D. V. (2010). *Cloud security a comprehensive guide to secure cloud computing*. Wiley.

Kuiper, E., Van Dam, F., Reiter, A., & Janssen, M. (2014, October). Factors influencing the adoption of and business case for Cloud computing in the public sector. In *eChallenges e-2014 Conference Proceedings* (pp. 1-10). IEEE.

Kumari, A., Behera, R. K., Sahoo, B., & Sahoo, S. P. (2022). Prediction of link evolution using community detection in social network. *Computing*, *104*(5), 1–22. doi:10.100700607-021-01035-4

Kumari, A., Sahoo, B., Behera, R. K., Misra, S., & Sharma, M. M. (2021). Evaluation of integrated frameworks for optimizing QoS in serverless computing. In *Computational Science and Its Applications–ICCSA 2021: 21st International Conference, Cagliari, Italy, September 13–16, 2021* [Springer International Publishing.]. *Proceedings*, *21*(Part VII), 277–288.

Lee, H., Satyam, K., & Fox, G. (2018, July). Evaluation of production serverless computing environments. In *2018 IEEE 11th International Conference on Cloud Computing (CLOUD)* (pp. 442-450). IEEE. 10.1109/CLOUD.2018.00062

Lee, Y. C., & Zomaya, A. Y. (2012). Energy efficient utilization of resources in cloud computing systems. *The Journal of Supercomputing*, *60*(2), 268–280. doi:10.100711227-010-0421-3

Li, Y., Lin, Y., Wang, Y., Ye, K., & Xu, C. (2022). Serverless computing: State-of-the-art, challenges and opportunities. *IEEE Transactions on Services Computing*, *16*(2), 1522–1539. doi:10.1109/TSC.2022.3166553

Lynn, T., Rosati, P., Lejeune, A., & Emeakaroha, V. (2017, December). A preliminary review of enterprise serverless cloud computing (function-as-a-service) platforms. In *2017 IEEE International Conference on Cloud Computing Technology and Science (CloudCom)* (pp. 162-169). IEEE. 10.1109/CloudCom.2017.15

Mainka, C., Mladenov, V., Schwenk, J., & Wich, T. (2017, April). SoK: single sign-on security—an evaluation of openID connect. In *2017 IEEE European Symposium on Security and Privacy (EuroS&P)* (pp. 251-266). IEEE. 10.1109/EuroSP.2017.32

Manvi, S. S., & Shyam, G. K. (2014). Resource management for Infrastructure as a Service (IaaS) in cloud computing: A survey. *Journal of Network and Computer Applications*, *41*, 424–440. doi:10.1016/j.jnca.2013.10.004

McGrath, G., & Brenner, P. R. (2017, June). Serverless computing: Design, implementation, and performance. In *2017 IEEE 37th International Conference on Distributed Computing Systems Workshops (ICDCSW)* (pp. 405-410). IEEE.

Mete, M. O., & Yomralioglu, T. (2021). Implementation of serverless cloud GIS platform for land valuation. *International Journal of Digital Earth*, *14*(7), 836–850. doi:10.1080/17538947.2021.1889056

Miloslavskaya, N., & Tolstoy, A. (2016). Big data, fast data and data lake concepts. *Procedia Computer Science*, *88*, 300–305. doi:10.1016/j.procs.2016.07.439

Patra, M. K., Patel, D., Sahoo, B., & Turuk, A. K. (2020, January). A randomized algorithm for load balancing in containerized cloud. In *2020 10th International conference on cloud computing, data science & engineering (confluence)* (pp. 410-414). IEEE. 10.1109/Confluence47617.2020.9058147

Patra, M. K., Sahoo, S., Sahoo, B., & Turuk, A. K. (2019, December). Game theoretic approach for real-time task scheduling in cloud computing environment. In *2019 International Conference on Information Technology (ICIT)* (pp. 454-459). IEEE. 10.1109/ICIT48102.2019.00086

Pogiatzis, A., & Samakovitis, G. (2020). An event-driven serverless ETL pipeline on AWS. *Applied Sciences (Basel, Switzerland)*, *11*(1), 191. doi:10.3390/app11010191

Rashid, A., & Chaturvedi, A. (2019). Cloud computing characteristics and services: A brief review. *International Journal on Computer Science and Engineering*, *7*(2), 421–426.

Sbarski, P., & Kroonenburg, S. (2017). *Serverless architectures on AWS: with examples using Aws Lambda*. Simon and Schuster.

Sen, J. (2015). Security and privacy issues in cloud computing. In *Cloud technology: concepts, methodologies, tools, and applications* (pp. 1585–1630). IGI global. doi:10.4018/978-1-4666-6539-2.ch074

Sewak, M., & Singh, S. (2018, April). Winning in the era of serverless computing and function as a service. In *2018 3rd International Conference for Convergence in Technology (I2CT)* (pp. 1-5). IEEE. 10.1109/I2CT.2018.8529465

Shafiei, H., Khonsari, A., & Mousavi, P. (2022). Serverless computing: A survey of opportunities, challenges, and applications. *ACM Computing Surveys*, *54*(11s), 1–32. doi:10.1145/3510611

Sharma, S., Shakya, H. K., & Mishra, A. (2022). Medical Data Classification in Cloud Computing Using Soft Computing With Voting Classifier: A Review. *The Internet of Medical Things (IoMT) Healthcare Transformation*, 23-44.

Singh, M. P., Hoque, M. A., & Tarkoma, S. (2016). A survey of systems for massive stream analytics. *arXiv preprint arXiv:1605.09021*.

Stieninger, M., & Nedbal, D. (2014). Characteristics of cloud computing in the business context: A systematic literature review. *Global Journal of Flexible Systems Managment*, *15*(1), 59–68. doi:10.100740171-013-0055-4

Sun, W., Zhang, K., Chen, S. K., Zhang, X., & Liang, H. (2007). Software as a service: An integration perspective. In *Service-Oriented Computing–ICSOC 2007: Fifth International Conference*. Springer Berlin Heidelberg.

Takabi, H., Joshi, J. B., & Ahn, G. J. (2010). Security and privacy challenges in cloud computing environments. *IEEE Security and Privacy*, *8*(6), 24–31. doi:10.1109/MSP.2010.186

Trupthi, M., Pabboju, S., & Narasimha, G. (2017, January). Sentiment analysis on twitter using streaming API. In *2017 IEEE 7th international advance computing conference (IACC)* (pp. 915-919). IEEE. 10.1109/IACC.2017.0186

Wang, Z. (2011, October). Security and privacy issues within the Cloud Computing. In *2011 International Conference on Computational and Information Sciences* (pp. 175-178). IEEE. 10.1109/ICCIS.2011.247

Chapter 8
Detection of Damage in Composite Materials Using Hybrid Fuzzy Logic Technique in Aerospace

Jenifer Mahilraj

https://orcid.org/0000-0002-6257-9682

Department of AI and DS, NPR College of Engineering and Technology, Natham, India

T. Avudaiappan

Department of AI and DS, K. Ramakrishnan college of Technology, Trichy, India

Sivaram Ponnusamy

https://orcid.org/0000-0001-5746-0268

Department of Artificial Intelligence, G.H. Raisoni College of Engineering, Nagpur, India

ABSTRACT

In the past two decades, the use of various materials for various structural and mechanical aspects has become increasingly important. Scientists in today's high-tech world have a vested interest in exotic materials with novel features. Composite material utilisation has increased dramatically during the past two decades to satisfy the needs of the aerospace, nuclear, and aeronautics industries. Fibre reinforced polymer matrix composites are increasingly being used in place of traditional metallic materials due to their superior performance in a number of areas, including fatigue, damage tolerance, and greater resistance to oxidation. In this investigation, the authors set out to develop and characterise a polymer-based composite packed with nano-micro particles for use in aerospace. In this chapter, the authors employ a hybrid of the FAHP and FTOPSIS to assign an overall rating to various dental composites. The research results presented here enhance the development of effective and precise damage detection techniques for composite materials.

DOI: 10.4018/978-1-6684-8306-0.ch008

INTRODUCTION

Aluminum, titanium, and nickel alloys and other time-honored construction materials have made significant contributions to the aviation sector. Different innovative engineered materials continually produced to meet the demands of the aerospace industry for materials that are lower in weight and higher in strength (Hörrmann et al., 2016). Many industries, including aviation, agriculture, textiles, automobiles, military, electronics and electricity, sports, civic infrastructures, and the maritime industry, are switching to composites from more traditional materials. The aerospace and space sectors place the highest demands on composite materials due to their need for highly developed high-performance components (Bard et al., 2018). The aerospace industry's primary goal is to reduce bulk while simultaneously increasing damage tolerance. Lighter composites can be used in place of heavier metal alloys, cutting costs in the aircraft industry by decreasing fuel consumption and, in turn, reducing operating expenses (Bakis et al., 2021). Composites' superior metals, is another important benefit of their use in aerospace, as it reduces the number of inspections needed and the overall cost of maintaining an aircraft (Jolly et al., 2015).

Polymer matrix composites (PMC) have seen rapid growth in popularity within the aerospace industry in recent years due to its ability to significantly cut down on weight while increasing reliability and security (Kempf et al., 2014). PMCs were employed in several parts of commercial, military, and even civilian aircraft. Due to their low density, good strength, and stiffness, PMCs, particularly fibre reinforced polymer or plastic (FRP) amalgams, are being used to replace aircraft metallic components, resulting in a weight reduction (Kiyoshi et al., 2013). Lighter aircraft use less fuel, produce fewer emissions, and can manoeuvre more quickly and precisely (Bang et al., 2020). The aerospace industry's insistence on PMCs as a high-performance material has not changed over time. Their use in planes of all stripes, both civilian and military, is on the rise (Chulkov et al., 2021).

For key aerospace structures including fuselages, vertical tails, rudders, empennage boxes, and wings, FRPs, especially CFRP composites, are able to relocate the traditional materials Al-, Ni-, and Tialloys, due to their better performance characteristics (Marani et al., 2021). Since FRPs are lighter than traditional metallic materials, using them has helped cut aircraft weight by half, which has resulted in reduced fuel consumption and a 20% decrease in cost overall (Eder et al., 2021). Since then, other new composite materials composites, have emerged as viable alternatives to aluminium and steel structural aerospace parts. Low-strength, low-load aircraft components are ideal candidates for GFRPs and AFRPs (Gornet et al., 2013).

Fragile, weak, and easily broken, FRP composites are often damaged. Damages like as delamination and impact cracking are common in FRP complex aircraft constructions and can lead to a catastrophic collapse at any time. Invisible or hardly visible structures can sometimes acquire damage over time. Crack existence, size, position, and growth rate must be determined at an early stage to ensure public safety. In order to quickly and affordably estimate invisible damage in machine parts and aircraft structures, several currently available non-destructive procedures employ artificial intelligence approaches (Peyrac et al., 2015). In this study, we look at the benefits of using composite materials for aeroplane components rather than traditional metals and alloys. By using hybrid fuzzy logic concept for damage detection, this research work focused on composite materials of aerospace. The remaining paper is designed as: Section 2 presents the importance of composite materials; the study of related work is given in Section 3 and the description of proposed work is presented in Section 4. Finally, the experimental analysis with conclusion are depicted in Section 5 and 6.

2. IMPORTANCE OF COMPOSITE MATERIALS IN AEROSPACE

When more than two materials with different mechanical, physical, and chemical properties are joined, a new designed material is created that has improved properties above those of either of the original materials. This new material is called a composite. Composites not only retain the advantages of their individual constituents' qualities, but they may also compensate for any shortcomings that would be introduced by using any one of them on its own. Low density, toughness, flame retardant qualities, and ductility are just some of the changed features that emerge when two or more materials are combined to form a composite (Kien & Zhuang, 2021). Composites have a scattered phase called reinforcement and a continuous phase called a matrix. The composite's reinforcement is responsible for carrying the weight. In order to keep the fibres in the right place and with the right orientation, the matrix bonds them together. The fibres themselves are shielded from environmental degradation by the matrix. Matrix material transmits and distributes the external stress to the fibres. Matrix also acts as a stopper for the spread of cracks. The matrix can be made of a polymer, ceramic, metal, carbon, or hybrid, and the reinforcement can take the form of fibres or particles. Composites can be broken down into several different types based on the reinforcement structure, including "Fibre-reinforced composites," "Particulate composites," "whisker reinforced composites," "structural composites," and "Nano-composites" (Nanthakumar et al., 2016). Composites are classified as either polymer matrix composites (PMC), metal matrix composites (MMC), or ceramic matrix composites based on the matrix material used.

2.1. Composites for Aerospace Request

This study provides a concise overview of the composite materials utilised in the aerospace industry, along with information on how to spot damage in these components. Below (Ciałkowski & Grysa, 2010) is a list of some of the design necessities for aircraft constructions.

❖ High electrical conductivity,
❖ Inherent damping stuff,
❖ Low density,
❖ Superior specific strength and exact stiffness,
❖ Large toughness and reliability,
❖ Thermal and chemical constancy,
❖ High corrosion and erosion confrontation,
❖ Less abrasive in nature,
❖ All weather process,
❖ Large aerodynamic demonstration,
❖ Low manufacturing and life period inspection price,
❖ Have high fatigue and fracture resistance,
❖ Must Provide required passenger care,
❖ Capability that can be fine-tuned to meet the specific needs of a given environmental load in terms of directional strength or stiffness

Aerospace structural design requires a special set of properties from the materials used, so that they can meet the aforementioned challenges. The qualities that composite materials possess make them ideal for use in aeroplane parts. All these factors are substantial justifications for using composites in aeronautical construction. In particular, high-tech FRPs made of carbon fibre or aramid provide most of these benefits. Thus, aircraft applications favour these composites to a large extent.

Figure 1. Resources used in modern Airbus A350 XWB

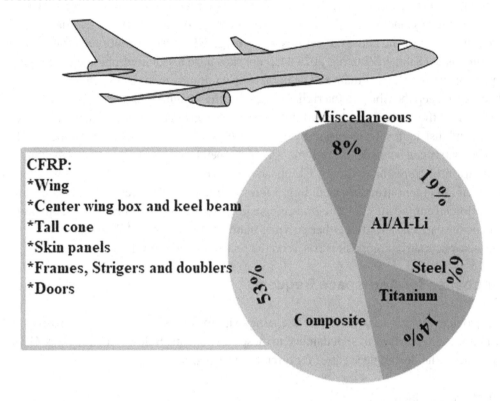

Figure 1 displays the percentage breakdown of the materials used to construct the cutting-edge Airbus A350XWB, which includes 19% AL or AL-Li. Intelligent airframe design and a carbon fibre reinforced plastic (CFRP) wing structure are only two of the many recent modifications and improvements to the aircraft. Airbus was able to extend the service life of their aircraft from 6 to 8 years by using more composite mechanisms and taking into account advanced design considerations when creating the A350XWB. Table1 provides a synopsis of the use of composites in numerous civilian and military aircraft (Schwartz, 1997; Ye et al., 2005).

3. RELATED WORKS

In order to identify internal delamination in carbon fibre reinforced polymers, Wu et al. (2021) offer a original technique that combines a CNN with a continuous wavelet transform. This data-driven approach can make use of the abundant data without the need for laborious feature extraction. Using the continuous wavelet transform method, we transform the time series signal into a time-frequency image, and then use a CNN model to assign categories to the images. A damage localization method for ply delamination is also proposed, and it is based on the model's predicted routes. In order to prove this method's worth, an experimental study is conducted. The outcome demonstrates that this methodology is helpful for accurate identification and localization of delamination damage in composite constructions.

EMW-NDT, proposed by Ni et. al. (2021), is a novel approach to non-destructive testing (NDT) that makes use of electromagnetic wave (EMW) technology. Defects in CFRP composites, like delamination, cracks, and others, can be found using the proposed EMW-NDT approach. Researchers looked into how well the EMW-NDT approach could spot slits, delamination's, and delamination thicknesses in carbon fibre reinforced plastic (CFRP) composites. The ratio of the damage area to the change in thickness, 12.6%/dB, and the change in thickness, 5.5 dB/mm, both indicate a decent alteration in delamination. Due to the skin effect in CFRP composites, incident angle of the EM wave was discovered to have a crucial role in detecting sensitivity. The outcomes validated the high detection sensitivity of the suggested approach regardless of delamination size or thickness. In this investigation, using the properties of the EMI shielding anisotropy in CFRPs, we were able to detect the slit, its length, and the slit's orientation, all of which pertain to crack damage. In addition, there is no need for a coupling medium with the suggested EMW-NDT approach with a specially constructed free-space measuring apparatus, therefore it has great potential as a novel damage detection tool for CFRP composites.

Authors Papa et al. (2021) Using ultrasonic technology, the effectiveness of detecting damage in low-velocity collisions in a variety of compound laminates, at varying energies, is studied. The latter method was used to ensure it could provide data on the delamination's shape and size despite the presence of various factors. It was helpful especially for investigating how various variables affected the dynamic behaviour of the composites under investigation. Ultrasound was transmitted and received using a pulse-echo technology and a facing array of transducers operating at a frequency of 5 MHz. The findings helped researchers better comprehend damage's origins, development, and spread.

The research of Lee et al. (2022) The DAE model's architecture and hyperparameters are improved, and a statistical detection baseline is developed to collect damage indications, all with the goal of improving the model's accuracy and sensitivity in damage diagnosis. The ultrasonic signals collected after additional fatigue cycles are included to validate the trained automatically obtained from the DAE model's bottleneck layer are used to categorise fatigue damage mode. Singular value decomposition is then used to further reduce the dimensionality of the features (SVD). For this analysis, we utilise a technique called density-based spatial clustering of applications with noise (DBSCAN) to look for regularities in the simplified characteristics. Results show that the proposed method can accurately detect and classify fatigue damage in composite structures, without requiring the time-consuming and error-prone procedure of manually or computationally extracting damage-sensitive features from ultrasonic signals for damage analysis.

The ANN-RDT method introduced by Mojtahedi et al. (2022) is evaluated against the MRDT and the AMD-RDT for use in damage detection, with both types of error indices taken into account. It is demonstrated that the current approach outperforms the MRDT and the AMD-RDT. The findings demonstrate the efficacy of the proposed method in detecting the presence of damage in the two designated support systems. The trained algorithm fared well in pinned settings where the damage was located closer to the supports. As was previously said, damage location, sensor placement, and support type all play significant roles in the method's overall effectiveness. It is shown that using a simpler linear equation and gaining the dynamic features of the system is greatly aided by the experimental non-contact data.

4. DAMAGE DETECTION IN COMPOUND MATERIALS FOR AIRCRAFT MECHANISMS

Composite materials have gained popularity in the aerospace industry over the past two decades due to its exclusive qualities, such as a high strength-to-weight ratio and the ability to be shaped into complex configurations without the need for any special tools. However, they are easily broken due to their construction. Whenever a composite structure is damaged, the geometry and material characteristics of the structure are altered, resulting in a decrease in the structure's strength, stiffness, and stability, all of which negatively impact the structure's performance and safety. To prevent sudden and catastrophic failures of structural systems, it is crucial to conduct damage assessment at an early stage. During production, aeroplane composites parts can be harmed by inclusions of foreign substances and delaminations between composite laminae. Impacts and mechanical stresses are the main causes of damage to aircraft while in flight.

Unexpected impact forces of varying velocities are experienced by FRP aircraft structural parts during the fabrication and working period. These include low velocity intermediate velocity (between 10 m/s and 50 m/s), high or ballistic velocity (between 50 m/s and 1000 m/s). As a result of impact stresses, FRP composite aircraft structures can sustain damage such as matrix cracking, fibre breakage, debonding at the fiber-matrix interface, and delamination in piles. Because structural flaws like fatigue cracks, impact damage, and delamination are so pervasive and harmful in aircraft composite materials (), spotting them is a major challenge for aircraft designers and engineers. Composite aircraft parts typically fail catastrophically when subjected to any impact force more than trivial. In order to avoid a catastrophic structural breakdown, it is essential to detect damage on aircraft structures as soon as feasible and to evaluate the amount of that damage.

Both active and passive methods, respectively, can be used to detect damage in aircraft composite constructions. This is the active method of non-destructive testing that has been used for decades. The conventional NDT approaches rely on costly and time intensive experiments. When dealing with massive structures like aeroplane wings and stabilisers, conventional NDT techniques can be a real pain. A passive method is used to identify impact damage, such as locating the point of impact. It significantly reduced the cost of maintenance for huge buildings. This technology is ideal for use aboard spacecraft because conventional NDT techniques are unsuitable for use in such environments. The field of Artificial Intelligence (AI) has recently produced a powerful online device for anticipating the location of damage and to evaluate composite constructions in air, rail, and marine vehicles, and civil infrastructures. Artificial intelligence (AI) approaches are commonly used in enterprise-level software due to their capacity to provide answers rapidly and accurately, reducing the likelihood of failure.

4.1. AI Used for Documentation of Damage on Aircraft Composite Components

These days, AI methods play a pivotal role in solving difficult structural and engineering problems that are unsolvable with more traditional, logical approaches. The evaluation of structural damage at an early stage and the monitoring of structural health have become major challenges is best achieved through the use of artificial intelligence methods including neural networks (NN), Genetic Algorithms (GA), fuzzy logic, and Adaptive Neuro Fuzzy Inference System (ANFIS). The following is a definition of the hybrid fuzzy approach utilised in this study:

4.1.1. Procedure of Hybrid FAHP-FTOPSIS Optimization Procedure

Figure 2. The flow chart of the hybrid FAHP-FTOPSIS procedure

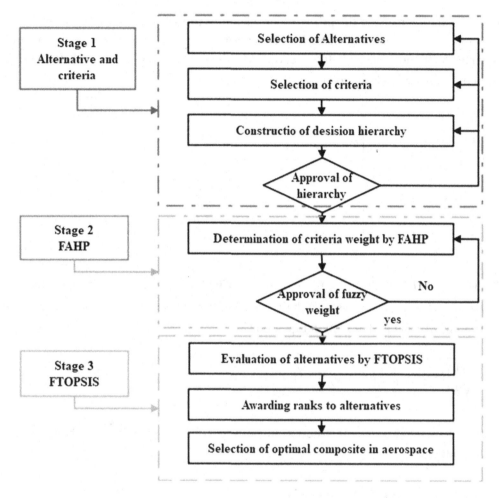

In this investigation, we used a combined FAHP and FTOPSIS MCDM approach to select and rank a group of candidates, which is shown in Figure 2. Using FAHP and FTOPSIS, we can ensure that each criterion is given its proper weight and then rank the available options accordingly. It is possible to illustrate the various steps of this procedure using:

Stage I: Identifying the characteristics or measures that define performance.
Stage II: The FAHP method for evaluating weight criteria.
Stage III: Using linguistic values and fuzzy triangular numbers, the FTOPSIS method ranks options.

In the following part, we will examine the stages in depth.

Stage I: Acknowledgement of the characteristics that define performance PDAs are decision factors used to determine how well a composite defect performs in outer space.

Stage II: Evaluation of weight standards using the FAHP technique.

The membership degree was the primary consideration in fuzzy sets (ranging from 0 to 1). The membership range was a positive integer. A TFN is a triangular fuzzy number, which is a special kind of fuzzy quantity with three facets. In the interval [0,1], the membership function of the fuzzy quantity $\mu_{\tilde{A}}(K)$ can be expressed as Equation (1)

$$\mu_{\tilde{A}}(K) = \begin{bmatrix} 0 & k < z \\ \dfrac{k - zz}{y - z} & z \le k \le y \\ \dfrac{k - x}{y - x} & y \le k \le x \\ 0 & k > x \end{bmatrix} \tag{1}$$

Let $\tilde{A} = (z_1, y_1, X_1)$ and $\tilde{A}_1 = (z_2, y_2, X_2)$ are two triangular fuzzy numbers.

Assuming that $\tilde{A}$ and $\tilde{A}_1$ are the true digits, etc. Vertex representation of the Euclidean distance between two points Ae and Ae1 is seen in Equation (2).

$$D(\tilde{A}, \tilde{A}_1) = \sqrt{\frac{1}{3}\left\{(z_1 - z_2)^2 + (y_1 - y_2)^2 + ((X_1 - X_2))^2\right\}} \tag{2}$$

Linguistic values stand in for the criterion in every possible choice. Table 1 shows the linguistic values of fuzzy numbers.

Table 1. Linguistic values and range of fuzzy facts

Linguistic standards	Range of fuzzy facts
L (Low)	(0.14, 0.29, 0.46)
M (Medium)	(0.34, 0.49, 0.66)
VL (Very-low)	(0.00, 0.11, 0.26)
VH (Very-high)	(0.74, 0.89, 1.00)

Following are the steps depicted to determine the weight requirements using the FAHP method.:

Phase 1: The problem is organised hierarchically in FAHP. The primary decision objective of the case study is shown at the top of the hierarchy, followed by the study's qualities in the middle, and the case study's alternate criterion at the bottom.

Phase 2: Sattay's nine-point scale is used to compare all of the criteria with one another, and the results are derived by the pair-wise comparison matrix, as shown in Equation (3). The dimensions of the comparison matrix (P) will be dd, where d is the attribute number.

$$P = \begin{bmatrix} p_{11} & p_{12} & \cdots & p_{1d} \\ p_{21} & p_{22} & \cdots & p_{2d} \\ \vdots & \vdots & \ddots & \vdots \\ p_{d1} & p_{d1} & \cdots & p_{dd} \end{bmatrix} \tag{3}$$

Where $p_{ii} = 1, p_{ji} = \dfrac{1}{p_{ij}}, p_{ij} \neq 0$.

In Equation we have a representation for fuzzy comparison matrices between pairs (4).

$$\tilde{P} = \begin{bmatrix} \widetilde{p_{11}} & \widetilde{p_{12}} & \cdots & \widetilde{p_{1d}} \\ \widetilde{p_{21}} & \widetilde{p_{22}} & \cdots & \widetilde{p_{2d}} \\ \vdots & \vdots & \ddots & \vdots \\ \widetilde{p_{d1}} & \widetilde{p_{d1}} & \cdots & \widetilde{p_{dd}} \end{bmatrix} \tag{4}$$

Phase 3: Equations (5) and (6) represent, respectively, the fuzzy geometric mean and the fuzzy weights of each criterion.

$$\tilde{q}_1 = \left[\tilde{p}_{i1} \times \tilde{p}_{i2} \times \ldots . \tilde{p}_{id} \right]^{1/b} \tag{5}$$

$$\tilde{W}_i = \tilde{q}_1 \times [\widetilde{q_1} \times \widetilde{q_2} \times \widetilde{q_d}]^{-1} \tag{6}$$

Stage III: Using the Five-Task Analysis of Preferences, Strengths, and Interests

If you're having trouble making a decision based on multiple factors, the TOPSIS method can help. An outline of FTOPSIS's sequential procedures is as follows:

Step 1: After the PDAs of a given study are made clear, a decision matrix is constructed. The size of the decision matrix is deduced as cd, where c is the number of alternative criteria and d is the number of performances defining qualities (7).

$$B_{c \times d} = \begin{bmatrix} b_{11} & b_{12} & \cdots & b_{1d} \\ b_{21} & b_{22} & \cdots & b_{2d} \\ \vdots & \vdots & \ddots & \vdots \\ b_{c1} & b_{c1} & \cdots & b_{cd} \end{bmatrix} \tag{7}$$

Step 2: Equations (8) and (9) for the benefit criterion and the cost criterion represent the normalised decision matrix of the decision matrix.

$$r_{ii} = \frac{b_{ij} - \min\left(b_{ij}\right)}{\max\left(b_{ij}\right) - \min\left(b_{ij}\right)} \text{ for benefit criterion} \tag{8}$$

And

$$r_{ij} = \frac{\max\left(b_{ij}\right) - b_{ij}}{\max\left(b_{ij}\right) - \min\left(b_{ij}\right)} \text{ for cost criterion} \tag{9}$$

Step 3: C) Selecting linguistic options based on their attributes (d). In the realm of language, fuzzy values might fall anywhere from 0 to 1.

Step 4: The FAHP technique provides the weight of several PDAs that are used to calculate the fuzzy linguistic normalised matrix. In Equation (10), we find the formula for the weighted normalised fuzzy matrix:

$$\tilde{F}_{ij} = \tilde{B}_{ij} \times \tilde{W}_i \tag{10}$$

Step 5: In order to compare and contrast the FPIS, A + and the FPIS, A -, we need to perform an evaluation. $\left(FPIS, \tilde{A}^-\right)$ by Equations (11) and (12).

$$\tilde{A}^+ = \left(\tilde{F}_1^+, \tilde{F}_2^+, \dots \tilde{F}_d^+\right) \tag{11}$$

$$\tilde{A}^- = \left(\tilde{F}_1^-, \tilde{F}_2^-, \dots \tilde{F}_d^-\right) \tag{12}$$

where $\tilde{F}_j^+ = (1,1,1)$ and $\tilde{F}_j^- = (0,0,0)$ and $j=1,2,\dots,d$

Step 6: Calculate the Euclidean distances between each solution to the problem; Equations (13) and (14) show how to arrive at the fuzzy positive ideal and fuzzy negative ideal solution:

$$\tilde{D}_i^+ = \sqrt{\sum_{j=1}^{d} D\left(\tilde{F}_1^+ - \tilde{F}_{ij}^+ \right)^2} \tag{13}$$

$$\tilde{D}_i^- = \sqrt{\sum_{j=1}^{d} D\left(\tilde{F}_{ij}^- - \tilde{F}_i^- \right)^2} \text{ for } i = 1, 2, \ldots, c \tag{14}$$

Step 7: Finally, Intimacy Index $\widetilde{Cl}_i$ of options are tallied and computed for. Equation (15) can be used to calculate the fuzzy closeness index of the options.:

$$\widetilde{Cl}_i = \frac{\tilde{D}_i^-}{\tilde{D}_i^+ + \tilde{D}_i^-} \text{ for } i = 1, 2, \ldots, c \tag{15}$$

Step 8: Create an ascending/descending order that reflects the final ranking of all options according to the proximity index.

5. RESULTS AND DISCUSSION

Performance Measure

Regular measurements of findings and outcomes provide reliable data on the efficacy of a method, and hence a high kappa index performance metric. The kappa index and the overall formula for identifying the composite are given by the equations (16), (17), (18), and (19).

$$Sensitivity = \frac{TP}{TP + FN} \times 100 \tag{16}$$

$$Specificity = \frac{TN}{TN + FP} \times 100 \tag{17}$$

$$Accuracy = \frac{TP + TN}{TP + TN + FP + FN} \times 100 \tag{18}$$

$$Kappa\ index = \frac{Accuracy - Accuracy_T}{1 - Accuracy_T} \tag{19}$$

False positive (FP), true negative (TN), true positive (TP), and false negative (FN) are all denoted here.

Table 2. Comparative analysis of proposed classifier with existing techniques

Methodologies	Sensitivity (%)	Specificity (%)	Accuracy (%)	Kappa index (%)
DT	72.33	76.55	72.03	86
Rule based	86.95	83	87.33	79.86
Fuzzy logic	91.77	88.4	92	85.45
Proposed model	**97.34**	**97.49**	**96.89**	**88**

In the above Table 2 represent that the Comparative Analysis of proposed classifier with existing techniques. In this comparisons analysis, we have used different techniques as DT, Rule based, Fuzzy logic with Proposed model. By this analysis the proposed model reaches the better results than the other comparing models. The proposed model accuracy of 97.49% and kappa score of 88% respectively. Figure 3 to 6 presents the graphical analysis of proposed model with existing techniques.

Figure 3. Sensitivity comparison

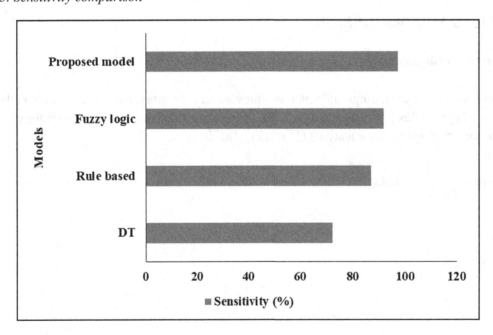

Figure 4. Specificity comparison

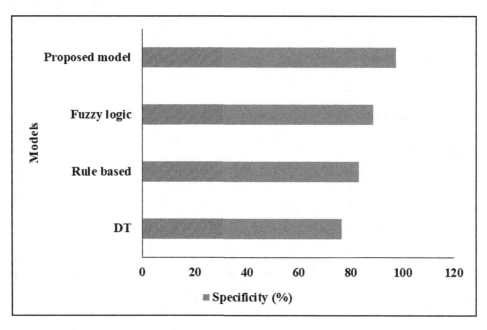

Figure 5. Accuracy comparison

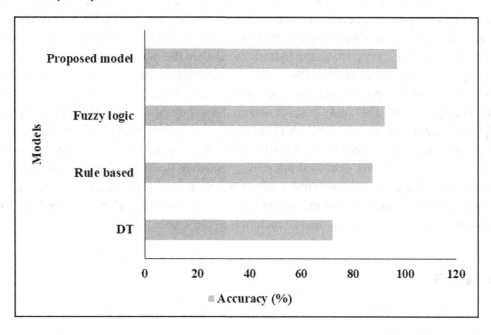

Figure 6. Kappa index comparison

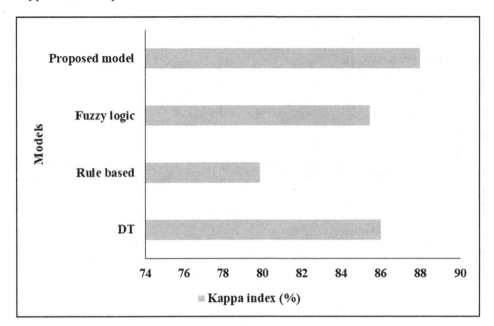

6. CONCLUSION

Even though composites, and particularly PMCs, can be utilised as direct replacements for old, heavy metallic materials, they are also developing their own identities in many fields. Because of their superior mechanical capabilities and lightweight nature, composites are the most in-demand structural components. carbon fibre, aramid fibre, boron fibre, and hybrids thereof are the most common choices for these applications of polymer matrix composites (PMCs). Aerospace applications make better use of CFRPs than traditional metallic material because of their superior creep resistance, excellent ability to be tailored into any required complex form. This study looks at several composite materials with specific application to the aerospace sector. Visual assessments don't always pick up on structural problems. In this case, both NDT and AI procedures are applied in order. Artificial intelligence methods are discovered to be a rapid and reliable method of checking structural integrity, even when damage is imperceptible to the naked eye. However, there is a lack of research into damage detection for composites. Crack detection is often carried out using time-consuming and inefficient conventional methods. There is a need to investigate damage detection technologies for composite materials in the future.

REFERENCES

AZO Team. (n.d.). The A350 XWB – Advanced Materials and Design. AZO. https://www.azom.com/article.aspx?ArticleID=7858

Bakis, G., Wendel, J. F., Zeiler, R., Aksit, A., Häublein, M., Demleitner, M., Benra, J., Forero, S., Schütz, W., & Altstädt, V. (2021). Mechanical properties of the carbon nanotube modified epoxy–carbon fiber unidirectional prepreg laminates. *Polymers*, *13*(5), 770. doi:10.3390/polym13050770 PMID:33801511

Bang, H., Park, S., & Jeon, H. (2020). Defect identification in composite materials via thermography and deep learning techniques. *Composite Structures, 246*, 112405. doi:10.1016/j.compstruct.2020.112405

Bard, S., Demleitner, M., Häublein, M., & Altstädt, V. (2018). Fracture behaviour of prepreg laminates studied by in-situ sem mechanical tests. *Procedia Structural Integrity, 13*, 1442–1446. doi:10.1016/j.prostr.2018.12.299

Bricout, S. (2020). *Environmental analysis of innovative sustainable composites with potential use in aviation sector—A life cycle assessment review.* Research Gate. https://www.researchgate.net/figure/Materials-used-in-a-modern-aircraftthe-Airbus-A350-XWB-5_fig6_318923824

Chulkov, A. O., Nesteruk, D. A., Vavilov, V. P., Shagdirov, B., Omar, M., Siddiqui, A. O., & Prasad, Y. L. V. D. (2021). Automated procedure for detecting and characterizing defects in gfrp composite by using thermal nondestructive testing. *Infrared Physics & Technology, 114*, 103675. doi:10.1016/j.infrared.2021.103675

Ciałkowski, M. J., & Grysa, K. (2010). Trefftz method in solving the inverse problems. *Journal of Inverse and Ill-Posed Problems, 18*(6), 595–616. doi:10.1515/jiip.2010.027

Eder, M. A., Sarhadi, A., & Chen, X. (2021). A novel and robust method to quantify fatigue damage in fibre composite materials using thermal imaging analysis. *International Journal of Fatigue, 150*, 106326. doi:10.1016/j.ijfatigue.2021.106326

Gornet, L., Wesphal, O., Burtin, C., Bailleul, J., Rozycki, P., & Stainier, L. (2013). Rapid determination of the high cycle fatigue limit curve of carbon fiber epoxy matrix composite laminates by thermography methodology: Tests and finite element simulations. *Procedia Engineering, 66*, 697–704. doi:10.1016/j.proeng.2013.12.123

Hörrmann, S., Adumitroaie, A., Viechtbauer, C., & Schagerl, M. (2016). The effect of fiber waviness on the fatigue life of CFRP materials. *International Journal of Fatigue, 90*, 139–147. doi:10.1016/j.ijfatigue.2016.04.029

Jolly, M., Prabhakar, A., Sturzu, B., Hollstein, K., Singh, R., Thomas, S., Foote, P., & Shaw, A. (2015). Review of Non-destructive Testing (NDT) Techniques and their Applicability to Thick Walled Composites. *Procedia CIRP, 38*, 129–136. doi:10.1016/j.procir.2015.07.043

Kempf, M., Skrabala, O., & Altstädt, V. (2014). Acoustic emission analysis for characterisation of damage mechanisms in fibre reinforced thermosetting polyurethane and epoxy. *Composites. Part B, Engineering, 56*, 477–483. doi:10.1016/j.compositesb.2013.08.080

Kien, D. N., & Zhuang, X. (2021). A deep neural network-based algorithm for solving structural optimization. *Journal of Zhejiang University. Science A, 22*(8), 609–620. doi:10.1631/jzus.A2000380

Kiyoshi, K., Hiroshi, H., & Gouki, K. (2013). Eddy current nondestructive testing for carbon fiber-reinforced composites. *Journal of Pressure Vessel Technology – Transactions of the ASME.* 10.1115/1.4023253

Lee, H., Lim, H. J., Skinner, T., Chattopadhyay, A., & Hall, A. (2022). Automated fatigue damage detection and classification technique for composite structures using Lamb waves and deep autoencoder. *Mechanical Systems and Signal Processing, 163*, 108148. doi:10.1016/j.ymssp.2021.108148

Marani, R., Palumbo, D., Galietti, U., & D'Orazio, T. (2021). Deep learning for defect characterization in composite laminates inspected by step-heating thermography. *Optics and Lasers in Engineering*, *145*, 106679. doi:10.1016/j.optlaseng.2021.106679

Mojtahedi, A., Hokmabady, H., Kouhi, M., & Mohammadyzadeh, S. (2022). A novel ANN-RDT approach for damage detection of a composite panel employing contact and non-contact measuring data. *Composite Structures*, *279*, 114794. doi:10.1016/j.compstruct.2021.114794

Nanthakumar, S. S., Lahmer, T., Zhuang, X., Zi, G., & Rabczuk, T. (2016). Detection of material interfaces using a regularized level set method in piezoelectric structures. *Inverse Problems in Science and Engineering*, *24*(1), 153–176. doi:10.1080/17415977.2015.1017485

Ni, Q. Q., Hong, J., Xu, P., Xu, Z., Khvostunkov, K., & Xia, H. (2021). Damage detection of CFRP composites by electromagnetic wave nondestructive testing (EMW-NDT). *Composites Science and Technology*, *210*, 108839. doi:10.1016/j.compscitech.2021.108839

Papa, I., Lopresto, V., & Langella, A. (2021). Ultrasonic inspection of composites materials: Application to detect impact damage. *International Journal of Lightweight Materials and Manufacture*, *4*(1), 37–42. doi:10.1016/j.ijlmm.2020.04.002

Peyrac, C., Jollivet, T., Leray, N., Lefebvre, F., Westphal, O., & Gornet, L. (2015). Self-heating method for fatigue limit determination on thermoplastic composites. *Procedia Engineering*, *133*, 129–135. doi:10.1016/j.proeng.2015.12.639

. Schwartz, M. M. (1997). *Journal of Composite Materials*. Prentice Hall PTR.

Wu, J., Xu, X., Liu, C., Deng, C., & Shao, X. (2021). Lamb wave-based damage detection of composite structures using deep convolutional neural network and continuous wavelet transform. *Composite Structures*, *276*, 114590. doi:10.1016/j.compstruct.2021.114590

Ye, L., Lu, Y., Su, Z., & Meng, G. (2005). Functionalized composite structures for new generation airframes: A review. *Composites Science and Technology*, *65*(9), 1436–1446. doi:10.1016/j.compscitech.2004.12.015

Chapter 9
Disease Diagnosis Interface Using Machine Learning Technique

D. Rajeswari

https://orcid.org/0000-0002-2677-4296

Department of Data Science and Business Systems, School of Computing, College of Engineering and Technology, SRM institute of Science and Technology, Kattankulathur, India

Athish Venkatachalam Parthiban

Department of Data Science and Business Systems, School of Computing, College of Engineering and Technology, SRM Institute of Science and Technology, Kattankulathur, India

S. S. Sree Nandha

Department of Data Science and Business Systems, School of Computing, College of Engineering and Technology, SRM Institute of Science and Technology, Kattankulathur, India

ABSTRACT

Self-care has acquired relevance, especially in light of the COVID-19 scenario. For anyone to diagnose underlying disorders without a doctor's involvement, improved remote healthcare equipment was required. Due to recent technical breakthroughs, this mission is no longer insurmountable. The objective is to develop an interactive application that can identify potential reasons for a person's discomfort. The primary objective is to carry out a trustworthy machine learning technique that can accurately predict a person's status depending on their symptoms. The collection includes 5000 individual cases and 133 distinctive symptom types. On the same dataset, three alternative models (support vector classification, random forest and Naive Bayes) were instructed to achieve maximum accuracy. The second part involves developing a web application and integrating the model with it. The primary aim of the project is to implement a machine learning based web application that is user-friendly and easy to understand, so that patients can detect their problems before visiting a doctor.

DOI: 10.4018/978-1-6684-8306-0.ch009

INTRODUCTION

Online Disease Diagnosis (ODD) are smart medical tools that are frequently used in health care. ODD uses techniques like machine learning (ML) to enable self-disease identification through symptoms reported by medical persons. The fast advancement of the digital community and the medical industry has increased the demand for symptom checkers (SC) in the application (app) market. Tens of millions of people have downloaded the Symptom Checkers (SC) apps from app shops, including Apollo. These SCs collect user-submitted symptoms and provide users with a provisional diagnosis via a chatbot or a form that mimics a questionnaire. Some SCs equate themselves to knowledgeable medical professionals who offer reliable and accurate information. However, particularly in high-stakes industries like healthcare, the lack of transparency and understandability in intelligent systems may have unintended consequences like misleading consumers. Consumers of healthcare risk their health if they blindly accept the SCs' diagnosis.

The economy and the welfare of humanity depend on a functional healthcare system. There are a lot of changes between the current scenario and the one we did a few decades ago. Everything has become more disorganised and uglier. In this case, medical professionals are risking their own lives in order to save as many lives as they possibly can. Approved doctors can do online consultation instead of offline consultations when they can. However this is not always possible in an emergency. In this situation pre-trained machines can do disease diagnosis.

Without involving a person, a disease predictor, also referred to as a virtual doctor, can correctly forecast a patient's illness. In severe cases, like COVID-19 and EBOLA, ODD can help patients to identify their health without the need for physical contact.

According to estimates, more than 70% of Indians are susceptible to common illnesses including the flu, cold, and other viral infections every two months. 25% of the population passes away as a result of disregarding the early general body symptoms because many individuals are unaware that these illnesses could be indicators of something more dangerous. This situation has the potential to be worrisome and harmful for the populace. It is hard to detect or identify the illness in the early stages to prevent the worst condition. The systems that are currently in use are either those that are focused on a specific ailment or are in the research stage for algorithms when it comes to generalised disease.

When something goes wrong inside of us, our bodies will exhibit symptoms. Sometimes these symptoms will indicate a little issue, but other times they may indicate a serious illness. If the symptoms are not analysed it will lead to the worst disease. So, the ODD is helped to identify the worst disease by analysing the symptoms in order to treat them at an early stage. It reduces the time and complexity to analyse the symptoms to get diagnosis and recommendations in the early stages itself. So, the patients can diagnose the necessary disorders.

The Proposed ODD has a Dialog Box which asks the user to enter the symptoms faced by them. They can select from a drop-down list that consists of all the major symptoms. Once Done entering the Symptoms the user can then view the diagnosis results of the given symptoms which would suggest the kind of Disease and it's severity based on the symptoms given.

The accuracy of the symptom checkers (SC) model and the symptom checkers (SC) app's usability by users of all ages are highlighted in this chapter. The study of the literature reveals the most precise ML models that can be applied to the problem. To attain very low error possibilities in this project, 3 of these high accuracy producing models have been implemented simultaneously.

Given the Rapid Growth of Digitalization and Connectivity, and access to high-speed data from small villages to Metro's, this application can be used by anyone who has a smartphone at any point of time, by simply downloading the application. The ODD can also be used offline without access to the internet, therefore making it accessible in remote places that do not have access to the internet.

LITERATURE REVIEW

Kumar et al., (2022) illustrated how symptoms are provided as input to a ML method in order to forecast the disease. Utilizing a random forest method, the disease is predicted. In the database, both the anticipated disease as well as its related symptoms were included. It is built using Python; they also developed a GUI to display the results. Illness can be anticipated by categorising the provided dataset. A tool to help users identify their ailment using this forecast is provided, along with medical advice and strategies (Reddy et al., 2022). If the user only has to know the disease's fundamentals and also the patient is not in danger, they can utilize this system to gain a basic understanding about mild illnesses. For Disease Prediction using Symptoms, the authors employed ML techniques, using Python programming along with a User Interface built on Tkinter, and even a hospital-collected data set. The illnesses of users were predicted by Radhika et al., (2020) according to their symptoms. To do this, the Decision Tree (DT) Classifier was utilised, which aids in diagnosing the health condition of the patient after obtaining the specific symptoms by presenting the expected ailment. The collection consists of physiological measurements, each of which has 132 variables and 40 instances. The proper patient's EHR is also collected in order to synthesise the prescription or test report using NLTK.

As a novel approach to pattern recognition, an automated sickness detection model using ML models were developed (Farooqui & Ahmad, 2020). In this case, 95 out of 132 independent symptoms that were strongly connected with the stated disorders were selected and further optimised. Sample records of patients with diagnoses of 41 different diseases were taken into consideration for analysis. The data are entered into a Tkinter GUI in the proposed paradigm, where they are analysed and a disease prognosis is created. Decision trees and Naive Bayes techniques are deployed for prognosis. It is feasible to predict diseases early and subsequently enhance patient care and services by using reliable medical database analysis. Venkatesh et al., (2021) employs Multilinear Regression (MLR) and Support Vector Machine (SVM) ML approaches in efficiently detecting possible illnesses. The proposed approach can generate results that are up to 87 percent accurate. The technique has incredible promise for more accurately forecasting future illnesses. The primary objective of this particular research is in assisting non-technical persons and also new professionals establish reliable judgements about disorders.

The creation of classifier systems by using ML algorithms seeks in greatly contributing to the resolution of difficulties related to health by helping physicians and also patients promptly forecast and identify the ailments at a very nascent stage. One Sample dataset of 4920 patient files along with diagnoses for forty-one diseases was chosen for analysis. The variable that was dependent consisted forty-one diseases. Ninety-Five of the 132 variables that were independent (symptoms) were chosen in an effort to condense the number of symptoms into closely related categories. In the research project by Keniya et al., (2020), a system that will be able to predict diseases was developed using ML techniques such as Random Forest (RF) classifier, Naive Bayes classifier, DT classifier, SVM, and KNN is shown. Dahiwade et al., (2019) employed a hand-full of ML approaches to create an illness prediction system. The data set analysed was contained information about more than 230 diseases. Based on the patient's symptoms, age, and gender, the diagnosis process outputs the ailment that the patient may be suffering. The weighted KNN technique delivered the best outcomes in comparison to the other algorithms. Prediction accuracy for the weighted KNN method was 93.5%. In this research project, a classifier constructed using ML methods such as RF classifier, SVM, DT classifier, Naive Bayes classifier, and KNN is shown.

Divya et al., (2018) presented a general prognosis for the patient's illness relying on his or her symptoms. High accuracy illness prediction is achieved using convolutional neural networks (CNN) and the K-Nearest Neighbour (KNN). The usual disease forecast considers a person's lifestyle decisions along with their medical history for an accurate diagnosis. CNN's general illness prediction accuracy is 84.5%, which is better than KNN's. KNN requires more time and memory than CNN as well. This method can show if the risk of general disease is higher or lower after the prediction of general disease. The goal is to construct a healthcare chatbot with artificial intelligence which can identify the patient's illness and offer a brief summary of it before the patient calls a physician (Ghosh et al., 2018). The purpose of the medical chatbot is to provide access to medical knowledge while reducing healthcare costs. Some chatbots act as virtual encyclopaedias for medicine, teaching users about their ailments and encouraging improved health. A chatbot is only beneficial to a user if it can identify all ailments and offer the required information. A text-to-text interactive diagnostic bot engages individuals in dialogue with their health concerns to provide a tailored treatment according to their ailment. Consequently, individuals would be conscious of their condition and obtain the required treatment.

Mathew et al., (2019) presented the construction and testing of such an autonomous chatbot that uses input from the user and natural language to evaluate symptoms and perform triage. The installed bot helps patients by conversing with them about their issues and provides a pre-diagnosis that is specific to each person's symptoms and profile. With 2 sets of patient test cases, our chatbot system was successfully able to recognize user symptoms with an average accuracy of 0.82. With the help of simple symptom analysis and a conversational approach, our application demonstrates how a chatbot used in the medical field may help with the pre-assessment and automatic triage of patients, without the need for time-consuming form-based data entry. The proposed strategy will offer an alternative to the prevalent method of obtaining a diagnosis by visiting a clinic and booking an appointment (Chen et al., 2017). This work aims to create a chatbot application by fusing ML and natural language processing concepts. The chatbot will recognise the symptoms of the user, through a series of questions, identify the ailment, and make therapy recommendations. The chatbot allows users to interact with it exactly as they would a real person. This method may be highly useful for encouraging people to perform daily check-ups, educate themselves about their health, and take the appropriate steps to maintain their health. People can avoid the arduous procedure of visiting physicians by utilising this free application anywhere and using the suggested framework.

Kohli & Arora, (2019) deconstructed ML approaches for precise chronic illness outbreak forecasting in areas with high disease incidence. Actual hospital data that was acquired in central China between 2013 and 2015 was assessed using improved prediction models. To address the issue of data gaps, the authors employed a veiled component model to fill in the gaps and suggested a unique multimodal ailment prediction technique employing unstructured and structured hospital data and convolutional neural networks (CNNs). When compared to various traditional algorithms, the proposed method has a predictive precision of 94.8% and a time of convergence which is faster than the unimodal illness prediction algorithm that is based on CNN. Various categorization strategies were used to three distinct illness databases namely Diabetes, Heart and Breast cancer from the UCI repository in order to predict disease. Each dataset's characteristics were chosen using the p-value test and backward modelling. The study's conclusions lend credence to the idea that early disease detection may be possible using ML.

Proposed System

Dataset Description

From kaggle, the dataset was downloaded. The Full Dataset is separated into 2 CSV files. The first is utilized for model training, whilst second is utilised for model validation. In the CSV file, 133 columns are present. In the file 132 columns are the person's symptoms, and the concluding column has to be the prognosis. The dataset is already balanced, thus there is no need to rebalance it. These signs and symptoms are corresponding to 42 different types of diseases. This dataset is already in binary form, with "1" denoting the presence of the symptom in the patient and "0" denoting its absence.

Data Visualization

After the dataset has been imported, it is visually inspected to check for noise or data gaps. Seaborn library is used for this. The data visualisation stage verifies consistency and makes sure that it is balanced. For each symptom, the data are balanced.

Proposed Architecture

The proposed architecture contains a data set, pre-processing techniques, a Chabot application and a diagnosis system as shown in Figure 2.

Figure 1. Proposed diagnosis system

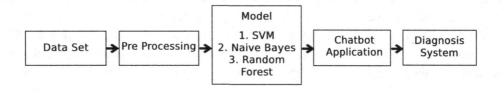

Pre-Processing

Label Encoding

Explicitly training the model on the dataset itself is not possible, because almost all of the data points in the dataset are strings. To enable the model to be trained using the data, label encoding is done on the data to turn the strings into integers.

K-Fold Cross Validation

Cross-validation(CV) is considered as a arithmetical technique used to evaluate the performance of ML models. It is most prevalently in use in applied ML to analyze and pick a model for a given predictive modelling problem since it is very easy to interpret, straightforward to put into practice, and generally produces skill estimates with less bias than other techniques. The procedure has an argument, k, which specifies the no. of groups to be produced from a specified sample data. Consequently, the technique is commonly known as k-fold CV. Whilst a constant value for the argument k is selected, it is possible to be replaced for the value of k within the reference of the model, let's take an instance when $k = 12$ refers to indicate CV with a 12-fold factor.

CV is typically employed within applied ML to assess the performance of a ML model using untrained data. This is, to utilise a small sample to determine the output of the technique when the model predicts the data which wasn't used during the training phase. Fivefold cross validation is employed here.

Support Vector Machine (SVM)

The mathematical technique SVM is meant to classify difficult data. This function is capable of learning the data distribution and providing a non-linear classification line (or ideal hyper plane).

As in context of support vector machines, one data point is seen and we wish to determine if any such points may be segregated by a hyper plane of a given dimension. A linear classifier is known as such. There are various potential classification hyper planes for the data. The hyperplane that shows most difference within the classes could be the best one. Therefore, the hyper plane is selected so as to maximise the interval to the next data-point on every side. When this type of hyper plane occurs, it is referred to as the maximum-margin hyper plane, and the linear classifier it generates is referred to as the maximum-margin classifier or, correspondingly, the perceptron of higher stability.

SVM generates a hyper plane or group of them in such a higher or infinite search area that may be used for classification, outlier detection and regression among other jobs. Naturally, a decent separation is acquired by a hyper plane with the largest distance to the nearest training-data point of any class, since the classifier's generalisation error decreases as the margin increases.

Through projecting raw data to something like a feature space with a high dimensions, SVM classifies data points even if they cannot be split in a linear fashion. Once a divider among the categories has been identified, then the data are transformed as in the divider may be represented by a hyper plane. Consequently, the group to which a new record should belong may be predicted using the characteristics of the new data. The entering data are divided into 42 different categories by the hyper plane's drawing in this manner.

Naïve Bayes

Naive Bayes is a group of classification techniques that depends on Bayes' Theorem. It is a group of techniques based on the concept that each pair of characteristics being categorised is autonomous of the other. These are a type of "probabilistic classifiers" constructed by using Bayes' theorem under the (naive) assumption of strong feature independence. These are few basic Bayesian network techniques, however when merged with kernel density assessment, they may attain great tiers of precision.

The quantity of variables needed by Naive Bayes techniques in a learning task is dependent on the number of variables. Maximum-likelihood training could be carried out in linear time through interpreting a closed-form expression, rather in contrast to the expensive iterative approximation required by the majority of different types of classifiers. According to statistical literature, naive Bayes models can also be called as Independence Bayes or also simple Bayes. Both the names allude to applying the Bayes' theorem to the classifier's determination rule, whereas naive Bayes is generally not a Bayesian approach. Simply speaking, naive Bayes is just a conditional probability method: provided a case that can be categorised, expressed using a vector 'A = (a1, a2...an)' comprising 'n' characteristics (independent parameters), it allocates probabilities to the occurrence of the issue instance.

Each attribute's frequency table has data in it. Let the independent variables (133 characteristics) be B and the event "prognosis" be A for Bayes' theorem. Let's determine the probability for one of the diseases included in the "prognosis" variables.

Random Forest (RF)

Random forests or random decision is a supervised strategy used for regression, classification as well as other problems that includes building a significant amount of decision trees during training phase. The outcome of the random forest for classification issues is that class which is picked by bulk of trees. In regression tasks, the mean prediction for each and every tree is returned. The RF reduces the propensity for decision trees to over fit its training set. RF is a supervised technique that may be used for regression, classification, and other problems. During training, a significant amount of decision trees are constructed. The result of a random forest for classification problems is the class selected by the majority of trees. In regression tasks, the mean prediction of each tree is calculated. RF lower the likelihood of decision trees overfitting their training set. On an Average, RF is better than choice trees, but their precision is inferior to gradient-boosted trees.

The phases that characterise the functioning of the Random Forest Algorithm are as follows:

1. Select random samples out of a specified data or training set.
2. Using this method, a decision tree is constructed from each data set used for training.
3. The choice tree will be averaged during voting.
4. As a final step, select the result that garnered the highest number of votes as the actual prediction result.

RESULTS AND DISCUSSION

The Full Dataset is separated into two files in CSV format. The first is utilised for training the model, whereas the second is utilised for model validation. In the CSV file, 133 columns are present. A person's symptoms are listed in the first 132 columns, and the final column contains the prognosis. The dataset is already balanced, thus there is no need to rebalance it. These signs and symptoms are corresponding to 42 different types of diseases. Dataset is in the binary format, with "1" denoting the presence of the symptom in the patient and "0" denoting its absence.

Following pre-processing, the data are ready for ML models, training data are given to the ML algorithms so that they can learn how to create predictions for the defined task. The Random Forest Classifier, the Naive Bayes Classifier, and the Support Vector Classifier have been selected as the three most accurate models for this project after noting that different models have different levels of accuracy in predicting the prognosis. Once the data has been cleansed, these models will all be trained on it. SVM achieves 93%, Naive Bayes achieves 98% and random forest achieves 96% accuracy. All the three models are combined and produced 98.7% accuracy.

Table 1. Model with accuracy

Model	Accuracy
SVM	93%
Naïve Bayes	98%
Random Forest	96%
Combined model	98.7%

Interface Module

To receive a diagnosis from the models, the patient or user must input all of their symptoms into the web application. It is likely that the user will develop at least one symptom. The user may search for and select as many symptoms as needed. The objective of GUI development is to create the most user-friendly interface possible, one that can be easily understood by individuals of all ages. When developing medical applications, the design of user-friendly systems becomes vital. The user's input is then placed into the model to generate the forecast. The projected prognosis is displayed directly on the user interface for ease of access.

On the basis of the user's input stream of symptoms, a disease is identified and fed into the model. Since each of the three models predicts the outcome separately, the web application then displays the mathematical mode of the three results. The outcome more closely matches a one-word forecast of the precise condition the user may be experiencing shown in figure 2.

Figure 2. Disease diagnosis interface

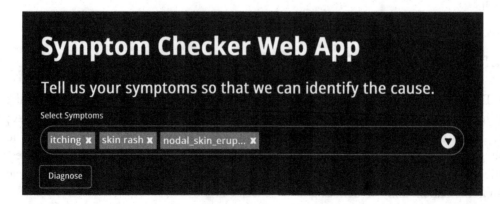

The application integrates the models extremely precisely into the GUI. It is quite effective at using the precise models and delivering the expected prognosis on a clear and straightforward GUI. The application's predicted output can be predicted in a very short amount of time, which increases the usability of the design.

The following procedures have been developed and put into practise using Python and several ML libraries: From the web app, symptoms are inputted. The technique of receiving the input worked well. The ML models are then given the input symptoms. The three predicted outputs' mathematical models are then processed and shown on the GUI. To create the GUI, Python's streamlit module was used.

CONCLUSION

A functional application to examine and classify symptoms has been put in place. Naive Bayes, Random Forest classification and Support Vector Classification, have all been shown to work well together to produce extremely accurate diagnoses with 98.7%. The system can be updated in the future to function as a chatbot or voice assistant that can directly accept symptom inputs in the form of conversational text or verbal speech. A user will find it much simpler to explain their symptoms and issues as a result. In the same manner that a patient would consult a doctor, this also makes the conversation seem more natural.

Instead of only displaying plain text, the application additionally has the ability to audibly or textually tells the user about the diagnosis. To make it simple for the user to keep track of their symptoms and to provide a better reference for a doctor to understand, a report of the same can be provided. In the future, the app will also be able to prescribe medication and find the closest hospital or drugstore. The technology can be utilised as SOS applications and can be integrated into mobile devices. In order to assist patients who would not require extensive doctor consultation and could be diagnosed and supplied basic medication instantly, mobile gadgets can be set up in hospitals.

REFERENCES

Chen, M., Hao, Y., Hwang, K., Wang, L., & Wang, L. (2017). Disease prediction by machine learning over big data from Healthcare Communities. *IEEE Access : Practical Innovations, Open Solutions, 5,* 8869–8879. doi:10.1109/ACCESS.2017.2694446

Dahiwade, D., Patle, G., & Meshram, E. (2019). Designing disease prediction model using machine learning approach. *2019 3rd International Conference on Computing Methodologies and Communication (ICCMC).* 10.1109/ICCMC.2019.8819782

Divya, A., Deepika, B., Durga Akhila, C. H., Tonika Devi, A., Lavanya, B., & Sravya Teja, E. (2022). Disease prediction based on symptoms given by user using machine learning. *SN Computer Science, 3*(6), 504. doi:10.100742979-022-01399-0

Divya, S., Indumathi, V., Ishwarya, S., Priyasankari, M., & Devi, S. K. (2018). A Self-Diagnosis Medical Chatbot Using Artificial Intelligence. *Journal of Web Development and Web Designing, 3*(1). https://core.ac.uk/download/pdf/230494941.pdf

Farooqui, M. E., & Ahmad, D. J. (2020). Disease prediction system using support vector machine and multilinear regression. *International Journal of Innovative Research in Computer Science & Technology*, *8*(4), 331–336. doi:10.21276/ijircst.2020.8.4.15

Ghosh, S., Bhatia, S., & Bhatia, A. (2018). Quro: Facilitating User Symptom Check Using a Personalised Chatbot-Oriented Dialogue System. In E. Cummings, A. Ryan, & L. K. Schaper (Eds.), Connecting the System to Enhance the Practitioner and Consumer Experience in Healthcare (Vol. 252, Ser. pp. 51–56). IOS Press.

Keniya, R., Khakharia, A., Shah, V., Gada, V., Manjalkar, R., Thaker, T., Warang, M., & Mehendale, N. (2020). Disease prediction from various symptoms using machine learning. SSRN *Electronic Journal*. doi:10.2139/ssrn.3661426

Kohli, P. S., & Arora, S. (2019). Application of machine learning in disease prediction. *2018 4th International Conference on Computing Communication and Automation (ICCCA)*. 10.1109/CCAA.2018.8777449

Kumar, K. S., Sai Sathya, M., Nadeem, A., & Rajesh, S. (2022). Diseases prediction based on symptoms using database and GUI. *2022 6th International Conference on Computing Methodologies and Communication (ICCMC)*. 10.1109/ICCMC53470.2022.9753707

Mathew, R. B., Varghese, S., Joy, S. E., & Alex, S. S. (2019). Chatbot for Disease Prediction and treatment recommendation using machine learning. *2019 3rd International Conference on Trends in Electronics and Informatics (ICOEI)*. 10.1109/ICOEI.2019.8862707

Radhika, S., Shree, S. R., Divyadharsini, V. R., & Ranjitha, A. (2020). Symptoms Based Disease Prediction Using Decision Tree and Electronic Health Record Analysis. *European Journal of Molecular and Clinical Medicine*, *7*(4), 2060–2066. https://ejmcm.com/pdf_1944_cb7aaa34894c921618817c5c40cdaf5d.html

Rajdhan, A., Agarwal, A., Sai, M., Ravi, D., & Ghuli, D. P. (2020). Heart disease prediction using machine learning. [IJERT]. *International Journal of Engineering Research & Technology (Ahmedabad)*, *09*(04), 659–662. doi:10.17577/IJERTV9IS040614

Reddy, M. V., Abhijith, G. V. P. S., Nath, K. S., & Sathyanarayana, M. (2022). Disease predictor based on symptoms using machine learning. *International Journal for Research in Applied Science and Engineering Technology*, *10*(6), 2549–2555. doi:10.22214/ijraset.2022.44408

Venkatesh, K., Dhyanesh, K., Prathyusha, M., & Teja, C. H. N. (2021). Identification of Disease Prediction Based on Symptoms Using Machine Learning. *Journal of Advanced Composition*, *14*(6), 86–93. https://drive.google.com/file/d/1lunpeHjQcZUHWiZt24pMd72Y0pUEw6jI/view

Chapter 10
Fabrication of Dental Implants Using MIMICS Software

G. Krishnakanth
SASTRA University, India

M. Malini Deepika
Sathyabama University, Chennai, India

M. Yuvaraja
SASTRA University, India

ABSTRACT

The major problem while treating the tumor is that each responds differently to drug therapies. 3D printing is an aid to solve the difficulty faced in radiation therapy that enables personalized treatment by creating mimic models with micro information to facilitate complex therapies like implanting and tumor structural analysis. The data from modern imaging modalities are combined to construct the 3D structure. In the chapter, 3D construction is done with MIMICS software, and the printing is done with Ultimaker 3 ext to produce the vitro implant model as a reference for pre-operative planning and allows the creation of patient-specific models.

INTRODUCTION

Cancer is found to be a second deadly disease in the world, and it is predicted new cases likely to increases by 70% by the next two decades. Thus, the development of a rigorous framework is required for early detection and planning therapies with less adverse effects on the patients. The heterogeneity nature of Tumor is the major problem in cancer treatment response for the drugs varies from person to person. Prototyping or 3D printing lets fabricate the 3D models of the desired region through computer-generated designs helps in personalized treatment planning (Daniel, 2011). The medical image prototyping was introduced in 1980 in japan. In recent, the construction of vitro models resolves difficulties faced in therapeutic planning.

DOI: 10.4018/978-1-6684-8306-0.ch010

The present work develops implant for oral cancer treatment. Oral cancer is developed in mouth, tongue, lips, and throat tissues early detection lets key to surviving the pathology disease. Treatment includes surgery and radiation therapy. The surgeon removes the affected tumor region and margin of a few surrounding healthy tissues in case of tumors with big size requires removal of jawbones. Requires reconstructive surgery to rebuild jaws to regain the regular involuntary movements. The medical practitioner transplants some part of bone and skin muscle from other body parts. Dental implants are also used to reconstruct the mouth after surgery. The present work involves mimics software for segmentation of ROI from medical imaging modalities CT and MRI image slices for 3D construction. The 3D model is printed; it aids reference for surgery planning and making implants. The work is done in SASTRA University, Thanjavur. Trichy Medical College; Trichy validate it, and it is used for treating patients.

Challenges in Bioprinting

Unique 3D anatomy of the specimen is constructed through Mimics software from images obtained through CT image slices. Masks of cortical bones and teeth are built through thresholding, and morphological operates from inbuild operations. The surface model of the selected bone is constructed with tetrahedral mesh.

Result and Discussion

Figure 1. Sample CT slices

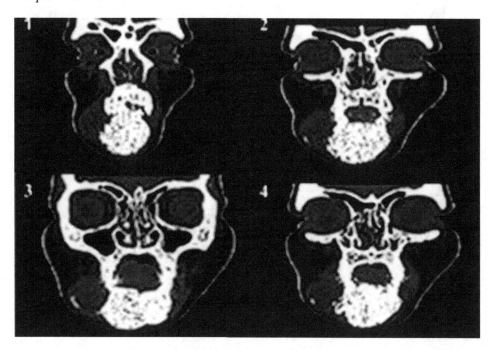

Figure 1 shows the sample image slices obtained from Trichy Medical College, Trichy. The picture shows the Tumor located at the jaw. The images are CT slices of a female patient with mouth cancer. The abnormality is identified in the jaw region.

Figure 2. Segmented and 3D modelled tumor

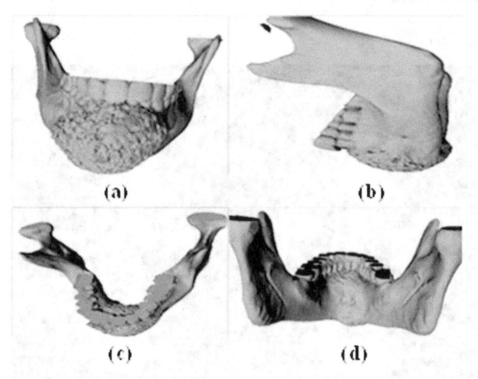

Figure 2 shows the 3D constructed jaw region with Tumor obtained from CT image slices shown in Figure 1. The inferences show the tumor present chin region of the mouth with the structure and size. The segmentation and 3D modelling are done with the mimic software.

Figure 3. Printed Jaw model with implant

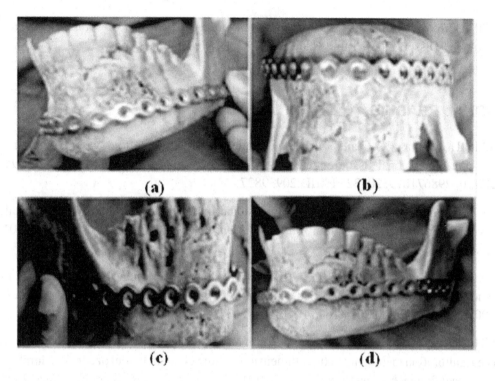

(a)   (b)

(c)   (d)

Figure 3 (a) (b) (c) (d) Shows the 3D printed model of the jaw with removed tumor region with the fixed dental implant fixed that act as a pre-operative reference for surgery and aids in making the implants with correct measurements that of the patients' jaw. The model of the jaw in Figure 3 is printed with Ultimaker 3 with the flexibility to print complex geometric curves in the input image.

CONCLUSION

The model-based pre-operative let's direct interface with the individual patient data through 3D structure and easily customize the implants for all dental surgical proceedings. The forward research with mimics software lets studies on personalized prosthesis development.

ACKNOWLEDGMENT

The authors would like to thank the technical support on implementing the study of Mimics software. TBI of SASTRA University for providing facilities for printing the 3D constructed data. The Trichy medical College for providing the data and implement our method.

REFERENCES

Daniel. (2011). *Role of Mimics a CAD Software in 3D Reconstruction of CT Data in Oral and Maxillofacial Surgery* [Dissertation]. Tamil Nadu Dr. M. G. R. Medical University.

ADDITIONAL READING

Bram Feldt, H., Sabra, G., Centis, V., & Vermette, P. (2010). Scaffold vascularization: A challenge for three-dimensional tissue engineering. *Current Medicinal Chemistry*, *17*(33), 3944–3967. doi:10.2174/092986710793205327 PMID:20939827

Hakim, N. S., & King, A. I. (1979). A three-dimensional finite element dynamic response analysis of a vertebra with experimental verification. *Journal of Biomechanics*, *12*(4), 277–285. doi:10.1016/0021-9290(79)90070-8 PMID:468853

Li, D., Xiao, Z., Wang, G., & Zhao, G. (2014). Novel, fast and efficient image-based 3D modeling method and its application in fracture risk evaluation. *Experimental and Therapeutic Medicine*, *7*(6), 1583–1590. doi:10.3892/etm.2014.1645 PMID:24926348

Schmidt, H., Heuer, F., Simon, U., Kettler, A., Rohlmann, A., Claes, L., & Wilke, H.-J. (2006). Application of a new calibration method for a three-dimensional finite element model of a human lumbar annulus fibrosus. *Clinical Biomechanics (Bristol, Avon)*, *21*(4), 337–344. doi:10.1016/j.clinbiomech.2005.12.001 PMID:16439042

Chapter 11
Face Mask and Social Distancing Detection in Real Time

Madhumita Choudhury
St. Xavier's College, Kolkata, India

Durba Paul
St. Xavier's College, Kolkata, India

Anal Acharya
St. Xavier's College, Kolkata, India

Nisha Banerjee
St. Xavier's College, Kolkata, India

Debabrata Datta
St. Xavier's College, Kolkata, India

ABSTRACT

With the recent outbreak and rapid transmission of the COVID-19 pandemic, the need for the people to follow social distancing and wear masks in public is only increasing. So, the main objective of this chapter is to build a machine learning model based on TensorFlow object detection API and YOLO Objection Detection that will determine a green and red rectangle around the face if the person detected in the camera wears or does not wear a mask, along with an email alert being sent to the authority in charge informing about a person's violation of face mask policy and will return a green or red bounding box accordingly if social distancing is maintained between two people and at the same time alert others by a beep alarm. The accuracy of the model is nearly 97% so it can be used by governments to alert people if the situation turns serious.

DOI: 10.4018/978-1-6684-8306-0.ch011

1. INTRODUCTION

The emergence of coronavirus disease (COVID-19), in Wuhan, China (Raghuvir, 2020) in December 2019, has infected about millions of people and claimed many lives globally. The virus is known to transmit from person to person primarily via respiratory droplets. Hence the use of several measures, such as wearing a face mask, physical distancing, etc., have been implemented by the government bodies of most of the pandemic-affected countries to reduce the viral transmission. However, negligence in following rules has been observed both at individual and community levels. Physical distancing, face masks are basic mechanical barriers effective in reducing viral transmission (Advice for the public, n.d.). A few studies have been conducted, which shows the effectiveness of wearing mask and maintaining social distance in controlling the viral spread. Physical distancing has also been an effective measure as it helps avoid any direct contact amongst individuals and assists in reducing any sorts of transmission of the droplets containing the virus. Studies conducted shows that the droplets transfer via human breathing, coughing, talking, sneezing and eating. Here arises the questions like "what is a safe distance to maintain social distancing?" and "what further can stop this transmission?". Other biological, medical and engineering factors also needed to be considered to answer the above-mentioned questions. Finally, it was suggested by WHO that distance for a safe social distance was recommended to be at least 6 feet, that is, 2 meters (COVID-19, n.d.).

Yet, now the distance has been reduced to 1 meter in some of the recovering countries. This research paper proposes an AI based detection system that helps in detecting any kinds of violations. This research intends on building a model that can be applied in real-time systems and thus help in avoiding the spread of the virus. A significant positive change has been observed between the people wearing mask and the others not wearing a mask. The study conducted using a logistic and statistical model has shown that the highest significant control over viral transmission can be achieved with increase in face mask wearing and social distance maintaining habit. On the other hand, low level of community transmission control has been seen in states with self-reported mask-wearing but limited social distancing. So, this proposed AI (Artificial Intelligence) based Face Mask Detection and Social Distancing Detection System can be implemented in public places like the banks, airports, schools, colleges, offices, etc., to monitor physical movements of people and alert people to take necessary steps in case of violations.

2. RELATED LITERATURE

This section previews some of the related research works on Object Detection, Object Recognition, Face detection and identification based on Artificial Intelligence, Convolution Neural network, YOLO Object detection algorithm, TensorFlow Object Detection API, OpenCV package, etc., and implementation of these models in real world applications. Several works have been done successfully in this domain. Many of these significant works have been thoroughly examined to gain knowledge in this field and build the proposed model for our research paper:

Zhong-Qiu Zhao, Peng Zheng, Shou-tao Xu, and Xindong Wu (2019) attempted to provide deep learning-based object detection frameworks in a research paper and compared various object detection methods on three benchmark datasets, including PASCAL VOC 2007 (n.d.), PASCAL VOC 2012 (n.d.) and Microsoft COCO. This paper also focussed on the modifications that can be made to typical generic object detection architectures and also surveyed tasks like face detection, pedestrian deletion etc.

The main research work of the article put forward by Sheng Ding and Kun Zhao (2018) was to collect a small data set of daily objects and using the TensorFlow framework, build different models of object detection, and use this data set for training model and finally effect of the model was improved by fine-tuning the model parameters.

S. Bartlett, G. Littlewort, I. Fasel and J. R. Movellan in their paper "Real Time Face Detection and Facial Expression Recognition: Development and Applications to Human Computer Interaction" (2003) proposed a system that automatically detects frontal faces in the video stream and codes them with respect to 7 dimensions in real time: neutral, anger, disgust, fear, joy, sadness, surprise. The system was tested on the Cohn-Kanade datasetof posed facial expressions. Most interestingly the outputs of the classifier change smoothly as a function of time and the system has been deployed on a wide variety of platforms including Sony's Aibo pet robot, ATR's RoboVie, and CU animator, and is currently being evaluated for applications including automatic reading tutors, assessment of human-robot interaction.

Considering there are a lot of mobile computing devices available, Zhongjie Li and Rao Zhang (n.d.) implemented a CNN based object detection algorithm on Android devices. The model architecture was based on SqueezeNet to get image feature maps and a convolutional layer to detect bounding boxes for recognized objects. The total model size was around 8 MB while most other object detection model takes more than 100 MB's storage. The model architecture makes the calculation more efficient, which enables its implementation on mobile devices.

As existing manual attendance system is time consuming and cumbersome to maintain, so Smitha,PavithraHegde and Afshin proposed a "Face Recognition based Attendance Management System" (2020) that also removes the chances of proxy attendance. Face detection and recognition is performed from live video of the classroom using Haar-Cascade classifier and Local Binary Pattern Histogram algorithm respectively and finally attendance is mailed to the respective faculty at the end of the session.

MagantiManasa, Vikas B and K. Subhadra (2019) described a technique to detect drowsiness among car drivers using Open CV and alert them whenever they tend to sleep has been proposed. The algorithm is based on eye-blink and yawn frequency.

The work described in research paper by Sandesh R, AvinashSridhar, Rishikesh T, Saniya Farheenand Sara Tameem (n.d.) deals with the proposed system for smart and savvy door lock recognition system which is essentially for identification of human faces and mainly for home security. Open CV is mainly used for Face Recognition and finally automatic door access which can replace the use of standard passwords, pins and patterns, adding more security to our life. The process was carried out by raspberry pi.

In a research paper by Anudeep Gandam and Dr.Jagroop Singh Sidhu (2016), various video processing techniques have been discussed along with their application in traffic environment, real time video capturing through mobiles. This paper also provided a brief description on the various approaches used for stabilizing or enhancing the quality of captured video.

The proposed system by Amit Chavda, Jason Dsouza, Sumeet Badgujar, Ankit Damani (2021) consisted of a dual stage Convolutional Neural Network (CNN) architecture capable of detecting masked and unmasked faces and integrated with pre-installed CCTV cameras. This helps to track safety violations, promote the use of face masks, and ensure a safe working environment.

Research conducted by IshaShete (n.d.) proposed a novel method of an Artificial Intelligence-based real-time social distancing and face mask detection system. In this article, pre-trained deep neural network models such as ResNet Classifier, DSFD, and YOLOv3 were used in the detection of individuals and face masks with the help of bounding boxes.

Chhaya Gupta and Nasib Singh Gill (2020) developed "CoronaMask", a highly effective face mask detector to contribute towards welfare of human beings during this pandemic situation. The proposed model used the deep learning convolutional neural network (CNN) algorithm as a base for detecting faces and the dataset has been created which consists of 1238 images divided into two classes as "mask" and "no_mask". The convolutional neural network is trained on the dataset and it gives 95% of accuracy. CoronaMask, a two-phase face mask detector works in identifying masks in images and also in real-time video streams.

In another work as put forward by Saman Almufti, Ridwan Marqas, Zakiya Nayef and Mohamed (2021), mask-less people were avoided from entering to desired places (i.e., mall, university, etc.,) by detecting face mask using deep learning, TensorFlow, Keras, and OpenCV and sending a signal to Arduino device that was connected to the gate to be opened. The method attained accuracy up to 97.80% and identified whether the person wear mask or not in real time. The dataset provided in this paper, was collected from various sources.

Joby K. J. &Priyanga K. K. in a paper (2021), proposed "RetinaFaceMask", which is a high-accuracy and efficient face mask detector. The proposed RetinaFaceMask is a one-stage detector, which consisted of a feature pyramid network to fuse high-level semantic information with multiple feature maps, and a novel context attention module to focus on detecting face masks. In addition, the paper also proposed a novel cross-class object removal algorithm to reject predictions with low confidences and the high intersection of union. In this project, the researchers proposed a mask detector using image processing, the manual system automated. An IOT Component is connected to display the real time update of the image. The technique used for segmentation and classification of images was Convolutional Neural Network.

A face mask detection model using RaspberryPi was developed by Ashish Choudhary (n.d.) to control the spread of Covid 19. For this project the dataset consisted of 500 images belonging to two classes-with and without mask and after training the recognizer with and without masks, in the last phase trainer data was used to classify each face into the two categories. To see real-time COVID-19 face mask detector in action, Raspberry Pi Camera module was connected with Pi for facial landmark and face mask detection.

The purpose of the work in the paper "Monitoring social distancing under various low light conditions with deep learning and a single motionless time of flight camera" by Rahim A, Maqbool A, Rana T (2021) was to provide an effective social distance monitoring solution in low light environments in a pandemic situation. Low light environments can become a problem in the spread of disease because of people's night gatherings. So, in this paper, a deep learning-based solution is proposed which utilizes YOLO V4 model for real-time object detection and the social distance measuring approach is introduced with a single motionless time of flight (ToF) camera. The risk factor is indicated based on the calculated distance and safety distance violations are highlighted. Experimental results showed that the proposed model exhibited good performance with 97.84% mean average precision (mAP) score and the observed mean absolute error (MAE) between actual and measured social distance values is 1.01 cm.

Mahdi Rezaei and Mohsen Azarmi (2020) contributed to build a hybrid Computer Vision and YOLOv4-based Deep Neural Network (DNN) mode for automated people detection in the crowd in indoor and outdoor environments using common CCTV security cameras. The proposed DNN model in combination with an adapted inverse perspective mapping (IPM) technique and SORT tracking algorithm led to a robust people detection and social distancing monitoring. The model has been trained against two most comprehensive datasets—the Microsoft Common Objects in Context (MS COCO) and Google Open Image datasets. The system has been evaluated against the Oxford Town Centre dataset (including 150,000 instances of people detection.The evaluation has been conducted in challenging conditions, including occlusion, partial visibility, and under lighting variations and also provided an online infection risk assessment scheme by statistical analysis of the spatio-temporal data from people's moving trajectories and the rate of social distancing violations.

Gokul Sudheesh Kumar and Sujala D. Shetty (2021) proposed an Android app named "StaySafe" where the user will be notified if face mask and social distancing violation is detected. For this purpose, Firebase was used as the backend service. Firebase Cloud Messaging service was used to send notifications which will be handled in the android app. The app offers various features like viewing history, saving the image to the device, deleting the images from the cloud etc. A heat map can also be viewed which highlights crowded regions which can help officials identify the regions that need to be sanitized more often.

3. PROPOSED METHODOLOGY

In this paper we are suggesting a model to handle the basic mandatory step to be taken by the society to control the COVID transit i.e., wearing the facemask and maintaining proper physical distances while out in public places. It is not feasible to manually track the implementation of the basic Anti-Covid protection policies so technology plays an important role in this aspect.

The main objective of this paper is to build a real-time detection model which will detect if a person is wearing a face mask or not i.e., if a person is following proper face mask policy or not and at the same time will keep a track of people who are maintaining the necessary social distancing norms i.e., maintaining minimum physical distance from another person while out in public.

The proposed method consists of a binary classifier and a pre-trained Convolutional Neural Network (CNN) (n.d.) which contains two 2D convolution layers connected to layers of dense neurons that helps us in the classification of masked and unmasked people. Deep Learning is a subset of machine learning in Artificial Intelligence that contains networks which is capable of learning features from unstructured or unlabelled data without the need of prior knowledge about it. Transfer Learning (n.d.) is the process of reusing a pre-trained model to build a more powerful new model by fine-tuning different parameters of the existing trained model. Generally training an object detection model takes several days on a CPU so Transfer learning approach is used to train the object detection models as it takes few hours or less. Therefore, in this paper, Social Distancing and Face Mask Detection models utilize Transfer learning approach and YOLO Object Detection algorithm to detect if a person while walking maintains social distance or not and if the person does/doesn't wear a mask in real time. This application can be implemented using any system in-built camera or CCTV cameras or security cameras to identify if an individual is maintaining the proper face mask and social distancing guidelines.

Python based image processing (n.d.) is used for real time object detection in each frame and machine learning techniques are used to achieve the real time implementation. Violation can take place at any point of time, so this paper suggests a cloud-based approach that counts the total number of human beings tracked in the frame, the total number of violations of social distancing by people in the frame regardless of age, location, and classifies people into two categories of with-mask and without-mask. Such real time application of the model can create awareness to global users and by increasing the system accuracy, there is a possibility of improving the current pandemic situation.

The proposed method makes use of Sequential CNN (Yang et al., 2017) where the First Convolution layer is followed by Rectified Linear Unit (ReLU) and MaxPooling layers. The Convolution layer learns from 200 filters. Kernel size is set to 7 x 7 which specifies the height and width of the 2D convolution window. To insert the data into CNN, the long vector of input is passed through a Flatten layer which transforms matrix of features into a vector that can be fed into a fully connected neural network classifier. Then a Dense layer of 128 neurons with a ReLu activation function is added. To reduce overfitting a Dropout layer with a 50% chance of setting inputs to zero is added to the model. The final layer (Dense) with 2 outputs for two categories uses the Softmax activation function (Softmax Activation Function with Python, n.d.). The whole Sequential CNN architecture (consisting of several layers) uses TensorFlow (An end-to-end open-source machine learning platform, n.d.) (which is an interface for expressing machine learning algorithms and developing and training ML models) at backend. It is also used to reshape the data (image) during the data processing.

The entire implementation of the proposed model is shown in a flowchart:

Figure 1. Flowchart of the proposed model

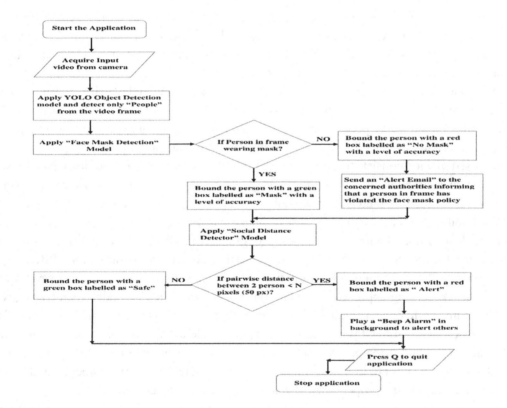

Figure 2. Visual representation of the proposed model

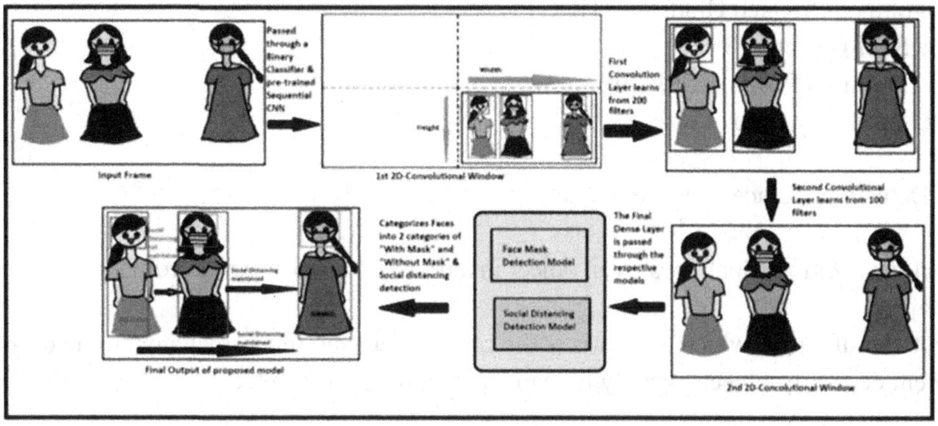

Keras (n.d.) gives fundamental reflections and building units for creation and transportation of ML arrangements with high iteration velocity. It takes full advantage of the scalability and cross-platform capabilities of TensorFlow. The core data structures of Keras are layers and models. All the layers used in the CNN model in this paper are implemented using Keras. Along with the conversion of the class vector to the binary class matrix in data processing, it also helps to compile the overall model.

Kaggle Face Mask Dataset (n.d.) containing 3861 image samples have been used to train the proposed model for face mask detection. This is a balanced dataset containing faces, with and without masks with a mean height of 283.68 and mean width of 278.77.

a)   With_mask (1931 Images sample)
b)   Without_mask (1930 Images Sample)

The proposed model which helps in detecting if a person is wearing mask or not and at the same time if the person is maintaining proper social distance or not, is based upon three algorithms:

a)   Object Detection Algorithm
b)   Object Tracking Algorithm
c)   Euclidean Distance between detected objects

3.1 Object Detection Algorithm

Object Detection is an automated method of computer vision which helps us to locate different objects present in an image or a frame of a video. There are different object detection algorithms that identify the location of an object in an image or video and output the coordinates of the location of an object in the frame. Some of the popular object detection algorithms are:

a)   Region based Convolutional Neural Network (R-CNN)
b)   Region based Fully Convolutional Network (R-FCN)
c)   Fast R-CNN

d)   Faster R-CNN
e)   Histogram of Oriented Gradients (HOG)
f)   Single Shot Detector (SSD)
g)   Spatial Pyramid Pooling (SPP-net)
h)   YOLO (You Only Look Once)

Object Detection includes two techniques:

a)   Object localization which locates an object in a frame and return the coordinates of the position of the object.
b)   Object classification which categorizes the objects detected in an image or frame of a video into different classes of objects namely human, cars, building, dog, etc.

The various methods of Object Detection can be categorized into (i) Two Stage detector and (ii) One Stage Detector.

- The Two Stage Detectors (Soviany & Ionescu, 2018) use two neural networks for detecting objects. The first neural network is used to generate the region proposal i.e., to generate the region of interests in a frame. The second neural network is used to refine these region proposals for object classification and bounding box regressions. Such models result in high detection performance but compromises speed. Although these models reach highest accuracy rates but they are much slower. R-CNN and Faster R-CNN are examples of Two- Stage object detectors.
- The One Stage Detector (Soviany & Ionescu, 2018) uses a single neural network layer for region proposals and detection. The single stage detector requires only one pass to go through the neural network and predict the bounding boxes. For this, the bounding boxes should be predefined. Such models have lower accuracy rates but are much faster than Two stage detectors. Although the one stage detectors trade off the detection performance, they are preferred over two stage detectors for object detection. Some primary examples of one stage detectors are Single Shot Multi-Box Detector (SSD) and You Only Look Once (YOLO).

In this paper, we have used the *YOLO Object detection Algorithm.*

3.1.1. YOLO Object Detection Algorithm:

YOLO Objection Detection (n.d.) algorithm is used for real-time object detection. It is popular because of its speed and accuracy. YOLO Object Detection algorithm finds all the objects in a frame of a digital image or video and predicts the different classes of the objects like Person, car, building, etc. Object detection in YOLO is considered as a regression problem that provides the probabilities of detected classes of the different objects in an image.

This algorithm involves the detection of an object in a single forward pass through the convolutional neural network so that the object detection can be done in real time in a faster manner. The prediction of the object in the entire frame is done in a single execution of the algorithm. The algorithm applies a single CNN to the entire image at once and then divides the image into different regions. It then draws bounding boxes around the different regions. The bounding box is an outline that highlights the different objects present in an image and consists of width, height, bounding box centre and are weighted by the predicted probability that establish the occurrence of an object in the image. A single CNN detects multiple bounding boxes around an object and predicts the class probabilities of the bounding box. Intersection over Union is a method that eliminates unnecessary overlapping bounding boxes which do not meet the object's actual bounding box coordinates. After the different objects in an image are bounded by multiple boundary boxes, it is necessary to select the best boundary box with higher IoU score from the multiple predicted boundary boxes and eliminate or suppress the less likely ones. This technique of rejection of less IoU scored boundary boxes and selection of the best one is known as non-maximum suppression, So, after non-maximum suppression that makes sure that object detection algorithm detects each object exactly once, the final detection consists of unique bounding boxes around the object that surrounds the object perfectly. In Fig.3., it is noticeable that after application of CNN on the input image, the different objects in the image are bounded by various boundary boxes along with their class and IoU scores like Person class with three different IoU scores of 0.43,0.95 and 0.98. Now after application of non-maximum suppression, the box with less IoU score is deleted and the objects in the image are finally detected by unique boundary box around them.

Figure 3. Elimination of multiple bounding boxes over a single object by method of intersection over union

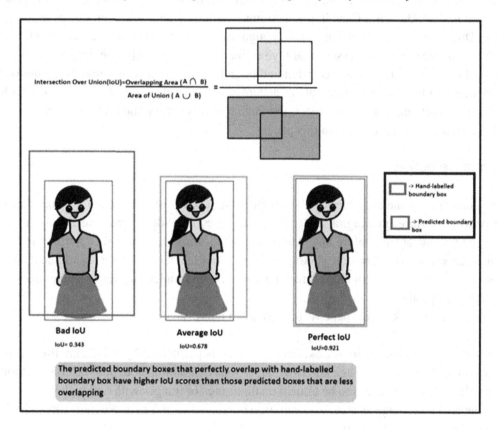

Figure 4. YOLO object detection mechanism

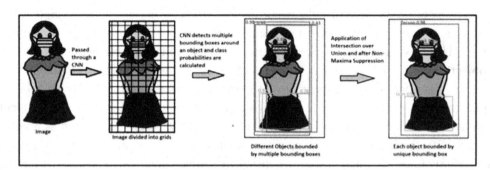

There are different implementations of YOLO algorithm in web platform. One of the noted examples is the Darknet (n.d.) which is an open-source neural network framework that enables computations on a GPU platform faster as it is an essential for real- time predictions.

The different variations of this approach are- YOLOv1, YOLOv2, YOLOv3. In this proposed model, we have used the YOLOv3 i.e., You Only Look Once Version 3, as it can identify the objects in live feeds, videos, images reallyfast. In particular, YOLO is trained on the COCO Dataset (n.d.) which consists of 80 labels like People, Bicycles, Cars, Trucks, Animals including cats, dogs, birds, horses, Aeroplanes, Stop signs, Dining objects and many more. Although the accuracy may not be precise, YOLO can predict nearly up to 9000 separate classes. YOLOv3 refined the design of the previous versions of YOLO by using tricks such as multi-scale prediction and bounding box prediction through the use of logistic regression which in turn increased the rate of accuracy of object detection but trading off with speed. From among the different classes of object, the Person class of pretrained YOLOv3 is used to detect people from each frame of the video in this paper.

3.1.2. Face Detection

Face detection is one of the examples of object detection. It is a computer vision method which is used to detect presence of faces in a digital image or a in a frame of a video. Face detection is the technique which is usually done at first before any face related applications like face recognition or verification for criminal detection, driverless car, photography, etc. An ideal face detector should be able to detect any faces regardless of age, skin colour, facial expression and under any set of lightening conditions and upon any background.

The face detection task in this paper is broken down into 2 steps:

a) The first step is a classification task. Face detection is performed by using classifiers which is an algorithm that divides an image into two classes -one containing faces and the other without faces. Generally, a classifier needs to be trained on thousands of images with and without faces. Thus, it takes an arbitrary image as input and outputs a binary value of Yes or No indicating whether there are any faces present in the image.

b) The second task is the face localization task that takes an image as input, search for the faces in the image and if face is present then returns the location of the face with bounding box around it.

Previously face detection models were implemented using edge, line and centre near features and patterns were recognized from those features. These approaches are used to find binary patterns locally. These approaches are very effective to deal with Gray-scale images and the computation effort required is also very less. So, the researchers used pattern recognition to predict faces based on prior face models.

A breakthrough face detection technology was then developed using Haar-Cascade Algorithm (Padilla et al., 2012) also known as Viola Jones Detector algorithm that proposed a real-time object model, used to detect different classes of objects and is also implemented in this paper. Since a video consists of multiple images in each frame, it uses 24x24 base window size to evaluate any image with edge, line and four rectangular features. Harr-like features are like convolutions to check weather given feature is available in the image or not. This model fails to work in when image brightness varies and even it exhibits poor performance when images are in different orientations.

Open- CV (Mahamkali & Ayyasamy, 2015) is an Open-source Computer Vision library which is used for image processing, identifying and differentiating faces, recognizing group movements in recordings, following eye gestures, detecting objects in real time, tracking camera points etc., and already consists of two pre-trained face detection classifiers as- Haar classifier and Local Binary Pattern (LBP) classifier. Since in Open- CV, we have several trained Haar Cascade models which are saved as XML files so instead of creating and training the model from scratch, these XML files are used for face detection. OpenCV always uses BGR image format so the proposed method makes use of the features of OpenCV in resizing and color conversion of data images.

The SSD i.e., Single Shot Multi-Box Detector (Liu et al., 2016) is a single convolutional network that is capable of predicting bounding box locations and classifying these locations in one forward propagation through the neural network unlike regional proposal network (RPN) based approaches such as R-CNN series which need two shots. Since SSD is much faster compared with two-shot RPN-based approaches so in this paper, we have used Pre-trained SSD model to detect faces of people from each frame of the video in real-time.

Figure 5. Architecture of a convolutional neural network with a SSD detector

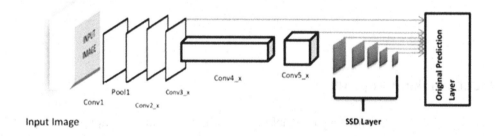

3.1.3. Face Mask Detection

The face mask detection model is designed so that it is able to recognize faces with and without mask and draw bounding box around the face with level of accuracy of detection.

The face mask detection is divided into 2 phases:

a) The first phase is the training of the face mask detector model. In this phase, first we load the face mask dataset from the disk. Then we train the model on 80% of the dataset using Keras/ Tensorflow. Finally, we serialize the face mask classifier to the disk. MobileNet is an object detector which was released in 2017 as an efficient CNN architecture designed for mobile and embedded vision application. Here in this proposed model, the Trained MobileNet V2 model is used as the binary face mask classifier i.e., to classify people with and without masks. The MobileNet V2 is fine-tuned with pre-trained ImageNet weights (n.d.) for data augmentation.

b) The second phase is the actual implementation of the face mask detection model in real time. In this phasethe face mask classifier is first loaded from the disk. After detecting faces of people in the frame of a video or in the camera, the main features of each face are extracted like eyes, nose, mouth, ears. These features are considered as the ROI (Regions of Interest). The face mask classifier which is loaded from the disk is then applied on the detected face ROIs. This binary classifier classifies people into "with mask" and "without mask" and shows the results on the output frame.

Figure 6. Block diagram of face mask detection system of the proposed model

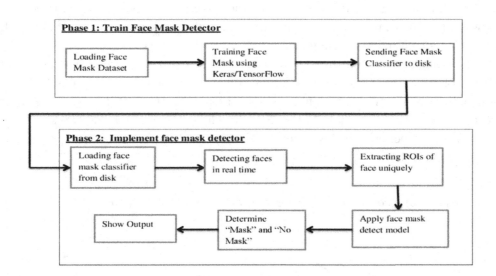

3.2. Object Tracking Algorithm

After detection of the object, the Object Tracking Algorithm allows us to apply a unique ID to each tracked object making it possible to count unique objects moving around the frames in a video. The Object Tracking algorithm using Open CV is also known as centroid -tracking in which a new ID is assigned to every detected person, a box is drawn over them and the centroid is computed.

Figure 7. Object tracking algorithm

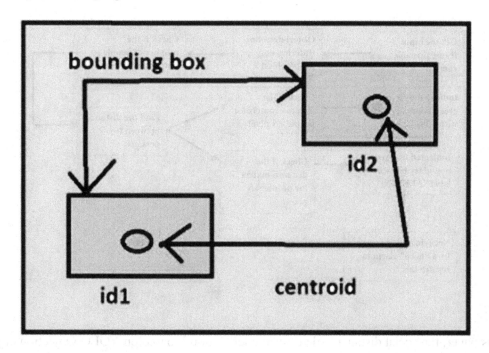

3.3. Distance Measured Between Detected Objects

This object tracking algorithm relies on the Euclidean distance (Kumar & Shetty, 2021) between (a) existing object centroids and (b) new object centroids between subsequent frames in a video. Euclidean distance is calculated as the square root of the sum of the squared differences between the two vectors.

$$)) = \sqrt{\left(xi - xj\right)^2 + \left(yi - yj\right)^2}$$

3.3.1. Social Distancing Detection

Social distancing is a method used to control the spread of contagious diseases. As the name suggests, social distancing implies that people should physically distance themselves from one another, reducing close contact, and thereby reducing the spread of the contagious disease of Corona Virus.

In this model, webcam is used for social distance monitoring using CV2(latest version of Open CV package).

The following block diagram depicts the implementation of the social distancing detection process:

Figure 8. Block diagram of social distancing detection process

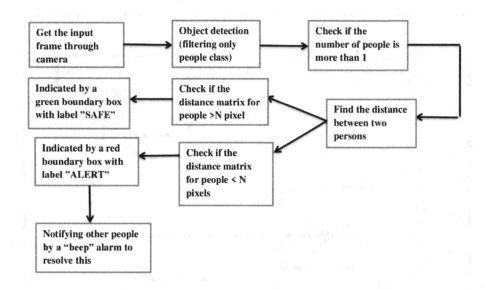

In this paper, the social distancing detector model was built based on YOLO Objection algorithm. This real time object detection algorithm is used to detect only people in the frame of a videostream and at least 2 people should be detected in the frame for the proposed model to compute distance between them. Based on the calculated Euclidean distance between two people, it is checked if any two people are less than N pixels apart and the corresponding results are shown on the output frame. For this proposed model, the minimum safe distance is assumed to be 50px. So, if the computed distance between two people is less than 50px, then those two people are bounded with a red alert box and if the calculated distance is more than 50px i.e., minimum safe distance is maintained, then those people are bounded with a green safe box.

With OpenCV's DNN (Deep Neural Network) module compiled with GPU support, our method was able to run in real-time, making it usable as a simultaneous face mask and social distancing detector.

4. RESULTS AND ANALYSIS

The proposed methodology discussed in the previous section have been implemented with a system having the following hardware and software configurations:

a) Software Used:
   Software: Anaconda + Python 3.8
   Editor: Sublime Text 3
   Environment: TensorFlow
b) Hardware Used:
   OS Version: Windows 10, x64
   Camera: Webcam

The discussed model runs faster in a GPU-enabled environment. Since GPU drivers, NVIDIA (n.d.) graphics processor or any GPU enabled processors were not available in the system, so the proposed model has been executed in a CPU environment of AMD Ryzen 5 3500U processor with relatively slow computation by creating an isolated python virtual environment.

4.1. Model Training

The proposed model has been trained with Kaggle dataset which contains image samples of people with and without masks on their face as described in the proposed procedures.80% of our total custom dataset is used to train our model with a single shot detector, which takes only one shot to detect multiple objects that are present in an image using multi-box and the rest 20% goes for testing purposes.

The model is trained for 20 epochs (iterations) which maintains a trade-off between accuracy and chances of overfitting.

Figure 9. Depicts the 20 epochs

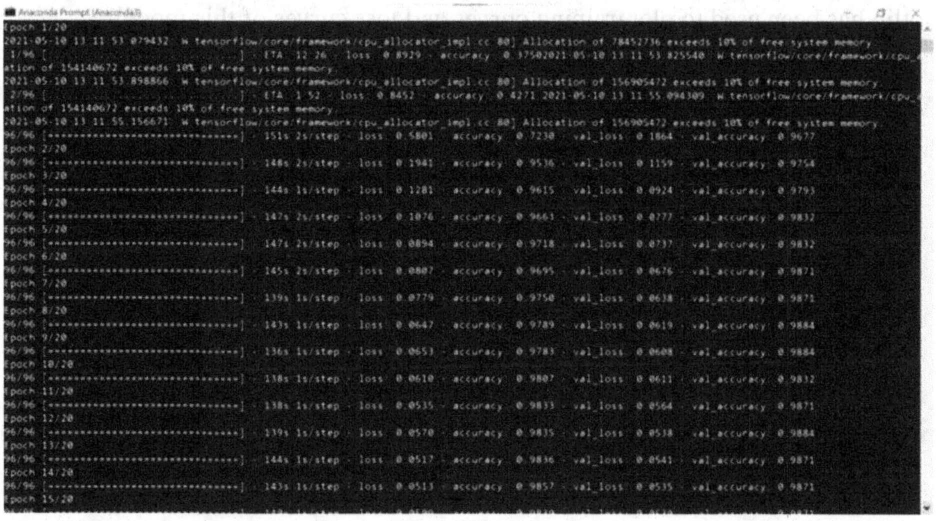

Figure 10. Depicts 20 epochs along with accuracy results

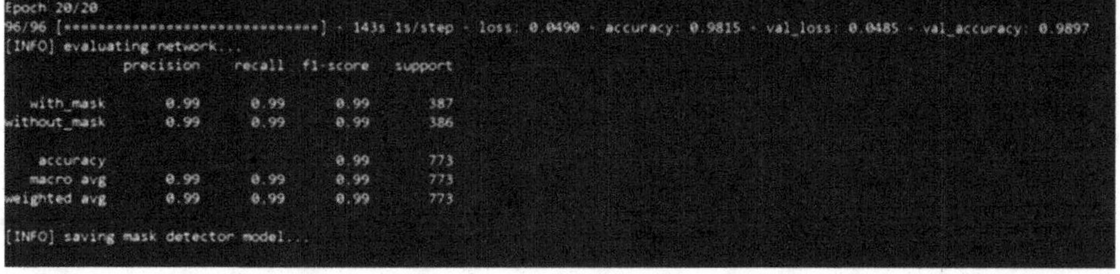

- The custom data set is loaded into the project directory and the algorithm is trained on the basis of the labelled images.
- In pre-processing steps, the image is resized to 224×224 pixels, converted to NumPy (van der Walt et al., 2011) array format and the corresponding labels are added to the images in the dataset before using our SSD model as input to build our custom model with MobileNetV2 as the backbone and train our model using the TensorFlow Object Detection API.
- Before model training begins, TensorFlow helps in Data augmentation and pre-trained ImageNet weights are downloaded to make the algorithm's prediction efficiency accurate. After downloading the pre-trained weights and creating a new fully-connected (FC) head, the SSD algorithm is trained with both the pre-trained ImageNet weights and the annotated images in the custom data set by tuning the head layer weights of the CNN without updating weights of base layers.
- Finally, "Adam optimizer" (Keras Optimizers, n.d.) is used for compiling the model and binary_ crossentropy which is also known as log loss (the cost function used in Logistic Regression) is used as a loss function (the objective that the model tries to minimize).In this paper, scikit-learn (sklearn) (n.d.) is used for binarizing class labels, segmenting our dataset, and printing a classification report. As the problem is a classification problem, metrics is set to "accuracy". Finally, matplotlib has been used to plot training curves and loss curves of this model.

Figure 11. Model training accuracy/loss curves

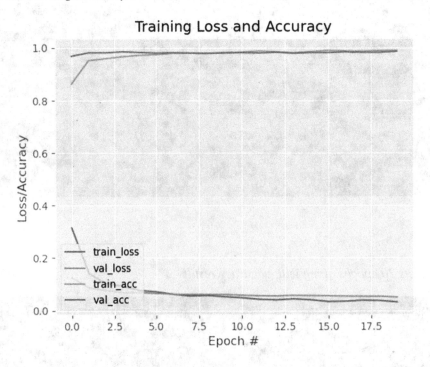

Python comes with built-in smtplib module for sending emails using Simple Mail Transfer Protocol. The same has been used in this paper for sending alert email to the authority-in-charge when face mask policy is violated. For beep alert during violation of social distancing norms, the mixer component imported from pygame package has been initialised which plays an alarm sound when person detected in frame is very close to another person.

4.2. Final Outcomes of the Model

Since, NVIDIA CUDA-capable GPU was unavailable in our system, so the configuration option of using GPU has been set to False so that our CPU is the processor used.

The proposed model has been tested by taking inputs through system in-built webcam and also implemented on 2 downloaded videos from internet.

This research model uses a binary classifier which after determining the accuracy of the model, draws a green bounding box with label "MASK" around the face of the person wearing mask and a red bounding box with label "NO MASK" around the face of the person not wearing a face mask. If the person is not wearing mask, then this model sends an alert email to the concerned authorities in charge informing about the detection of a person violating the face mask policy.

Figure 12. Outputs with mask

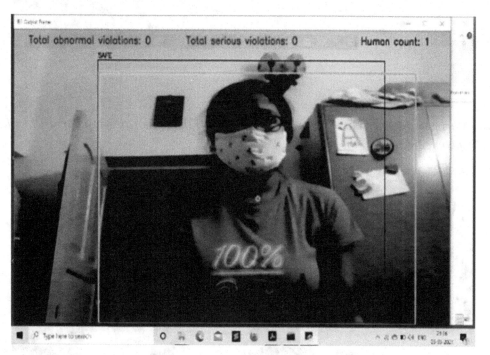

Figure 13. Outputs without mask

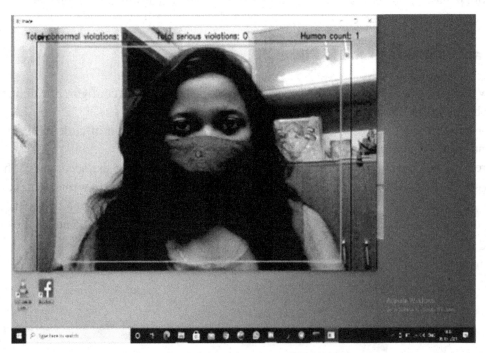

Figure 14. Alert email being sent to the common mail id of the authorities-in-charge when face mask not worn by people detected in the camera

Our model is also responsible for identifying people who are maintaining proper social distance between each other. Red bounding boxes with label "ALERT" around a person indicate that the person is in close proximity of another person by violating the minimum safe distance and green box with label "SAFE" indicates that the person is maintaining social distance. If the person is not maintaining minimum safe distance which is assumed to be at least 1m, then a beep alarm is played in background to alert the person and others moving near him. The total human count tracked in the frame is also displayed.

Figure 15. Social distance detection output on 1ˢᵗ video (Oxford Street Dataset, n.d.)

The proposed model is supposed to detect face mask and social distancing simultaneously in real time. So, the following output on another video (Male and Female walking on street wearing face masks, n.d.) give us such results:

Figure 16. The two people are bounded by red alert box as they are in close proximity of one another thus violating social distancing norms (output from 2ⁿᵈ video (Male and Female walking on street wearing face masks, n.d.))

Figure 17. Light green box around the two person indicates that they are wearing face mask

The model also records the time taken for prediction of the face mask and social distancing detection in each frame of a video stream before closing the application:

Figure 18. Time taken to predict the results in each frame of the input video

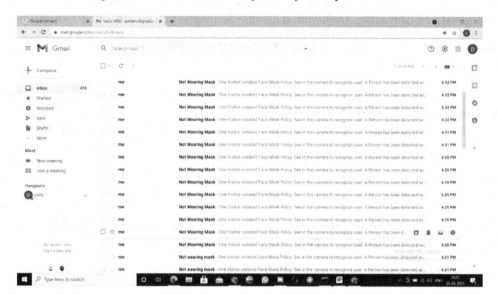

5. CONCLUSION AND FUTURE SCOPE

The study of this research is to understand the social distancing and face mask detection for protection against Covid-19. The object detection for social distancing which is based on persons and face mask detection that is based on faces, was done by using YOLO. Protecting oneself from the critical virus is most important. We are currently facing the coronavirus pandemic of 2019-21. In this paper, we propose a face mask recognition model that captures in real time if a person is wearing a face mask or not and also maintains social distance norms especially at public places such as airports and schools and hospitals, marketplace, etc. Such application can be particularly useful for security purposes in checking if the disease transmission is being kept in check especially for children and the elderly. Real-time application of our model can be used in public places such as offices, markets, and airports etc. where properly wearing mask and maintaining social distancing is compulsory. This model can be further enhanced with any external source such as CCTV or IOT Renders Solution during this pandemic. For a future study, we can work on finding a pattern to detect or predict the time at which it gets crowded the most and the heat map can be plotted in a more accurate manner. By enhancing our proposed solution with body gesture analysis to understand if an individual is coughing and sneezing in public places while breaching facial mask and social distancing guidelines and based on outcome enforcement agencies can be alerted. The proposed use-case can be equipped with thermal camera-based screening to analyse body temperature of the peoples in public places that can add another helping hand to enforcement agencies to tackle the pandemic effectively.

REFERENCES

Advice for the public: Coronavirus disease (COVID-19). (n.d.). Available at: https://www.who.int/emergencies/diseases/novel-coronavirus-2019/advice-for-public

Almufti, S., Marqas, R., Nayef, Z., & Mohamed, T. (2021). Real Time Face-mask Detection with Arduino to Prevent COVID-19 Spreading. *Qubahan Academic Journal, 1*(2), 39–46. doi:10.48161/qaj.v1n2a47

An end-to-end open-source machine learning platform-TensorFlow. (n.d.). Available at: https://www.tensorflow.org/

Bartlett, S., Littlewort, G., Fasel, I., & Movellan, J. R. (2003). Real Time Face Detection and Facial Expression Recognition: Development and Applications to Human Computer Interation. *2003 Conference on Computer Vision and Pattern Recognition Workshop*, 53-53. 10.1109/CVPRW.2003.10057

Chavda, A., Dsouza, J., Badgujar, S., & Damani, A. (2021). Multi-Stage CNN Architecture for Face Mask Detection. *6th International Conference for Convergence in Technology(I2CT)*, 1-8. 10.1109/I2CT51068.2021.9418207

Choudhary, A. (n.d.). *Face Mask Detection using Raspberry Pi and OpenCV*. Available at: https://circuitdigest.com/microcontroller-projects/face-mask-detection-using-raspberry-pi-and-opencv.May13,2021

COCO-Common Objects in Context. (n.d.). Available at: https://cocodataset.org/#download

Convolutional Neural Networks. (n.d.). Available at: https://www.ibm.com/cloud/learn/convolutional-neural-networks

COVID-19: Physical distancing. (n.d.). Available at: https://www.who.int/westernpacific/emergencies/covid-19/information/physical-distancing

Darknet: Open-Source Neural Networks in C. (n.d.). Available at: https://pjreddie.com/darknet/

Ding, S., & Zhao, K. (2018). Research on Daily Objects Detection Based on Deep Neural Network. *Materials Science and Engineering, 322*(6).

Face Mask Detection. (n.d.). Available at: https://www.kaggle.com/andrewmvd/face-mask-detection

Gandam & Sidhu. (2016). Video processing & its applications. *International Research Journal of Engineering and Technology, 3*(8).

Gupta & Gill. (2020). Coronamask: A Face Mask Detector for Real-Time Data. *International Journal of Advanced Trends in Computer Science and Engineering, 9*(4).

Image Processing in Python: Algorithms, Tools, and Methods You Should Know. (n.d.). Available at: https://neptune.ai/blog/image-processing-in-python-algorithms-tools-and-methods-you-should-know

ImageNet Classification. (n.d.). Available at: https://pjreddie.com/darknet/imagent/

Joby, K. J., & Priyanga, K. K. (2021, June). Face Mask Detection System. *International Journal of Innovative Research in Science, Engineering and Technology, 10*(6).

Keras. (n.d.). Available at: https://keras.io/

Keras Optimizers. (n.d.). Available at: https://keras.io/api/optimizers/

Kumar, G. S., & Shetty, S. D. (2021). Application Development for Mask Detection and Social Distancing Violation Detection using Convolutional Neural Networks. *Proceedings of the 23rd International Conference on Enterprise Information Systems (ICEIS 2021)*, 1, 760-767. 10.5220/0010483107600767

Kumar, G. S., & Shetty, S. D. (2021). Application Development for Mask Detection and Social Distancing Violation Detection using Convolutional Neural Networks. *Proceedings of the 23rd International Conference on Enterprise Information Systems (ICEIS 2021)*, 1, 760-767. 10.5220/0010483107600767

Li & Zhang. (n.d.). *Object Detection and Its Implementation on Android Devices.* Department of Electrical Engineering, Stanford University.

Liu, W., Anguelov, D., Erhan, D., Szegedy, C., Reed, S., Fu, C.-Y., & Berg, A. C. (2016). SSD: Single Shot MultiBox Detector. *Lecture Notes in Computer Science*, *9905*, 21–37. doi:10.1007/978-3-319-46448-0_2

Mahamkali, N., & Ayyasamy, V. (2015). OpenCV for Computer Vision Applications. *Proceedings of National Conference on Big Data and Cloud Computing(NCBDC'15).*

Male and Female walking on street wearing face masks-An Asian couple wearing face masks walk down the street. (n.d.). Available at: https://www.videvo.net/video/male-and-female-walking-on-street-wearing-face-masks/464817/

Manasa, Vikas, & Subhadra. (2019). Drowsiness detection using Eye-Blink frequency and Yawn count for Driver Alert. *International Journal of Innovative Technology and Exploring Engineering, 9*(2).

NVIDIA. (n.d.). Available at: https://www.nvidia.com/en-in/

Oxford Street Dataset. (n.d.). Available at: https://www.youtube.com/watch?v=osaJ2oaOiV8

Padilla, R., Filho, C., & Costa, M. (2012). Evaluation of Haar Cascade Classifiers for Face Detection. *International Conference on Digital Image Processing.*

Pascal VOC 2007. (n.d.). Available at: https://www.kaggle.com/zaraks/pascal-voc-2007

Pascal VOC 2012. (n.d.). Available at: https://www.kaggle.com/huanghanchina/pascal-voc-2012

Raghuvir. (2020). *COVID-19: Emergence, Spread, Possible Treatments, and Global Burden* (Vol. 8). Frontiers in Public Health.

Rahim, A., Maqbool, A., & Rana, T. (2021, February 25). Monitoring social distancing under various low light conditions with deep learningand a single motionless time of flight camera. *PLoS One, 16*(2), e0247440. Advance online publication. doi:10.1371/journal.pone.0247440 PMID:33630951

Rezaei, M., & Azarmi, M. (2020). DeepSOCIAL: Social Distancing Monitoring and Infection Risk Assessment in COVID-19 Pandemic. *Applied Sciences (Basel, Switzerland), 10*(21), 7514. doi:10.3390/app10217514

Sandesh, Sridhar, Rishikesh, Farheen, & Tameem. (n.d.). Smart Door Lock/Unlock Using Raspberry Pi. *International Journal of Scientific Research in Computer Science, Engineering and Information Technology*, 543-548. doi:10.32628/CSEIT2063135

Scikit-learn, Machine Learning in Python. (n.d.). Available at: https://scikit-learn.org/stable/

Shete. (n.d.). *Social Distancing and Face Mask Detection using Deep Learning and Computer Vision* [MSc. diss.]. National College of Ireland, Dublin.

Smitha, Afshin, & Hegde. (2020). Face Recognition based Attendance Management System. *International Journal of Engineering Research & Technology (Ahmedabad)*, *9*(5). Advance online publication. doi:10.17577/IJERTV9IS050861

Softmax Activation Function with Python. (n.d.). Available at: https://machinelearningmastery.com/softmax-activation-function-with-python/

Soviany & Ionescu. (2018). *Optimizing the Trade-off between Single-Stage and Two-Stage Deep Object Detectors using Image Difficulty Prediction*. doi:10.1109/SYNASC.2018.00041,2018

Transfer Learning in Keras with Computer Vision Models. (n.d.). Available at: https://machinelearningmastery.com/how-to-use-transfer-learning-when-developing-convolutional-neural-network-models/

van der Walt, Colbert, & Varoquaux. (2011). The NumPy Array: A Structure for Efficient Numerical Computation. *Computing in Science & Engineering*, *13*, 22 - 30. . doi:10.1109/MCSE.2011.37,2011

Yang, H., Yuan, C., Xing, J., & Hu, W. (2017). SCNN: Sequential convolutional neural network for human action recognition in videos. *IEEE International Conference on Image Processing (ICIP)*, 355-359. 10.1109/ICIP.2017.8296302

YOLO: Real Time Object Detection. (n.d.). Available at: https://pjreddie.com/darknet/yolo/

Zhao, Z., Zheng, P., Xu, S., & Wu, X. (2019, November). Object Detection with Deep Learning: A Review. *IEEE Transactions on Neural Networks and Learning Systems*, *30*(11), 3212–3232. doi:10.1109/TNNLS.2018.2876865 PMID:30703038

Chapter 12
Generative Adversarial Networks the Future of Consumer Deep Learning?
A Comprehensive Study

N. Prabakaran

*School of Computer Science and Engineering,
Vellore Institute of Technology, Vellore, India*

Aditya Deepak Joshi

*School of Computer Science and Engineering,
Vellore Institute of Technology, Vellore, India*

Rajarshi Bhattacharyay

*School of Computer Science and Engineering,
Vellore Institute of Technology, Vellore, India*

R. Kannadasan

*School of Computer Science and Engineering,
Vellore Institute of Technology, Vellore, India*

A. S. Anakath

*Depatment of CSE, Saveetha School of
Engineering, Chennai, India*

ABSTRACT

In recent years, deep learning and its subtopics have found a near gold-rush stature in the industry. This booming response has not been restricted to niche applications, but rather to titanic domains such as healthcare, self-driving cars, cybersecurity, and more. This "rise" has consequently led to a large influx of practitioners and users to this domain. One such subdomain is generative adversarial networks (GANs), an application of deep learning centered on image segmentation. The researchers aim to study the trajectory of and attempt to extrapolate the future of this subdomain in an attempt to discern if the meteoric rise of this technique is based on concrete positive results or a trend deemed to ebb. This study aims to first gather the most salient aspects and recent advancements of GANs. Specifically, the study emphasizes the importance of GANs and presents differing types utilized in various domains. Finally, the researchers present the current research gaps and the difficulties that could potentially be faced in the attainment of the aforementioned trajectory of this field.

DOI: 10.4018/978-1-6684-8306-0.ch012

INTRODUCTION

In the last few years, Machine Learning (ML) has transformed the very way we look at data in more ways than one. It has widened the span of research by augmenting the predictions made from data in domains ranging from information retrieval to recommender systems, from predicting stock prices to predicting the outcome of the FIFA World Cup! (T. Phung, 2022; Sansone & Sperlí, 2022; Marappan & Bhaskaran, 2022; Soni et al., 2022). It has allowed us to get outcomes and decisions from scopes well beyond those of human competence, in fact allowing us to do so in the case of the stock market and the world cup through unsupervised means. Within the subgenre of ML, generative models hold an eminent spot partly due to their presence in the domain spanning multiple decades. Their primary role stems from situations where directly learning/ training for a goal is computationally inefficient (intractable) using discriminative models. For this exact purpose, as the name suggests a joint distribution is generated of the goal and the training dataset. Their importance is seen primarily in two domains, firstly, they help to better depict data and to model lifelike data through the use of Markov chains or Generative Iterative Processes (Harshvardhan et al., 2020). The second and more popular application of these is their ability to generate realistic samples in a wide array of topics, perhaps most eminently in transforming and translating images, for instance, converting The Starry Night as if it were drawn by Botticelli. Furthermore, upon training amply, they possess the ability to generate photorealistic realism in their representations of objects, and sceneries enough to stump even human experts. In this paper, the researchers will be providing an overview of Generative Adversarial Networks (GANs) from the multi-vantage-point of the background of GANs, the common architectures, the challenges, and the applications. One might be tempted to ask what differentiates this paper from the absolute crowd of papers on and around the topic of Generative Adversarial Networks. Several papers have been published around the review of architectures, predicting diseases in crops, medical imaging techniques, and object detection. However, these have centered around their singular topics as opposed to providing a complete, updated one-stop destination to all these facets. An extensive amount of time has been dedicated to reviewing and filtering a large number of papers. The final goal for what this paper is meant to be is a diving board, a marquee mile marker for beginners and advanced practitioners alike to dive into the topic of GANs. It will empower prospective researchers to take informed decisions while remaining cognizant of the consequences of the same.

BACKGROUND AND SURVEY

The researchers have embraced the literature review approach that aligned with previous studies such as (Alzubaidi et al., 2021). This also yielded us a chance to evaluate and understand the growth trend and the growing research interest into the field of GANs. Following this we experimented with various other keyword searches such as, 'GANs in healthcare', "Applications of GANs", "GANs Architectures", "GANs in the metaverse", Deepfake detection. In addition to these preliminary searches, we also performed a depth-first style search by manually reading the suggested articles of the articles previously shortlisted. The analysis was conducted encompassing the past 6 years (2018- 2023 inclusive). In all openness there were articles preceding these years all the way back to 2016, that being said we believe in creating a research paper that stands the test of time and computational advancements for as long as possible. Hence we decided to target the very bleeding edge of GANs. Before taking a deep dive into the field and popularity of GANs it is quintessential to understand the inner workings and functioning of the GAN itself. Being a generative modeling architecture GANs in their most prevalent form are a form of unsupervised learning, depending on the richness of the underlying data this could be a collection of video clips, textual documents, and even GIFs. That being said, there are streaks of supervised learning present in GANs as well, this is easily seen in the Discriminator where the decision-making regarding the distinction between a falsey image and the truthy image is a supervised learning problem. Furthermore, the generator then betters its understanding of this and generates adversarially better examples. To understand this adversarial generation better we take a look at the structure of a GANS in Figure 1.

Figure 1. A vanilla depiction of the generative adversarial network

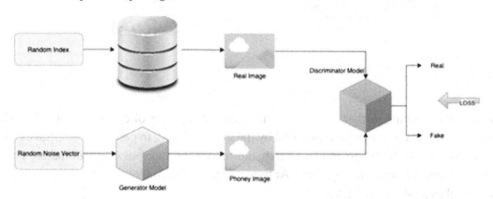

The primary parts of the GAN are split into two deep learning models, the Generator and the Discriminator. Let's understand this functioning with an elegant example, being fans of the movie CZ12, the researchers analogize the Generator to a ring of Art counterfeiters and the Discriminator to be the Interpol authorities hot on their tail to distinguish the phony art from the authentic. The Generator being untrained and inexperienced generates random art which to a high degree does not represent the art at all. For instance, the phony depiction of the self-portrait of Van Gogh in Figure 2 looks as if it were drawn by a toddler. This fake would fairly easily get detected by the Discriminator and in return would provide the necessary Loss value for the model in consideration.

Figure 2. A demonstrative example of early stage GANs

However, upon training further, we see the emergence of a series of chess matches. The Generator learns from its previous mistakes (as quantified by the loss function), to generate better fakes after every cycle of confrontations. In this to and fro, parry and repose the Interpol (Discriminator) get progressively more capable at discriminating fakes. At the same time, the counterfeiters (Generators) get better at generating fakes as shown in Figure 3.

Figure 3. A demonstrative example of a GANs after sufficient training

To clarify the 'Chess games' further, this scenario computationally is called a min-max game played by two players, as introduced in (Aggarwal A, 2021) and wonderfully explained in (Mao L, 2020).

$$K(Q,T) := F_{x \sim q_{data}(x)}\Big[\log T(x)\Big] + F_{z \sim p(z)}\Big[\log\big(1 - T(q(z))\big)\Big] \tag{1}$$

Equation 1 represents the loss function for the discriminator of the GANs represented by K. The first term calculates the average of the log of the discriminator's output for data sample x, sampled from the real data distribution $q_{data}(x)$. The average represents the extent of the discriminator's ability to classify a real image as real. The question then arises, how does the discriminator in fact differentiate fake and real images? The answer lies in the question, the discriminator in essence becomes a binary classifier, able to output probability values representing the chances that an image it receives is real. It does this by learning to capture underlying patterns and features present in the real data distribution in a manner so as to generalise these patterns to, in a sense characterise that entire category of images to then be able to pick out the existence or non-existence of these characteristics from even fake images.

The second term represents the ability of the discriminator to identify the phony content generated by the generator. It has the output of the discriminator (by applying parameters T) when identifying the generated output (represented by q) produced from synthetic data z sampled from a noise distribution $p(z)$. Essentially this objective function represents the discriminator's performance in identifying a real image as real, and a phony image as phony. The training of the discriminator is aimed at minimising this loss, we attempt to maximise the probability of the 'correct log' $F_{x \sim q_{data}(x)}\left[\log T(x) \right]$ while also maximising the probability of correctly classifying the fakes as fakes.

$$L_G := -F_{z \sim p(z)}\left[\log\left(1 - T\left(q(z)\right)\right) \right] \tag{2}$$

The training of the GANs also includes accounting for the generator's loss function represented by L_G in equation 2. The generator takes a random noise vector z from a noise distribution, as input and generates a synthetic sample $q(z)$. The generator consists of learnable parameters Q which are updated during the aforementioned training. Based on the nature of the input images the generator learns to map the data vector z to a high dimensionality generated object such as an image. The generator's loss hence is the negative of the discriminator's output as it accounts for probability of the discriminator incorrectly classifying the generated image as real.

$$\min_Q \max_T V\left(Q, T\right) \tag{3}$$

The training process then becomes an iterative competitive game as shown in equation 3. The adversarial aspects comes in where we train with an objective of maximising the parameters T(discriminator) and minimise the parameters Q(generator). This leads to the generator trying to better its ability to produce increasingly realistic images and the discriminator trying to become better at distinguishing fake and real images. This proceeds until we reach a point of equilibrium, the Nash Equilibrium. It is considered reached when an "It's anyone's guess" situation is reached, and the discriminator begins making random guesses when faced with generated data being so realistic that it is unable to tell the two apart. This is ideally how GANs are trained and how they function, though we must state in advance that in practicality reaching this point is highly intractable and challenging to achieve. This will further be explained when the researchers discuss the asymptotic convergence and the lack thereof in the challenges of GANs.

Types Of GANs

Post establishing the importance of the GAN paradigm, we can move on to discuss the various other popular variations of GANs, these range from being specialized for certain applications to being more accurate in certain scenarios. The motivation behind elaborating on these specific cases is to encourage the reader beyond the status quo while remaining grounded in terms of usefulness.

Conditional Generative Adversarial Networks (CGANs)

This divagation of GANs is considered by most to be an extension of the conventional GANs as shown in Figure 5, Interestingly enough it (Mirza, 2014) was also published in the year 2014. Secondly, a differentiating factor is a class/modal label this model accommodates from its users. The added data denoted by y plays two roles. Firstly it can act as a filter thereby generating samples of that entered label while at the same time, it acts as an added source of information improving the overall quality of the samples generated. To drive this point home we found two absolutely elegant implementations of CGANs in applications as depicted in Figure 4 (D. Wu et al., 2021; Bird et al., 2022) . The first (D. Wu et al., 2021), deals with the fine-grained recolouring of ethnic clothing. A topic in and of itself a highly essential one dealing with the recolouring and image processing, furthermore the researchers provided the semantics/labelling of the constituent clothing sections in terms of the components they represent for instance, sleeves, belts, pants, accessories, etc. Because of this and other optimizations, they received a performance of 91.4% while other comparable automated colouring methods received a max of 91.3%. Secondly, the attractiveness to the human eye yielded to these native Chinese dresses is truly phenomenal.

Figure 4. Architectural diagram of a conditional GAN (CGAN)

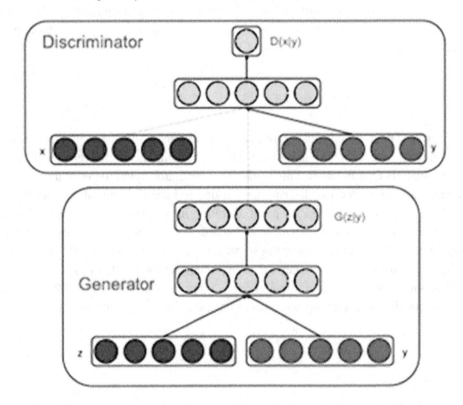

Figure 5. Architectural diagram of a deep convolutional GAN (DCGAN)

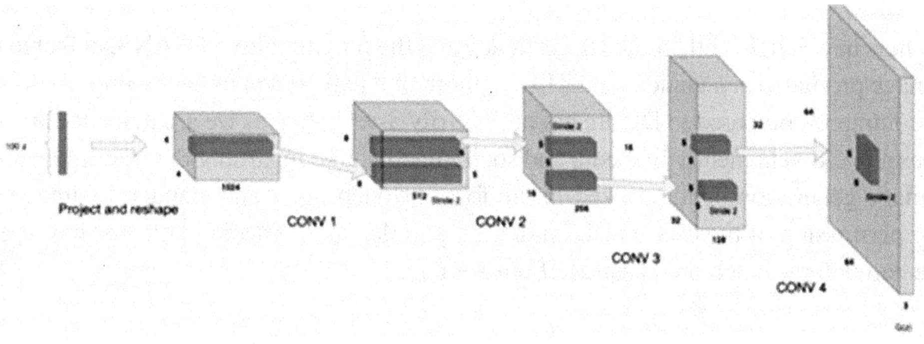

The researchers in the paper (Bird et al., 2022) provide additional class label data in the form of a binary column, they classify whether the fruit is healthy or unhealthy. This data on inherent healthiness or lack thereof allowed them to generate images of lemons riddled with diseases like gangrene and mold while also generating ones without them as well. These researchers possess a recognition accuracy of 88.75%

Deep Convolutional Generative Adversarial Networks DCGANs

A year after the momentous release of the original GANs in 2014, in the year 2015 DCGANs were introduced. Its primary modification over the vanilla GANs was the proposal to remove the dense layers present in fully connected GANs and swap them out for the Convolutional layers, hence the name.

This in essence due to the inherent benefits that Convolutional layers yield to image processing and filtering in addition to matrix-like operations allowing DCGANs to function extremely well in both image translations and Data modeling alike. Upon surveying the recent examples of the DCGANs being used we found; For the purpose of determining disease and quality of yield in agriculture (Q. Wu et al., 2020; Ni et al., 2022).

Challenges of GANs

All of this being said, the reader might be encouraged to assume the GAN to be a one size fits all silver bullet, but that not being the case, the architecture does indeed possess limitations. Not only that but as highlighted by Dwivedi et al. (2022) for the field of the Metaverse, being an evolving and emerging field warrants the multifaceted research of the domain and its challenges for greater adoption. A study of such fashion by contributors and researchers of this domain forms a substantial research endeavour. Furthermore, Börner et al. (2018) emphasise on the varying forecasts for any particular technological domain depending on stakeholder nature of the forecaster. By the very nature of the researchers of this study being from academia makes 'Understanding Science', also called the 'science of science' as the motivation behind forecasting the future of technologies. Therefore by understanding and potentially root cause analysing these challenges could lead to widespread adoption of GANs as the face of consumer deep learning. These challenges are elaborated in the subsections below.

The Reality Paradox

The researchers have sufficiently touted the efficacy and the functionality of GANS, in fact in more cases than one image produced at a glance seems like a photo of a real person or happening. As highlighted in Figure 6 we humans compared to DL are not necessarily as effective as we are made to think. Concerns have been expressed vehemently in media and social media alike regarding the fraudulent and spurious usage of image generation being utilized in the form of deep fakes and slanderous images generated without the permission of the user. Furthermore, on popular social media platforms have been utilized to replicate and defame celebrated figures of our society.

Figure 6. Performance of humans against popular deep learning frameworks

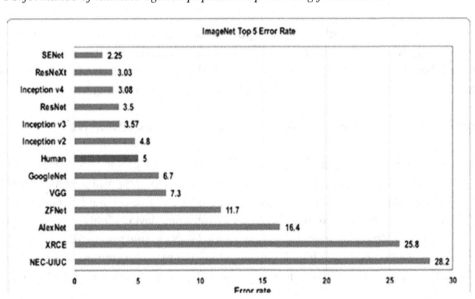

The question, therefore, arises how does one combat something that is essentially doing its job too well, how does one penalize the model for generating data that is too real? Simply put one does not, one penalizes the creator of the GAN. As things stand, as stated in (Dauer, 2022)the premise and the ease of generating deep fakes are not as prevalent as they should be, law enforcement agencies and people alike are simply not aware of these technological advancements. That being said, as of 2020 defence advanced research projects agency (DARPA) reportedly possesses software that cracks down on these bogus accounts, we are optimistic in assuming their progress in the subsequent three years and the years to come. Secondly, law enforcement agencies in the states of Texas, Virginia, and California in the United States do have specific laws targeting certain crimes that could be committed through the manhandling of elections, pornography, and both respectively. As with all things, however, the solutions to most problems do exist in the problems themselves. The researchers of the paper (Mallet, 2022) use various features such as Spectral, Temporal, Geometric, and Visual to then separately identify areas of interest in the subject data in question. They received accuracies of 99.95% however as researchers of (Passos, 2022) rightly state the end of this cat-and-mouse game between the increasingly powerful deep fake generators and the evaluating mechanisms is a non-deterministic one. The culmination of this conflict is yet to be seen. However, the solution lies in more concrete mechanisms to semi-supervised perform the task thereby successfully evolving abreast with the deep fake technology while also not having a shoot-in-the-dark approach as with unsupervised learning. Our predictions of possible solutions are the targeted effort in making the technologies and tools for deep fake detection far more accessible, in fact we believe they should be in the hands of the public and law enforcement so as to provide a distributed verifying mechanism for deep fakes.

The Non-Convergence Problem

As discussed in the previous sections, in practical situations it is nearly impossible for there to be a guaranteed solution for the generator's generated data to be guaranteed in a way that all subsequent images not be detected (equilibrium).

Vanishing Gradient Problem There are two main means by which the generator may reach a threshold and plateau in their improvement, the first and slightly more likely occurrence is such that though the most optimal solution exists, the other parameters and conditions disallow the gradient descent training to proceed further.

The second unlikelier but equally damaging scenario is a modification of the first, in the sense that the slope along which the model is to be trained gets limited and squeezed down to a single point. It becomes immediately apparent that except for that single point, there is nothing to be learned from this gradient, hence the name Vanishing Gradient Problem (Barnett, 2018).

Now we explain why we named this issue unlikely, the reason is simply because, to get backed into this corner one must make a suite of consecutive mistakes to do so. Firstly, the repeated training of the discriminator i.e. its overtraining causes the probability of rejecting to move farther away from the Nash Equilibrium value of 50% that we desire to a far "surer" value closer to 100% probability of rejecting the phony data.

Before we enter into the technicalities of the Mode Collapse problem, we encourage the reader to put on their thinking caps. As we all know diversity is the keyword and sometimes the root of all problems in all biological situations where deep learning is meant to be employed. What this means is that predictive modelling as the name suggests involves predictions made on the basis of probability, this becomes a logical fallacy in our case as in certain critical scenarios one must not ignore even the smallest of possible events however unlikely. Take for instance the human population of the earth, of these 8 billion people only about 9-10% make up left-handed people (Searing L, 2019; Jarry, 2021). In fact, (Searing L, 2019) even goes on to state that this number used to be 2-4% in the late 19th and early 20th centuries. Another study (Frothingham, 2019) states the following increased likelihoods of left-handed individuals.

- Left-handed women are more likely to develop breast cancer than right- handed women
- Left-handed people are more likely to develop psychotic disorders like
  - schizophrenia
  - bipolar disorder
  - Post-Traumatic Stress Disorder (PTSD)
- Left-handed people tended to drink more alcohol.
- Tend to have learning disabilities such as dyslexia and overall a lack of skill at work

Keeping all of these things in mind, probabilistically speaking this is a disastrous situation to be in considering all the various domains the handedness of a person affects. Therefore the generator could potentially catastrophically fail and repeatedly give a sense of false readings due to the larger number of entries on one end of the spectrum (Mode).

Both the above problems are variants of overfitting, both models Generator and Discriminator have the potential to be overtrained without the adversary being updated. This imbalance can cause a lack of convergence. During the training cycles, the Discriminator has only updated on the basis of the inputs it gets from the Generator, i.e. its behaviour is reactive in a sense. Hence it is far less likely to be overfitted perchance and by accident. In all practical senses, our understanding of the occurrence of this issue is fairly limited and we can owe this to the fact that we do not possess the faculties to process that data beforehand and detect the skewness and the mode. It is due to this that solutions for collapses are fairly trial and error, empirical based. One must find the best of a bad situation and minimize the likelihood of collapse, while also accepting the fact that a partial collapse is commonplace. On the other hand when performing image translations or style transfers from one image style to another we in fact prefer the deterministic and overfitted nature of the outputs to the more random output.

Lastly, when discussing the vanishing gradient problem we must discuss the pointers to be kept in mind while training the discriminator. The authors of (Aggarwal et al., 2021) suggest that we must aim to sidestep the overtraining of the discriminator and must seek to interleave the updates between the two on a blow-by-blow, one-by-one basis.

Applications of GANs

To establish the validity of studying the current applications of GANs, one must establish the need for analysing the applications of any domain. Firstly analysing applications gives us a tangible proof of a domain's practical relevance. It veritably establishes the need for that domain while also providing a performance evaluation of said technological domain out in the real world. By examining how GANs are currently being used the researchers can analyse the performance factors of the technology in said application while also studying the current boundaries and limitations of the same. Finally, studying current applications also holds the potential to uncover untapped and previously unknown facets to existing applications. This explorative form of analysis has led and can lead to the discovery of new and unconventional forms of deploying said technology, extending the aforementioned boundaries to new limits. Bringing the focus back to GANs, as we are well aware at this point, the creation and training of supervised DL models demand enormous quantities of data, not to mention the unforeseen time, effort, and monetary investments to assimilate them. In fact, after pouring it in, it is a very real possibility that publicly available data may not exist, if it does in fact. GANs find a very real application in this scenario to fill in these gaps with generated data.

GANs as a Service (GaaS)

This subsection of the research paper constitutes a blanket term for the applications created using GANs are created by an entity for another entity entirely, thereby creating a GANs model and then offering it as a service. As we are aware at this not everyone has the interest, time or mental faculties to learn an entirely new skill to reap the benefits it offers, the best example of this being cloud service providers such as Azure and Amazon Web Services(AWS) being leased to us for the reason that we ourselves might not be able to maintain the elevated computation resources and could much rather offload this responsibility in exchange for a price tag.

We see a similar trend in terms of fashion in the case of Amazon, the e-commerce giant. As we observe in (Wiggers, 2020), Amazon as a company does not have the incentive to participate in the creation process of the GAN-based functionality their primary function is to sell as many products as they possibly can while also offering their customers new and exciting experiences. In this scenario, one must take a look at the revolutionary paper (Choi et al., 2021)and its updated counterpart (Lee et al., 2022) are functionalities that Amazon could then fine-tune to inculcate into their virtual wardrobe offerings. Furthermore, it allows for a research direction to thrive that does not initially have a commercial side-benefit and then provides the required boost for it to be so.

Let's discuss a bit about shoes while in the domain of fashion, to a certain extent it would be fair to state that a threshold, a saturation point has been reached in terms of novel designs. A solution, as suggested in (Lee S, 2022) though old holds immense sway in the way that industry is going. One does not have to look too far to find examples such as thissneakerdoesnotexist.com, created by Stan Van Der Vossen, an ML engineer at Stavos using StyleGANS2 to generate random and new creations of sneakers that do not exist in the real world. Furthermore, it provides a 3d rendering of the shoe in question using a conditional diffusion model, a hat tip to the above paragraph. This application is so successful in fact there turned out to be a successful business venture built on the demonstration of products using AI called commerce.ai. Lastly one of if not the most famous examples are the shoe brand New Balance employing the generative models of the company Runwayml. This company also provides low-code to no-code solutions for creating GANs as a service, simply provide the details and you have a code ready.

Last but not least we have Imaginaire by NVIDIA, in their words, it is a PyTorch-based GAN module. Its job is to integrate optimal versions of some or all image and video generation modules covered under NVIDIA's software license into one. One such example is pix2pixHD (T. Wang et al., 2018; Maithani, 2021) a High Resolution (HighRes) Image Synthesis tool that allows semantic manipulation using CGANs. It also provides pre-trained models for a multitude of purposes.

GANs Used to Support Computer Vision Applications

In the studies conducted in (Dziugaite et al., 2015), the authors introduce a revolutionary Posture Guided Person Generation Network (PG2) that can create person images in any stance based on a person's image and a creative pose. Position integration and picture refining are the two main phases that made their generation framework, PG2, which expressly makes use of pose information. The condition image and the target pose were fed into a network resembling a U-Net in the first stage to create an initial but crude image of the subject in the target pose. The second stage then clarified the initial, hazy outcome by adversarially training a U-Net-like generator.

In the field of Generating videos with scene dynamics, the authors of (Ma et al., 2017) made use of a significant amount of unlabelled video for the purpose of learning and creating a model of scene dynamics for both video recognition tasks (such as action categorization) and video production tasks for futuristic applications(e.g. future prediction). Their research and efforts offer a spatiotemporal convolutional architecture for a generative adversarial network for a video that separates the foreground and background of the scene. We demonstrate this model's effectiveness in forecasting likely futures of static images, and experiments to date indicate that it can make mini films up to a second at full frame rate better than basic baselines. Additionally, tests and visualizations demonstrate that the model internally picks up helpful details for identifying actions with little guidance, indicating that scene dynamics are a suitable signal for representation learning.

The authors of (Vondrick et al., 2016) proposed a method for multi-scale neural patch synthesis that matches and adapts patches with the most similar mid-layer feature correlations of a deep classification network, preserving contextual structures while also providing high-frequency details. The in-painted areas would appear hazy and ugly boundaries would show up even on slightly bigger photographs. This approach is based on jointly optimizing the limitations on the image content and texture. Results were reached with state-of-the-art inpainting accuracy and were evaluated using the ImageNet and Paris Streetview datasets.

The authors of the paper (Yang et al., 2017)) presented some novel techniques for generative adversarial networks (GANs) for probabilistic image synthesis training. They built a GANs variation that uses label conditioning to produce global coherent picture samples with a resolution of 128 x 128. They built on earlier research for evaluating the quality of images by offering two novel techniques for evaluating the diversity and discriminability of samples from class-conditional image synthesis models. According to these analyses, they also concluded that high-resolution samples offer class information that low-resolution alternatives do not.

The researchers (Odena et al., 2017) posited a method that leads to the creation of an independent sample using a single feed-forward pass through a multilayer perceptron. To train a generative adversarial network, a challenging mini-max program must be carefully optimized to prevent hazards of any kind. Instead, they decided to employ the maximum mean discrepancy (MMD) method from statistical hypothesis testing, which yielded a straightforward aim that can be translated as matching all orders of statistics between a dataset and samples from the model and can be trained via back-propagation. By merging their generative network with an auto-encoder network and learning to create codes using MMD that can then be decoded to produce samples, they further improved the performance of this method by a significant amount.

It is well established that realistic picture modification is an arduous task since it calls for changing the image's appearance in a way that the user can manage while maintaining the result's reality. Without significant artistic talent, during editing, it is simple to "slip off" the variety of natural images. In this paper, the authors suggested utilizing a generative adversarial neural network to learn the natural picture manifold directly from the dataset, define a class of image editing operations, and constrain their output to always lie on the learned manifold. The model they deployed automatically modifies the output, maintaining the highest level of realism in all modifications. All modifications were applied in close to real-time and were represented in terms of limited optimization.

A generative model of people in clothing The first image-based full-body generative model of people wearing garments is presented in a recent study elucidated in (Zhu et al., 2016). Researchers avoid the necessity for high-quality 3D scans of dressed persons as well as the frequently employed complicated graphics rendering pipeline. Instead, they use a big image database to learn generative models. Dealing with the wide range of human position, shapes, and look is the key challenge. Purely image-based methods have not yet been taken into consideration because of this (Prabakaran.N, et al., 2022; Prabakaran.N., & Kannan.RJ, 2017). They demonstrate how this difficulty can be solved by dividing the generating process into two steps. They first acquire the ability to produce a meaningful segmentation of the body and clothing. Secondly, On the generated segments, we learn a conditional model that yields realistic visuals. The entire model can be differentiated based on position, shape, or colour. As a result, the suggested model can create whole new individuals wearing real-world attire thereby providing examples of people wearing diverse varieties of attire.

Metaverse Applications of GANs

The Metaverse is akin to an immersive world where users can communicate with one another, go to a concert, and do other things thanks to AR and VR technology. The authors (Prabakaran.N, et al., 2021; Kannadasan.R., et al, 2018) seek to make this goal more realistic by building things based on actual beings with which these models (people) can interact. According to the authors, in this VR world, we may make our models and react to such various models. Thus, a fully connected neural network with an autoencoder is an intriguing version. It has three components: an encoder, a bottleneck, and a decoder. The bottleneck only has three neurons, therefore the encoder compresses the input before storing the spatial data there. As a result, the bottleneck stores the spatial data in a smaller dimension. The original image is created once this data is subsequently fed into the decoder, which is once more a completely linked layer. The bottleneck is compelled to acquire crucial knowledge in order to reduce the data's dimensions so that the original image may be created with the same data. Similar to GAN, the autoencoder offers a wide range of modifications depending on the fully connected layer, which is occasionally substituted with pooling layers. The loss function can then vary depending on the Autoencoder variant.

The GANverse 3D model, proposed in created by NVIDIA's AI Research, transforms 2D photos into animated 3D counterparts using deep learning. The technology, which was first described in a research article presented at ICLR and CVPR last year, performs simulations more quickly and for less money. To automatically create various views from a single image, the model used StyleGANs. To accurately render 3D objects in the virtual environment, the application can be imported as an extension in the NVIDIA Omniverse.

The success of a platform is heavily influenced by its content, and the Metaverse is no different. Who would want to hang out in a barren virtual world? Recent models like Google Imagen or Open AI DALL-E 2 demonstrated outstanding picture-generating results, indicating that AI will soon be able to produce 3D assets. But to train, these models require enormous amounts of data and processing power. Diffusion-based models and Generative Adversarial Networks (GAN) demonstrated remarkable performance on this test. For instance, StyleGAN NADA, the most recent StyleGAN model, can produce highly realistic human faces and change the domain of the images it produces without collecting further information. Lately, DALL-E 2 from OpenAI and Google Imagen has achieved astounding success in the deep learning and metaverse community by showcasing their image editing capabilities, and their models which are primarily based on Diffusion.

CONCLUSION

The researchers have established that GANs as they are, are a strong component of not just DL but ML as a whole. That being said, this comprehensive study has also yielded that GANs do not come without their shortcomings. They are of prime importance in providing data where it truly does not exist (generatively). In this paper, we went over multiple applications of, disadvantages of, and popular alternatives of GANs. As researchers in 2023, we do not have to predict that cloud-based computing websites and as-a-service platforms will have a strong role to play. They are already commercially viable at the time of writing and will only go up henceforth. Utilizing these platforms will yield never-before-like flexibility in processing big data by reducing costs and increasing efficiency in the training of here and mentioned DL models. Lastly, this paper delivers an opening statement for future engineers, scientists, and users of DL. It should be taken as kick-off point to then start one's own research journey into the field of GANs.

ACKNOWLEDGMENT

This research received no specific grant from any funding agency in the public, commercial, or not-for profit sectors.

REFERENCES

Aggarwal, A., Mittal, M., & Battineni, G. (2021, April). Generative adversarial network: An overview of theory and applications. *International Journal of Information Management Data Insights*, *1*(1), 100004. doi:10.1016/j.jjimei.2020.100004

Alzubaidi, L., Zhang, J., Humaidi, A. J., Al-Dujaili, A., Duan, Y., Al-Shamma, O., Santamaría, J., Fadhel, M. A., Al-Amidie, M., & Farhan, L. (2021, March 31). Review of deep learning: Concepts, CNN architectures, challenges, applications, future directions. *Journal of Big Data*, *8*(1), 53. Advance online publication. doi:10.118640537-021-00444-8 PMID:33816053

BarnettS. A. (2018, June 29). *Convergence Problems with Generative Adversarial Networks (GANs)*. https://arxiv.org/abs/1806.11382v1

Bird, J. J., Barnes, C. M., Manso, L. J., Ekárt, A., & Faria, D. R. (2022, February). Fruit quality and defect image classification with conditional GAN data augmentation. *Scientia Horticulturae*, *293*, 110684. doi:10.1016/j.scienta.2021.110684

Börner, K., Rouse, W. B., Trunfio, P., & Stanley, H. E. (2018, December 10). Forecasting innovations in science, technology, and education. *Proceedings of the National Academy of Sciences of the United States of America*, *115*(50), 12573–12581. doi:10.1073/pnas.1818750115 PMID:30530683

Cheng, J., Yang, Y., Tang, X., Xiong, N., Zhang, Y., & Lei, F. (2020, December 31). Generative Adversarial Networks: A Literature Review. *KSII Transactions on Internet and Information Systems*, *14*(12), 4625–4647. doi:10.3837/tiis.2020.12.001

Choi, S., Park, S., Lee, M., & Choo, J. (2021, June). VITON-HD: High-Resolution Virtual Try-On via Misalignment-Aware Normalization. *2021 IEEE/CVF Conference on Computer Vision and Pattern Recognition (CVPR)*. 10.1109/CVPR46437.2021.01391

Dauer, F. (2022, June 29). Law Enforcement in the Era of Deepfakes. *Police Chief Magazine*. https://www.policechiefmagazine.org/law-enforcement-era-deepfakes/?ref=cdc285c5f3355599c05402cb647b0694

Deverall, J., Lee, J., & Ayala, M. (2017). Using Generative Adversarial Networks to Design Shoes: The Preliminary steps. *CS231n in Stanford*. http://cs231n.stanford.edu/reports/2017/pdfs/119.pdf

Dwivedi, Y. K., Hughes, L., Baabdullah, A. M., Ribeiro-Navarrete, S., Giannakis, M., Al-Debei, M. M., Dennehy, D., Metri, B., Buhalis, D., Cheung, C. M., Conboy, K., Doyle, R., Dubey, R., Dutot, V., Felix, R., Goyal, D., Gustafsson, A., Hinsch, C., Jebabli, I., ... Wamba, S. F. (2022, October). Metaverse beyond the hype: Multidisciplinary perspectives on emerging challenges, opportunities, and agenda for research, practice and policy. *International Journal of Information Management, 66*, 102542. doi:10.1016/j.ijinfomgt.2022.102542

Dziugaite, G. K., Roy, D. M., & Ghahramani, Z. (2015, May 14). *Training generative neural networks via Maximum Mean Discrepancy optimization.* arXiv.org. https://arxiv.org/abs/1505.03906v1

Frothingham, S. (2019, April 30). *Are Left Handers Less Healthy Than Right Handers?* Healthline. https://www.healthline.com/health/left-handers-and-health-risk

Gil, G. (2020, May 14). *AI to design new products using Deep Product Learning.* https://www.commerce.ai/blog/ai-to-design-new-products-using-deep-product-learning

Gm, H., Gourisaria, M. K., Pandey, M., & Rautaray, S. S.GM. (2020, November). A comprehensive survey and analysis of generative models in machine learning. *Computer Science Review, 38*, 100285. doi:10.1016/j.cosrev.2020.100285

Hockaday & Bühler. (2019, July 18). *GANs. Comparing machine learning techniques.* Avira Blog. Retrieved January 11, 2023, from https://www.avira.com/en/blog/gans-comparative-with-machine-learning

Ioffe, S., & Szegedy, C. (2015, June 1). *Batch Normalization: Accelerating Deep Network Training by Reducing Internal Covariate Shift.* PMLR. https://proceedings.mlr.press/v37/ioffe15.html

Jarry, J. (2021, September 17). *Are You Left-Handed? Science Still Yearns to Know Why.* Office for Science and Society. https://www.mcgill.ca/oss/article/health-general-science/are-you-left-handed-science-still-yearns-know-why

Kahng, M., Thorat, N., Chau, D. H. P., Viegas, F. B., & Wattenberg, M. (2019, January). GAN Lab: Understanding Complex Deep Generative Models using Interactive Visual Experimentation. *IEEE Transactions on Visualization and Computer Graphics, 25*(1), 310–320. doi:10.1109/TVCG.2018.2864500 PMID:30130198

Kannadasan, R., Prabakaran, N., Boominathan, P., Krishnamoorthy, A., Naresh, K., & Sivashanmugam, G. (2018). High Performance Parallel Computing with Cloud Technologies. *Procedia Computer Science, 132*, 518–524. doi:10.1016/j.procs.2018.05.004

Lassner, C., Pons-Moll, G., & Gehler, P. V. (2017, October). A Generative Model of People in Clothing. *2017 IEEE International Conference on Computer Vision (ICCV).* 10.1109/ICCV.2017.98

Lee, S., Gu, G., Park, S., Choi, S., & Choo, J. (2022, October 24). *High-Resolution Virtual Try-On with Misalignment and Occlusion-Handled Conditions.* doi:10.1007/978-3-031-19790-1_13

Li, Y., Swersky, K., & Zemel, R. (2015, June 1). *Generative Moment Matching Networks.* PMLR. https://proceedings.mlr.press/v37/li15.html

Ma, L., Jia, X., Sun, Q., Schiele, B., Tuytelaars, T., & Van Gool, L. (2017). Pose Guided Person Image Generation. In *Neural Information Processing Systems* (Vol. 30, pp. 406-416). https://papers.nips.cc/paper/2017/file/34ed066df378efacc9b924ec161e7639-Paper.pdf

Maithani, M. (2021, January 6). Hands-On Guide To Nvidia Imaginaire: Image & Video translation GAN Library. *Analytics India Magazine*. https://analyticsindiamag.com/guide-to-nvidia-imaginaire-gan-library-in-python/

MalletJ.DaveR.SeliyaN.VanamalaM. (2022, July 27). *Using Deep Learning to Detecting Deepfakes*. doi:10.1109/ISCMI56532.2022.10068449

Mao. (2020, July 10). *Minimax Game for Training Generative Adversarial Networks*. Lei Mao's Log Book. Retrieved January 13, 2023, from https://leimao.github.io/blog/Generative-Adversarial-Networks-Minmax-Game/

Marappan, R., & Bhaskaran, S. (2022, May 6). Movie Recommendation System Modeling Using Machine Learning. *Trends Journal of Sciences Research*, *1*(1), 12–16. doi:10.31586/ijmebac.2022.291

McCandless Farmer, B. (2022, July 31). The impact of deepfakes: How do you know when a video is real? *CBS News*. https://www.cbsnews.com/news/deepfakes-real-fake-videos-60-minutes-2022-07-31/

MirzaM.OsinderoS. (2014, November 6). *Conditional Generative Adversarial Nets*. https://arxiv.org/abs/1411.1784v1

Model Training | Runway. (n.d.). https://runwayml.com/training/

Ni, J., Liu, B., Li, J., Gao, J., Yang, H., & Han, Z. (2022, January 22). Detection of Carrot Quality Using DCGAN and Deep Network with Squeeze-and-Excitation. *Food Analytical Methods*, *15*(5), 1432–1444. doi:10.100712161-021-02189-9

Odena, A., Olah, C., & Shlens, J. (2017, July 17). *Conditional Image Synthesis with Auxiliary Classifier GANs*. PMLR. https://proceedings.mlr.press/v70/odena17a.html

Passos, L. A., Jodas, D., & da Costa, P. (2022, February 12). *A Review of Deep Learning-based Approaches for Deepfake Content Detection*. https://arxiv.org/abs/2202.06095v1

Phukan, S., Singh, J., Gogoi, R., Dhar, S., & Jana, N. D. (2022). COVID-19 Chest X-ray Image Generation Using ResNet-DCGAN Model. *Lecture Notes in Networks and Systems*, 227–234. doi:10.1007/978-981-19-0825-5_24

Prabakaran, N., & Kannan, R. J. (2016, September 14). Sustainable life-span of WSN nodes using participatory devices in pervasive environment. *Microsystem Technologies*, *23*(3), 651–657. doi:10.100700542-016-3117-7

Prabakaran, N., Palaniappan, R., Kannadasan, R., Dudi, S. V., & Sasidhar, V. (2021, August 24). Forecasting the momentum using customised loss function for financial series. *International Journal of Intelligent Computing and Cybernetics*, *14*(4), 702–713. doi:10.1108/IJICC-05-2021-0098

Prabakaran, N., Sai Kumar, S. S., Kiran, P. K., & Supriya, P. (2022, January 22). A Deep Learning Based Social Distance Analyzer with Person Detection and Tracking Using Region Based Convolutional Neural Networks for Novel Coronavirus. *Journal of Mobile Multimedia*. doi:10.13052/jmm1550-4646.1834

Radford, A., Metz, L., & Chintala, S. (2016). *Unsupervised Representation Learning with Deep Convolutional Generative Adversarial Networks*. Cornell University. https://arxiv.org/pdf/1511.06434

Sansone, C., & Sperlí, G. (2022, May). Legal Information Retrieval systems: State-of-the-art and open issues. *Information Systems*, *106*, 101967. doi:10.1016/j.is.2021.101967

Searing, L. (2019, August 12). The Big Number: Lefties make up about 10 percent of the world. *Washington Post*. https://www.washingtonpost.com/health/the-big-number-lefties-make-up-about-10-percent-of-the-world/2019/08/09/69978100-b9e2-11e9-bad6-609f75bfd97f_story.html

Soni, P., Tewari, Y., & Krishnan, D. (2022, January 1). Machine Learning Approaches in Stock Price Prediction: A Systematic Review. *Journal of Physics: Conference Series*, *2161*(1), 012065. doi:10.1088/1742-6596/2161/1/012065

Thien Phung. (2022, October 27). *Predicting FIFA World Cup 2022™ using Machine Learning*. TGM Research. Retrieved January 27, 2023, from https://tgmresearch.com/predicting-fifa-world-cup-2022.html

This Sneaker Does Not Exist! (2021). https://thissneakerdoesnotexist.com/

VondrickC.PirsiavashH.TorralbaA. (2016, January 1). *Generating Videos with Scene Dynamics*. doi:10.13016/m26gih-tnyz

Wang, T. C., Liu, M. Y., Zhu, J. Y., Tao, A., Kautz, J., & Catanzaro, B. (2018, June). High-Resolution Image Synthesis and Semantic Manipulation with Conditional GANs. *2018 IEEE/CVF Conference on Computer Vision and Pattern Recognition*. 10.1109/CVPR.2018.00917

Wang, Z., Wang, C., Cheng, L., & Li, G. (2022, November). An approach for day-ahead interval forecasting of photovoltaic power: A novel DCGAN and LSTM based quantile regression modeling method. *Energy Reports*, *8*, 14020–14033. doi:10.1016/j.egyr.2022.10.309

Wiggers, K. (2020, June 5). *Amazon's new AI technique lets users virtually try on outfits*. VentureBeat. https://venturebeat.com/ai/amazons-new-ai-technique-lets-users-virtually-try-on-outfits/

Wu, D., Gan, J., Zhou, J., Wang, J., & Gao, W. (2021, November 12). Fine-grained semantic ethnic costume high-resolution image colorization with conditional GAN. *International Journal of Intelligent Systems*, *37*(5), 2952–2968. doi:10.1002/int.22726

Wu, Q., Chen, Y., & Meng, J. (2020). DCGAN-Based Data Augmentation for Tomato Leaf Disease Identification. *IEEE Access : Practical Innovations, Open Solutions*, *8*, 98716–98728. doi:10.1109/ACCESS.2020.2997001

Xiao, Z., Lu, J., Wang, X., Li, N., Wang, Y., & Zhao, N. (2022, December 3). WCE-DCGAN: A data augmentation method based on wireless capsule endoscopy images for gastrointestinal disease detection. *IET Image Processing*, *17*(4), 1170–1180. doi:10.1049/ipr2.12704

Yang, C., Lu, X., Lin, Z., Shechtman, E., Wang, O., & Li, H. (2017). *High-Resolution Image Inpainting Using Multi-scale Neural Patch Synthesis*. doi:10.1109/CVPR.2017.434

Zhu, J. Y., Krähenbühl, P., Shechtman, E., & Efros, A. A. (2016). Generative Visual Manipulation on the Natural Image Manifold. *Computer Vision – ECCV 2016*, 597–613. doi:10.1007/978-3-319-46454-1_36

Chapter 13
Investigations on the Swiftness of a Quantum and a Classical Processor

Sumathi Rajyam
SASTRA University, India

N. R. Raajan
SASTRA University, India

G. Samyuktha
SASTRA University, India

V. Priyadharshini
SASTRA University, India

M. Sindhujaa
SASTRA University, India

ABSTRACT

The cutting-edge technologies cloud computing and IoT are taking an upper hand in every domain. A huge and wide variety of data is being handled and processed by clouds. The cloud federation technique further adds up to this. In the coming years, quantum computers will replace the conventional computers. Pulling out particular data from the gigantic data set processed by clouds in a conventional computer would take a considerable amount of time. In the chapter, Grover's algorithm, a search algorithm, is implemented on traditional computers on IBM quantum simulator and also on QUIRK quantum simulator. Three qubit data is considered in the proposed scheme. The objective of this chapter is to compare the execution time taken to run the Grover's algorithm on IBM and Quirk quantum simulators and on classical computers. The work carried out proves that quantum computer execution speed is high compared to the classical counterpart. This could be effectively used in the future in searching for specific data from a mammoth data set using quantum simulators.

DOI: 10.4018/978-1-6684-8306-0.ch013

INTRODUCTION

The widely used recent technologies include Cloud Computing (Naved et al., 2022)(Gupta et al., 2022), Internet of Things (Dhingra et al., 2021), Quantum Computing (Seegerer et al., 2021),..etc. The scalability, automation, speed and cost efficient features of them have enabled many organizations, corporate's, government sectors and companies to implement them in handling the data, processing the data, maintaining their databases and in achieving their intended goals. The Clouds (Kannadasan et al., 2018)used by organizations and corporate's these days, generally are dumped with huge and a wide variety of data.

The most significant usage of any database is information storage and recovery. With the Cloud's handling huge amount of data (Li et al., 2022), locating a particular item in a given database is generally time consuming. The faster the required data is determined, further processing of the same is carried out without any delay.

The work carried out confirms that the quantum processor finds out the required item very much faster than the conventional processors in searching a particular item from the given database. Grover's algorithm is executed on a quantum processor and also on a traditional processor. The processing time taken to perform the execution in both the processors are also recorded and compared.

Any classical computer generally takes (N/2) iterations to locate a specific data or at the worse would require (N-1) iterations for a given data base. Identifying an item $O(N)$ with N being the size of the database can be executed using brute force search technique. However, 'binary search' is a search algorithm which requires sorting of the data. The unsorted database cannot be searched with the binary search technique. The significant drawback of binary searching is filtering and then searching. The most difficult moment finding an object using this method is $O(\log N)$. In real time scenario however, sorting the data all the time is not possible. Hence, an efficient system is required to hunt for the precise data from the given record without sorting. This would also be appreciable if it could take less time than the conventional computing. Accomplishing this task, is a challenging job.

Implementation of Grover's algorithm using a quantum computer is the answer to this. Quantum computer makes use of quantum computing concepts which have been influenced by quantum mechanics. Quantum computing (Abd El-Aziz et al., 2022b; Golestan et al., 2023) is an emerging technology where the speed of its computing is very high. The days are not far away when quantum computers will replace the conventional computers.

A Quantum computer (S et al., 2022) is a one which uses the principle of quantum mechanics to do the computation (*IBM - India | IBM*, n.d.; *IBM Quantum Computing | Tools*, n.d.). It is Feynman, the American physicist who introduced the concept of quantum mechanics. A quantum computer (S et al., 2022) takes ($\sqrt{N}$) iterations to find the required data from a given length of database 'N=2^n', where 'n' is the number of bits used. Quantum computing is an interesting area of research which finds its applications in the areas of cyber security, artificial intelligence, computational chemistry, machine learning, drug design, logistics and scheduling, data management, financial services etc. Quantum computing makes use of quantum mechanical effects such as superposition, entanglement and quantum tunneling to perform a computation more effectively. Quantum computation provides the possibility to significantly decrease both runtime (Wack et al., 2021) and power usage compared with traditional digital computation. However, the quantum programming differs substantially from traditional computer programming. Classical or Conventional computing makes use of laws of mathematics while Quantum computing makes use of the laws of physics. All the significant quantum algorithms found to date execute functions exponentially quicker than their classical peers. A classical computer makes use of bits to perform computation while a quantum computer uses 'qubits' to do the computation. A 'qubit' takes a state of |0 and |1 at the same time in quantum computation unlike a bit in the classical computation which takes either only a '0' or '1' state at a given time. It is this ability of the 'qubit' to appear as a |0 and |1 at the same time which gives it the potential to execute the things very much faster than the classical computers. This capability of the 'qubit' to appear as a |0 and |1 simultaneously is called 'superposition' which is one of the important characteristics of quantum computing. The other prime feature of quantum computing is 'entanglement'.

A Classical computer (Mutibara & Refianti, 2010) can be made to run Grover's search algorithm by making it work as an emulator. The features of Quantum computing and also the working of Grover's search algorithm (*Grover's Algorithm | CNOT*, n.d.), are taken into account to accomplish this job.

Related Work

The websites (*IBM Quantum Computing*, n.d.; *IBM Quantum Computing | Tools*, n.d.) gives an idea about the IBM Q Network, the IBM Quantum simulator and also gives us an option to sign up for IBM Quantum Experience, the quantum simulator. It also briefs about quantum computing. (*Grover's Algorithm | CNOT*, n.d.; Mandviwalla et al., 2019; Jiayu et al., 2014; Wright & Tseng, 2015) explains about Grover's algorithm, introduction to it, steps involved in it and its implementation, also shares some examples on it. (*IBM Quantum Computing | Tools*, n.d.) takes us to IBM Quantum Experience signed in page, where one is allowed to create a quantum circuit and run it. The resources tab provides us with a lot of options. It helps us to choose to learn about different quantum gates, learn to build up a quantum circuit, run it, learn different algorithms, etc. (*GitHub - Strilanc/Quirk: A Drag-and-Drop Quantum Circuit Simulator That Runs in Your Browser. A Toy for Exploring and Understanding Small Quantum Circuits.*, n.d.), takes us to a quantum simulator called 'QUIRK' which walks us through the working of it. Surprisingly, the circuit need not be run separately, the instant the building up of the circuit is over and the output appears. (*Explorations in Quantum Computing*, n.d.) deals with the working of different quantum gates. It explains 'reversible and irreversible gates' and also their computing. (Wright & Tseng, 2015) work concentrates exclusively on the working of Grover's algorithm. It also deals with amplitude amplification process involved in the execution of the algorithm. Also, it speaks about highlighting a particular data from a database. (Ozols & Walter, 2018) deals with the qubits, quantum gates and their working and explains Quirk Quantum simulator. Also, it explains various quantum algorithms viz Grover's algorithm, Deutsch's algorithm, Deutsh-Joza algorithm and Bernstein-Vazirani algorithm. It also explains quantum entanglement. (McMahon, 2007) deals with qbits, quantum states, matrices, operators, tensor products, quantum measurement, entanglement, quantum gates and circuits, quantum algorithms, applications of quantum entanglement, quantum cryptography, quantum noise and error correction and cluster state quantum computing. (Jiayu et al., 2014) focuses on implementing Grover's search algorithm on a classical computer. Due to the difficulties in the execution of the Grover's algorithm on a quantum computer, the work in this paper highlights on a quantum computation emulator in classical computer which satisfies the requirements of a quantum computer.

(Mandviwalla et al., 2019) implements grover's algorithm on IBM quantum computer. It also highlights on the various effects of the choices made in the number of bits, qubits and the device chosen to operate. It implements a 4qubit grovers algorithm. (Seegerer et al., 2021) discusses about quantum computing, explains about different approaches to make quantum computing comprehensible. (Gates, n.d.) explains about the symbols and the working of different quantum gates. (Wack et al., 2021) considers quality, speed and scale as the parameters to measure the performance of quantum computing.

(Mutibara & Refianti, 2010) executes Grover's search algorithm on a classic computer. (Abd El-Aziz et al., 2022a) proposes a new deep residual learning based quantum–classical neural network (Res-QCNN). (Gupta et al., 2022) creates a sustainable health care system by identifying the role of quantum computing. (Naved et al., 2022) discusses importance of cloud computing in educational institutions. Congestion control and management of the traffic is taken care of in (Dhingra et al., 2021). Different software and techniques used in cloud computing are compared based on the data handling capacities and speed in (Kannadasan et al., 2018). (Guanlei et al., 2020) suggests searching algorithm that makes use of features of quantum image to compare and search the image. (S et al., 2022) presents ideas about quantum computing. Solutions to problems in artificial intelligence, logic design and machine learning is discussed in (Perkowski, 2022). (Golestan et al., 2023) suggests quantum computing as a potential solution to address challenges in power systems.

Preliminaries

Qbit

The bit used in the quantum circuit is a Qbit.

Quantum State

It's a vector in a two dimensional vector space known as 'state space'.

Quantum Circuit

This is a combination of quantum gates that are put up in a particular fashion to obtain some specific output. However, the simplest Quantum circuit is a quantum wire.

Quantum Gates

Like the logic gates that we have in classical computation viz. AND gate, OR gate,NOT gate, EX-OR gate etc... Quantum computation also makes use of Quantum gates (Gates, n.d.; Ozols & Walter, 2018; Feynman et al., n.d.; Gates, n.d.; Gorbatsevich & Shubin, 2018). Only few Quantum gates viz. Hadamard gate, X gate and CNOT gate used in the execution of Grover's Algorithm for 3 qubits is explained below. The circuit for the gate and the state vector output for the Hadamard gate, X gate and CNOT gates are discussed below.

Hadamard Gate

The Hadamard gate in the Figure 1 puts the qbit $|0\rangle$ or $|1\rangle$ state into a superposition of $|0\rangle$ and $|1\rangle$. If the qubit takes the value $|0\rangle$, the output is

$$H \quad H \cdot |0\rangle = \frac{|0\rangle + |1\rangle}{\sqrt{2}} \tag{1}$$

If the qubit takes the value $|1\rangle$, the output is

$$\text{H} \quad \text{H} \cdot |1\rangle = \frac{|0\rangle - |1\rangle}{\sqrt{2}} = \qquad\qquad (2)$$

The circuit for Hadamard gate operation with input qubit |0 and the corresponding state vector output are as in Figures 2 and 3 respectively.

Figure 1. Appearance of a Hadamard gate

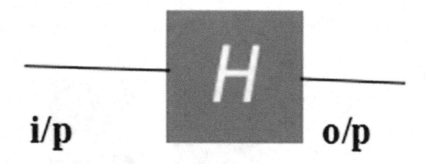

Figure 2. Circuit for Hadamard gate operation with qubit |0>

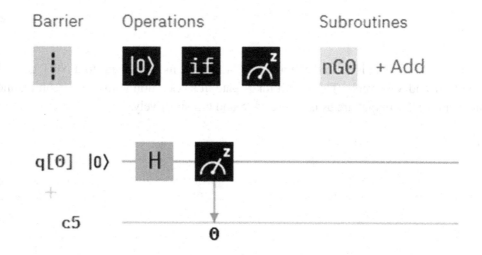

Figure 3. State vector output for Hadamard gate operation with qubit |0>

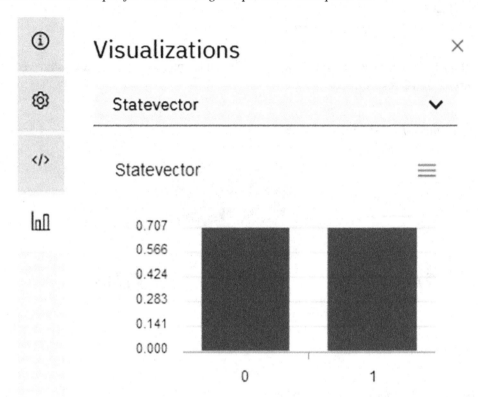

X Gate

The appearance of X gate is as in the figure 4. Classically, its equivalent to a NOT gate. A state |0 is converted to |1 and Vice versa. The circuit for X gate, it's operation with input qubit |0, and the corresponding state vector output are as in figures 4, 5 and 6 respectively.

$$X |0 = |1 \tag{3}$$

$$X |1 = |0 \tag{4}$$

Figure 5. Circuit for X gate operation

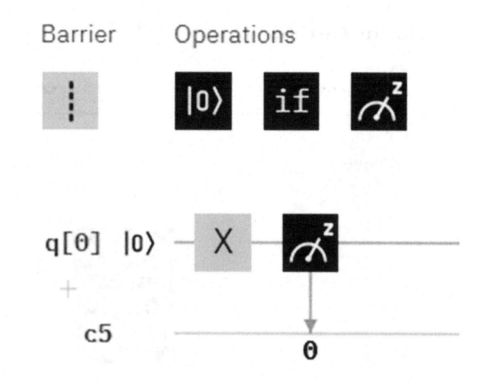

Figure 4. Appearance of X gate

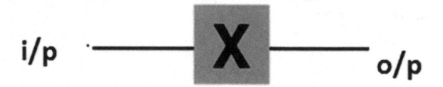

Figure 6. State vector output for X gate operation

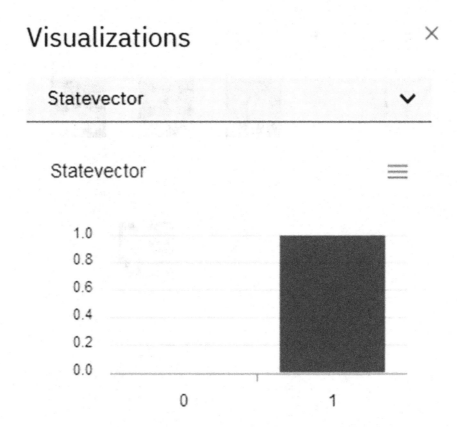

Controlled Not Gate

It is also known as Controlled X gate. It works on a pair of qubits with the first one being 'control' bit and the other one being 'target' bit.

Figure 7. Two qubit CNOT GATE

Control Bit

Target Bit

Two bit CNOT gate

Table 1. Behaviour of 2 qubit CNOT gate

Control Bit	Target Bit	Output
0	0	00
0	1	01
1	0	11
1	1	10

The target bit will flip its state when the control bit is one. The appearance of two qubit CNOT gate is as in Figure 7 and its working is as in table 1. The circuit for the two qubit CNOT operation and its corresponding state vector output are as shown in Figures 8 and 9 respectively.

Figure 8. Circuit for 2 qubit CNOT gate

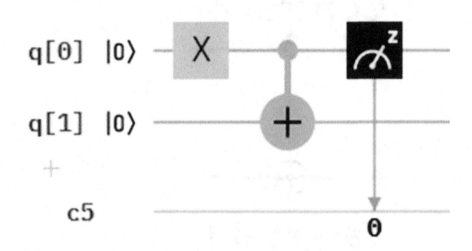

Figure 9. State vector output of 2 qubit CNOT gate

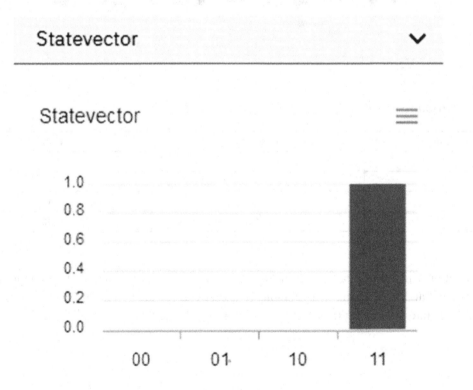

Table 2. Behaviour of 3 qbit CNOT gate

Control Bit 1	Control Bit 2	Target Bit	Output
0	0	0	000
0	0	1	001
0	1	0	010
0	1	1	011
1	0	0	100
1	0	1	101
1	1	0	111
1	1	1	110

Figure 10. Three qbit CNOT gate or Toffoli gate

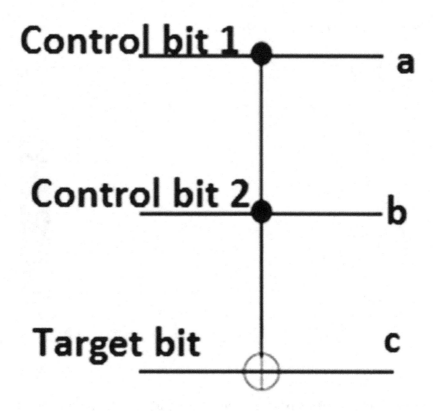

Figure 11. Circuit for a 3qubit CNOT gate

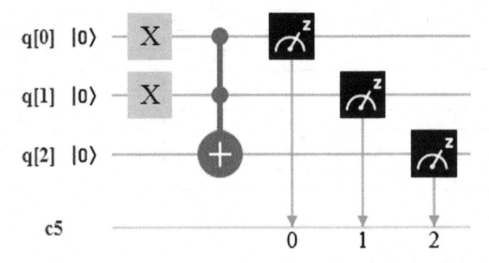

Figure 12. State vector output of 3qubit CNOT gate

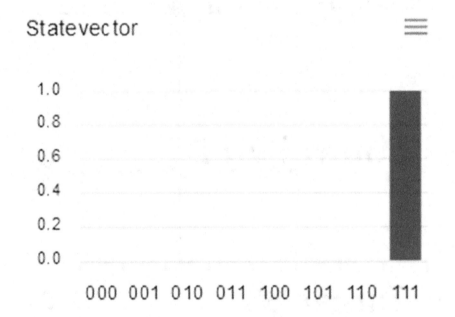

The representation of a 3 qubit CNOT gate and its working are shown in Figure 10 and table 2 respectively. The circuit for the 3 qubit CNOT operation and its corresponding state vector output are as in Figures 11 and 12 correspondingly.

Superposition

Superposition (Sun et al., 2021) is a phenomenon in quantum computing where a qubit can exist in two quantum states simultaneously. This simultaneous existence of the quantum states is the reason that gives the quantum computer the necessary exponential speed which helps to do the computing faster. This superposition is achieved using a Hadamard gate. The circuits for the superposition of 1 qubit, 2 qubits and 3 qubits, their state vector outputs and probability measurements are as indicated in figures from 13 to 21:

Figure 13. Circuit for one qubit in superposition

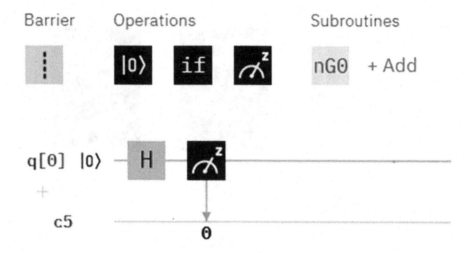

Figure 14. State vector output for one qubit when put in superposition

Figure 15. Probability measurement for one qubit, when put in superposition

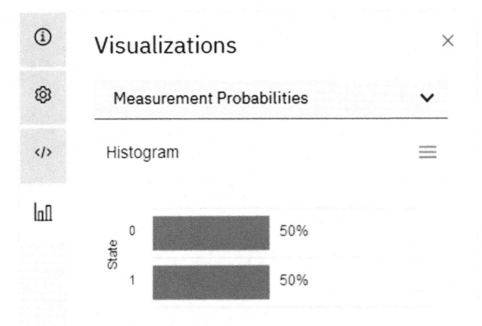

Figure 16. Circuit for two qubit superposition

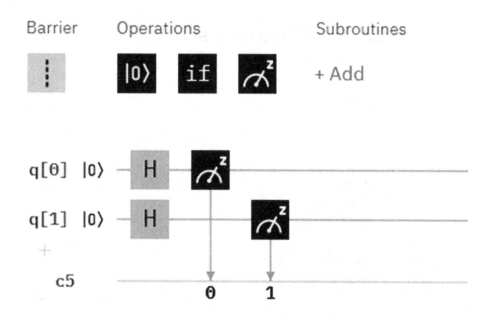

Figure 17. State vector output for two qubits, when put in superposition

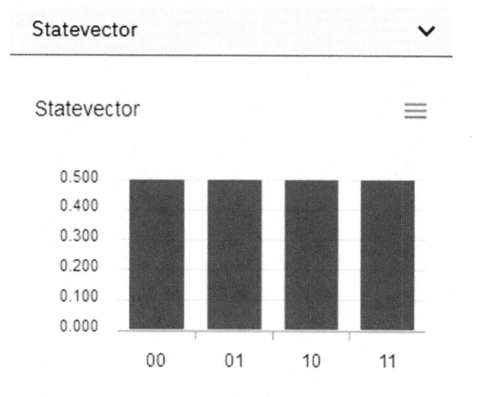

Figure 18. Probability measurement of two qubits, when put in superposition

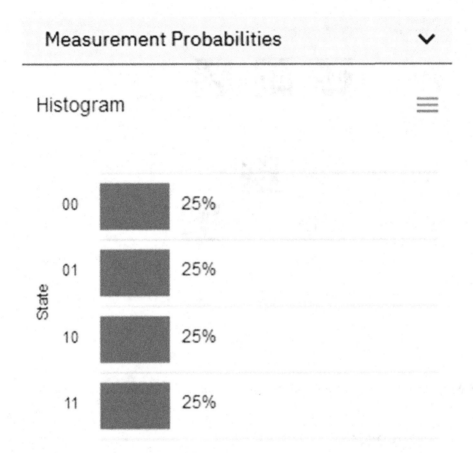

Figure 19. Circuit for three qubit super position

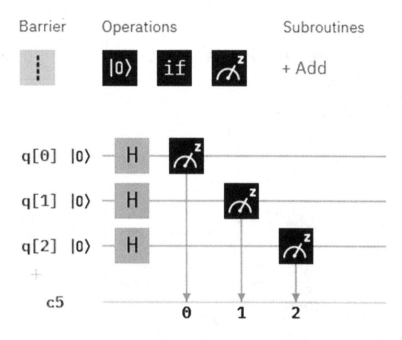

Figure 20. State vector output for three qubit, when put in superposition

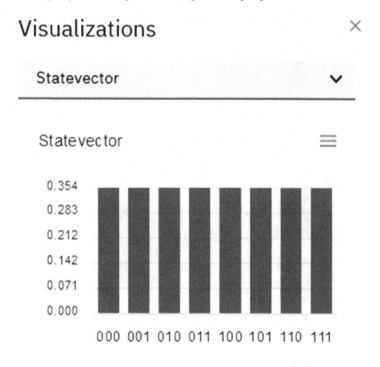

Figure 21. Probability measurement for three qubits, when put in superposition

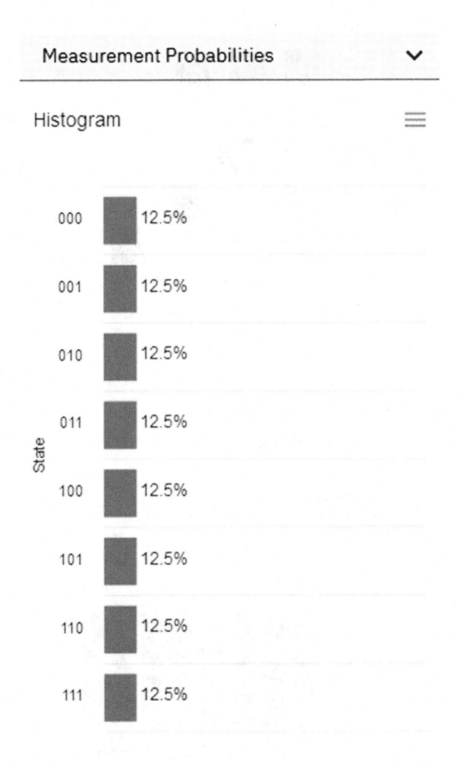

It is this superposition of the states which allows all the states to be accessed parallely and hence the computation becomes faster.

Grover's Algorithm

This quantum search algorithm (Jiayu et al., 2014) attempts to amplify the amplitude of the target state. The word amplification here implies to raise the desired state's possibility of occurrence as the output. The main idea in the Grover's algorithm (*Grover's Algorithm*, n.d.; Jiayu et al., 2014) is to execute a phase flip on the searching element and then to perform an inversion about the average of the amplitudes. The algorithm is iterative and creates the same rotation in each iteration.

Steps Involved in Grover's Algorithm

1. The number of qubits is fixed, the database thus obtained is (2^n) states. The qubits is fixed to 3 qubits.
2. Uniform superposition using Hadamard gates is created.
3. The desired element to be searched in the Oracle is arranged. The searching element (Guanlei et al., 2020) considered here is '011'. The quantum circuit to measure the specific state '011' is as in the Figure 22.
4. The Grover diffusion operator to store each state in the database is created.
5. The measurement is added to display the probability values of each state.

Figure 22. Complete quantum circuit to measure state 011

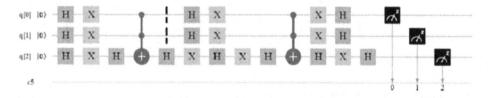

The Phases of the Grover's Algorithm

The algorithm has four phases:

1. Initialization

Step1 is executed here. All the three qubits are put in superposition using Hadamard gates. The amplitude of every state measures $1/\sqrt{N}$ which turns out to 0.354. The state of a qubit is a vector in a complex vector space.

Figure 23. State vector output for three qubit, when put in superposition

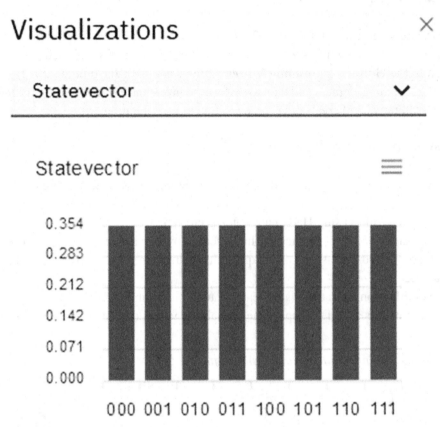

After superposition, the amplitudes of all the states is $1/\sqrt{8} = 0.3535$ as in the Figure 23.

2.   Oracle

The searching element is indicated here. The ORACLE (Perkowski, 2022) performs the operation $|x> = (-1)^{f(x)} |x>$. Function f(x) which will return '0' if x ǂ x′ and will return '1', if x = x′, where x′ is the searching element or target element and x is the element in the database.

The marked state is indicated, by performing a phase toss, once the condition f(x) = 1 is satisfied. This phase flip is reflection about zero which is the same as negating the amplitude on any of the basis states. This negation of the amplitude is performed by using a combination of Hadamard and NOT gates. The Oracle for the state '011' is as shown in Figure 24.

Figure 24. The Oracle for the state '011'

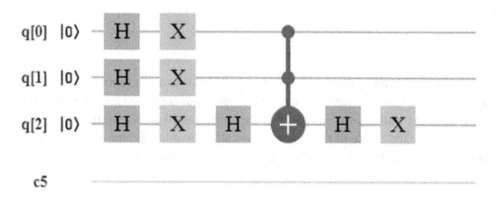

Figure 25. State vector output for the above Oracle

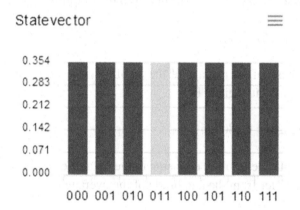

The figure 25 confirms that the target state '011''s amplitude is inverted while the amplitude of the other states are not disturbed. The inverted amplitude of the searching element is indicated in yellow while the undisturbed amplitudes of all the other states are indicated in blue in the state vector representation. This is then passed on to Grover's diffusion operator where it undergoes a lot of iterations and the amplitude of the target state is enhanced.

3. Amplification

The step 4 of Grover's algorithm (Wright & Tseng, 2015) is executed here. Also, the inversion about the average of the amplitudes is carried out. From the previous step, we know that the amplitude of the target state is reversed while that of the other states is maintained at their initial levels. This spin leads the amplitude of the target state to rise. Hence it is called 'amplitude amplification'. The state vector output obtained after the amplitude amplification is as in the Figure 26.

The average amplitude of the all the states is given by

$$\alpha_{avg} = [7(0.35)-0.35] / 8$$

$$\alpha_{avg} = 0.2651625 \tag{5}$$

The amplitude of the searching element differs from the amplitude of the average by

$$\alpha_x' = 0.2651625-(-0.35) = 0.6151625 \tag{6}$$

On doing an inversion about the average of the amplitudes for the searching element, the final amplitude of the searching element is given by

$$\alpha_x' = 0.2651625+0.6151625 = 0.880325 \tag{7}$$

On computing the amplitude of other elements in the database, we have, the amplitude of the other elements in the database differ from the amplitude of the average by

$$\alpha_x' = (0.2651625-0.35) = -0.08839 \tag{8}$$

On doing an inversion about the average of the amplitudes for the other elements in the database, the final amplitude of them is given by

$$\alpha_x' = 0.17677 \tag{9}$$

Figure 26. State vector output after the amplitude amplification

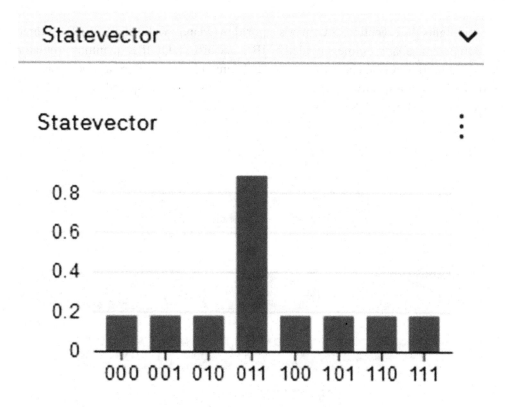

4. Measurement

The measurements are placed in all the three quantum wires at the end of the quantum circuit to measure the searching element.

Work Done

This paper highlights the execution of Grover's algorithm (Mandviwalla et al., 2019) for three qubits on a quantum computer available online provided by IBM and also on QUIRK quantum simulator. Also, the Grover's algorithm for three bits is run on a classical computer with different processors. Their speeds of execution in locating a specific data are also noted and are then compared. The process flow of the work carried out is as shown in the Figure 27.

Figure 27. The process flow of the work carried out

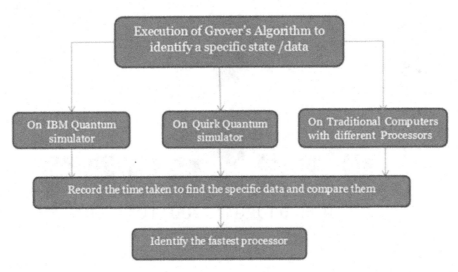

'Superposition', a distinctive feature of quantum computing enables a quantum computer to address a family of issues quicker than the conventional computers as in looking for an item in a database. The quantum search technique uses quantum parallelism to build a superposition of all feasible state components and then improves the probability of occurrence of the target state.

Quantum Simulator

IBM Q Experience

The IBM Q Experience is an online platform that allows all of us to the access IBM's quantum processors via cloud. These quantum processors can be used to run the quantum circuits to serve a purpose. Ibmq_qasm simulator is a quantum assembly language simulator. Grover's Alogorithm for 3qubit mentioned in the work carried out, is run on "Ibmq_qasm_simulator in ibm-q/open/main" and the output is captured. The oracle output, the amplitudes of the searching element and other states, the probability of the searching element are all explained in section 5.

Quirk (Quantum Simulator)

It's a drag and drop quantum circuit simulator that reacts and simulates. It has inline state displays. It has no run procedure. It is always evaluating the circuit. It is a part of drawing code. Hence, there is no running time that it takes to execute the circuit. The output is obtained the instant, the circuit is connected completely. The same 3qubit Grover's algorithm circuit is implemented on the QUIRK (*GitHub - Strilanc/Quirk: A Drag-and-Drop Quantum Circuit Simulator That Runs in Your Browser. A Toy for Exploring and Understanding Small Quantum Circuits.*, n.d.),a quantum simulator. Surprisingly, the run time is zero as the searching element is identified the moment the building of the circuit is completed. The circuit implemented and the output obtained is discussed in section 5.

Implementation of Grover's Algorithm on Classical Processor

Emulation is the ability of a computer to imitate another device. The working of Grover's search algorithm is mimicked on a Classical computer, thus making it work as an emulator. The time taken for the execution of a 3 qubit Grover's search algorithm on classical computers are noted and tabulated in the Table 4. It is observed that the execution time of the classical processor varies with the internal features such as RAM, frequency, etc.,

Matlab software is used to implement Grover's search algorithm on classical computer's and is simulated to get the output as indicated in Figure 32.

Steps in Grover's Search Algorithm for Classical Processors

1. The number of qubits is entered, the database thus obtained is $N=2^n$ states. 3 qubits were considered for the experimentation.
2. The desired element to be searched is entered. The searching element considered is '010' which is equivalently '2'.
3. The diffusion transform is applied.
4. A function eye(n) for creating the Oracle is defined.
5. The amplitude is negated by assigning the value of the Oracle to be -1.
6. The optimal number of iterations is calculated.
7. The Grover diffusion operator is created to store each state in the database.
8. The probability values of each state is displayed.
9. Tic tock is used for calculating the time taken.

RESULTS AND DISCUSSION

IBM Q Experience Output

The Probability of Occurrence

The probability of occurrence of the searching state and other states when run on "Ibmq_qasm_simulator in ibm-q/open/main" is as shown in the Figure 28. This result shows that there is a high probability of occurrence for the searching element '011' which is 79.39%. While the probability of occurrence of other states is very less compared to the above. Hence, the prospectus of the getting the searching element as the output is very high. This confirms that the Quantum circuit for 3 qubit Grover's Algorithm identifies the searching element appropriately.

Figure 28. The probability of occurrence of the searching state and other states

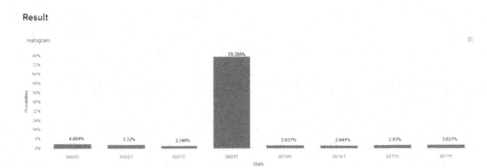

State Vector Output

The state vector output of the searching state and other states with the details of the amplitude is as shown in the Figure 29. The obtained result confirms that the searching element has the highest amplitude than the other states which goes well with the description of the Grover's search algorithm.

Figure 29. The state vector output with amplitude details

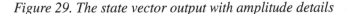

Run Time Details

The run time details obtained after running the quantum circuit on the IBM Quantum Simulator for 3 qubit Grover's Algorithm with '011' as the searching element is as shown in Figure 30.

Figure 30. Run time details of the output obtained on IBM simulator

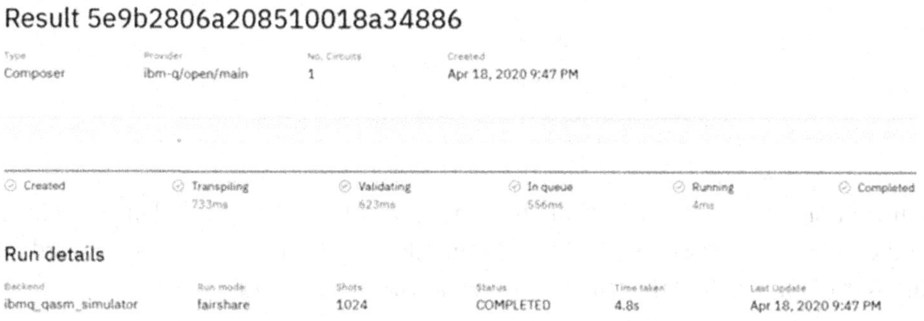

Result 5e9b2806a208510018a34886

Type	Provider	No. Circuits	Created
Composer	ibm-q/open/main	1	Apr 18, 2020 9:47 PM

⊘ Created	⊘ Transpiling	⊘ Validating	⊘ In queue	⊘ Running	⊘ Completed
	733ms	623ms	556ms	4ms	

Run details

Backend	Run mode	Shots	Status	Time taken	Last Update
ibmq_qasm_simulator	fairshare	1024	COMPLETED	4.8s	Apr 18, 2020 9:47 PM

The run time details of the quantum circuit viz date of execution, the backend used and the time taken for the execution etc., are obtained after running on the simulator. The execution time includes time taken for transpiling, validating, being in queue and running the circuit. Though the total time taken exhibits 4.8s, the actual time taken to run the circuit is 4ms. However, the run time is not the same when the quantum circuit is executed by taking different states as the search element. It can be observed that the time taken is all in terms of milliseconds. The run time obtained for different states is put up in the Table 3:

Table 3. Run time details for different states as search elements

Search Element (Target State)	Run Time Taken in the IBM Quantum Simulator
000	3ms
001	10ms
010	2ms
011	4ms
100	5ms
101	8ms
110	5ms
111	6ms

Quirk Quantum Simulator Output

The output obtained after running the 3qubit Grover's algorithm with the searching element as '111' on Quirk simulator is as shown in Figure 31.

Figure 31. Output obtained on running 3qubit Grover's algorithm on Quirk

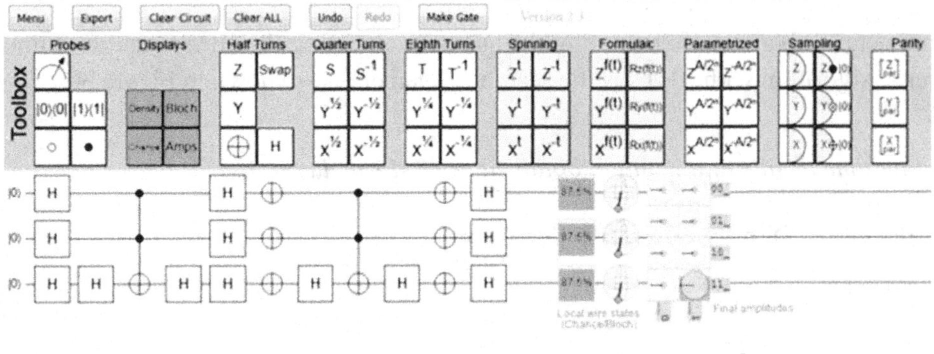

The Figure 31 shows that the state '111' is identified and is highlighted. This searching element is recognized the moment we are done with completing the quantum circuit. In other words the run time is zero. This is true for any 3bit element considered as the target element.

Implementation of Grover's Algorithm on Classical Processor

The details of execution time on running a 3bit grover search algorithm on different classical processors are listed in Table 4.

Table 4. Run time details of the search algorithm on a Classical computer

Name of the Processor	Frequency of Processor	Ram	Execution Time
Intel®Core™i5-2520M CPU	2.50GHz	4.00GB	8.91 seconds
Intel®Core™i5-6200U CPU	2.30GHz	8.00GB	2 seconds
Intel®CORE™i7-7700Q CPU	2.8GHz	8.00GB	0.18 seconds
Intel®Core™i7-3517U CPU	1.90GHz	8.00GB	4 seconds

Figure 32. The probability of occurrence of the searching state 010(2)

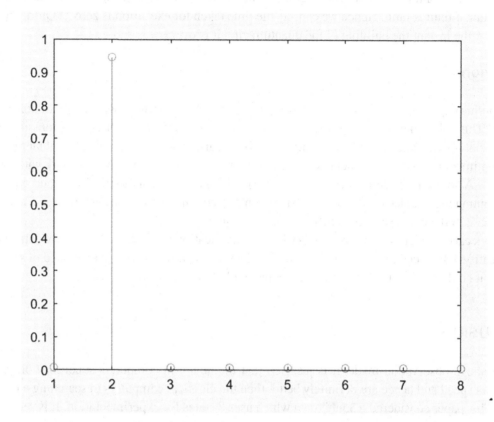

The Figure 32 shows the result of Grover's search algorithm for 3 bits on a Classical Processor. The x-axis in the Figure 32 represents the states and the y-axis represents the probability of occurrence of the states. On running the algorithm with the search element as '010'(2) with eight states in the database, the MatLab output is as shown in Figure 32. The output clearly shows that the probability of occurrence of state '010'(2) to appear as the output is high as compared to the other states.

Observations Made

1. The probability of occurrence of the searching state is maximum than the other states when the quantum circuit is run on the IBM quantum simulator.
2. The state vector output of the quantum circuit confirms that the searching element has the highest amplitude than the other states.
3. Table 3 gives the run time details of running the 3qubit quantum search circuit on IBM simulator, "Ibmq_qasm_simulator in ibm-q/open/main". Table 4 gives the run time details of running the 3qubit Grover's search algorithm on different Classical Processors. On comparing the two tables, it can be concluded that the Classical Processors identify the target state in 'seconds' while the quantum search algorithm identifies the target state in 'milliseconds'.

4. The Quirk quantum simulator distinguishes the element we are looking out for, the instant the quantum circuit is built. Hence we can say the time taken for execution is zero as Quirk yields the output, the instant the building of the quantum circuit is over.

Applications

The computing capabilities and the speed of a quantum computer is far more superior to the conventional computer. This salient feature of it could be harnessed to carry out different applications in domains viz... artificial intelligence and machine learning, cybersecurity and cryptography, financial modelling, logistics optimization and so on. Not far away are the days when each one of us would work with quantum computers . Also the increase in the usage of the most happening technologies like cloud computing, edge computing has enabled corporate's, organization's, academic institutions, enterprises..etc to put up their database in the cloud servers to manage them efficiently.

The work carried out fits in the scenario's where the application deals with a large set of data. It allows one to identify a distinct data in the gigantic data set handled by a server without the need of sorting the data. Also it could be used to align and sort the data with ease.

CONCLUSION

From the above observation made, it is justified that the quantum computers superposition property enhances its speed and hence are definitely better than the classical computers in searching a particular element. This paper considered a 3qubit data which uses 8 states for experimentation. It is seen that the speed of execution is for sure, better on a quantum computer. However, this experimentation would find its advantage when the data base is sufficiently large enough which is achieved using cloud computing technology. Even with sufficiently large data base, the Quantum Processors would surely take less time to execute than the Classical Processors as it exploits superposition property. The best result is obtained when the quantum circuit is run on Quirk simulator as the state we are looking out for is discovered, the moment the circuit is built. Hence Quantum processors outperform their classical counterparts.

REFERENCES

Abd El-Aziz, R. M., Taloba, A. I., & Alghamdi, F. A. (2022). Quantum Computing Optimization Technique for IoT Platform using Modified Deep Residual Approach. *Alexandria Engineering Journal*, *61*(12), 12497–12509. doi:10.1016/j.aej.2022.06.029

Dhingra, S., Madda, R. B., Patan, R., Jiao, P., Barri, K., & Alavi, A. H. (2021). Internet of things-based fog and cloud computing technology for smart traffic monitoring. *Internet of Things (Netherlands)*, *14*, 100175. Advance online publication. doi:10.1016/j.iot.2020.100175

Explorations in Quantum Computing. (n.d.). Retrieved January 21, 2023, from https://www.amazon.com/Explorations-Quantum-Computing-Colin-Williams/dp/038794768X

FeynmanR. P.FeynmanR.SocietyA. P. (n.d.). *Gate1*. doi:10.1007/978-1-84628-887-6

GitHub - Strilanc/Quirk: A drag-and-drop quantum circuit simulator that runs in your browser. A toy for exploring and understanding small quantum circuits. (n.d.). Retrieved January 18, 2023, from https://github.com/Strilanc/Quirk

Golestan, S., Habibi, M. R., Mousazadeh Mousavi, S. Y., Guerrero, J. M., & Vasquez, J. C. (2023). Quantum computation in power systems: An overview of recent advances. *Energy Reports*, *9*, 584–596. doi:10.1016/j.egyr.2022.11.185

Gorbatsevich, A. A., & Shubin, N. M. (2018). Quantum logic gates. *Physics Uspekhi*, *61*(11), 1100–1115. doi:10.3367/UFNe.2017.12.038310

Grover's Algorithm | CNOT. (n.d.). Retrieved January 17, 2023, from https://cnot.io/quantum_algorithms/grover/grovers_algorithm.html

Grover's Algorithm. (n.d.). Retrieved January 18, 2023, from https://qiskit.org/textbook/ch-algorithms/grover.html

Guanlei, X., Xiaogang, X., Xun, W., & Xiaotong, W. (2020). A novel quantum image parallel searching algorithm. *Optik*, *209*(May), 164565. doi:10.1016/j.ijleo.2020.164565

Gupta, S., Modgil, S., Bhatt, P. C., Chiappetta Jabbour, C. J., & Kamble, S. (2022). Quantum computing led innovation for achieving a more sustainable Covid-19 healthcare industry. *Technovation*. Advance online publication. doi:10.1016/j.technovation.2022.102544

IBM - India | IBM. (n.d.). Retrieved January 18, 2023, from https://www.ibm.com/in-en

IBM Quantum Computing | Tools. (n.d.). Retrieved January 18, 2023, from https://www.ibm.com/quantum/tools

IBM Quantum Computing. (n.d.). Retrieved January 17, 2023, from https://www.ibm.com/quantum

Jiayu, Z., Junsuo, Z., Fanjiang, X., Haiying, H., & Peng, Q. (2014). Analysis and simulation of grover's search algorithm. *International Journal of Machine Learning and Computing*, *4*(1), 21.

Kannadasan, R., Prabakaran, N., Boominathan, P., Krishnamoorthy, A., Naresh, K., & Sivashanmugam, G. (2018). High Performance Parallel Computing with Cloud Technologies. *Procedia Computer Science*, *132*, 518–524. doi:10.1016/j.procs.2018.05.004

Li, N., Yan, F., & Hirota, K. (2022). Quantum data visualization: A quantum computing framework for enhancing visual analysis of data. *Physica A*, *599*, 127476. doi:10.1016/j.physa.2022.127476

Mandviwalla, A., Ohshiro, K., & Ji, B. (2019). Implementing Grover's Algorithm on the IBM Quantum Computers. *Proceedings - 2018 IEEE International Conference on Big Data*, 2531–2537. doi:10.1109/BigData.2018.8622457

McMahon, D. (2007). *Quantum computing explained.* John Wiley & Sons. doi:10.1002/9780470181386

Mutibara, A. B., & Refianti, R. (2010). Simulation of Grover algorithm Quantum search in a Classical Computer. *International Journal of Computer Science and Information Security*, *8*(9).

Naved, M., Sanchez, D. T., Dela Cruz, A. P., Peconcillo, L. B. Jr, Peteros, E. D., & Tenerife, J. J. L. (2022). Identifying the role of cloud computing technology in management of educational institutions. *Materials Today: Proceedings, 51*, 2309–2312. doi:10.1016/j.matpr.2021.11.414

Ozols, M., & Walter, M. (2018). The *quantum quest.* www.quantumquest.nl

Perkowski, M. (2022). Inverse problems, constraint satisfaction, reversible logic, invertible logic and Grover quantum oracles for practical problems. *Science of Computer Programming, 218*, 102775. doi:10.1016/j.scico.2022.102775

S, N., Singh, H., & N, A. U. (2022). An extensive review on quantum computers. *Advances in Engineering Software, 174*(September), 103337. doi:10.1016/j.advengsoft.2022.103337

Seegerer, S., Michaeli, T., & Romeike, R. (2021). Quantum Computing As a Topic in Computer Science Education. In *ACM International Conference Proceeding Series* (*Vol. 1*, Issue 1). Association for Computing Machinery. 10.1145/3481312.3481348

Sun, Y., Zeng, Y., & Zhang, T. (2021). Quantum superposition inspired spiking neural network. *iScience, 24*(8), 102880. Advance online publication. doi:10.1016/j.isci.2021.102880 PMID:34401664

WackA.PaikH.Javadi-AbhariA.JurcevicP.FaroI.GambettaJ. M.JohnsonB. R. (2021). *Quality, Speed, and Scale: three key attributes to measure the performance of near-term quantum computers.* https://arxiv.org/abs/2110.14108

Wright, J., & Tseng, T. (2015). *Lecture 04: Grover's Algorithm.* Academic Press.

Chapter 14
Optimization of MPPT Controller for Standalone Photovoltaic Systems

Jatin Soni
ⓘ https://orcid.org/0000-0002-4939-8481
Nirma University, India

Kuntal Bhattacharjee
Nirma University, India

ABSTRACT

A photovoltaic (PV) system uses the maximum power point tracking (MPPT) controller used in a photovoltaic (PV) system to get the maximum power operating point at different temperatures and irradiance conditions. Several optimization methods from conventional to soft computing methods have been applied to software and hardware platforms to generate duty cycles and optimize fuzzy membership functions. The PV system with partial shading condition is also considered for better tracking of power peaks. Merits and demerits of different MPPT optimization methods have been discussed to conclude better. The results obtained by recently developed algorithms in the MPPT controller have been compared to show better performance and effectiveness of the algorithm. This chapter references undertaking research work to optimize MPPT controllers in PV systems under partial shading conditions.

1. INTRODUCTION

In recent years, researchers have shown significant interest in renewable energy sources due to their abundant availability across a broad spectrum (Shah et al., 2023). The photovoltaic (PV) system's power generation has no impact on pollution, has no moving components, and doesn't deplete materials (Shah et al., 2023; J. Soni & Bhattacharjee, 2023). The ambient temperature and solar irradiation have an impact on the performance of the PV system. Furthermore, the PV system achieves its highest output power at a specific operating point (Bhattacharjee et al., 2021). Clouds, vegetation, structures, and birds

DOI: 10.4018/978-1-6684-8306-0.ch014

all have an impact on how much electricity a PV system can produce. Consequently, the PV system's efficiency and dependability are reduced (Bhattacharjee et al., 2021; J. Soni & Bhattacharjee, 2022). Many tracking techniques have been devised to get the most out of the solar panels (Verma et al., 2022). Some of the commonly used techniques include hill-climbing approaches, perturb and observe (P&O), and incremental conductance (INC) (J. M. Soni et al., 2020; Verma et al., 2022).

Because they are straightforward, inexpensive, and simple to apply, traditional methods are more suited for practical applications (Ferreira & van Wyk, n.d.; J. M. Soni et al., 2020; Verma et al., 2022). When power monitoring is being done, it is difficult to get to the precise tracking location. Following each sample period, these techniques are utilized to monitor the output voltage and current of the PV system (Hattu, 2019). The settings will provide incorrect tracking directions if the atmospheric conditions change (Hattu, 2019; Reay, 2004). To address the shortcomings of conventional approaches, optimization techniques and soft computing machine intelligence (AI) tools have been created. Without obtaining a perfect mathematical model, AI techniques can determine the PV unit's precise functioning point. As a result, these techniques rely on the PV system's features and behaviour. However, in shadowed situations, the PV module's output power is impacted (Syafaruddin et al., 2010). Evolutionary optimization methods like 'Genetic Algorithm' (GA), 'Particle Swarm Optimization (PSO), 'Cuckoo Search' (CS), and 'Firefly Algorithm' (FA) have been used to get global maxima point. However, the algorithm's efficiency decreases after using random variables in algorithms. The desired optimum solution cannot be obtained due to an increment in uncertainty (Kosgi & Kulkarni, 2022; Syafaruddin et al., 2010). By adjusting the control parameters of the power converter, such as voltage, current, and duty cycle, the algorithms' parameters can influence and modify them. MPPT techniques monitor the PV system's characteristics, and the DC-DC converter receives the resulting control signal (Ayad et al., 2021; Kosgi & Kulkarni, 2022; Syafaruddin et al., 2010). Given in 1.1 is the system chart of the PV unit with a DC load.

The ambient temperature and solar irradiation have a direct impact on the output power of the PV module (Bayeh & Moubayed, 2014). To achieve the maximum power point, it is necessary to modify the duty cycle of the converter, similar to how the maximum power point tracker operates (Waghmare-Ujgare et al., 2022). Because of this, the MPPT point may be attained gradually. The point of operation for a PV system directly connected to a load is determined by the intersection of the I-V characteristics. Therefore, the most possible power cannot be generated. The MPP alters when climatic conditions vary, increasing unit oversizing and expense (Lee & Sohn, 2011; Waghmare-Ujgare et al., 2022). By integrating power converters like buck, boost, buck-boost, and SEPIC converters, the PV system can be effectively enhanced in its performance. Incorporating a DC-DC converter enables the PV system to operate with improved efficiency (Hegazy et al., 2020; Lee & Sohn, 2011; Waghmare-Ujgare et al., 2022).

The single-phase PWM converters may change the frequency at which DC input voltage is converted to AC output voltage. The ON and OFF times of switching devices determine the AC voltage's output frequency (Yamamoto & Shinohara, 1996). The H-bridge inverter gives the non-sinusoidal output voltage suitable for the low and medium voltage levels. The unwanted signals available in the voltage waveform are called harmonics (Georgakopoulos et al., 2018). The electrical equipment becomes overheated due to excessive harmonics. Therefore, the high power system requires the sinusoidal voltage with fewer harmonics. The multi-level inverter can get smooth output voltage (Hosseini et al., 2015).

1.1. Overview of PV System

The sun is considered an endless reliable and eco-friendly energy source. The PV panel receives the radiated energy from the sun and produces power. The PV system converts this sunlight into electricity. The main block of producing electricity is called a solar cell (Hosseini et al., 2015; Sprenger et al., 2016). The efficiency of the PV modules is about 12 to 29% which is converted from sunlight into electricity. The efficiency of solar cells for gallium arsenide is around 29%, whereas silicon is around 12 to 14%. As a result, the 'maximum power point' (MPPT) controller is required to obtain the maximum output power from the PV system (Hosseini et al., 2015; M. Y. A. Khan, 2019; Sprenger et al., 2016).

1.1.1. Modeling of PV System

A single solar cell produces an output of around 0.5V and 2W, respectively. In order to attain the desired output voltage and power, multiple solar cells are interconnected in both series and parallel configurations (Badapanda et al., 2022). This configuration is referred to as a solar panel, and multiple solar panels are combined to form a solar array (Badapanda et al., 2022; A. Mahmoud et al., 2018). These solar arrays are linked in series to get high output voltage. In the absence of solar irradiance, the solar cell functions as a p-n junction diode. The holes are generated due to the interaction between the cell atom and incident photon. Electrons migrate from the n-region to the p-region. The speed of the electron depends upon the intensity and wavelength of solar irradiation. Therefore, the electric field is produced in the solar cells (Bhattacharjee et al., 2014b). The solar cell produces dark current I_D when the solar cell is directly connected to the external power supply.

Hence, the PV system comprises an MPPT controller, series-parallel PV modules, a DC-DC converter, and a power inverter (Bhattacharjee et al., 2014c). The DC voltage generated by the PV module is amplified through a DC-DC converter and subsequently converted into AC voltage by the inverter. Therefore, the rating of the PV panel must be selected as per load demand (Bhattacharjee et al., 2014a). The equivalent circuit of the solar unit is given in 1.2.

The total current I is generated current Ipv minus ID and current through parallel resistance Rp.

$$I = I_{pv} - I_d - I_{sh}$$

The mathematical equation of the diode current and shunt resistance current is given in

$$I_d = I_0 \left\{ \exp\left[\frac{q}{mkT_c} \left(V + IR_s \right) \right] - 1 \right\}$$

$$I_{sh} = \frac{V + IR_s}{R_p}$$

The equation (1) is formulated as

$$I = I_{pv} - I_d = I_0 \left\{ \exp\left[\frac{q}{mkT_c}\left(V + IR_s\right)\right] - 1 \right\} - \frac{V + IR_s}{R_p}$$

The shunt resistance value is usually high. Such that the shunt current is eliminated.

$$I = I_{pv} - I_d = I_0 \left\{ \exp\left[\frac{q}{mkT_c}\left(V + IR_s\right)\right] - 1 \right\}$$

The mathematical equation of the curve fitting parameter is given below.

$$A = \frac{mkT_c}{q}$$

The modified equation of output current of PV module in the standard condition is given below.

$$I = I_{pv} - I_0 \left[\exp\left(\frac{V}{a} \right) - 1 \right]$$

If the PV cell is short-circuited, the mathematical equation of short circuit current is given below.

$$I_{sc} = I_{pv} - I_0 \left[\exp\left(\frac{0}{a} \right) - 1 \right] = I_{pv}$$

For the ideal state,

$$I_{sc} \approx I_{pv}$$

The photocurrent of a solar cell is influenced by the ambient temperature and solar irradiance, as depicted in the following mathematical equation.

$$I_{pv} = \frac{G}{G_{ref}}\left(I_{pv} + \alpha\Delta T \right)$$

The mathematical equation of maximum voltage and current is given below.

$$I_{sc} = I_{pv} - I_0 \left[\exp\left(\frac{I_{sc} R_s}{A} \right) - 1 \right]$$

$$0 = I_{pv} - I_0 \left[\exp\left(\frac{V_{oc}}{A} \right) - 1 \right]$$

$$I_{pm} = I_{pv} - I_0 \left[\exp\left(\frac{V_0}{A} \right) \right]$$

The (-1) term in the equation can be eliminated compared to the exponential term. The modified equation is given below.

$$0 = I_{sc} - I_0 \left[\exp\left(\frac{V_0}{A} \right) \right]$$

Figure 17.3 illustrates the I-V characteristics, while Figure 1.4 represents the P-V characteristics of the PV module.

1.2. DC-DC Converter

The DC-DC converter is utilized to increase or decrease the output DC voltage of the PV system based on specific requirements. It also produces the regulated output voltage from uncontrolled sources for the load (Farghally et al., 2018). The high-frequency switching device, capacitors, inductors, and transformers are used in the DC-DC controller to get smooth and constant output. The efficiency of the DC-DC converter is around 90%, such that It is much more efficient than regular regulators (Farghally et al., 2018; A. Kumar et al., 2021). The converter can be connected to the ground as per the requirements. Therefore, it links the load and solar panels (Nangia et al., 2021). The buck-boost, and SEPIC converters are among the prominent types of converters utilized in DC-DC converter systems (Ghazi et al., 2022; Nangia et al., 2021). The buck converter reduces the voltage to a level lower than the input voltage. It is primarily employed to regulate the charge of a 4.2 V lithium-ion battery. The boost converter receives a higher voltage than the input voltage (Jouda et al., 2017). The boost converter is primarily used to drive LEDs from cells. The 'buck-boost converter' gets lower or higher output voltage from the input voltage. The primary purpose of the 'buck-boost converter' is to maintain a constant output voltage from the battery. The SEPIC converter also has a lower or higher output voltage from the input voltage (Parthiban & Durairaj, 2015). The SEPIC converter is employed in a comparable manner to the 'buck-boost converter' for similar applications. Isolated converters like forward and 'flyback converters' are widely used in the industry (Bennis et al., 2015). The 'forward converter' is a buck converter with isolation, while the flyback converter is an isolated boost converter (Bennis et al., 2015; John et al., 2017). The isolated converters are mainly used to get the positive or negative voltage as per requirements. The DC-DC converter can be additionally linked to the inverter in order to obtain an AC output.

1.3. Multi-Level Inverter

The power altering from DC to AC is done by the multi-level inverter (Bennis et al., 2015; Gameti & Vairagi, 2021; John et al., 2017). The inverter is also used in the home as an emergency power backup. The conventional H-bridge inverter is mainly prone low and average approach (Hamdi et al., n.d.). The multi-level inverter is primarily used in average and excessive level approach. There is a high deviation in voltage dV / dt in the single-phase inverter (Prajapati & Shah, 2021). The harmonic losses are also available in the single-phase inverter, which a tuned LC filter can remove. As a result, multi-level inverters are extensively employed in applications that require high voltage and current levels (Kapur et al., 2020; Prajapati & Shah, 2021). The MLI was firstly proposed in 1975. By increasing the number of voltage levels, the total harmonic distortion (THD) of the system can be reduced. The classification of the multi-level inverter is provided in Figure 1.5.

1.4. Maximum Power Point Tracking (MPPT)

The MPPT serves as a control system employed to achieve optimal power output from the PV modules (Ayad et al., 2022). The MPPT is an electronic system that adjusts the operating point of the PV module to attain the maximum power output (Ayad et al., 2022; Stosovic et al., 2013). The 'MPPT' is used in conjunction with the tracking method (Ramu & Sobhana, 2018).

1.4.1. Tracking Efficiency of MPPT Methods

The duty cycle of the converter can enhance the speed at which the tracking shaft operates. The tracking speed is the ratio between the PV array's practical and theoretical power (Rekioua & Matagne, 2012). The GMPPT has been proposed by Chakkarapani Manickam et al. (Arumugam & Chakkarapani, 2019), which combines the PSO and P&O methods. The slanted shading condition has also been considered in the later stage. The GMPPT is mainly used due to its ability to restrict convergence time and power oscillations.

1.4.1.1. Hill Climbing Method

The HC technique is straightforward and flexible in MPPT controllers (Sarkar et al., 2012). The HC method produces a perturbation in the converter's duty cycle (Sarkar et al., 2012; Tan et al., 2014). The flowchart of the HC method is given in 1.6. The PV voltage and current are initially measured, followed by the calculation of generated power. This power is then compared with the voltage and current values from the previous iteration. After reaching it, the PWM duty cycle is generated, and past data is stored in the memory.

1.4.1.2. Perturb and Observe (P&O) Algorithm

The P&O technique is mainly used in battery charging by PV modules. The instant voltage of the PV unit is perturbed, and generated power is used to get the direction of upcoming modification in current or voltage (John et al., 2017). If the power is increased by perturbation, the voltage or current is kept on varying in an identical direction until the energy decreases. After that, the power is calculated and compared with an estimated value (Panda et al., 2020). This method is widely used for monitoring voltage with restricted flexibility and implementation cost. The P&O method decreases the time complexity and tries to attain MPP (Z. Fan et al., 2021). This feature helps the P&O method to get solutions in less time.

1.4.1.3. Incremental Conductance (INC)

The INC technique uses two current-voltage output for calculating the output current and voltage of the PV array (Mahmood et al., 2020). If the instantaneous value matches the solar conductance value, the MPP will be obtained.

1.4.1.4. Fuzzy Logic Controls

The FLC gives an exact mathematical model and also deals with nonlinearities available in the controller (Mendel et al., 2014). The FLC is based on information and recognition. The PV modules have nonlinear relation between voltage and current (Bai et al., 2007; Mendel et al., 2014). Therefore, the operating point is dependent on higher output power which deflects from the atmospheric conditions. The FLC is classified as

1) Fuzzification
2) Inference, rule-based
3) Defuzzification

1.4.1.5. Neural Network

The NN is used in microcontrollers for obtaining MPPT (Dong & Duan, 2023). The three layers in the NN are input, hidden, and output layers (Dong & Duan, 2023; Wang et al., 2022). The input data are PV array, irradiance, and temperature. The NN is applied in the MPPT controller by Ali Chikh & Ambrish Chandra. The complexity of the hardware setup is reduced by NN (Santos de Araújo et al., 2022).

1.4.1.6. Particle Swarm Optimization

PSO is a population-formed search method inspired by bird flocking activities. The swarms of individuals are considered as particles in which each individual is viewed as a solution (Dar & Imtiaz, 2023; Santos de Araújo et al., 2022). The particles move around search space which follows the neighboring particles. The isolated particles calculate their fitness according to their positions (Teferra et al., 2023). After consecutive iterations, the particles converge to one point. Therefore, PSO is an effective method for MPPT controller.

1.4.1.7. Differential Evolution (DE)

The initial population is generated in a random manner. After that, the subsequent process is done to get solutions. There are three processes in the DE method (Tzani-Tzanopoulou et al., 2022; Wu et al., 2023).

1) Selection
2) Mutation
3) Crossover

1.4.1.8. Cuckoo Search Algorithm

The CSA method is presented by Xin-She Yang and Suash Deb in 2019 (Tzani-Tzanopoulou et al., 2022; Wu et al., 2023; Zhan et al., 2023). The CSA method has been inspired by obligate brood parasitism of some cuckoos. The host bird nteracts with other intruding cuckoos.

2. RELATED WORKS

The formation of solar energy into electrical power by the PV system is the most usual method (Wahab & Mohamed, 2022). The MPPT is employed to achieve the maximum power output from the PV system. The MPPT can be used in applications like charging electric vehicles or batteries, powering the electric motor, and positioning control on the grid (Chitra et al., 2022). Many power maximization method has been performed to increase PV unit output. The energy conversion is reliant on on the application and dynamics of solar irradiance (Govindharaj & Mariappan, 2019). Several MPPT techniques have already been applied to increase the competence of the solar modules. However, there are many drawbacks to previous methods (Chao & Rizal, 2021; Govindharaj & Mariappan, 2019). Therefore, several research papers have been analysed to improve efficiency (Rekioua & Matagne, 2012).

Steven L Brunton et al. has first described the MPPT algorithm to upgrade the act of the PV unit (Precup et al., 2019; Rekioua & Matagne, 2012). The robust and unreliable solar irradiance has been considered. The ripple effect is present in the natural inverter employed by the extremum seeking (ES) controller. The ES controller has improved efficiency with transient time (Kamalakannan et al., 2014).

Another method has created a PV module function at MPP (Ghazi et al., 2022; Kamalakannan et al., 2014). The operating point has been assigned using an approximation of short-circuit current (Farajdadian & Hassan Hosseini, 2019). The boost converter has been used to check the tracking method. However, the issues on the irradiance and temperature remain untouched in this method.

The newton-based ES method has been developed by Azad Ghaffari et al. (Farajdadian & Hassan Hosseini, 2019; Villegas-Mier et al., 2021). This method has utilized gradient and hessian for tracking MPP (Farajdadian & Hassan Hosseini, 2019; K & Punitha, n.d.; Villegas-Mier et al., 2021). The convergence rate was self-governing of hessian. The estimated hessian has been used to restrict the reliance on the ES method (Farajdadian & Hassan Hosseini, 2019; K & Punitha, n.d.; Venkateshkumar, 2018; Villegas-Mier et al., 2021). This method has been used in transient form with alternation of irradiance and temperature (Gonal & Sheshadri, 2016). The response time of this method is increased, which results in poor tracking of MPP (Gonal & Sheshadri, 2016; Shobanadevi & PheminaSelvi, n.d.).

The adaptive neuro-fuzzy (ANFIS) solar model has been proposed by Ali Chikh & Ambrish wasandra (Y. A. Ali & Ouassaid, 2019). The analytic model has also been presented to estimated hardware circuitry and measurement of noise wavelets (Y. A. Ali & Ouassaid, 2019; Govindharaj & Mariappan, 2019). However, the competence of the MPPT method is not up to the wanted mark.

The modified PSO method has been published to improve the MPPT controller's competence by Vivek Nandan Lal & Sri Niwas Singh. The single-stage PV system has been controlled to inject reactive power into the grid (Hai et al., 2022). This single-stage method has also been used to improve the converter's efficiency. However, energy utilization has not been performed well in this method.

The tracking controller has been proposed for the PV water pumping system by Mohamed A Enany (Chao & Rizal, 2021; Hai et al., 2022). The PV array and controlled converter have been connected with an external DC motor and centrifugal pump. This controller has been widely used for searching, predicting, and identifying with the CS method. The accuracy is higher by minimizing energy utilization. However, the tracking controller has not given desired solution level.

The two-axis sun tracking system has been presented by Sebastijan Seme et al. (Chao & Rizal, 2021; Hai et al., 2022; G. V. Kumar & Vinodh kumar, 2012). This system has been implemented with an optimization method to generate electricity in the PV system. The tilt and azimuth angles have also been considered to represent a nonlinear system (El-Khatib et al., 2023). The DE method has been employed to get a solution in less time (Ba et al., 2023; El-Khatib et al., 2023). The path for both angles based on irradiance, efficiency, tracking system has also been provided in this method. However, the MPPT has not been obtained efficiently through this method.

The JX crystals have been proposed for implementation in solar tracker by Lewis Fraas et al. (Ba et al., 2023; Chalh et al., 2022; El-Khatib et al., 2023). The solar track has been employed for rooftop without roof dissemination. The low-cost mirror has been replaced for silicon solar cells . The JX crystals have not been used for getting maximum carousels. Moreover, there is also time complexity.

The performance of various reflectors has been discussed by Rizk & Trial (Gong et al., 2022) discussed the performance of various reflectors. The effect of excessive sunlight on solar cells has also been discussed. The efficiency and performance have been improved by solar intensifiers (Gong et al., 2022; Hu et al., 2022). However, the power has been decreased due to reflectors.

The P&O method has been implemented by Mohammed A. Elgendy et al. (Dagal et al., 2022; Gong et al., 2022; Hu et al., 2022). This method is dependent on energy consumption, performance, and system strength. The characteristics of the PV system have been discussed on various parameter values (Jagwani & Venkatesha, 2019). The issue of every method has been recognized for various weather circumstances. However, the system's stability has been reduced in a high perturbation operation.

Hugues Renaudineau et al. (Jagwani & Venkatesha, 2019; Pandey, 2022) presents the algebra of the DC-DC converter with real-time inhibited optimization. The practical restriction has been considered for obtaining the operating point (Jagwani & Venkatesha, 2019; P. Kumar et al., 2018; Pandey, 2022). The real-time issue with PV system with optimization methods have also been presented. However, the efficiency of the converter is poor in this method.

The modified INC for identifying GMPP has been presented by Kok Soon Tey & Saad Mekhilef (Jagwani & Venkatesha, 2019; P. Kumar et al., 2018; Pandey, 2022; Vasant et al., 2019). The converter's duty cycle calculation has also been presented to improve the MPPT process. The GMPP method in various shading conditions has also been presented (Jagwani & Venkatesha, 2019; P. Kumar et al., 2018; Pandey, 2022; Rekioua & Matagne, 2012; Vasant et al., 2019). The response time in various conditions has also been presented. However, the consequential oscillations have not been removed in this method.

The shuffled frog leap algorithm (SFLA) has been presented to obtain MPPT proposed by Sridhar et al. (Vasant et al., 2022). This method does not need any mathematical computation in hardware implementation. The algorithm has been tested in various shading conditions (Lakshmi & Reddy, 2022; Vasant et al., 2022).

The investigation and computation method for getting voltage has been presented by Xinyu Fan et al. The GMPP in various irradiance values has been presented (Rouabah et al., 2022). The investigation of GMPP has been performed in various regions. However, the computation complexities have not been presented in this method.

The nonlinear MPPT controller has been presented by Hamed Taheri & Shamsodin Taheri (L. Fan & Ma, 2022). This method independent on the two-diode model. This method has been tested in combination with a Z-source converter. The modeling of nonlinear MPPT controller has also been presented with considering PV model and converter. The adaption scheme has also been presented as a PV model concerning PV characteristics. However, the response time is more in this method.

The PV array 'Integrated Unified Power Quality Conditioner' (PV-UPQC-S) has been presented by Sachin Devassy & Bhim Singh (Alrowaili et al., 2021). This method is dependent on the p-q theory. The positive sequence frequency in p-q theory has been presented to produce grid currents (Alrowaili et al., 2021; Oussama et al., 2022). The shunt compensators have been connected to this controller. Clean energy has been produced for improvement of power quality. The dynamics of PV-UPQC-S have also been presented. However, the output efficiency was not effective.

The three-phase UPQC-S with voltage compensators has been presented by Sachin Devassy & Bhim Singh (Alrowaili et al., 2021; Liu et al., 2022; Oussama et al., 2022). The shunt compensators have been connected with DC-link. The synchronous reference frame has been used to attain active current. The power quality troubles have been solved by a series compensator. However, the variation in irradiance has not been considered in UPQC-S.

The maximum electrical power tracker (MEPT) has been presented by Hassan Fathabadi (M. N. Ali et al., 2021). MEPT has been used to get maximum electrical output power, whereas MMPT has been used to get higher mechanical turbine output. MEPT method is efficient, cheap, and better in response. However, the computational burden has not been considered.

The Maximum Power Trapezium (MPT) has been presented by Artur MS Furtado et al. (M. N. Ali et al., 2021; Kamalakannan et al., 2014). This method has been compared with GMPPT. The method has been developed with MPT to obtain GMPP time. The bottom sampling time has been considered as a function. However, the shading conditions have not been considered.

The Maximum Power Point Estimation (MPPE) has been presented by Mahdi Jedari & Hamid Fathi (M. N. Ali et al., 2021; Kamalakannan et al., 2014; Precup et al., 2019). The power loss and complexity have been pointed out.

The perturbation step size models and perturbation frequency have been presented by Jyri Kivimaki et al. (M. N. Ali et al., 2021; Hua et al., 2022; Kamalakannan et al., 2014; Precup et al., 2019). The PV generator vital resistance is significant for settling time. The stable area of power has been considered for evaluating perturbation frequency. However, the performance efficiency has been reduced due to irradiance.

The contra-rotating Power Split Transmission (CR-PST) has been presented by Xiang Luo & Shuangxia Niu for wind power generation (Chtita et al., 2022). The contra-rotating rotors have been fitted with blades for absorbing wind energy. This system is straightforward and generates maximum power from wind. The finite element strategy has also been considered to check characteristics. However, the optimization issue has not been resolved in this method.

The Wave Energy Converter (WEC) for MPPT has been conferred by Joon Sung Park et al. (Ahmed et al., 2022; Chtita et al., 2022). The multiplication of wave speed and force gives the output power. Therefore, the wave energy has been removed by excitation force. The wave period represents the time phase between speed and force. The wave has been considered for several periods and amplitude. Therefore, the MPPT method has been developed by adding speed and acceleration. However, the output power has not been increased.

The transfer function, steady-state, and dynamic condition of MPPT have been presented by Yu Zou et al. (Ahmed et al., 2022; Banakhr & Mosaad, 2021; Chtita et al., 2022). It also explains the effect of wind speed on the rotor. The power curve model has also been presented to analyse the MPPT operation. However, the tracking efficiency is not up to the desired level.

Efstratios has presented the state space PV characteristics I Batzelis et al. (Andújar & Melgar, 2020). The dynamic PV model has also been integrated with MPP. The Lambert function has been presented to get the PV generator's formula. The efficiency and accuracy have also been improved. However, the oscillations have not been reduced.

The stand-alone PV system has been presented by Hadeed Ahmed Sher et al. with hybrid MPPT (Andújar & Melgar, 2020; Eltamaly & Abdelaziz, 2019). The hybrid MPPT is incorporated with P&O and the short current approach. The instantaneous current value has selected the parameters of the SCP. The flyback converter has been used for power conversion. However, the hybrid MPPT method decreases the convergence rate and tracking speed.

The enhanced PV system has been proposed by Bhim Singh et al. (Andújar & Melgar, 2020; Eltamaly & Abdelaziz, 2019; Femia et al., 2017). The boost converter has been used in operation. The voltage source converter has been used to increase power quality. The dynamic response has achieved the feed-forward. However, the losses have not been sufficiently minimized in a PV system.

The hybrid Jaya and DE algorithm has been presented by Nishant Kumar et al. (Rekioua & Matagne, 2012). This method has been applied for testing in various atmospheric conditions. The Jaya algorithm helps to get a nearly global solution. DE method helps to examine closely and to get a final and exact answer. This hybrid method has also been verified effectively. However, the hardware implementation of MPPT has not been discussed.

2.1 Neural Network-Based MPPT

The single-stage PV system with three-phase voltage has been presented by Ikhlaq Hussain et al. (Haq et al., 2022; Rekioua & Matagne, 2012). The MLP with NN has been employed in the control structure. The DSTATCOM has been utilized with the PV system to increase power quality. The presented system has given better performance for weak grids with voltage fluctuations. The MLP has many advantages, like alleviate and compact in size. However, The unstable conditions have not been addressed.

The fuzzy polynomial model with MPPT control has been presented by Mohsen Rakhshan et al. The PDC has also been added. The Takagi-Sugeno (T-S) fuzzy has been presented with LMI to reduce tracking time. The Direct Maximum Power method has been added with FPM model to get better MPPT control. However, the time complexity has not been sufficiently reduced by the FMP method.

The FOFLC has been presented for MPPT control by Shiqing Tang et al. (Z. A. Khan et al., 2021). The accuracy of tracking MPPT has been tested by fuzzy logic in various weather conditions. The dynamic nature of the fuzzy controller has been discussed. The alpha factor has been added in MPPT to minimize oscillation around MPP. This technique has a very high degree of precision. However, optimized fractional-order has not been used to get better performance.

2.2 PV System-Based Power Controlling Methods

The digital control scheme has been presented by Ahmad Al Nabulsi & Rached Dhaouadi (Wani et al., 2018). For the PV panel to get greater solar irradiation, the altitude and azimuthal have been given. The MPPT regulates the PV panel's and load's output. The P&O and FLC have been executed to increase MPP. The discrete PI controller has been used to alter the duty cycle. The PV panel function has been obtained. The oscillation around MPP has also been restricted. However, the system's stability has not to be obtained up to the desired level.

Sathish Kumar Kollimalla & Mahesh Kumar Mishra (V.v. et al., 2018). Both the temperature and the short-circuit current have been calculated. The current perturbation has been used as voltage perturbation. The robust stability has been obtained (Priya et al., 2018; V.v. et al., 2018). The constant oscillation has been avoided. Global power has not been received by this method (M et al., 2015; Priya et al., 2018; V.v. et al., 2018).

3. METHODS

PV technology has successfully turned solar power into electricity (Unde et al., 2020). The MPPT technique is utilized to optimize the power extraction from the PV panel, ensuring the maximum power output. Many researchers have developed and presented optimized MPPT methods in PV systems. Various algorithms have been implemented to enhance the performance of the MPPT system and maximize its efficiency.

3.1. PV System With Modified Structure and Reflector-Based System

The MPPT controller has the real-time derived P&O mechanism in place. The flowchart of this algorithm has been shown. The fixed panel gives variable output (Li & Feng, n.d.). Therefore, the reflectors have been modified by changing the diameter and size of the reflector. The power is generated with the height of the reflector. This method helps to reduce power wastage in variations of atmospheric conditions. For the converter to produce a constant DC voltage, the MPP tracker supplies a duty cycle. Figure 17.7 depicts the P&O algorithm's flowchart for the MPPT controller.

3.2. Hyper-Heuristic and Meta-Lamarckian Memetic Algorithm for MPPT

The lagrangian interpolation has been implemented to present the MPPT controller (Y. Mahmoud, 2022). To maximise the MPP of solar panels, the HHMLMO approach has been suggested. The iteration process gives the maximum output power (Y. Mahmoud, 2022; Singh & Shukl, 2021). The temperature and irradiance have been determined initially at different time periods. The n-bit chromosomes have been considered. The selection, crossover, and mutation processes have been proposed to get optimized output power. Figure 17.8 depicts the flowchart for the HHMLMO algorithm used by the MPPT controller.

3.3. Experimental Setup

The presented DP&O algorithm has been implemented in MATLAB 2021a with a 3.4 GHz intel core i5 processor, 4GB RAM, and Windows ten platform. The solar panel converts power into voltage or current level as per requirements. The experimental setup of the presented DP&O algorithm has been shown in Figure 17.9. The parameter has been set initially. The two 100 W solar panel has been fixed in the experiment. The parameter of the solar panel has been shown in Table 1.

Table 1. Parameters of solar array

Parameter of Solar Array	
Voc	21.5V
Isc	6.55A
Vmp	17.1V
Imp	5.85A
Maximum power	100 W

The modified solar panels with 100W have been shown in Figure 17.10. The maximum and optimum energy has been produced in the time of 8.45 AM to 4.45 PM.

4. RESULTS AND DISCUSSION

The output voltages at various temperature and solar irradiance obtained by various algorithm in MPPT controller have been presented in Table 2. The output voltage results have been represented in graph as shown in Figure 17.11. The output currents obtained by various algorithm have been presented in Table 3. The output current's results have been presented in graph as shown in Figure 17.12. The output powers obtained by algorithm have been presented in Table 4. The output power's results have been presented in graph as shown in Figure 17.13.

Table 2. Output voltage obtained by various algorithm

Time	Output Voltage			
	Modified INC	Modified PSO	Presented DP&O	Presented HHMLMO
8.45	13.1	13.9	15	14.1
9.45	13.6	14.5	15.5	14.3
10.45	14.5	15.3	16.4	15.1
11.45	14.8	15.7	17	15.3
12.45	15.2	16	17.34	16
13.45	15.6	16.4	17.34	16.1
14.45	14.6	15.8	17.21	15.8
15.45	14.3	15.3	16.74	15.6
16.45	14.1	14.9	16.1	14.7

Table 3. Output current obtained by algorithms

Time	Output Current (A)		
	Modified INC	Modified PSO	Presented DP&O
8.45	4.23	4.56	5.2
9.45	4.42	4.85	5.35
10.45	4.67	4.98	5.43
11.45	4.98	5.31	5.63
12.45	5.14	5.49	5.87
13.45	5.37	5.61	5.87
14.45	5.06	5.34	5.61
15.45	4.87	5.16	5.52
16.45	4.46	4.75	5.02

Table 4. Output power obtained by algorithms

Time	Output Power (W)		
	Modified INC	Modified PSO	Presented DP&O
8.45	62	69	78
9.45	67.2	75.6	82.9
10.45	72.5	79.9	89
11.45	78.3	83.4	95.74
12.45	86.9	93	101.7
13.45	89.6	95.4	101.7
14.45	82.4	91.3	96.5
15.45	79.6	86.2	92.4
16.45	68.9	75.1	80.8

5. CONCLUSION

The main problem of the solar unit is to obtain the optimal prong where the solar panel gives maximum output power under various atmospheric conditions. Recently, many researchers have proposed a number of algorithms to get optimum solutions by MPPT controller. Initially, the P&O algorithm was proposed in the PV system for obtaining MPPT with panels is getting The presented derived P&O panels were tested in various atmospheric conditions, even shading conditions. The reflectors along with mirrors have given better performance in the presented DP&O method. The Hyper-Heuristic and Meta-Lamarckian Memetic Optimization have been presented for the MPPT controller to get the compound in fewer concurrence time. The algorithm has undergone testing during different time periods to showcase its effectiveness and superior performance. In order to demonstrate its superiority, the results were compared with those obtained from other widely recognized algorithms. The following are the chapter's key contributions:

- The modeling of the PV system, DC-DC converter, overview of MPPT methods, and optimization methods have been discussed. The various MPPT methods like the P&O method, I & C method, Neural network, PSO, DE, and CSA methods have been discussed to get an overview of their application in the MPPT controller.
- The previously applied optimization techniques have been considered. A comprehensive analysis of the advantages and disadvantages of these optimization techniques has been conducted. The merits of hybrid optimization techniques are also discussed. The comparisons between these above-mentioned optimization techniques have been given.
- The flowchart and steps of recently developed algorithms applied in the MPPT controller have been given. The mathematical modeling of these algorithms has also been given for better understanding.
- Recently developed methods have provided the voltage output, current, and power of the Photovoltaic in tabular form. These algorithms can still be improved upon by other more modern algorithms, according to a comparison of their performance.
- For easier comprehension, the output voltage, current, and power from the algorithms have been shown in graphical form.

6. FUTURE RESEARCH DIRECTION

For MPPT in the PV system, the DP&O and HHMLMO algorithm has been given. The PV system produces an infinite amount of energy. However, it is impossible to create power at night. Solar panels are made in a fairly basic manner. However, it is unable to store the electricity produced. The quality and output level of PV electricity may be enhanced by designing the solar panel. To get the most out of the PV panel, apply the other designed algorithm. Other electrical optimization issues, such as efficient power flow, economical load dispatch, and electric cars, can be resolved using the optimization techniques.

REFERENCES

Ahmed, M., Harbi, I., Kennel, R., Rodríguez, J., & Abdelrahem, M. (2022). Maximum Power Point Tracking-Based Model Predictive Control for Photovoltaic Systems: Investigation and New Perspective. *Sensors (Basel)*, 22(8), 3069. Advance online publication. doi:10.339022083069 PMID:35459055

Ali, M. N., Mahmoud, K., Lehtonen, M., & Darwish, M. M. F. (2021). Promising MPPT Methods Combining Metaheuristic, Fuzzy-Logic and ANN Techniques for Grid-Connected Photovoltaic. *Sensors (Basel)*, 21(4), 1244. Advance online publication. doi:10.339021041244 PMID:33578777

Ali, Y. A., & Ouassaid, M. (2019). Sensorless MPPT Controller using Particle Swarm and Grey Wolf Optimization for Wind Turbines. *2019 7th International Renewable and Sustainable Energy Conference (IRSEC)*. 10.1109/IRSEC48032.2019.9078151

Alrowaili, Z. A., Ali, M. M., Youssef, A., Mousa, H. H. H., Ali, A. S., Abdel-Jaber, G. T., Ezzeldien, M., & Gami, F. (2021). Robust Adaptive HCS MPPT Algorithm-Based Wind Generation System Using Model Reference Adaptive Control. *Sensors (Basel)*, *21*(15), 5187. Advance online publication. doi:10.339021155187 PMID:34372423

Andújar, J. M., & Melgar, S. G. (2020). *Energy Efficiency in Buildings: Both New and Rehabilitated*. MDPI.

Arumugam, S., & Chakkarapani, L. D. (2019). Metal nanoparticles functionalized carbon nanotubes for efficient catalytic application. In Materials Research Express (Vol. 6, Issue 10, p. 1050e3). doi:10.1088/2053-1591/ab42ff

Ayad, I. A., Elwarraki, E., & Baghdadi, M. (2021). Intelligent Perturb and Observe Based MPPT Approach Using Multilevel DC-DC Converter to Improve PV Production System. In Journal of Electrical and Computer Engineering (Vol. 2021, pp. 1–13). doi:10.1155/2021/6673022

Ayad, I. A., Elwarraki, E., & Baghdadi, M. (2022). MPPT Comparison of Standalone Photovoltaic System using Multi-level Boost Converter. In *2022 4th Global Power, Energy and Communication Conference (GPECOM)*. 10.1109/GPECOM55404.2022.9815738

Ba, A., Ndiaye, A., Ndiaye, E. H. M., & Mbodji, S. (2023). Power optimization of a photovoltaic system with artificial intelligence algorithms over two seasons in tropical area. *MethodsX*, *10*, 101959. doi:10.1016/j.mex.2022.101959 PMID:36545542

Badapanda, M. K., Tripathi, A., Upadhyay, R., & Lad, M. (2022). High Voltage DC Power Supply with Input Parallel and Output Series Connected DC-DC Converters. In IEEE Transactions on Power Electronics (pp. 1–5). doi:10.1109/TPEL.2022.3233257

Bai, Y., Zhuang, H., & Wang, D. (2007). *Advanced Fuzzy Logic Technologies in Industrial Applications*. Springer Science & Business Media.

Banakhr, F. A., & Mosaad, M. I. (2021). High performance adaptive maximum power point tracking technique for off-grid photovoltaic systems. *Scientific Reports*, *11*(1), 20400. doi:10.103841598-021-99949-8 PMID:34650159

Bayeh, C. Z., & Moubayed, N. (2014). Comparison between PV farms, solar chimneys and CSP towers in Lebanon: Influence of temperature and solar irradiance on the output power. *International Conference on Renewable Energies for Developing Countries 2014*. 10.1109/REDEC.2014.7038558

Bennis, G., Karim, M., & Lagrioui, A. (2015). Optimization of the performance of a photovoltaic system with MPPT controller. *2015 3rd International Renewable and Sustainable Energy Conference (IRSEC)*. 10.1109/IRSEC.2015.7455115

Bhattacharjee, K., Bhattacharya, A., & Dey, S. H. N. (2014a). Chemical reaction optimisation for different economic dispatch problems. In IET Generation, Transmission & Distribution (Vol. 8, Issue 3, pp. 530–541). doi:10.1049/iet-gtd.2013.0122

Bhattacharjee, K., Bhattacharya, A., & Dey, S. H. N. (2014b). Oppositional Real Coded Chemical Reaction Optimization for different economic dispatch problems. In International Journal of Electrical Power & Energy Systems (Vol. 55, pp. 378–391). doi:10.1016/j.ijepes.2013.09.033

Bhattacharjee, K., Bhattacharya, A., & Dey, S. H. N. (2014c). Solution of Economic Emission Load Dispatch problems of power systems by Real Coded Chemical Reaction algorithm. In International Journal of Electrical Power & Energy Systems (Vol. 59, pp. 176–187). doi:10.1016/j.ijepes.2014.02.006

Bhattacharjee, K., Shah, K., & Soni, J. (2021). Solving Economic Dispatch using Artificial Eco System-based Optimization. In Electric Power Components and Systems (Vol. 49, Issues 11-12, pp. 1034–1051). doi:10.1080/15325008.2021.2013995

Chalh, A., Chaibi, R., Hammoumi, A. E., Motahhir, S., Ghzizal, A. E., & Al-Dhaifallah, M. (2022). A novel MPPT design based on the seagull optimization algorithm for photovoltaic systems operating under partial shading. *Scientific Reports*, *12*(1), 21804. doi:10.103841598-022-26284-x PMID:36526663

Chao, K.-H., & Rizal, M. N. (2021). A Hybrid MPPT Controller Based on the Genetic Algorithm and Ant Colony Optimization for Photovoltaic Systems under Partially Shaded Conditions. In Energies (Vol. 14, Issue 10, p. 2902). doi:10.3390/en14102902

Chitra, A., Indragandhi, V., & Razia Sultana, W. (2022). *Smart Grids and Green Energy Systems*. John Wiley & Sons. doi:10.1002/9781119872061

Chtita, S., Motahhir, S., El Hammoumi, A., Chouder, A., Benyoucef, A. S., El Ghzizal, A., Derouich, A., Abouhawwash, M., & Askar, S. S. (2022). A novel hybrid GWO-PSO-based maximum power point tracking for photovoltaic systems operating under partial shading conditions. *Scientific Reports*, *12*(1), 10637. doi:10.103841598-022-14733-6 PMID:35739302

Dagal, I., Akın, B., & Akboy, E. (2022). MPPT mechanism based on novel hybrid particle swarm optimization and salp swarm optimization algorithm for battery charging through simulink. *Scientific Reports*, *12*(1), 2664. doi:10.103841598-022-06609-6 PMID:35177713

Dar, S. A., & Imtiaz, N. (2023). Classification of neuroimaging data in Alzheimer's disease using particle swarm optimization: A systematic review. *Applied Neuropsychology. Adult*, 1–12. doi:10.1080/23279095.2023.2169886 PMID:36719791

Dong, J., & Duan, X. (2023). A Robust Control via a Fuzzy System with PID for the ROV. *Sensors (Basel)*, *23*(2), 821. Advance online publication. doi:10.339023020821 PMID:36679618

Dynamic Behavior Analysis of ANFIS Based MPPT Controller for Standalone Photovoltaic Systems. (2020). In International Journal of Renewable Energy Research (Issue v10i1). doi:10.20508/ijrer.v10i1.10244.g7897

El-Khatib, M. F., Sabry, M.-N., El-Sebah, M. I. A., & Maged, S. A. (2023). Hardware-in-the-loop testing of simple and intelligent MPPT control algorithm for an electric vehicle charging power by photovoltaic system. *ISA Transactions*, *137*, 656–669. Advance online publication. doi:10.1016/j.isatra.2023.01.025 PMID:36725414

Eltamaly, A. M., & Abdelaziz, A. Y. (2019). *Modern Maximum Power Point Tracking Techniques for Photovoltaic Energy Systems.* Springer.

Fan, L., & Ma, X. (2022). Maximum power point tracking of PEMFC based on hybrid artificial bee colony algorithm with fuzzy control. *Scientific Reports, 12*(1), 4316. doi:10.103841598-022-08327-5 PMID:35279691

Fan, Z., Li, S., Cheng, H., & Liu, L. (2021). Perturb and Observe MPPT Algorithm of photovoltaic System: A Review. *2021 33rd Chinese Control and Decision Conference (CCDC).* 10.1109/CCDC52312.2021.9602272

Farajdadian, S., & Hassan Hosseini, S. M. (2019). Optimization of fuzzy-based MPPT controller via metaheuristic techniques for stand-alone PV systems. In International Journal of Hydrogen Energy (Vol. 44, Issue 47, pp. 25457–25472). doi:10.1016/j.ijhydene.2019.08.037

Farghally, H., Ahmed, N., & Fahmy, F. (2018). Design and optimization of standalone photovoltaic system based on MPPT FLC controller for electric bikes charging station. In *The International Conference on Electrical Engineering* (Vol. 11, Issue 11, pp. 1–24). 10.21608/iceeng.2018.30177

Femia, N., Petrone, G., Spagnuolo, G., & Vitelli, M. (2017). *Power Electronics and Control Techniques for Maximum Energy Harvesting in Photovoltaic Systems.* CRC Press. doi:10.1201/b14303

Ferreira, J. A., & van Wyk, J. D. (n.d.). Transistor inverter optimization employing self-oscillation for low cost and simplicity. *Conference Record of the 1988 IEEE Industry Applications Society Annual Meeting.* 10.1109/IAS.1988.25177

Gameti, N., & Vairagi, B. D. (2021). Artificial intelligence technique based MPPT controller for stand-alone solar energy conversion system. In International Journal of Technical Research & Science (pp. 15–21). doi:10.30780/IJTRS.V06.I12.002

Georgakopoulos, D., Budovsky, I., Benz, S. P., & Gubler, G. (2018). Josephson Arbitrary Waveform Synthesizer as a Reference Standard for the Measurement of the Phase of Harmonics in Distorted Signals. *2018 Conference on Precision Electromagnetic Measurements (CPEM 2018).* 10.1109/CPEM.2018.8501223

Ghazi, A., Ghazi, G. A., Al-Ammar, E. A., Hasanien, H. M., & Turky, R. A. (2022). Transient Search Optimization Based Fuzzy-PI Controller for MPPT of Standalone PV System. *2022 23rd International Middle East Power Systems Conference (MEPCON).* 10.1109/MEPCON55441.2022.10021781

Gonal, V. S., & Sheshadri, G. S. (2016). Solar energy optimization using MPPT controller by maximum conductance method. *2016 IEEE 7th Power India International Conference (PIICON).* 10.1109/POWERI.2016.8077445

Gong, L., Hou, G., & Huang, C. (2022). A two-stage MPPT controller for PV system based on the improved artificial bee colony and simultaneous heat transfer search algorithm. *ISA Transactions.* Advance online publication. doi:10.1016/j.isatra.2022.06.005 PMID:35753811

Govindharaj, A., & Mariappan, A. (2019). Adaptive Neuralback Stepping Controller for MPPT in Photo Voltaic Systems. *2019 IEEE International Conference on Intelligent Techniques in Control, Optimization and Signal Processing (INCOS).* 10.1109/INCOS45849.2019.8951363

Hai, T., Zhou, J., & Muranaka, K. (2022). An efficient fuzzy-logic based MPPT controller for grid-connected PV systems by farmland fertility optimization algorithm. In Optik (Vol. 267, p. 169636). doi:10.1016/j.ijleo.2022.169636

HamdiT.ElleuchK.AbidH.ToumiA. (n.d.). *Sliding mode controller with fuzzy supervisor for MPPT of Photovoltaic Pumping system.* doi:10.21203/rs.3.rs-2021791/v1

Haq, I. U., Khan, Q., Ullah, S., Khan, S. A., Akmeliawati, R., Khan, M. A., & Iqbal, J. (2022). Neural network-based adaptive global sliding mode MPPT controller design for stand-alone photovoltaic systems. *PLoS One, 17*(1), e0260480. doi:10.1371/journal.pone.0260480 PMID:35051183

Hattu, E. (2019). Colling System Application In PV Module Toward Output Voltage And Current PV Module. *Proceedings of the 1st International Conference on Engineering, Science, and Commerce, ICESC 2019, 18-19 October 2019, Labuan Bajo, Nusa Tenggara Timur, Indonesia.* 10.4108/eai.18-10-2019.2289921

Hegazy, E., Saad, W., & Shokair, M. (2020). Studying the Effect of Using a Low Power PV and DC-DC Boost Converter on the Performance of the Solar Energy PV System. *2020 15th International Conference on Computer Engineering and Systems (ICCES).* 10.1109/ICCES51560.2020.9334581

Hosseini, S. H., Varesi, K., Ardashir, J. F., Gandomi, A. A., & Saeidabadi, S. (2015). An attempt to improve output voltage quality of developed multi-level inverter topology by increasing the number of levels. *2015 9th International Conference on Electrical and Electronics Engineering (ELECO).* 10.1109/ELECO.2015.7394622

Hu, Z., Norouzi, H., Jiang, M., Dadfar, S., & Kashiwagi, T. (2022). Novel hybrid modified krill herd algorithm and fuzzy controller based MPPT to optimally tune the member functions for PV system in the three-phase grid-connected mode. *ISA Transactions, 129*(Pt B), 214–229.

Hua, R., Marin-Quiros, S., Mohan, H. K., & Wang, Y. (2022). Maximum power point tracking for a multi-layered piezoelectric heel charger with a levered mechanism toward impact-based energy harvesting. *The Review of Scientific Instruments, 93*(9), 095001. doi:10.1063/5.0091254 PMID:36182488

Implementasi Perbandingan Algoritma Simple Hill Climbing Dan Algoritma Ascent Hill Climbing Pada Permainan 8-Puzzle. (2021). In *Edik Informatika* (Vol. 8, Issue 1, pp. 41–52). doi:10.22202/ei.2021.v8i1.5054

Jagwani, S., & Venkatesha, L. (2019). Particle Swarm Optimization-Based MPPT Controller for Wind Turbine Systems. In *Data* (pp. 313–319). Engineering and Applications. doi:10.1007/978-981-13-6351-1_25

John, R., Sheik Mohammed, S., & Zachariah, R. (2017). Variable step size Perturb and observe MPPT algorithm for standalone solar photovoltaic system. *2017 IEEE International Conference on Intelligent Techniques in Control, Optimization and Signal Processing (INCOS).* 10.1109/ITCOSP.2017.8303163

Jouda, A., Elyes, F., Rabhi, A., & Abdelkader, M. (2017). Optimization of Scaling Factors of Fuzzy–MPPT Controller for Stand-alone Photovoltaic System by Particle Swarm Optimization. In Energy Procedia (Vol. 111, pp. 954–963). doi:10.1016/j.egypro.2017.03.258

K, P., & Punitha, K. (n.d.). *Horse Herd Optimization Algorithm based MPPT controller for Solar Tree Application*. doi:10.22541/au.167285877.71885740/v1

Kamalakannan, C., Padma Suresh, L., Dash, S. S., & Panigrahi, B. K. (2014). Power Electronics and Renewable Energy Systems*: Proceedings of ICPERES 2014*. Springer.

Kapur, I., Jain, D., Jain, A., & Garg, R. (2020). Adaptive Neuro Fuzzy Inference System for MPPT in Standalone Solar Photovoltaic System. *2020 IEEE 17th India Council International Conference (INDICON)*. 10.1109/INDICON49873.2020.9342105

Khan, M. Y. A. (2019). Design and Analysis of Maximum Power Point Tracking (MPPT) Controller for PV System. In Journal of Mechanics of Continua and Mathematical Sciences (Vol. 14, Issue 1). doi:10.26782/jmcms.2019.02.00019

Khan, Z. A., Khan, L., Ahmad, S., Mumtaz, S., Jafar, M., & Khan, Q. (2021). RBF neural network based backstepping terminal sliding mode MPPT control technique for PV system. *PLoS One*, *16*(4), e0249705. doi:10.1371/journal.pone.0249705 PMID:33831094

Kosgi, D., & Kulkarni, V. V. (2022). To Investigate the Failure in Sensor Assembly Due to Temperature Variational Loading, and to Provide Optimum Material Solution to Avert This Failure. SAE Technical Paper Series. doi:10.4271/2022-28-0369

Kumar, A., Rizwan, M., & Nangia, U. (2021). Development of ANFIS-based algorithm for MPPT controller for standalone photovoltaic system. In International Journal of Advanced Intelligence Paradigms (Vol. 18, Issue 2, p. 247). doi:10.1504/IJAIP.2021.112906

Kumar, G. V., & Vinodh Kumar, G. (2012). Performance Enhancement in PV System usingIntelligent Controller based MPPT Controller. In *IOSR Journal of Engineering* (Vol. 2, Issue 2, pp. 284–287). doi:10.9790/3021-0202284287

Kumar, P., Singh, S., Ali, I., & Ustun, T. S. (2018). *Handbook of Research on Power and Energy System Optimization*. IGI Global. doi:10.4018/978-1-5225-3935-3

Lakshmi, G. V., & Reddy, K. H. (2022). Improved tunicate swarm search-based MPPT for photovoltaic on a "grid-connected" inverter system. *Environmental Science and Pollution Research International*, *29*(52), 78650–78665. doi:10.100711356-022-21157-2 PMID:35691948

Lee, E.-H., & Sohn, B.-J. (2011). Recent increasing trend in dust frequency over Mongolia and Inner Mongolia regions and its association with climate and surface condition change. In Atmospheric Environment (Vol. 45, Issue 27, pp. 4611–4616). doi:10.1016/j.atmosenv.2011.05.065

LiY.FengY. (n.d.). *Power Prediction Method of PV System Based on Bifacial PV Modules*. doi:10.21203/rs.3.rs-2145030/v1

Liu, S., You, H., Liu, Y., Feng, W., & Fu, S. (2022). Research on optimal control strategy of wind-solar hybrid system based on power prediction. *ISA Transactions*, *123*, 179–187. doi:10.1016/j.isatra.2021.05.010 PMID:33994212

M, D., Dharani, M., & Usha, P. V. (2015). A Novel Topology for Controlling a Four Port DC-DC Boost Converter for a Hybrid PV/PV/Battery Power System. In *TELKOMNIKA Indonesian Journal of Electrical Engineering* (Vol. 14, Issue 3). doi:10.11591/telkomnika.v14i3.7854

Mahmood, M., Ali, I., & Ahmed, O. (2020). Comparative Study of Perturb & Observe, Modified Perturb & Observe and Modified Incremental Conductance MPPT Techniques for PV Systems. In Engineering and Technology Journal (Vol. 38, Issue 4A, pp. 478–490). doi:10.30684/etj.v38i4A.329

Mahmoud, A., Fath, H., & Ahmed, M. (2018). Enhancing the performance of a solar driven hybrid solar still/humidification-dehumidification desalination system integrated with solar concentrator and photovoltaic panels. In Desalination (Vol. 430, pp. 165–179). doi:10.1016/j.desal.2017.12.052

Mahmoud, Y. (2022). New Approach for Controlling PV-PV Differential Power Processing Converters. *2022 13th International Renewable Energy Congress (IREC)*. 10.1109/IREC56325.2022.10001944

Mendel, J., Hagras, H., Tan, W.-W., Melek, W. W., & Ying, H. (2014). *Introduction To Type-2 Fuzzy Logic Control: Theory and Applications*. John Wiley & Sons. doi:10.1002/9781118886540

Nangia, U., Kumar, A., & Rizwan, M. (2021). Development of ANFIS based Algorithm for MPPT Controller for Standalone Photovoltaic System. In International Journal of Advanced Intelligence Paradigms (Vol. 18, Issue 1, p. 1). doi:10.1504/IJAIP.2021.10017382

Oussama, M., Abdelghani, C., & Lakhdar, C. (2022). Efficiency and robustness of type-2 fractional fuzzy PID design using salps swarm algorithm for a wind turbine control under uncertainty. *ISA Transactions*, *125*, 72–84. doi:10.1016/j.isatra.2021.06.016 PMID:34167819

Panda, S., Gupta, M., & Malvi, C. S. (2020). Advances in perturb and observe based MPPT algorithm. In *WEENTECH Proceedings in Energy* (pp. 21–27). 10.32438/WPE.060245

Pandey, S. (2022). *MATLAB Model of an Optimized Battery Charge Controller*. SUBRATA PANDEY.

Parthiban, S., & Durairaj, D. (2015). Standalone photovoltaic system with MPPT techniques on single-phase eleven-level inverter for utility applications. *2015 International Conference on Electrical, Electronics, Signals, Communication and Optimization (EESCO)*. 10.1109/EESCO.2015.7253884

Prajapati, S., & Shah, M. T. (2021). Novel MPPT Algorithm for Standalone Solar Photovoltaic System. *2021 International Conference on Advance Computing and Innovative Technologies in Engineering (ICACITE)*. 10.1109/ICACITE51222.2021.9404599

Precup, R.-E., Kamal, T., & Hassan, S. Z. (2019). *Advanced Control and Optimization Paradigms for Wind Energy Systems*. Springer. doi:10.1007/978-981-13-5995-8

Priya, M. A. J., Ashok Kumar, B., & Senthilrani, S. (2018). Phase Locked Loop for controlling inverter interfaced with grid connected solar PV system. *2018 National Power Engineering Conference (NPEC)*. 10.1109/NPEC.2018.8476728

Ramu, E., & Sobhana, O. (2018). Standalone PV system with Fuzzy MPPT controller. *2018 International Conference on Recent Innovations in Electrical, Electronics & Communication Engineering (ICRIEECE)*. 10.1109/ICRIEECE44171.2018.9009379

Reay, D. S. (2004). New Directions: Flying in the face of the climate change convention. In Atmospheric Environment (Vol. 38, Issue 5, pp. 793–794). doi:10.1016/j.atmosenv.2003.10.026

Rekioua, D., & Matagne, E. (2012). *Optimization of Photovoltaic Power Systems: Modelization, Simulation and Control*. Springer Science & Business Media. doi:10.1007/978-1-4471-2403-0

Rouabah, B., Toubakh, H., Kafi, M. R., & Sayed-Mouchaweh, M. (2022). Adaptive data-driven fault-tolerant control strategy for optimal power extraction in presence of broken rotor bars in wind turbine. *ISA Transactions*, *130*, 92–103. doi:10.1016/j.isatra.2022.04.008 PMID:35450727

Santos de Araújo, J. V., Villanueva, J. M. M., Cordula, M. M., Cardoso, A. A., & Gomes, H. P. (2022). Fuzzy Control of Pressure in a Water Supply Network Based on Neural Network System Modeling and IoT Measurements. *Sensors (Basel)*, *22*(23), 9130. Advance online publication. doi:10.339022239130 PMID:36501831

Sarkar, K., Sharma, R., & Bhattacharyya, S. P. (2012). A constrained variational approach to the designing of low transport band gap materials: A multiobjective random mutation hill climbing method. In International Journal of Quantum Chemistry (Vol. 112, Issue 6, pp. 1547–1558). doi:10.1002/qua.23119

Shah, K., Soni, J., & Bhattacharjee, K. (2023). Artificial Electric Field Algorithm Applied to the Economic Load Dispatch Problem With Valve Point Loading Effect. In International Journal of Swarm Intelligence Research (Vol. 14, Issue 1, pp. 1–23). doi:10.4018/IJSIR.317136

Shobanadevi, N. (n.d.). Adaptive Black Widow Optimization Based MPPT Controller in High-Gain Non-Isolated DC-DC Converter for PV Applications. doi:10.21203/rs.3.rs-2473630/v1

Singh, B., & Shukl, P. (2021). Seamless Power Transfer of Solar PV Based Grid Interactive System. *2021 National Power Electronics Conference (NPEC)*. 10.1109/NPEC52100.2021.9672533

Soni, J., & Bhattacharjee, K. (2022). Sooty Tern Optimization Algorithm for Solving the Multi-Objective Dynamic Economic Emission Dispatch Problem. In International Journal of Swarm Intelligence Research (Vol. 13, Issue 1, pp. 1–15). doi:10.4018/IJSIR.308292

Soni, J., & Bhattacharjee, K. (2023). Sine-Cosine Algorithm for the Dynamic Economic Dispatch Problem With the Valve-Point Loading Effect. In International Journal of Swarm Intelligence Research (Vol. 14, Issue 1, pp. 1–15). doi:10.4018/IJSIR.316801

Soni, J. M., Patel, D. V., Patel, R. V., & Modha, H. P. (2020). A Strategic Community Control-Based Power Flow Between Grid-Integrated PV Houses. In Lecture Notes in Electrical Engineering (pp. 1061–1071). doi:10.1007/978-981-15-7031-5_101

Sprenger, W., Wilson, H. R., & Kuhn, T. E. (2016). Electricity yield simulation for the building-integrated photovoltaic system installed in the main building roof of the Fraunhofer Institute for Solar Energy Systems ISE. In Solar Energy (Vol. 135, pp. 633–643). doi:10.1016/j.solener.2016.06.037

Stosovic, M. A., Dimitrijevic, M., & Litovski, V. (2013). MPPT controller design for a standalone PV system. In *2013 11th International Conference on Telecommunications in Modern Satellite, Cable and Broadcasting Services (TELSIKS)*. 10.1109/TELSKS.2013.6704427

Syafaruddin, S., Hiyama, T., & Karatepe, E. (2010). Investigation of ANN performance for tracking the optimum points of PV module under partially shaded conditions. *2010 Conference Proceedings IPEC.* 10.1109/IPECON.2010.5697002

Tan, C. Y., Selvaraj, J., & Abd Rahim, N. (2014). Improvement of hill climbing method by introducing simple irradiance detection method. *3rd IET International Conference on Clean Energy and Technology (CEAT) 2014.* 10.1049/cp.2014.1493

Teferra, D. M., Ngoo, L. M. H., & Nyakoe, G. N. (2023). Fuzzy-based prediction of solar PV and wind power generation for microgrid modeling using particle swarm optimization. *Heliyon*, *9*(1), e12802. doi:10.1016/j.heliyon.2023.e12802 PMID:36704286

Tzani-Tzanopoulou, P., Rozumbetov, R., Taka, S., Doudoulakakis, A., Lebessi, E., Chanishvili, N., Kakabadze, E., Bakuradze, N., Grdzelishvili, N., Goderdzishvili, M., Legaki, E., Andreakos, E., Papadaki, M., Megremis, S., Xepapadaki, P., Kaltsas, G., Akdis, C. A., & Papadopoulos, N. G. (2022). Development of an homeostasis model between airway epithelial cells, bacteria and bacteriophages: A time-lapsed observation of cell viability and inflammatory response. *The Journal of General Virology*, *103*(12). Advance online publication. doi:10.1099/jgv.0.001819 PMID:36748697

Unde, M., Hans, M., & Navghare, M. (2020). Grid Tie PV Inverter Using Buck-Boost Based Converter Maximizing Power Yield in Mismatched Environmental Condition Controlling Two Solar PV Arrays. *2020 IEEE International Symposium on Sustainable Energy, Signal Processing and Cyber Security (iSSSC).* 10.1109/iSSSC50941.2020.9358896

Vasant, P., Zelinka, I., & Weber, G.-W. (2019). *Intelligent Computing and Optimization: Proceedings of the 2nd International Conference on Intelligent Computing and Optimization 2019 (ICO 2019).* Springer Nature. 10.1007/978-3-030-00979-3

Vasant, P., Zelinka, I., & Weber, G.-W. (2022). *Intelligent Computing & Optimization: Proceedings of the 4th International Conference on Intelligent Computing and Optimization 2021 (ICO2021).* Springer Nature. 10.1007/978-3-030-93247-3

Venkateshkumar, M. (2018). Fuzzy Controller-Based MPPT of PV Power System. Fuzzy Logic Based in Optimization Methods and Control Systems and its Applications. doi:10.5772/intechopen.80065

Verma, D., Soni, J., Kalathia, D., & Bhattacharjee, K. (2022). Sine Cosine Algorithm for Solving Economic Load Dispatch Problem With Penetration of Renewables. In International Journal of Swarm Intelligence Research (Vol. 13, Issue 1, pp. 1–21). doi:10.4018/IJSIR.299847

Villegas-Mier, C. G., Rodriguez-Resendiz, J., Álvarez-Alvarado, J. M., Rodriguez-Resendiz, H., Herrera-Navarro, A. M., & Rodríguez-Abreo, O. (2021). Artificial Neural Networks in MPPT Algorithms for Optimization of Photovoltaic Power Systems: A Review. *Micromachines*, *12*(10), 1260. Advance online publication. doi:10.3390/mi12101260 PMID:34683311

V.V., R., Rajasegharan, V. V., L., P., & R., R. (2018). Modelling and controlling of PV connected quasi Z-source cascaded multilevel inverter system: An HACSNN based control approach. In *Electric Power Systems Research* (Vol. 162, pp. 10–22). doi:10.1016/j.epsr.2018.04.020

Waghmare-Ujgare, V., Goudar, M. D., & Kharadkar, R. D. (2022). Optimized maximum power point tracker for partially shaded PV system: adaptive duty cycle control. International Journal of Intelligent Robotics and Applications. doi:10.100741315-022-00249-9

Wahab, N. A., & Mohamed, Z. (2022). *Control, Instrumentation and Mechatronics: Theory and Practice.* Springer Nature. doi:10.1007/978-981-19-3923-5

Wang, C., Ma, Z., & Tong, S. (2022). Adaptive fuzzy output-feedback event-triggered control for fractional-order nonlinear system. *Mathematical Biosciences and Engineering*, *19*(12), 12334–12352. doi:10.3934/mbe.2022575 PMID:36654000

Wani, J. A. (2018). Different methods for controlling the power flow in RERs based power system. In International Journal of Trend in Scientific Research and Development (Vol. -2, Issue -3, pp. 1798–1803). doi:10.31142/ijtsrd11647

Wu, Z., Jiang, Z., Li, Z., Jiao, P., Zhai, J., Liu, S., Han, X., Zhang, S., Sun, J., Gai, Z., Qiu, C., Xu, J., Liu, H., Qin, R., & Lu, R. (2023). Multi-omics analysis reveals spatiotemporal regulation and function of heteromorphic leaves in Populus. *Plant Physiology*, *192*(1), 188–204. Advance online publication. doi:10.1093/plphys/kiad063 PMID:36746772

Yamamoto, K., & Shinohara, K. (1996). Analysis of AC Servo Motor Driven by PWM Inverter with Switching Dead-Time and Compensation for Output Voltage Deviation. In IEEJ Transactions on Industry Applications (Vol. 116, Issue 9, pp. 924–933). doi:10.1541/ieejias.116.924

Zhan, H., Zha, T., Hong, B., & Shan, L. (2023). Particle size distribution inversion using the Weibull-distribution adaptive-parameters cuckoo search algorithm. *Applied Optics*, *62*(1), 235–245. doi:10.1364/AO.476741 PMID:36606870

APPENDIX

List of Abbreviations

ANFIS	'Adaptive Neuro-Fuzzy Inference System'	CS	Cuckoo Search
AC	'Alternating Current'	DE	Differential Evolution
ACO	'Ant Colony Optimization	DAC	Digital-to-Analog Converter
BA	'Bat Algorithm'	DC	Direct Current
BSA	'Binary Search Algorithm'	DSTATCOM	Distributed Static Compensator
BL	'Bridge-linked'	FPGA	Field Programmable Gate Array
CR-PST	Contra-Rotating Power Split Transmission	FSA	Fish Swarm Algorithm
FPA	Flower Pollination Algorithm	FSCC	Fractional Short Circuit Current
FLC	'Fuzzy Logic controller'	GA	'Genetic Approach'
GMPP	'Global Maximum Power Point'	GWO	'Grey Wolf Optimization'
HC	'Hill Climbing'	HHMLMO	Hyper-Heuristic and Meta-Lamarckian Memetic Optimization
LMI	Linear Matrix Inequality	MMPT	'Maximum Mechanical Power Trackers'
MEPT	'Maximum Electrical Power Tracker'	MPPT	'Maximum Power Point Tracking
P&O	'Perturbation and Observation'	PSO	'Particle Swarm Optimization
PV	Photovoltaic	PCC	Point of Common Coupling
SEPIC	Single-ended primary-inductor converter	GMPPT	Global Maximum Power Point Tracking
PWM	Pulse-width modulation	DE	Differential Evolution
THD	Total harmonic distortion	FOFCL	Fractional-Order Fuzzy Logic Controller

Figure 1.

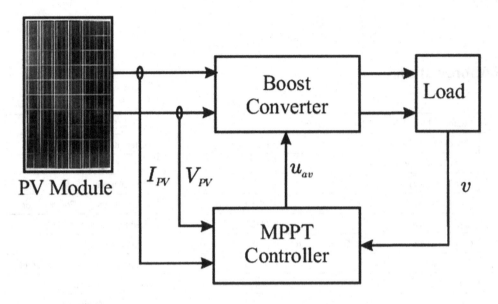

Figure 2.

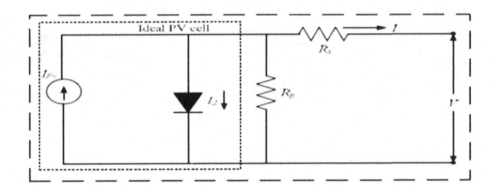

Figure 3.

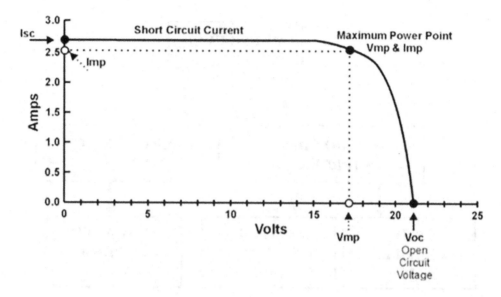

Figure 4.

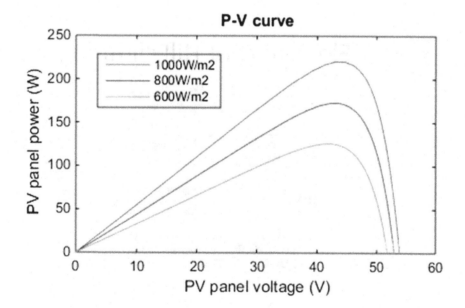

Figure 5.

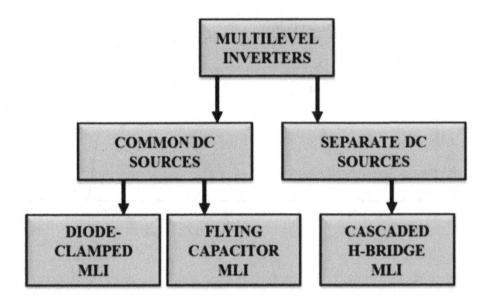

Figure 6.

Flowchart of Hill climbing

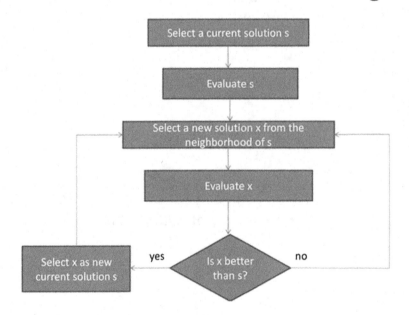

Figure 7.

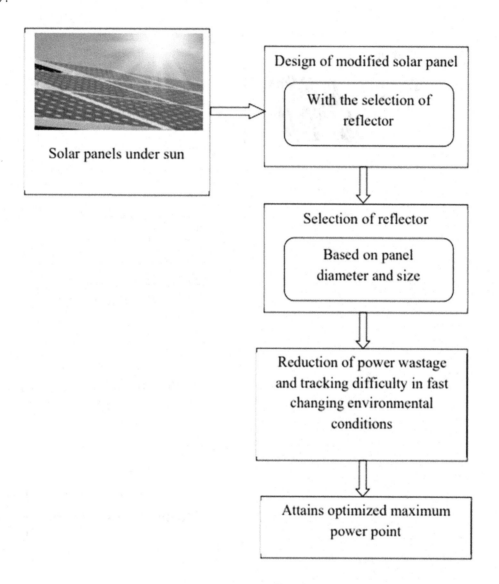

Figure 8.

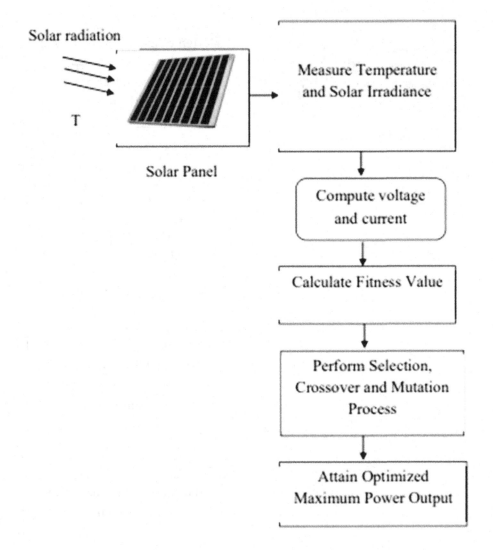

Figure 9.

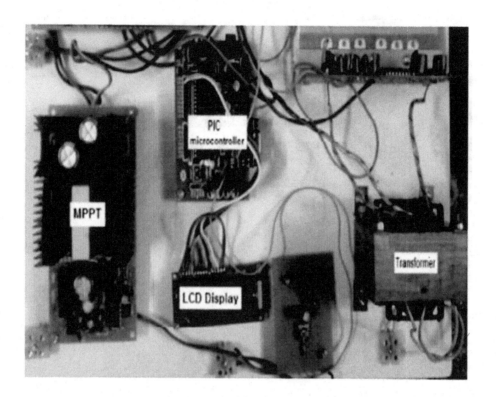

Figure 10.

Figure 11.

Figure 12.

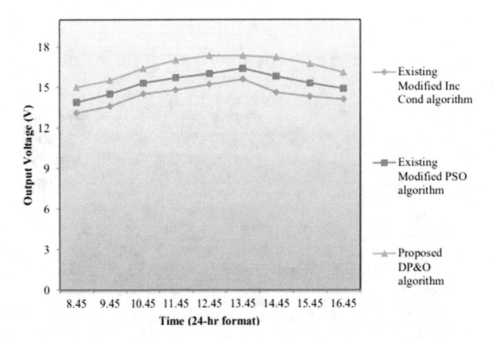

Figure 13.

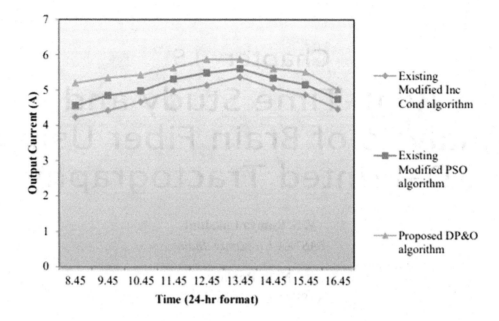

Figure 14.

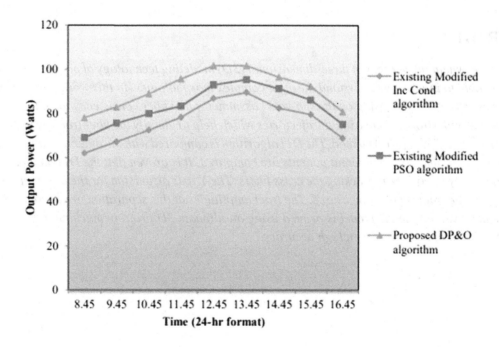

Chapter 15
Real-Time Study and Analysis of Brain Fiber Using 3D-Printed Tractography

V. S. Ramya Lakshmi
SASTRA University, India

N. R. Raajan
SASTRA University, India

Natarajan Prabaharan
SASTRA University, India

K. Hariharan
SASTRA University, India

ABSTRACT

With the overwhelming success of three-dimensional (3D) modeling technology of patient anatomy, surgeons are able to intuitively understand the most complex morphologies. In this work, the tractography model is constructed by focusing on the sub-voxel asymmetry and fiber consistency to enhance cortical tractography with strongly bent axonal trajectories which help to identify the fiber track by using the diffusion tensor imagining (DTI) method. The DTI algorithm is compared with the other tracking algorithms and the track parameters for different patients are compared. It is proven that the DTI method provides higher accuracy of 96.76% in tracking the cross fibers. The Y-axis dispersion for the different regions of interest from the tract center is measured. The tract amplitudes at this separation are decreased by 75% from the peak value. The 3D model is printed using an ultimate 3D printing machine at a diameter of about 0.025 mm at a low cost with high accuracy.

DOI: 10.4018/978-1-6684-8306-0.ch015

The tractography is the strategy of assessing, displaying, and remaking the directions of fiber tracts in white matter of the human cerebrum. This method outwardly depicts the nerve tracts with the Diffusion-Weighted Images (DWI) (Smith et al., 2012; Kamali et al., 2020; Qiu et al., 2012). Numerous techniques has been developed to perform tractography (Poupon et al., 2000; Reid et al., 2020; Siless et al., 2020; Wang et al., 2013; Ajoku et al., 2022; Coenen & Reisert, 2021). Diffusion MRI-based deterministic tractography is a useful method for the non-invasive investigation of normal cerebrum anatomy. Both the voxel-wise and the area-of-interest methods are responsible for combining population variations in range amplitude (streamline count or density) due to the proper arrangement of interest patterns. However, the quantification of variations in the tract (between classes or lengthwise inside particulars) has been complicated by double critical aspects of white matter. The first aspect is unclear about the stability of people vary in the exact position and direction of the expected tract. On the other hand, white matter lacks the gross neuroanatomical characteristics that makes it feasible for gray matter to be parceled to decide where the tracts may sit inside broader white matter systems.

Accurate quantifying the correlation of tractography between individuals is thus necessarily related to the difficulties of defining and aligning the exact direction of the route. Tractography is also used to identify neurological disorders in which specific structural connectivity anomalies are uncertain, emphasizing the significance of accounting for human variations in tract position while determining the extent of structural connectivity. The method of streamline tractography works under the principle of progressive venturing towards the guideline eigenvector (Smith et al., 2012), and subsequently, the outcomes will shift immensely, relying on the selected technique. Another method for streamline tractography is an unsupervised method (Smith et al., 2012) for clustering fiber tract of cerebrum nerves based on their proximate anatomical structures. The distinct tool for estimating the tract is Q-Ball Imaging (QBI) (Koike et al., 2022). In this method, approximate diffusion orientation distribution function(dODF) is determined using the Funk Radon transform directly from a single-shell High Angular Resolution Diffusion Imaging (HARDI) acquisition (Bauer et al., 2014). The extensions enable the automated development of bundle-specific tractograms that measure from a Gaussian distribution with a defined standard deviation based on each point, thereby allowing more detailed monitoring of the tract orientation maps (Wasserthal et al., 2019).

The limitation in supervised learning in the accuracy and availability of training data are considered. Tract alignment strengthens the current practice of entire cerebrum registration and checks weather this approach increases the efficiency of community contrasts (Waugh et al., 2019). The solutions focused on Atlas are helpful but may not understand the human tract size and type heterogeneity. We consider the error analysis carried out in the (Borkowski & Krzyżak, 2018) for determination of tract.

Some of the tractography Deterministic approaches were used for making a 3D cerebrum model in less time (Zhan et al., 2015). The radius of curvature fits the DT maxima by minimizing the predefined energy (Poupon et al., 2000). In addition to the development of the tractography algorithm, other imperative determinants of the subsequent tract images are existent. They are (a) the placement of seed voxels which is the beginning of the tractography, and (b) threshold connectivity. Improvements in image-based Medical data like CT, MRI and fMRI, have taken interest on both the side of medical and academic interest to create a 3D Printed galloping in a clinical context. Recent galloping of evidence enables to creates the development of somatic structures with varying density in microns and with the recent enculturation of medical image over segmentation, these prototype models were used to reprise inner and outer structures with higher degrees of precisions. The utilization of this improves the physician / surgical fields over surgical planning, diagnostic, enhancement and decreasing the diagnostics time for patients towards anesthesia, bleeding and wound divulging time. With this, it optimizes surgical results by lowering future costs and establishing clinical standards to enhance surgical assessment and planning outcomes, in the Thanjavur (government) medical college. Since its introduction, this aimed to allow physicians and surgeons requests for 3D models available within 12 to 24 hours. This method was used in research exertion to investigate the anatomy of human muscles and the usage of 3D printed models in the preparation of crucial brain procedures in conjunction with neurosurgical guidance models. The contagious success of this 3D fast design indulgence has resulted in its establishment as a vital function within the clinic, and its rapid illustration technology persists to have an incredible jolt on a growing number of aided surgical cases.

The Ultimaker 3D printer is used for printing 3D models. It enables high-quality printing, and the rate of printing is comparatively fast. Unlike other 3D printers, it is economically cheaper. Various printing materials were used such as nylon, PLA, Tough PLA, TPU 95A, etc. The chosen of material for printing tractography is Ultimaker breakaway as it is convenient to break and remove the support easily. Also, the need to anticipate the dissolution of the support.

This research work focuses on technology(engineering) contribution to medical science. This paper focuses on mathematically generated information using an MRI sequence that produces Diffusion Tensor Imagining for accurate tract information. 3D printed (using PLA) data assets the surgeon.

The paper is outlined as follows. Section II describes the data acquisition and preparation of MRI data used for the tractography. The methodology is discussed in Section III. The result outcomes are discussed in Section IV and the work is concluded in Section V.

DATA ACQUISITION AND PREPARATION

Data Stimulation

For the non-DWI, the SNR is approximated in the ratio of 40:2 to simulate diffusion data for a simulated pulse series comparable to the required in vivo sequence with a Camino data synth. A Twice-Refocused Spin-Echo (TRSE) series of b-value = 0 to 2,590 s/mm^2 was used for the simulated pulse sequence. In the same sequence, a non-diffusion weighted images was acquired for each b-value with the condition that none of the value is zero and this is used as a motion correction guide. The timing parameters were: $\delta1 = 9$ ms, $\delta2 = 23$ ms, and s = 6 ms for the diffusion gradients. For comparability, a EPI pulse series using the same b-values was used to take DW images using a diffusion gradient of $\delta1 = 33.2$ ms and $\delta2 = 39.8$ ms. Due to the signal-to-noise constraint, no parallel imaging approach was used. This constrain is affected only with the high b-value. Other key parameters for acquiring: TR/TE = 5,000/125ms, FOV = 25 cm, image matrix = 128 = 128 to 128, slice size = $2e^3$m and its distance between each slice is $2e^3$m, Number of excitations = 5, scans time = 90 sec for both two sequences. Four stable data sets of volunteers were gathered to validate the accuracy and reproductive.

MRI Data Acquisition

Subjects were scanned at the Thanjavur Medical College, Radiology department. A 3T MRI (Siemens, Germany) as scanned for fifty safe data; six subjects were scanned on MAGNETOM Prisma. For the next group studies were contrasted one by one and assured that these adjustments of the magnet have little effect on group comparisons XR 80/200 coil, the parallel TimTx true form transmission and 4G architecture. Images were obtained with certain parameters using the DTI sequence.

Preprocessing

For each subject, the initial pre-processing data is included radiological alignment, displacement correction and eddy correction, and elimination of non-cerebrum tissue. To identify the impact due to motion in the tract location, the parameter for motion correction is used in the subsequent steps. Drift was used to equip local diffusion tensors and to construct a 3D FA model of similar matrix size and resolution to the initial diffusion images. In native region of each subject, the bedpost was running on pre-processed DTI data to produce diffusion parameters on each voxel. The FA maps were inserted in standard spaces using serial affine or not-linear methods. All cerebrum registrations were checked for high quality. In subsequent steps, the corresponding whole-cerebrum activation matrix was used to record the tractography of subjects residing in a specific space. For subsequent tractography, the inverse of the corresponding matrix was used to record ROI. This is considered as a basic procedure for extension of all FA images and tracts and it was the first move towards improving registration (Waugh et al., 2019).

MATERIAL AND METHODS

A harmonization approach that can be extended directly to DWI and shows its effectiveness in diffusion scalars and tractography while minimizing inter-site variance (Huynh et al., 2019). The first stage in tractography is to fit the perturbation technique toward each voxel in the image, and the second step is to map the fibre across the voxels. The simplest method is to utilise a standard tensor prototype, which necessitates at least six DWIs plus one baseline image known as a non-diffusion-weighted image to identify the six unknown tensor parameters. The prevailing local fiber path is then measured at each voxel as a predictive vector with the tensor's greatest independent value. By using the Fiber Assignment by Continuous Tracking (FACT), the fibers are traced across the voxel. The image is built by the diffusion tensors' principal eigenvectors.

Non-Linear MRI Analysis Using 3D Stochastic Model

The algorithm for tractography with diffusion MRI is linked which is responsive to the diffusion of molecules and has its state in $\wp^3\ \Theta^2$. The $\wp$ and Θ represent the position and orientation of the water molecules, respectively. The nature of the movement is anisotropic which follows non-linearity. The R and S are sophisticated using the non-linear differential equation:

$$u' = \sin f.\cos g \tag{1}$$

$$v' = \sin f.\sin g \tag{2}$$

$$w' = \cos f \tag{3}$$

$$f' = O\left(0, \sigma_f^2\right) \tag{4}$$

$$g' = O\left(0, \sigma_f^2\right) \tag{5}$$

The equation (1) to equation(5) supports longer path track but the shorter paths are supported by (1-exp (-1)) to deteriorate per unit space (Mukherjee et al., 2008). The particle is advancing towards a path for reaching a point wherein the unrelated vector is turned by f in the kissing plane and g in the binomial plane. The main initiation is to use William and Jacob's machinery development completely to calculate probability p(u,v,w,f, g;t$_p$). At time t, the beginning coordinates of a particular source state (u$_0$,v$_0$,w$_0$,f$_0$,g$_0$) to erratic state (u,v,w,f,g) before deterioration. By exploiting the translation and rotational symmetries of a function, which is "the drive reaction of an in homogeneous straight differential condition characterized on space, with determined starting conditions or limit conditions," the convolution is used to find the necessary integral. The progress a probability of a Markov procedure which is characterized on the $\wp^3$ x Θ^2 5-D state space is represented by G. G is a rank ten tensor. This representation is done in the 3D setting, in order to satisfy the Eqn(1). This culminating to the notion of a speculative source field P(u,v,w,f,g;t$_p$) which represent the beginning coordinates of a particular source state (u$_0$,v$_0$,w$_0$,f$_0$,g$_0$) to erratic state (u,v,w,f,g) before deterioration. The product of these two stochastic fields gives the complete stochastic field. The above equation is the basis for the results that produce the fiber trajectories from the initial to the final state.

Consider a font voxel at p and ends at q. The molecules begin at *p* and end at *q*. It follows a path $\tilde{A}_p$ which comprise of "n" unit steps. At each progression, changes in orientations are observed *g* given by $\rho_1, \rho_2, \ldots, \rho_n$ and *f* are given by $\Omega_1, \Omega_2, \ldots, \Omega_n$. The density function for a set of paths leaving source voxel p is given in the equation (6),

$$x\left(\Gamma_i\right) = \prod_{i=1}^{n} e^{-\frac{1}{\tau}} \frac{1}{\vartheta_g \sqrt{2\pi}} e^{-\frac{\rho_i^2}{2\vartheta_g^2}} \frac{1}{\vartheta_f \sqrt{2\pi}} e^{-\frac{\Omega_i^2}{2\vartheta_g^2}} \tag{6}$$

The overall density function for the paths from font p to destination q ie. $\tilde{A}_{pq}$ is given by integrating f (Γp) and dividing from the above density function

$$\log y\left(\text{``}_{\{ij\}}\right) + C = \frac{-n}{\{\copyright\}} - n \setminus log\left(\left\{\{\upsilon_f\}\sqrt{\{2\pi\}}\right\}\right)$$

$$-nlog\left(\left\{\{\upsilon_g\}\sqrt{\{2\pi\}}\right\}\right) - \sum_{\{i=1\}}^{n} \frac{\left\{\{-k_i^2\}\right\}}{\left\{\{2\upsilon_{\{f\}}^2\}\right\}} - \sum_{\{i=1\}}^{n} \frac{\left\{\{-\copyright_i^2\}\right\}}{\left\{\{2\upsilon_g^2\}\right\}} \tag{7}$$

The energy in the continuous curves decries the energy in 3D, which is the straight blend of length, curvature squared κ and torsion squared τ. The energy in 3D is given as

$$\alpha \int_C \rho(t_p)^2 \, dt_p + \beta \int_C \copyright(t_p)^2 \, dt_p + \gamma \int_C dt_p$$

With

$$\alpha = \frac{1}{2v_f^2}; \gamma = \frac{1}{\tau} + \log\left(v_g \sqrt{(2\pi)}\right) + \log\left(v_f \sqrt{2\pi}\right); \beta = \frac{1}{2v_g^2};$$

The differential equation of the 3D random walk is given from the Fokker-Planck equation which explain the probability density of the molecule following a random walk in space. By exploiting this equation, the efficient implementation of a random walk is performed. Using Markov property, the probability density function is given by $P_{H+1}(I)$ for the I ∂P state is written as follows

$$P_{H+1}(I) = \int P_H(I|I') P_H(I') \, dI' \tag{9}$$

Characterizing a capacity $P(I,t_p)$ such that $P(I,H_p)=P_H(I)$, where $t_p = H\Delta t$ is a ceaseless time variable, a new transition probability function as

$$P\left(I, t_p + \Delta t_p | I', t_p\right) = P_H(I|I') \tag{10}$$

it follows that

$$P\left(I, t_p + \Delta t_p\right) = P\left(I, t_p + \Delta t_p | I', t_p\right) P\left(I'', t_p\right) dI' \tag{11}$$

A PDE can be derived from the function $I(I, t_p)$ as H goes to infinity. Plank's equation is given by

$$\frac{\partial I}{\partial \Delta t_p} + \sum_{i=1}^{H} \frac{\partial}{\partial I_i}\left(C_i^{(a)}(I,t_p)I\right) = \sum_{i=1}^{H} \frac{\partial^2}{\partial I_i^2}\left(C_i^b(I,t_p)I\right) \tag{12}$$

$$C_i^a(I,t_p) = \lim_{\Delta t \to 0} \frac{O_i^1(I,t_p)}{" t_p} \tag{13}$$

$$C_i^{(b)}(I,t_p) = \lim_{\Delta t_p \to 0} \frac{O_i^2(I,t_p)}{" t_p} \tag{14}$$

$$O_i^n\left(I,t_p\right)=\left(I_i'-I_i'\right)^n=\int I(I_i'\left(t_p+"\,t_p\right)|I_it_p)\left(I_i'-I_i\right)^n dI_i' \tag{15}$$

The random walk is implemented for 3D completion field with state has (u,v,w,f,g) is described by using the Eqn(1),the corresponding Fokker Planck equation can be stated as:

$$C_u^a\left(I,t_p\right)=\lim_{"\,t_p 0}\frac{\int I\left(u',\left(t_p+"\,t_p\right)|u,t_p\right)\left(u'-u\right)du'}{"\,t_p} \tag{16}$$

$$=\frac{\lim_{"\,t_p\to 0}\int\partial(u'-u-"\,t_p\sin f\cos g)\left(u'-u\right)du'}{"\,t_p} \tag{17}$$

$$=\lim_{"\,t_p\to 0}\frac{\int "\,t_p.\sin f.\cos g}{"\,t_p}=\sin f,\cos g \tag{18}$$

$$C_u^b\left(I,t_p\right)=\lim_{"\,t_p 0}\frac{\int I\left(u',\left(t_p+"\,t_p\right)|u,t_p\right)\left(u'-u\right)^2 du'}{2"\,t_p} \tag{19}$$

$$=\frac{\lim_{"\,t_p\to 0}\int\partial(u'-u-("\,t_p\sin f\cos g))\left(u'-u\right)^2 du'}{2"\,t_p} \tag{20}$$

$$I\left(u,v,w,f,g,t_p'\right)=I\left(u,v,w,f,g;0\right)+\frac{\int\partial I\left(u,v,w,f,g;t_p\right)}{\partial t_p}dt_p \tag{21}$$

$$\frac{\partial P}{\partial t_p}=-\sin f\cos g\frac{\partial P}{\partial u}-\sin f\sin g\frac{\partial P}{\partial v}-\cos f\frac{\partial P}{\partial v}+\frac{\sigma_g^2}{2}\frac{\partial^2 P}{\partial g^2}+\frac{\sigma_2}{2}\frac{\partial^2 P}{\partial f^2}-\frac{1}{\varsigma}P \tag{22}$$

Diffusion Tensor Imaging

The intensity level of the signal of each contrasted MRI sequence V results from the arbitrariness nature of water particles (called DWI images) in which the sensitivity of field is based on the Stejskal Tanner spin-echo scheme (Owens & Stoessel, 2008). The estimation of V is given by,

$$V_i = V_0 e^{-\varsigma^2 \gamma^2 G^2 \left(\delta - \frac{\gamma}{3}\right) M_{app}} \tag{23}$$

Equation (21) converts the DWI image into a DTI image. The M is the diffusion tensor matrix. It is the 3*3 symmetric positive semi-definite lattice. M in the scanner tensor casing and the neighborhood tissue outline have been connected by the accompanying condition *ML=LΛ*. Diffusion measures are changes related to the age of the person (Huynh et al., 2019).

The self-dispersion tensor eigenvalues are graded elements of the matrix 2 and E is the symmetrical rotational grid whose segment is eigenvector $\hat{l}_i$. The eigenvalues and eigenvector have found in the M matrix. The most substantial value of the eigenvector tract is the local fibers. The orientation forms of the eigenvalue should satisfy a $\geq$ b $\geq$c. The dissemination tensor has been evaluated from the slope vector. As the expansion in the slope vector has been observed, the quantity of dispersion-weighted images used to ascertain the dissemination tensor likewise intensified, which results in the precise estimation of dissemination (Qiu et al., 2012). Although it results in a more accurate tensor estimation, the time taken for evaluation is prolonged. The ellipsoid, formed by the orientation of eigenvalues, decides the effectiveness of diffusion. When the ellipsoid is thin and long, it means that the diffusion of water along the long axis is perfect.

In the Cartesian plane, the diffusion tensor matrix can be diagonalized by the ancient method of eigenvector- eigenvalue decomposition. There are three invariant J1, J2, J3} that are present in M. The characteristics equation of the M matrix is given by,

$$Det\left(M \rightarrow I_{3x3}\right) = \left(\lambda - a\right)\left(\lambda - b\right)\left(\lambda - c\right) = \lambda^3 - \lambda^2 J + \lambda J_2 - J_3 = 0 \tag{24}$$

where I indicate an identity matrix. From the Equation (21) the invariants are given by

$$J_1 = M_{xx} + M_{yy} + M_{zz} = a+b+c \tag{25}$$

$$J_2 = ab+bc+ac \tag{26}$$

$$J_3 = \det(M) = abc \tag{27}$$

The trace of matrix M is given by

$$Trace(M) = a+b+c = J_1 \tag{28}$$

The analytical description of eigenvalues is previously described [32]. From the three principle invariants J_1, J_2, J_3, the diagonalization of matrix M and the rotational orthogonal matrix A is derived, as discussed in the next section.

Determination of Eigenvalue and Eigenvector

The z and k are rotationally invariant to the 2nd and 3rd primary invariants of M_{an} with the 1st invariance which is represented as

$$M_{an} = M - \frac{J_1}{3} I_{3x3}$$
(29)

$$\tilde{} = \frac{acos\left(\frac{k}{z}\sqrt{\frac{1}{z}}\right)}{3}$$
(30)

The Θ is assumed to lie between $0 \leq \Theta \leq \pi/3$ for a positive-definite DT matrix. Thus, z and k can be considered as the variance and skewness of $Ma_{n,}$ and it is indicated as,

$$z = \frac{1}{6} Trace\left(M_{an}^2\right) = variance(\lambda) = \frac{J_2(M_{an})}{3}$$
(31)

$$k = \frac{1}{6} Trace\left(M_{an}^3\right) = skewness(\lambda) = \frac{J_{3(M_{an})}}{2} = \frac{\det(M_{an})}{2}$$
(32)

The orthonormal eigenvector is calculated from the eigenvalue from the linear equation $M\hat{l}_i = \hat{l}_i$ for the ratio $\hat{l}_{ix} : \hat{l}_{iy} : \hat{l}_{iz}$. For the ith vector, $\widehat{\hat{l}_i^T l_i} = 1$ and its variable is defined as

$$A_i = M_{xx} - \lambda_i; B_i = M_{yy} - \lambda_i; C_i = M_{zz} - \lambda_i;$$

$$\hat{l}_{ix} = \left(M_{xy}M_{yz} - B_iM_{xz}\right)\left(M_{xz}M_{yz} - C_iM_x\right)$$
(33)

$$\hat{l}_{iy} = \left(M_{xz}M_{yz} - C_iM_{xy}\right)(M_{xz}M_{xy} - A_iM_{yz})$$
(34)

$$\hat{l}_{iz} = \left(M_{xy}M_{yz} - B_i M_{xz} \right)\left(M_{xz}M_{xy} - A_i M_{yz} \right) \tag{35}$$

The normalized eigenvector corresponds to λi is given by,

$$\hat{l}_i = \frac{l_i}{\sqrt{l_i^T l_i}} \tag{36}$$

The steps are repeated for all orthonormalized sets for i=1,2 or 3 of the eigenvector that corresponds to the significant, moderate, and subordinate eigenvalues. The mathematical procedure may obtain the third eigenvector from two orthonormal eigenvectors l_i and l_i as

$$\hat{l}_3 = \left[l_{1y}l_{2z} - l_{1z} \quad l_{1z}l_{2x} - l_{1x}l_{2z} \quad l_{1z}l_{2x} - l_{1y}l_{2x} \right]^T \tag{37}$$

This algorithm can have implemented on the entire image volume array by using standard math library functions such as cos, acos, sqrt, etc. Before calculating the eigenvalue and eigenvector, it is necessary to select a positive-defined mask to incorporate all voxels that fulfill the condition to ensure the diffusion ellipsoid convexity:

$$J_3 > 0 \text{ and } \left(M_{ii} \text{ and } M_{ii}M_{jj} - M_{ij}^2 \right) \text{ for } i,j = x,y,z \text{ and } (a,b,c) > 0 \tag{38}$$

After the estimation of eigenvalues and eigenvectors, the most generally utilized criteria for DTI are Fractional anisotropy (FA) and mean diffusivity (MD), which represent the motional anisotropy of water molecules. These indices are more sensitive to the presence and integrity of white matter fiber and help to detect cerebrum diseases. The color-coded FA maps show directional information entrenched in DTI. MD and FA are shown as:

$$MD = \frac{a+b+c}{3} \tag{39}$$

$$FA = 1.2247 * \left[\frac{0.5\sqrt{\left((a-b)^2 + (b-c)^2 + (c-a)^2\right)}}{\left(a^2 + b^2 + c^2\right)} \right] \tag{40}$$

Lower limb amputees have been reported to have reduced fractional anisotropy (FA) values in the corpus callosum (CC), FA is considered to represent both the degree of myelination and the axonal density, and is also used as a predictor of WM integrity (Guo et al., 2019), which is utilized to depict the directionality of multimodal diffusion in the region where the fiber architecture is complex in the cerebrum. As it is mentioned earlier, the shading shows the bearing of diffusivity, and red implies left to right, which demonstrates the most extreme diffusivity course and green shows foremost-back and blue shows prevalent sub-par. This stage is additionally used to figure the following tensor.

Tractography Algorithm

The FACT is one of the first methods in deterministic DTI tractography. It is still presumably the most well-known way to deal with fiber following for both examination and clinical applications. The key concept is to trace the direction of the key path of the eigenvector of the diffusion tensor image while checking for abrupt changes in the local fiber orientation. FACT tracks pathways from the seeds region by tracking the main eigenvector from one voxel to another. In the second technique, the ROI-dependent tractography approach utilizes various masks, altering ROI channels and changing tractography parameters (step scale, curvature, anisotropic thresholds) to enhance the consistency of findings based on prior neuroanatomical information. An ROI-based seed approach is an easy way to easily target a bundle of value by reducing needless computations required for entire cerebrum tractography (Rheault et al., 2019).

Deterministic tractography was conducted to recreate subcortical relations using a fiber assignment. This process is continuous. Here, we consider FA threshold value as 0.1 and a turning angle of greater than 60 degrees for beginning and stopping monitoring. The White Matter (WM) atlas focused on voxel from Alexopoulos.et.al was used as a tool to classify the specific eloquent WM tracts in our research. This monitoring algorithm assumes that the fibers inside the voxel are oriented in the direction of the key value of the diffusion tensor (Alexopoulos et al., 2019).

At least two specific modes are employed based on tractography, i.e. examination of tracts and connectivity intensity within GM regions. The above is often computed by gathering the tracts together with an atomic parceling method for cerebrum connectivity (Zhan et al., 2015).

Tract Estimation

The performance of the tractography may not be specifically used for the study of the fibrous bundle, because the points required for the reconstruction of the fibers differ. Fiber points are then immediately rearranged between regions and the disjoined fibers are removed. As the final post-processing step, every fiber is resampled with the same number q = 105 points (Hunt et al., 2019; Stamile et al., 2019).

The extraction from the tensor field represents a coarse-scale property of the fiber bundles. The clustering calculation is based on the latitude and form comparability of fiber bundles for tracking the fiber (Yeh, 2020). The set of G_i of 3D curves in which each curve depicts a set of 3D points f_k, ie. $G_i = f_k$. Consider a two-pair fiber set G_a and G_b at distance d. The distance d is measured between G_a and G_b in G, where $a \neq b$. If $d(G_a and G_b) < r$ where re s, then the threshold is chosen. The outliers of the fiber are rejected. In class C, each fiber G_a will have at least one G_b with the condition $a \neq b$ such that $d(G_a and G_b) < r$. This measurement is followed by every adjacent fiber and propagates labels from neighboring fibers and benefits from a transitivity property. The threshold r depends on the examination data and distance metrics.

The white matter bundles should also include a geometric characteristic for their modeling. The use of a Frenet Frame is to derive the local shape descriptors. The curve C has a Frenet frame $(\vec{s}),(\vec{U}),(\vec{D})$ in which each point m of the curve C with differentiable parameter $o(t_p)$ is defined by the vector $\vec{S}$ represents the unit tangent vector, $\vec{U}$ represents the average unit vector, and $\vec{D}$ represents the supplements of the frame. The three vectors are orthonormal to each other. The curvature and torsion calculated for the local features at point m is measured by the Serret-Frenet formulae:

$$\frac{d\vec{S}}{dw} = \kappa\vec{S} \ and \ \frac{d\vec{D}}{dw} = -\tau\vec{U} \tag{41}$$

Where z is the curvilinear abscissa of C.

We design a simple analytical scheme to acquire the features across the fiber. Initially, the root for the arrangement of fibers is defined in each bundle based on the algebraic criteria, such as based on cerebrum data, and cross-section with minimal area. Then, the fibers are reparametrized with cubic B-splines such that the curves in the training set have an equidistant sampling. They additionally permit satisfactory inspecting of fiber with various by and extensive lengths. Homologous points have the same curved lines abscissae over the fiber set. The comparison has been made within an individually defined search volume. This search volume has been obtained by the union of white and grey matter segment images where the image is the threshold at r0.5 and restrained by r(white or gray) > r(CSF). The proportion of the voxel within the factually defined optical radiation that has labeled as

$$Sensitivity = \frac{\Sigma(k_{map} * tract)}{\Sigma k_{map}} \tag{42}$$

The False positive rate (FPR) has measured by the voxel value within the factually defined optical radiation

$$FPR = \frac{\left|\Sigma(1 - k_{map}) * tract\right|}{\Sigma(1 - k_{map})} \tag{43}$$

RESULT AND DISCUSSION

Result

By considering a series of MRI data from different patients to examine the fiber tract pattern, the DWI images have been acquired. The single-shot echo-planar sequence was engaged in attaining diffusion encoding. A clustering approach based on the similarity test between diffusion tensors was used to carry out segmentation and fiber tracking. Color maps were created from their combinations with traditional color coding. The diffusion signal is calculated in a linear shell and the data acquirement times are shorter than their corresponding equivalents. Diffusion patterns are determined by using their eigenvalues and eigenvectors. This detail can be shown as a glyph in Figure 1 including complete angular information of diffusion. The source and sink regions are extracted from the corpus callosum part of the cerebrum, as shown in Figure 2(a). The blue shadow represents the start and endpoint of the source and sinks in the DTI image. The yellow box represents the source, and the white box represents the sink in Figure 2(a). FIGURE 2(b) is the cingulum tract, Figure 2(c) is the callous corpus tract, and Figure 2(d) is the corticospinal tract. The 3D view of a Test data has shown in the next figures. Figure 3(a) represents the tracts of the left and right hemisphere, figure 3(b) indicates the tracts of anterior to posterior, and Figure 3(c) indicates the dorsal to ventral. Figure 4 presents the overall fiber tract of the cerebrum for patients 1 (Figure4(a)), patients 2 (Figure4(b)), patients 3 (Figure4(c)), patients 4 (Figure4(d)). The 3D printed tractography has shown in Figure 5. The algorithm method was a calculation-based method. At each stage, values such as eigenvalue, eigenvector, and the threshold for ROI have been measured. A bundle of fibers has formed from each voxel. The shape of the tracts is determined as discussed earlier in section 3. E.

Figure 1. Glyph images of cerebrum

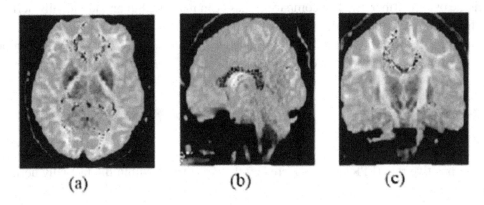

(a)   (b)   (c)

Figure 2. (a) Source and sink region, (b) DTI in the cingulum tract, (c) DTI in corpus callous, (d) DTI in corticospinal

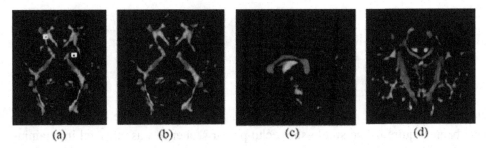

(a)   (b)   (c)   (d)

Figure 3. (a) Tracts of the left and right hemisphere, (b) tract of the dorsal to ventral, (c) tracts of anterior to posterior

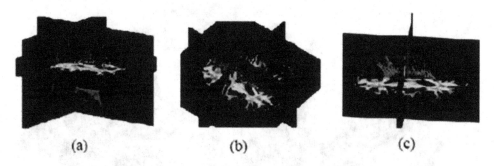

The comparison among several tensor-based algorithms is given in Table 1. For each simulated voxel is applied tensor-based algorithm and compared with the other two algorithms mentioned in (Lipp et al., 2020). The peak is obtained along with the true underlying directions and orthogonal to the long axis with an angle < 45° and reached the specific amplitude threshold. The CSD has a threshold greater than 0.1 and the DRL algorithm has a greater than 0.05. Cross- fiber is possible in both algorithms. Of all the algorithms everything works fine on the reconstruction of peak over virtual fiber predilection is 100% of components with an intracellular volumetric fraction < 20 percent, over a FA of approximately 0.5. The obtained successful reconstruction with true peaks is below 0.15. The remaining two algorithms clambered to overcome peak orientation accurately with intracellular volume value below 10 percent. A huge amount of false positive peaks is obtained in CSD. On the other hand, the tensor-based method provided a max of two percent of false positives. DRL developed less than 0.01 percent of false positives (Lipp et al., 2020).

Figure 4. Overall fiber tract of the cerebrum for (a) Patient 1, (b) Patient 2, (c) Patient 3, (d)Patient 4

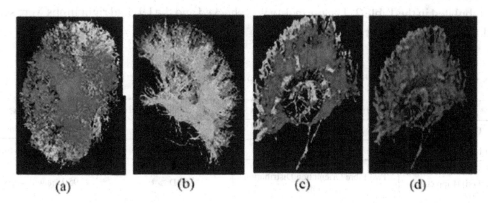

Figure 5. 3D printed tractography

We have shown the approach of utilizing a healthy volunteer. The data used in this paper is not the public data under the jurisdiction of the Ethical Committee. To distinguish improvements in the FA network after unilateral upper-limb amputation, we used separate U measures to measure distance, cluster coefficient, characteristic frequency, and intensity between cuts off in the limbs which are termed, amputees. The measurements of tensors such as Fractional Anisotropic, mean value, and the number of fibers are tabulated in the Table 2. The normality was checked and the left and right limbs were separately measured to null out the effect of WM asymmetry.

Table 1. Comparison of the fiber orientation reconstruction algorithms

	Parameter Set to Tract Fibers	Threshold Level	Accuracy
Proposed Tracking Method	**Fractional Anisotropy**	**>0.02**	**96.76% With Cross Fibers**
Tensor based tracking	Fractional Anisotropy	>0.02	96.76% without cross fibers
Probability based tracking [CSD Method] (Lipp et al., 2020)	Two Fibre Orientation Distribution (FOD)	CSD: > 0.1	95.18% with cross fibers
DRL based damped Richardson Lucy algorithm (Lipp et al., 2020)	Single fibre orientation distribution (FOD)	> 0.05	95.67% with cross fibers

Streamline counts declined exponentially with displacement from the middle of the tract. A disorder alignment of a few millimeters created major compromises in amplitude comparisons. This is shown in Table 3. The arrangement of "peak-to-peak" tracts is important for correct amplitude comparisons. The comparison for all transcallosal tracts was reported by the whole cerebrum method: the tract amplitudes at this separation were decreased by 75% from the peak value. On the other side, sub-cortical tract orientation was considerably higher than the orientation of cortical tracts; the whole cerebrum was adequate for these sub-cortical tracts. Increases in connectivity and fiber density in some left subfields were found in patients suspected of having foci in the left temporal lobe.

Table 2. Parameter of the fibre tract; P-Patient

Parameters	P1	P2	P3	P4
Num Points	14421	229072	239172	2507046
Num Fiber	763	1054	1156	1249
Mean Length	143.20315	108.11259	108.11259	108.75068
Tensor Fractional Anisotropy Mean	0.357201	0.49444	0.4849	0.000318
Tensor Linear Measure Mean	0.343346	0.478737	0.465479	0.000318
Tensor Max Eigenvalue Mean	0.001171	0.001163	0.001026	0.00001
Tensor Mean Diffusivity Mean	0.233175	0.000721	0.000663	0.545488
Tensor Mid Eigenvalue Mean	0.487598	0.000578	0.000429	0.231449
Tensor Min Eigenvalue Mean	0.002629	0.000422	0.000379	0.002028
Tensor Planar Measure Mean	0.1462158	0.146112	0.146102	0.7301530
Tensor Relative Anisotropy Mean	0.329412	0.328027	0.32541	0.768598
Tensor Spherical Measure Mean	0	0.375217	0.371590	0.001393
Tensor Trace Mean	0	0.002163	0.002015	0.0006760

Table 3. Y-axis dispersion by mm moved from tract center

Y-Axis Dispersion by mm Moved From Tract Center	Moving 0mm to 1mm	Moving 1mm to 2mm	Moving 2mm to 3mm	At 3mm From Tract Center
Corpus	21.7% - L	33.7% - L	40.4% - L	30.4% - L
Callosum	21.6% - R	37.9% - R	45.9% - R	23.7% - R
Cingulum	22.4% - L	34.7% - L	41.1% - L	29.6% - L
	22.7% - R	36.8% - R	46.3% - R	19.4% - R
Left and right Primary motor convex	20.9%-L 20.3%-R	37.4% - L 37.3% - R	43.5% - L 45.9% - R	26.0% - L 25.6% – R
Left and right Supplementary motor convex	19.2% - L 20.3% - R	32.3% - L 38.3% - R	38.7% - L 46.8% - R	33.5% - L 26.2% – R
Right and left	23.0%- L	40.1% - L	47.9% - L	24.0% - L
Visual convex	22.7% - R	40.1% - R	48.5% - R	23.9% – R
Mean for all	21.44% - L	35.64% - L	42.32% - L	28.7% - L
ROIs	21.52% - R	38.08% - R	46.68% - R	23.7% - R

Discussion

This process is validated by collaborating with neurosurgical planning at the Government hospital of a 30- year-old female with a tumor on the frontal lobe. Since, we had ethical clearance to access to the few data and also considering the willingness of the patients, we used only few data in this work. In this work, we demonstrated tensor-based algorithm for each voxel and compared CSD method and Richardson Lucy algorithm. The threshold level was fixed greater than 0.02 with the accuracy of 96.76%. The accuracy obtained was equal for both with and without cross fibers. The tract amplitudes at this separation were decreased by 75% from the peak value. On the other side, sub-cortical tract orientation was considerably higher than the orientation of cortical tracts; the whole cerebrum was adequate for these sub-cortical tracts. The various tensor measurements were measured and tabulated for the data we used. Finally, peak-to-peak tracts amplitude comparison was discussed and concluded that whole cerebrum was adequate for sub-cortical tracts. The 3D printing model gives raise to clinical outcomes and on other hand, it limits the surgeon to plan the surgery and encourages them to do more analysis of the patient data. Printed data offers significant advantages over conventional surgery and explains the understanding of the complex bio-structure and unanticipated challenges. This creates a specific model for each patient which make more clear and more complete discussion with the patients regarding their problem and upcoming procedure for surges. 3D printed model shown to improve the time required for operation, blood loss, etc., which tends to decrease infections generally claimed as Surgical Site Infections (SSIs) (Owens & Stoessel, 2008; Mann et al., 2021; Bagatti & Messina, 2020; Lefebvre et al., 2017). 3D models were already used by many used maxillofacial, spinal and orthopedic knee surgeries. The patient stays in the hospital after surgery have not been demonstrated to be significantly affected by the use of 3D-printed data and may need further investigation. After obtaining the 3D form of tractography, as explained in section 1, the Ultimaker® gives 0.025mm thickness of the model. As the obtained tractography has a diameter of about 0.025 mm, any modification in the model is not required. As the model is full of thin fibers, it is difficult to remove the supporting material when it is printed in other 3D printers even though the period for printing the period is less compared to Ultimaker. Hence, accuracy and quality are high in Ultimaker breakaway material.

CONCLUSION

3D printed prototypes and medical navigation systems can be integrated to boost operative training and planning. The work described here emphasizes the importance of planning before surgery. 3D printed models are feasible and provide complex operations. Additionally, this 3D printed model can shorten operation timing, contributes to the physician a practical training and better patient safety. Despite the fact that DTI is not a stable method it can still provide the neurologist with fiber tract in real time as 3D printed data using improved tumor sections and it improves postoperative deficits. Overall, this work shows that the reported 3D printing operation can be merged with DTI preparation and add important knowledge for neurosurgical preparation in conjunction with clinical systems. In future, using DTI many diseases such as traumatic brain injury for adult (Tallus et al., 2023) and children(Watson et al., 2019), epilepsy(Carlson et al., 2014), brain chronic pain (Owen et al., 2008), chronic (Auriat et al., 2015), acute stoke (Mukherjee, 2005) and ischemic stroke (Koenraads et al., 2016).

ACKNOWLEDGMENT

We, authors thank Dr. A. Srinivasan, Professor and Head of Neurology at Thanjavur Medical college (TMC), Thanjavur, Tamilnadu, India for providing us MRI data of brain to carry out the research performed in this work (Ethical commity clearance also approved by TMC).

Competing Interests: The authors of this publication declare there are no competing interests.

Funding: This research received no specific grant from any funding agency in the public, commercial, or not-for-profit sectors. Funding for this research was covered by the author(s) of the article. Out esteemed university "SASTRA Deemed University" supported us by providing Image research laboratory facilities to carry out the research.

REFERENCES

Ajoku, U., Almojuela, A., Kazina, C., Wilkinson, M., Ryner, L., & Dhaliwal, P. (2022). Maximizing surgical resection in revision surgery for an intramedullary spinal cord tumour using DTI/tractography and direct spinal cord stimulation: A technical note. *Interdisciplinary Neurosurgery : Advanced Techniques and Case Management*, *28*, 101467. doi:10.1016/j.inat.2021.101467

Alexopoulos, G., Cikla, U., El Tecle, N., Kulkarni, N., Pierson, M., Mercier, P., Kemp, J., Coppens, J., Mahmoud, S., Sehi, M., Bucholz, R., & Abdulrauf, S. (2019). The Value of White Matter Tractography by Diffusion Tensor Imaging in Altering a Neurosurgeon's Operative Plan. *World Neurosurgery*, *132*, e305–e313. doi:10.1016/j.wneu.2019.08.168 PMID:31494311

Auriat, A. M., Borich, M. R., Snow, N. J., Wadden, K. P., & Boyd, L. A. (2015). Comparing a diffusion tensor and non-tensor approach to white matter fiber tractography in chronic stroke. *NeuroImage. Clinical*, *7*, 771–781. doi:10.1016/j.nicl.2015.03.007 PMID:25844329

Bagatti, D., & Messina, G. (2020). Cytotoxic Lesion in the Splenium of Corpus Callosum Associated with Intracranial Infection After Deep Brain Stimulation. *World Neurosurgery*, *135*, 306–307. doi:10.1016/j.wneu.2019.12.114 PMID:31899396

Bauer, C. M., Heidary, G., Koo, B.-B., Killiany, R. J., Bex, P., & Merabet, L. B. (2014). Abnormal white matter tractography of visual pathways detected by high-angular-resolution diffusion imaging (HARDI) corresponds to visual dysfunction in cortical/cerebral visual impairment. *Journal of AAPOS*, *18*(4), 398–401. doi:10.1016/j.jaapos.2014.03.004 PMID:25087644

Borkowski, K., & Krzyżak, A. T. (2018). Analysis and correction of errors in DTI-based tractography due to diffusion gradient inhomogeneity. *Journal of Magnetic Resonance (San Diego, Calif.)*, *296*, 5–11. doi:10.1016/j.jmr.2018.08.011 PMID:30195248

Carlson, H. L., Laliberté, C., Brooks, B. L., Hodge, J., Kirton, A., Bello-Espinosa, L., Hader, W., & Sherman, E. M. S. (2014). Reliability and variability of diffusion tensor imaging (DTI) tractography in pediatric epilepsy. *Epilepsy & Behavior*, *37*, 116–122. doi:10.1016/j.yebeh.2014.06.020 PMID:25014749

Coenen, V. A., & Reisert, M. (2021). DTI for brain targeting: Diffusion weighted imaging fiber tractography—Assisted deep brain stimulation. In E*Emerging Horizons in Neuromodulation: New Frontiers in Brain and Spine Stimulation* (Vol. 159, pp. 47–67). Academic Press. https://doi.org/https://doi.org/10.1016/bs.irn.2021.07.001

Guo, X., Liu, R., Lu, J., Wu, C., Lyu, Y., Wang, Z., Xiang, J., Pan, C., & Tong, S. (2019). Alterations in Brain Structural Connectivity After Unilateral Upper-Limb Amputation. *IEEE Transactions on Neural Systems and Rehabilitation Engineering*, 27(10), 2196–2204. doi:10.1109/TNSRE.2019.2936615 PMID:31443033

Hunt, D., Dighe, M., Gatenby, C., & Studholme, C. (2019). Automatic, Age Consistent Reconstruction of the Corpus Callosum Guided by Coherency From In Utero Diffusion-Weighted MRI. *IEEE Transactions on Medical Imaging*, 39(3), 601–610. doi:10.1109/TMI.2019.2932681 PMID:31395540

Huynh, K. M., Chen, G., Wu, Y., Shen, D., & Yap, P.-T. (2019). Multi-site harmonization of diffusion MRI data via method of moments. *IEEE Transactions on Medical Imaging*, 38(7), 1599–1609. doi:10.1109/TMI.2019.2895020 PMID:30676953

Kamali, A., Sherbaf, F. G., Rahmani, F., Khayat-Khoei, M., Aein, A., Gandhi, A., Shah, E. G., Sair, H. I., Riascos, R. F., Esquenazi, Y., & ... (2020). A direct visuosensory cortical connectivity of the human limbic system. Dissecting the trajectory of the parieto-occipito-hypothalamic tract in the human brain using diffusion weighted tractography. *Neuroscience Letters*, 728, 134955. doi:10.1016/j.neulet.2020.134955 PMID:32278940

Koenraads, Y., Porro, G. L., Braun, K. P. J., Groenendaal, F., De Vries, L. S., & Van Der Aa, N. E. (2016). Prediction of visual field defects in newborn infants with perinatal arterial ischemic stroke using early MRI and DTI-based tractography of the optic radiation. *European Journal of Paediatric Neurology*, 20(2), 309–318. doi:10.1016/j.ejpn.2015.11.010 PMID:26708504

Koike, T., Tanaka, S., Kin, T., Suzuki, Y., Takayanagi, S., Takami, H., Kugasawa, K., Nambu, S., Omura, T., Yamazawa, E., Kushihara, Y., Furuta, Y., Niwa, R., Sato, K., Uchida, T., Takeda, Y., Kiyofuji, S., Saito, T., Oyama, H., & Saito, N. (2022). Accurate Preoperative Identification of Motor Speech Area as Termination of Arcuate Fasciculus Depicted by Q-Ball Imaging Tractography. *World Neurosurgery*, 164, e764–e771. doi:10.1016/j.wneu.2022.05.041 PMID:35595046

Lefebvre, J., Buffet-Bataillon, S., Henaux, P. L., Riffaud, L., Morandi, X., & Haegelen, C. (2017). Staphylococcus aureus screening and decolonization reduces the risk of surgical site infections in patients undergoing deep brain stimulation surgery. *The Journal of Hospital Infection*, 95(2), 144–147. doi:10.1016/j.jhin.2016.11.019 PMID:28081909

Lipp, I., Parker, G. D., Tallantyre, E. C., Goodall, A., Grama, S., Patitucci, E., Heveron, P., Tomassini, V., & Jones, D. K. (2020). Tractography in the presence of multiple sclerosis lesions. *NeuroImage*, 209, 116471. doi:10.1016/j.neuroimage.2019.116471 PMID:31877372

Mann, M., Wright, C. H., Jella, T., Labak, C. M., Shammassian, B., Srivatsa, S., Wright, J., Engineer, L., Sajatovic, M., & Selman, W. (2021). Cranial Surgical Site Infection Interventions and Prevention Bundles: A Systematic Review of the Literature. *World Neurosurgery*, 148, 206–219.e4. doi:10.1016/j.wneu.2020.12.137 PMID:33412319

Mukherjee, P. (2005). Diffusion Tensor Imaging and Fiber Tractography in Acute Stroke. *Neuroimaging Clinics of North America, 15*(3), 655–665. doi:10.1016/j.nic.2005.08.010 PMID:16360595

Mukherjee, P., Chung, S. W., Berman, J. I., Hess, C. P., & Henry, R. G. (2008). Diffusion tensor MR imaging and fiber tractography: Technical considerations. *AJNR. American Journal of Neuroradiology, 29*(5), 843–852. doi:10.3174/ajnr.A1052 PMID:18339719

Owen, S. L. F., Heath, J., Kringelbach, M., Green, A. L., Pereira, E. A. C., Jenkinson, N., Jegan, T., Stein, J. F., & Aziz, T. Z. (2008). Pre-operative DTI and probabilisitic tractography in four patients with deep brain stimulation for chronic pain. *Journal of Clinical Neuroscience, 15*(7), 801–805. doi:10.1016/j.jocn.2007.06.010 PMID:18495481

Owens, C. D., & Stoessel, K. (2008). Surgical site infections: Epidemiology, microbiology and prevention. *The Journal of Hospital Infection, 70*, 3–10. doi:10.1016/S0195-6701(08)60017-1 PMID:19022115

Poupon, C., Clark, C. A., Frouin, V., Regis, J., Bloch, I., Le Bihan, D., & Mangin, J.-F. (2000). Regularization of diffusion-based direction maps for the tracking of brain white matter fascicles. *NeuroImage, 12*(2), 184–195. doi:10.1006/nimg.2000.0607 PMID:10913324

Qiu, M., Zhang, J., Zhang, Y., Li, Q., Xie, B., & Wang, J. (2012). Diffusion tensor imaging-based research on human white matter anatomy. *TheScientificWorldJournal, 2012*, 2012. doi:10.1100/2012/530432 PMID:23226983

Reid, L. B., Cespedes, M. I., & Pannek, K. (2020). How many streamlines are required for reliable probabilistic tractography? Solutions for microstructural measurements and neurosurgical planning. *NeuroImage, 211*, 116646. doi:10.1016/j.neuroimage.2020.116646 PMID:32084566

Rheault, F., St-Onge, E., Sidhu, J., Maier-Hein, K., Tzourio-Mazoyer, N., Petit, L., & Descoteaux, M. (2019). Bundle-specific tractography with incorporated anatomical and orientational priors. *NeuroImage, 186*, 382–398. doi:10.1016/j.neuroimage.2018.11.018 PMID:30453031

Siless, V., Davidow, J. Y., Nielsen, J., Fan, Q., Hedden, T., Hollinshead, M., Beam, E., Bustamante, C. M. V., Garrad, M. C., Santillana, R., & ... (2020). Registration-free analysis of diffusion MRI tractography data across subjects through the human lifespan. *NeuroImage, 214*, 116703. doi:10.1016/j.neuroimage.2020.116703 PMID:32151759

Smith, R. E., Tournier, J. D., Calamante, F., & Connelly, A. (2012). Anatomically-constrained tractography: Improved diffusion MRI streamlines tractography through effective use of anatomical information. *NeuroImage, 62*(3), 1924–1938. doi:10.1016/j.neuroimage.2012.06.005 PMID:22705374

Stamile, C., Cotton, F., Sappey-Marinier, D., & Van Huffel, S. (2019). Constrained Tensor Decomposition for Longitudinal Analysis of Diffusion Imaging Data. *IEEE Journal of Biomedical and Health Informatics, 24*(4), 1137–1148. doi:10.1109/JBHI.2019.2933138 PMID:31395569

Tallus, J., Mohammadian, M., Kurki, T., Roine, T., Posti, J. P., & Tenovuo, O. (2023). A comparison of diffusion tensor imaging tractography and constrained spherical deconvolution with automatic segmentation in traumatic brain injury. *NeuroImage. Clinical, 37*, 103284. doi:10.1016/j.nicl.2022.103284 PMID:36502725

Wang, B., Fan, Y., Lu, M., Li, S., Song, Z., Peng, X., Zhang, R., Lin, Q., He, Y., Wang, J., & Huang, R. (2013). Brain anatomical networks in world class gymnasts: A DTI tractography study. *NeuroImage*, *65*, 476–487. doi:10.1016/j.neuroimage.2012.10.007 PMID:23073234

Wasserthal, J., Neher, P. F., Hirjak, D., & Maier-Hein, K. H. (2019). Combined tract segmentation and orientation mapping for bundle-specific tractography. *Medical Image Analysis*, *58*, 101559. doi:10.1016/j.media.2019.101559 PMID:31542711

Watson, C. G., DeMaster, D., & Ewing-Cobbs, L. (2019). Graph theory analysis of DTI tractography in children with traumatic injury. *NeuroImage. Clinical*, *21*, 101673. doi:10.1016/j.nicl.2019.101673 PMID:30660661

Waugh, J. L., Kuster, J. K., Makhlouf, M. L., Levenstein, J. M., Multhaupt-Buell, T. J., Warfield, S. K., Sharma, N., & Blood, A. J. (2019). A registration method for improving quantitative assessment in probabilistic diffusion tractography. *NeuroImage*, *189*, 288–306. doi:10.1016/j.neuroimage.2018.12.057 PMID:30611874

Yeh, F.-C. (2020). Shape analysis of the human association pathways. *NeuroImage*, *223*, 117329. doi:10.1016/j.neuroimage.2020.117329 PMID:32882375

Zhan, L., Zhou, J., Wang, Y., Jin, Y., Jahanshad, N., Prasad, G., Nir, T. M., Leonardo, C. D., Ye, J., & Thompson, P. M. (2015). Comparison of nine tractography algorithms for detecting abnormal structural brain networks in Alzheimer's disease. *Frontiers in Aging Neuroscience*, *7*, 48. doi:10.3389/fnagi.2015.00048 PMID:25926791

Chapter 16
Smart Hydroponic Monitoring System Using IoT

Shaminder Kaur

Chitkara University Institute of Engineering and Technology, Chitkara University, India

Lipika Gupta

Department of Electronics and Communication Engineering, Chitkara University Institute of Engineering and Technology, Chitkara University, India

Tripti Sharma

Chandigarh University, Punjab, India

Shilpi Birla

ⓘ https://orcid.org/0000-0002-4239-4912

Department of Electronics and Communication Engineering, Manipal University, Jaipur, India

Neeraj Kumar

Electrical Engineering Department, College of Engineering, King Khalid University, Abha, Saudi Arabia

ABSTRACT

The burden on agricultural productivity is growing as the global population continues to increase at a rapid rate. Due to the growth of metro areas, agricultural land is being lost daily, which could result in a shortage of arable land. Vertical farming (VF) is the answer to this issue. IoT system can be utilized to monitor and control these vertical farming systems. By using the latest technology such as IoT, it becomes very easy for the farmers to monitor the growth of their plants. It becomes easy for them to monitor plants in terms of what action is needed and how much care is required at appropriate time. It is important for determining the optimum growth of plants.

DOI: 10.4018/978-1-6684-8306-0.ch016

INTRODUCTION

For supporting human in the world farming plays a very vital role. Nowadays drinking water is scarce and out of which the largest part of it is being used in the farming process. As the population is growing the interest for both more food and more land is also increasing so we need a new method of farming that can bring conventional farming in urban areas (SDG-2).The idea of Vertical Farming (VF) was proposed by Dickson Despommier in 1999, he is professor of Public and Environmental Health at Columbia University (Bhowmick et al., 2019; Taha et al., 2022; Tatas et al., 2022). VF is the method of growing plants in vertically stacked layers with a controlled environment for proper growth of plants and this is a soilless farming technology such as hydroponics, aeroponics, and aquaponics. A major issue is the unpredictability of the weather and the uneven distribution of water resources throughout the entire year, both of which contribute to an inadequate yield and issue is addressed by VF. This scientific method's success in the realm of cultivation has the potential to significantly alter how crops are produced. By employing this technique, crop yield increase while utilizing much lesser space (Beacham et al., 2019; Vadivel et al., 2019).

Urban farming can be replaced by vertical framing. It is a method of industrial manufacturing that involves mass food production. These structures might produce fruit, vegetables, and other consumables throughout the year utilizing cutting-edge greenhouse technology and controlled environment. In contrast to the conventional rural farming approach, the concept calls for growing and harvesting a wide variety of plants in densely populated urban areas and selling these crops to the local population directly (bin Ismail & Thamrin, 2017; Crisnapati et al., 2017; Tatas et al., 2022). To raise plants, animals, fungus, and other living things for use as food, fuel, building materials, or other goods or services, VF, is a commercial agricultural approach. Further with the newer cutting-edge technologies such as IOT, Machine learning and Artificial Intelligence, VF, processes can be made automated as well as an healthy crop can be raised by taking necessary steps at required time.

VERTICAL FARMING (VF)

The technique of vertical farming (VF) involves layering plants vertically to increase food production per square foot of land. Plants are grown without soil via vertical farming while the plants receive the correct amount of water and nutrition for healthy growth using different techniques discussed in this chapter. Architecture of vertical farming is depicted in Figure 1. It makes use of Controlled Environment Agriculture (CEA) technology and indoor farming methods where a variety of variables, including humidity, temperature, light exposure, gases, and the quantity of nutrients to be given to the plants, may be managed (Bacco et al., 2018; Kumar et al., 2022).In difficult conditions, such as those where arable land is few or unavailable, vertical farms try to generate food. By combining skyscraper-like architecture and precision agriculture techniques, this style of vertical farming allows communities that are situated on mountainside, people who are living in the desert area, and cities grow various types of crops. VF grows plants using a variety of techniques, such as the hydroponic approach, which consumes up to 70% less water (Al-Chalabi, 2015; Ruengittinun et al., 2017; Salvi et al., 2017; Yusof et al., 2016). The amount of water needed is even less with the aeroponic approach. The artificial lighting used in VF is LED-based, with the ability to employ different coloured LEDs. The electricity needed for this method is generated by a sustainable energy source, like solar or wind energy.

Economic, Environmental, and Societal Benefits of Vertical Farming

- **Increased in crop production:** Vertical farming allow us to yield crops the whole year as it is not weather dependent. Plants are grown inside building and LED lights are being used by which photosynthesis process can occur entire time. Hence all-season farming increases the production of food (Belista et al., 2018; Wiangtong & Sirisuk, 2018).
- **Protection from weather related problem:** In vertical farming a controlled environment is being provided due to which the yield of vertical farms is mostly independent of weather and protected from severe weather events such as heavy rainfall, undesirable temperature, hailstorms, flooding, tornadoes, wildfires and severe drought. Also the plants are being protected from different kind of diseases (Lu & Shimamura, 2018; Mahesh et al., 2016; Puengsungwan & Jiraserccamomkul, 2018; Srivastav et al., 2023).
- **Transportation cost reduces:** Vertical farms can build in the middle of the cities by which there is reduction in transportation cost as we don't need to bring in the crops from different places. Transportation is decreased and ultimately pollution will be minimized hence vertical farming is eco-friendly (Sardare & Admane, 2013).
- **Growing higher quality produce:** In vertical farming no harmful herbicides or pesticides are used hence in vertical farming organic crops are grown which is good for human health.
- **Conservation of resources:** By using vertical farming the requirement of land is reduced as vertically stacked layers are being used for growing plants thus many natural resources is being saved. Deforestation and desertification would be reduced. In this method use of water is significantly less hence water conservation is done (Incemehmetouglu, 2012; Sardare & Admane, 2013).
- **Less use of water:** In vertical farming use of water is very less it only uses 10% of amount of water which is used in traditional farming process. The water which is used in vertical farming method is re-used hence most of the water doesn't get wasted.
- **Environmental benefits:** Increased land use with energy minimization, waste recycling and reduction, healthy food and green environment, improved air quality, reduced carbon footprint, more natural approaches to farming, reduced use of Herbicide and pesticide manufacture and many more (Gupta et al., 2022; Kaur et al., 2022).
- **Social Benefits:** Job creation for deploying the VF setup, reduction in stress and healthy environment, aesthetic benefits, consistent crop, vegetables, and fruits that have high nutritional values with added pesticides, artificial flavours and many more.

VERTICAL FARMING: TECHNOLOGY FOR SAVING WATER

Less Water Required in VF

Modern farming practices use the freshwater as per the availability. Due to artificial irrigation systems used in farms and the fact that most irrigation water evaporates, there is a water loss in modern farming. Evaporation is a natural process, but there is a bigger problem: the water that left on the land is contaminated by the pesticides and fertilizers which is again used in farming and thus the crop produced further has high amount of metallic, non-metallic components which are not suitable of human consumption. Indoor farming offers a solution to this issue as it reduces water waste and allows for water recycling for plant irrigation by ensuring that the plants receive the right amount of water necessary for sufficient production (Kalantari & Akhyani, 2021).

Water Reclamation by Recycling

The grey water from one-time uses like taking a shower or washing your hands can also be utilized by VF. Grey water can be easily filtered and treated with straightforward procedures. The initial step of the concept is to gather water from a building/ city/ township and store it in a cistern buried somewhere in the middle. Water will then be pushed to the tower, where it will then descend and irrigate the plants. The plants in VF can also be watered with water that has already been processed but doesn't need to be processed again to make it for drinking. By using this technique to recycle water, there will be control over water waste and the water table could be replenished.

Recovering Water Through Dehumidification

It is possible to collect and reuse the water that evaporates during transpiration. Water's nutrient content enters plants through their roots, where it is absorbed by the plants. The remaining water, which is clean water, is then transpired back to the air by plants' leaves. By using the dehumidification method in VF, the clean water that evaporates can be reused to water plants. The goal of getting this water back will be achieved by installing specific equipment on each floor of vertical farming. Statistics show that using hydroponics for agricultural requires 70% less water than using conventional methods (Naphtali et al., 2022).

Vertical Farming With IoT

Due to the rapidly increasing population, it is essential to enhance farming methods and agriculture production in order to produce more crops. At the same time, we must ensure that the system is automated, which could be accomplished with the help of the latest technologies such as Internet of Things (IoT), Machine learning and Artificial Intelligence. Implementation of various hardware sensors used to keep track of the factors during the process of growing plants, such as the appropriate temperature needed for the plants, soil moisture content, humidity measurement, light exposure, and intruder detection (Edwin et al., 2022). By automating the entire process, IoT in vertical farming increases the efficiency of the agricultural process while also reducing human involvement. The Internet of Things (IoT) method gathers data from sensors installed in farms, processes it using a controller, and then uses actuators to finish the process. This kind of strategy will ensure that all natural resources are used effectively. With the help of these contemporary methods, resource waste—such as the waste of water—may be reduced, as can the idea of giving plants in indoor systems the right atmosphere (Ramakrishnam Raju et al., 2022).

VF set-up: The deployment of a Hydroponic VF System is done in stages as shown in Figure 2 and 3. At the place where the entire hydroponic system is built, a stand made of PVC pipes with the necessary apertures is installed. The connectivity of all the pipes is completed for the proper flow of water, and net pots can be inserted into the apertures. The germinated plants are added to the system, and the pump is connected to the flow of nutritional solution through the pipes. In order to give the plants the correct light and encourage their quick growth, the LED connection is established. All the sensors are connected and prepared to sense different parameters. A mounted temperature and humidity sensor measures the environmental conditions, a pH sensor measures the pH of the nutrient solution, and a TDS sensor measures the amount of nutrient dissolved in water. The CO_2 sensor is used to gauge the CO_2 levels in the atmosphere. The amount of light being given to the plant is determined using a light intensity sensor. Tank water level is determined using a water level sensor.

The working model shown in Figure 3 has all the sensors fixed, and the connections are complete. The display board is then connected to all the sensors, and the readings from all the sensors are displayed there. The Arduino Mega 2560, pH sensor, TDS sensor, LDR sensor, temperature and humidity sensor (DHT 11), CO_2 sensor (MQ135), water level sensor and water pump are used in this model. Also, the LED strip is used to provide plants the right amount of light for their proper growth.

Design and Implementation

The connection of all the components is shown in Figure 4. In this hardware design connection is done between three LCDs with all the sensors. LCD1 displays the output from DHT 11 and MQ135, LCD2 displays the name on the unit, CO_2 sensor, LDR sensor and LCD3 displays the pH, TDS and water level indictor values.

The data generated by the sensors is then collected, visualized and examined over theThinkspeak Cloud. The data is sent to Thingspeak from the controller and Wi-Fi ESP8266 module.To control the Arduino Mega over the internet an App is used named as Blynk App is also developed. Through this app, all the readings from the sensors is made available to the user who can easily visualize the readings on their android phones or on the laptops. Flow chart shown in Figure 5 gives the overview of the control and implementation of the IOT based hydroponic system.

Smart Monitoring of Growth of Plants Through IoT

Initially all the deployed sensors were tested to establish the connection with the developed IoT system i.e. connection with Arduino Uno, ThinkSpeak Cloud and Blynk App. Further control mechanism through Blynk app i.e. LED switching, DC motor switching and growing media flow was tested and controlled successfully. The technique is used to track plant growth under various circumstances. The plant development is seen under various conditions; for example, if the light is inadequate, the LDR sends a signal to the user via the Blynk app and LCD display and through the control unit the LED strips are turned on. The system also kept track of how the amount of CO_2 in the air affected plant growth and adjusted the amount of nutrients given to the plants to observe how it affected plant growth. In the tank, a water level sensor is installed to measure the water level. Users will receive notifications three times a day initially at 70% of the water level, then at 50% and finally at 20%. To ensure that plants receive the right amount of nutrients for healthy growth, a pH sensor is installed in the tank.Additionally, a temperature-humidity sensor is included in the system to determine the temperature and humidity of the atmosphere.

CONCLUSION AND FUTURE SCOPE

This automated technology, which is controllable via a mobile device, can assist novice farmers and those who want to engage in farming but lack the time to handle it. A lot of different crops will be produced with the aid of this method. This method produces crops that are nutrient- and flavor-rich at the same time with minimal land use. The IoT based monitoring helps the provide the controlled environment to the hydronic crop which can be monitored automatically with least intervention from the user. People can create their own domestic plants using these easy to install vertical farms. Additionally, this approach aids in preventing diseases brought on by the usage of chemical fertilizers during food cultivation. This farming technique can be improved by measuring the plant height to monitor growth and forecast yield using image processing. The solar panel, which could tilt itself in the direction of the sun's rays, can be utilised to power this system. The analysis of data will reveal how much water the plant requires to grow, enabling farmers to plan their future crop production in accordance with water availability. Future work will involve adding more sensors, such as nitrogen, potassium, and phosphorus sensors, as well as providing insufficient nutrients.

REFERENCES

Al-Chalabi, M. (2015). Vertical farming: Skyscraper sustainability? *Sustainable Cities and Society*, *18*, 74–77. doi:10.1016/j.scs.2015.06.003

Bacco, M., Berton, A., Ferro, E., Gennaro, C., Gotta, A., Matteoli, S., Paonessa, F., Ruggeri, M., Virone, G., & Zanella, A. (2018). Smart farming: Opportunities, challenges and technology enablers. *2018 IoT Vertical and Topical Summit on Agriculture-Tuscany (IOT Tuscany)*, 1–6.

Beacham, A. M., Vickers, L. H., & Monaghan, J. M. (2019). Vertical farming: A summary of approaches to growing skywards. *The Journal of Horticultural Science & Biotechnology*, *94*(3), 277–283. doi:10. 1080/14620316.2019.1574214

Belista, F. C. L., Go, M. P. C., Luceñara, L. L., Policarpio, C. J. G., Tan, X. J. M., & Baldovino, R. G. (2018). A smart aeroponic tailored for IoT vertical agriculture using network connected modular environmental chambers. *2018 IEEE 10th International Conference on Humanoid, Nanotechnology, Information Technology, Communication and Control, Environment and Management (HNICEM)*, 1–4.

Bhowmick, S., Biswas, B., Biswas, M., Dey, A., Roy, S., & Sarkar, S. K. (2019). Application of IoT-enabled smart agriculture in vertical farming. *Advances in Communication, Devices and Networking. Proceedings of ICCDN*, *2018*, 521–528.

bin Ismail, M. I. H., & Thamrin, N. M. (2017). IoT implementation for indoor vertical farming watering system. *2017 International Conference on Electrical, Electronics and System Engineering (ICEESE)*, 89–94.

Crisnapati, P. N., Wardana, I. N. K., Aryanto, I. K. A. A., & Hermawan, A. (2017). Hommons: Hydroponic management and monitoring system for an IOT based NFT farm using web technology. *2017 5th International Conference on Cyber and IT Service Management (CITSM)*, 1–6.

Edwin, B., Veemaraj, E., Parthiban, P., Devarajan, J. P., Mariadhas, V., Arumuganainar, A., & Reddy, M. (2022). Smart agriculture monitoring system for outdoor and hydroponic environments. *Indonesian Journal of Electrical Engineering and Computer Science*, *25*(3), 1679–1687. doi:10.11591/ijeecs.v25. i3.pp1679-1687

Gupta, L., Malhotra, S., & Kumar, A. (2022). Study of applications of Internet of Things and Machine Learning for Smart Agriculture. *2022 IEEE International Conference on Current Development in Engineering and Technology (CCET)*, 1–5. 10.1109/CCET56606.2022.10080342

Incemehmetouglu, A. (2012). *Investigation the effects of different support medium on product with nutrient film technique*. Middle East Technical University.

Kalantari, F., & Akhyani, N. (2021). Community acceptance studies in the field of vertical farming—A critical and systematic analysis to advance the conceptualisation of community acceptance in Kuala Lumpur. *International Journal of Urban Sustainable Development*, *13*(3), 569–584. doi:10.1080/1946 3138.2021.2013849

Kaur, N., Kaushal, J., Mahajan, P., & Srivastav, A. L. (2022). *Design of hydroponic system for screening of ornamental plant species for removal of synthetic dyes using phytoremediation approach*. Academic Press.

Kumar, A., Malhotra, S., Kaur, D. P., & Gupta, L. (2022). Weather Monitoring and Air Quality Prediction using Machine Learning. *2022 1st International Conference on Computational Science and Technology (ICCST)*, 364–368.

Lu, N., & Shimamura, S. (2018). Protocols, issues and potential improvements of current cultivation systems. *Smart Plant Factory: The Next Generation Indoor Vertical Farms*, 31–49.

Mahesh, P. J., Naheem, M., Mubafar, R., Shyba, S., & Beevi, S. (2016). New aspect for organic farming practices: Controlled crop nutrition and soilless agriculture. *2016 IEEE Global Humanitarian Technology Conference (GHTC)*, 819–824. 10.1109/GHTC.2016.7857374

Naphtali, J. H., Misra, S., Wejin, J., Agrawal, A., & Oluranti, J. (2022). An Intelligent Hydroponic Farm Monitoring System Using IoT. In *Data, Engineering and Applications: Select Proceedings of IDEA 2021* (pp. 409–420). Springer. 10.1007/978-981-19-4687-5_31

Puengsungwan, S., & Jiraserccamomkul, K. (2018). IoT Based Stress Detection for Organic Lettuce Farms Using Chlorophyll Fluorescence (ChF). *2018 Global Wireless Summit (GWS)*, 354–357.

Ramakrishnam Raju, S. V. S., Dappuri, B., Ravi Kiran Varma, P., Yachamaneni, M., Verghese, D. M. G., & Mishra, M. K. (2022). Design and Implementation of Smart Hydroponics Farming Using IoT-Based AI Controller with Mobile Application System. *Journal of Nanomaterials*, *2022*, 1–12. doi:10.1155/2022/4435591

Ruengittinun, S., Phongsamsuan, S., & Sureeratanakorn, P. (2017). Applied internet of thing for smart hydroponic farming ecosystem (HFE). *2017 10th International Conference on Ubi-Media Computing and Workshops (Ubi-Media)*, 1–4.

Salvi, S., Jain, S. A. F., Sanjay, H. A., Harshita, T. K., Farhana, M., Jain, N., & Suhas, M. V. (2017). Cloud based data analysis and monitoring of smart multi-level irrigation system using IoT. *2017 International Conference on I-SMAC (IoT in Social, Mobile, Analytics and Cloud)(I-SMAC)*, 752–757. 10.1109/I-SMAC.2017.8058279

Sardare, M. D., & Admane, S. V. (2013). A review on plant without soil-hydroponics. *International Journal of Research in Engineering and Technology, 2*(3), 299–304. doi:10.15623/ijret.2013.0203013

Srivastav, A. L., Patel, N., Rani, L., Kumar, P., Dutt, I., Maddodi, B. S., & Chaudhary, V. K. (2023). Sustainable options for fertilizer management in agriculture to prevent water contamination: A review. *Environment, Development and Sustainability*, 1–25. doi:10.100710668-023-03117-z

Taha, M. F., ElMasry, G., Gouda, M., Zhou, L., Liang, N., Abdalla, A., Rousseau, D., & Qiu, Z. (2022). Recent Advances of Smart Systems and Internet of Things (IoT) for Aquaponics Automation: A Comprehensive Overview. *Chemosensors (Basel, Switzerland), 10*(8), 303. doi:10.3390/chemosensors10080303

Tatas, K., Al-Zoubi, A., Christofides, N., Zannettis, C., Chrysostomou, M., Panteli, S., & Antoniou, A. (2022). Reliable IoT-based monitoring and control of hydroponic systems. *Technologies, 10*(1), 26. doi:10.3390/technologies10010026

Vadivel, R., Parthasarathi, R. V., Navaneethraj, A., Sridhar, P., Nafi, K. A. M., & Karan, S. (2019). Hypaponics-monitoring and controlling using Internet of Things and machine learning. *2019 1st International Conference on Innovations in Information and Communication Technology (ICIICT)*, 1–6.

Wiangtong, T., & Sirisuk, P. (2018). IoT-based versatile platform for precision farming. *2018 18th International Symposium on Communications and Information Technologies (ISCIT)*, 438–441.

Yusof, S. S. S., Thamrin, N. M., Nordin, M. K., Yusoff, A. S. M., & Sidik, N. J. (2016). Effect of artificial lighting on typhonium flagelliforme for indoor vertical farming. *2016 IEEE International Conference on Automatic Control and Intelligent Systems (I2CACIS)*, 7–10. 10.1109/I2CACIS.2016.7885280

APPENDIX

Figure 1. Architecture of vertical farming

Figure 2. Hydroponic setup

Figure 3. Hydroponic setup with IoT-based monitoring

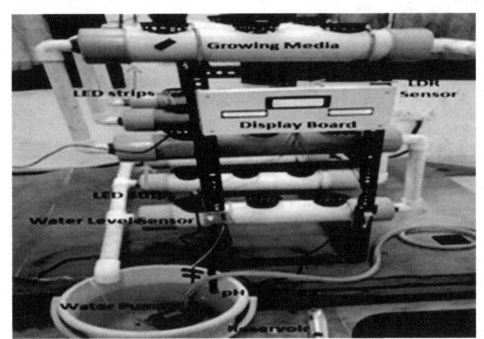

Figure 4. Component and connection diagram of the system

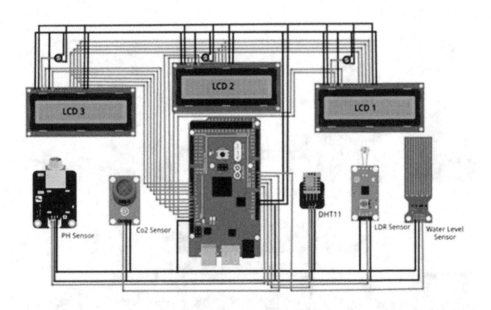

Figure 5. Overview of the control and implementation of the IoT-based hydroponic system.

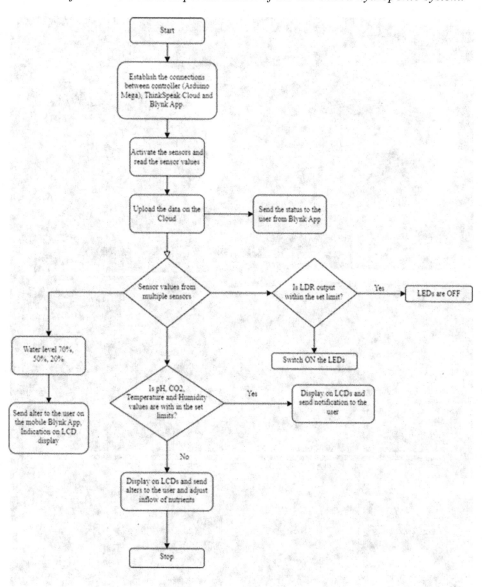

Figure 6. Blynk app showing pH valueFig

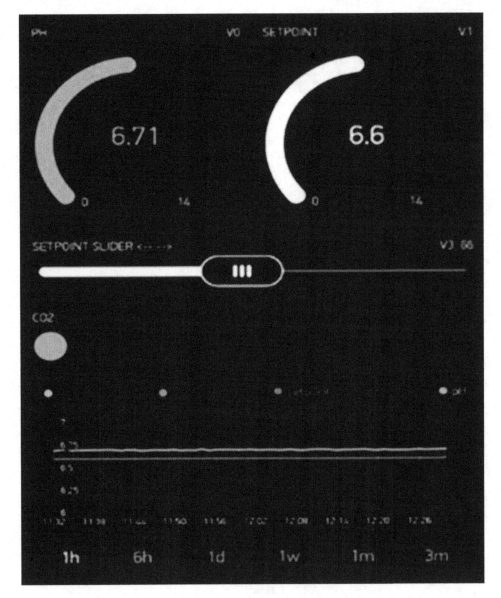

Figure 7. Blynk app showing CO$_2$ level

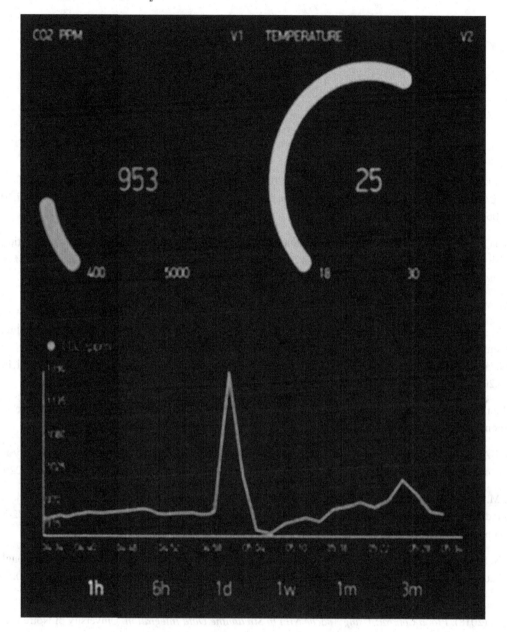

298

Compilation of References

Abd El-Aziz, R. M., Taloba, A. I., & Alghamdi, F. A. (2022). Quantum Computing Optimization Technique for IoT Platform using Modified Deep Residual Approach. *Alexandria Engineering Journal, 61*(12), 12497–12509. doi:10.1016/j.aej.2022.06.029

Abielmona, R., Groza, V., & Pretiu, W. (2003). Evolutionary neural network network-based sensor self-calibration scheme using IEEE1451 and wireless sensor networks. *International Symposium on Computational Intelligence for Masurement Systems and applications, CIMSA 2003*, Lugano, Switzerland. 10.1109/CIMSA.2003.1227198

Adadelta, M. D. (2012). *An adaptive learning rate method.* arXiv preprint arXiv:1212.5701.

Adams, M., Massey, F., Chastko, K., & Cupini, C. (2020). Spatial modelling of particulate matter air pollution sensor measurements collected by community scientists while cycling, land use regression with spatial cross-validation, and applications of machine learning for data correction. *Atmospheric Environment, 230*, 117479. doi:10.1016/j.atmosenv.2020.117479

Advice for the public: Coronavirus disease (COVID-19). (n.d.). Available at: https://www.who.int/emergencies/diseases/novel-coronavirus-2019/advice-for-public

Aggarwal, A., Mittal, M., & Battineni, G. (2021, April). Generative adversarial network: An overview of theory and applications. *International Journal of Information Management Data Insights, 1*(1), 100004. doi:10.1016/j.jjimei.2020.100004

Ahmed, M., Harbi, I., Kennel, R., Rodríguez, J., & Abdelrahem, M. (2022). Maximum Power Point Tracking-Based Model Predictive Control for Photovoltaic Systems: Investigation and New Perspective. *Sensors (Basel), 22*(8), 3069. Advance online publication. doi:10.339022083069 PMID:35459055

Ahmed, N. S. S., Acharjya, D. P., & Sanyal, S. (2017). A framework for phishing attack identification using rough set and formal concept analysis. *International Journal of Communication Networks and Distributed Systems, 18*(2), 186–212. doi:10.1504/IJCNDS.2017.082105

Ajamie, L. (2018). *Flood Control: Using Apache NiFi to Streamline Data Integration.* University of Notre Dame.

Ajoku, U., Almojuela, A., Kazina, C., Wilkinson, M., Ryner, L., & Dhaliwal, P. (2022). Maximizing surgical resection in revision surgery for an intramedullary spinal cord tumour using DTI/tractography and direct spinal cord stimulation: A technical note. *Interdisciplinary Neurosurgery : Advanced Techniques and Case Management, 28*, 101467. doi:10.1016/j.inat.2021.101467

Akyildiz, I., Su, Y., Sankarasubramaniam, W., & Cayirci, E. (2002). Wireless sensor networks: A survey. *Computer Networks, 38*(4), 393–422. doi:10.1016/S1389-1286(01)00302-4

Al-Chalabi, M. (2015). Vertical farming: Skyscraper sustainability? *Sustainable Cities and Society, 18*, 74–77. doi:10.1016/j.scs.2015.06.003

Alexopoulos, G., Cikla, U., El Tecle, N., Kulkarni, N., Pierson, M., Mercier, P., Kemp, J., Coppens, J., Mahmoud, S., Sehi, M., Bucholz, R., & Abdulrauf, S. (2019). The Value of White Matter Tractography by Diffusion Tensor Imaging in Altering a Neurosurgeon's Operative Plan. *World Neurosurgery*, *132*, e305–e313. doi:10.1016/j.wneu.2019.08.168 PMID:31494311

Ali, Y. A., & Ouassaid, M. (2019). Sensorless MPPT Controller using Particle Swarm and Grey Wolf Optimization for Wind Turbines. *2019 7th International Renewable and Sustainable Energy Conference (IRSEC)*. 10.1109/IRSEC48032.2019.9078151

Ali, M. N., Mahmoud, K., Lehtonen, M., & Darwish, M. M. F. (2021). Promising MPPT Methods Combining Meta-heuristic, Fuzzy-Logic and ANN Techniques for Grid-Connected Photovoltaic. *Sensors (Basel)*, *21*(4), 1244. Advance online publication. doi:10.339021041244 PMID:33578777

Al-Karaki, J., & Kamal, A. (2004). Routing techniques in wireless sensor networks: A survey, Wireless Sensor Networks. *IEEE Wireless Communications*, *4*(6), 6–28. doi:10.1109/MWC.2004.1368893

Almufti, S., Marqas, R., Nayef, Z., & Mohamed, T. (2021). Real Time Face-mask Detection with Arduino to Prevent COVID-19 Spreading. *Qubahan Academic Journal*, *1*(2), 39–46. doi:10.48161/qaj.v1n2a47

Alrowaili, Z. A., Ali, M. M., Youssef, A., Mousa, H. H. H., Ali, A. S., Abdel-Jaber, G. T., Ezzeldien, M., & Gami, F. (2021). Robust Adaptive HCS MPPT Algorithm-Based Wind Generation System Using Model Reference Adaptive Control. *Sensors (Basel)*, *21*(15), 5187. Advance online publication. doi:10.339021155187 PMID:34372423

Alzubaidi, L., Zhang, J., Humaidi, A. J., Al-Dujaili, A., Duan, Y., Al-Shamma, O., Santamaría, J., Fadhel, M. A., Al-Amidie, M., & Farhan, L. (2021, March 31). Review of deep learning: Concepts, CNN architectures, challenges, applications, future directions. *Journal of Big Data*, *8*(1), 53. Advance online publication. doi:10.118640537-021-00444-8 PMID:33816053

Amrutkar, C., Kim, Y. S., & Traynor, P. (2017). Detecting malicious mobile web pages in real-time. *IEEE Transactions on Mobile Computing*, *16*(8), 2184–2197. doi:10.1109/TMC.2016.2575828

An end-to-end open-source machine learning platform-TensorFlow. (n.d.). Available at: https://www.tensorflow.org/

Andújar, J. M., & Melgar, S. G. (2020). *Energy Efficiency in Buildings: Both New and Rehabilitated*. MDPI.

Arora, P., & Arora, P. (2019). Mining Twitter Data for Depression Detection. *2019 International Conference on Signal Processing and Communication (ICSC)*, (pp. 186-189). IEEE. 10.1109/ICSC45622.2019.8938353

Aroyehun, A., Olabiyisi, S., Omidiora, E., & Ganiyu, R. (2018). P. *Idowu Development of a Fuzzy Logic Model for Predicting the Likelihood of Cholera Disease WJERT*, *4*, 340–363.

Arumugam, S., & Chakkarapani, L. D. (2019). Metal nanoparticles functionalized carbon nanotubes for efficient catalytic application. In Materials Research Express (Vol. 6, Issue 10, p. 1050e3). doi:10.1088/2053-1591/ab42ff

Aspnes, K., Goldenberg, D., & Yang, Y. (2003). On the computational complexity of sensor network location. *Lecture Notes in Computer Science*, *3121*, 235–246.

Auriat, A. M., Borich, M. R., Snow, N. J., Wadden, K. P., & Boyd, L. A. (2015). Comparing a diffusion tensor and non-tensor approach to white matter fiber tractography in chronic stroke. *NeuroImage. Clinical*, *7*, 771–781. doi:10.1016/j.nicl.2015.03.007 PMID:25844329

Aurrecoechea, C., Campbell, A., & Hauw, L. (1998). A survey of QoS architectures. *Multimedia Systems*, *6*(3), 138–151. doi:10.1007005300050083

Ayad, I. A., Elwarraki, E., & Baghdadi, M. (2021). Intelligent Perturb and Observe Based MPPT Approach Using Multilevel DC-DC Converter to Improve PV Production System. In Journal of Electrical and Computer Engineering (Vol. 2021, pp. 1–13). doi:10.1155/2021/6673022

Ayad, I. A., Elwarraki, E., & Baghdadi, M. (2022). MPPT Comparison of Standalone Photovoltaic System using Multi-level Boost Converter. In *2022 4th Global Power, Energy and Communication Conference (GPECOM)*. 10.1109/GPECOM55404.2022.9815738

Azeez, N. (2020). Identifying phishing attacks in communication networks using URL consistency features. *International Journal of Electronic Security and Digital Forensics 12*(2), 200–213.

AZO Team. (n.d.). The A350 XWB – Advanced Materials and Design. AZO. https://www.azom.com/article.aspx?ArticleID=7858

Ba, A., Ndiaye, A., Ndiaye, E. H. M., & Mbodji, S. (2023). Power optimization of a photovoltaic system with artificial intelligence algorithms over two seasons in tropical area. *MethodsX, 10*, 101959. doi:10.1016/j.mex.2022.101959 PMID:36545542

Babu, P., & Parthasarathy, E. (2021). Optimized Object Detection Method for FPGA Implementation. *2021 Sixth International Conference on Wireless Communications, Signal Processing and Networking (WiSPNET)*, (pp. 72-74). IEEE. 10.1109/WiSPNET51692.2021.9419407

Bacco, M., Berton, A., Ferro, E., Gennaro, C., Gotta, A., Matteoli, S., Paonessa, F., Ruggeri, M., Virone, G., & Zanella, A. (2018). Smart farming: Opportunities, challenges and technology enablers. *2018 IoT Vertical and Topical Summit on Agriculture-Tuscany (IOT Tuscany)*, 1–6.

Badapanda, M. K., Tripathi, A., Upadhyay, R., & Lad, M. (2022). High Voltage DC Power Supply with Input Parallel and Output Series Connected DC-DC Converters. In IEEE Transactions on Power Electronics (pp. 1–5). doi:10.1109/TPEL.2022.3233257

Bagatti, D., & Messina, G. (2020). Cytotoxic Lesion in the Splenium of Corpus Callosum Associated with Intracranial Infection After Deep Brain Stimulation. *World Neurosurgery, 135*, 306–307. doi:10.1016/j.wneu.2019.12.114 PMID:31899396

Bailey, K., & Breslin, D. (2021, January). The COVID-19 Pandemic: What can we learn from past research in organizations and management? *International Journal of Management Reviews, 23*(1), 3–6. doi:10.1111/ijmr.12237

Bai, Y., Zhuang, H., & Wang, D. (2007). *Advanced Fuzzy Logic Technologies in Industrial Applications*. Springer Science & Business Media.

Bakis, G., Wendel, J. F., Zeiler, R., Aksit, A., Häublein, M., Demleitner, M., Benra, J., Forero, S., Schütz, W., & Altstädt, V. (2021). Mechanical properties of the carbon nanotube modified epoxy–carbon fiber unidirectional prepreg laminates. *Polymers, 13*(5), 770. doi:10.3390/polym13050770 PMID:33801511

Baldini, I., Castro, P., Chang, K., Cheng, P., Fink, S., Ishakian, V., & Suter, P. (2017). Serverless computing: Current trends and open problems. *Research advances in cloud computing*, 1-20.

Banakhr, F. A., & Mosaad, M. I. (2021). High performance adaptive maximum power point tracking technique for off-grid photovoltaic systems. *Scientific Reports, 11*(1), 20400. doi:10.103841598-021-99949-8 PMID:34650159

Bang, H., Park, S., & Jeon, H. (2020). Defect identification in composite materials via thermography and deep learning techniques. *Composite Structures, 246*, 112405. doi:10.1016/j.compstruct.2020.112405

Barbancho, J., Leo'n, C., Molina, F., & Barbancho, A. (2006). SIR: A new wireless sensor network routing protocol based on artificial intelligence. *Lecture Notes in Computer Science, 3842*, 271–275. doi:10.1007/11610496_35

Barbancho, J., Molina, F., Leo'n, D., Ropero, J., & Barbancho, A. OLIMPO, an ad-hoc wireless sensor network simulator for public utilities applications. In *Proceedings of the Second European Workshop on Wireless Sensor Networks* (pp. 419–424). IEEE. 10.1109/EWSN.2005.1462037

Bard, S., Demleitner, M., Häublein, M., & Altstädt, V. (2018). Fracture behaviour of prepreg laminates studied by in-situ sem mechanical tests. *Procedia Structural Integrity, 13*, 1442–1446. doi:10.1016/j.prostr.2018.12.299

BarnettS. A. (2018, June 29). *Convergence Problems with Generative Adversarial Networks (GANs)*. https://arxiv.org/abs/1806.11382v1

Bartlett, S., Littlewort, G., Fasel, I., & Movellan, J. R. (2003). Real Time Face Detection and Facial Expression Recognition: Development and Applications to Human Computer Interation. *2003 Conference on Computer Vision and Pattern Recognition Workshop*, 53-53. 10.1109/CVPRW.2003.10057

Bauer, C. M., Heidary, G., Koo, B.-B., Killiany, R. J., Bex, P., & Merabet, L. B. (2014). Abnormal white matter tractography of visual pathways detected by high-angular-resolution diffusion imaging (HARDI) corresponds to visual dysfunction in cortical/cerebral visual impairment. *Journal of AAPOS, 18*(4), 398–401. doi:10.1016/j.jaapos.2014.03.004 PMID:25087644

Bayeh, C. Z., & Moubayed, N. (2014). Comparison between PV farms, solar chimneys and CSP towers in Lebanon: Influence of temperature and solar irradiance on the output power. *International Conference on Renewable Energies for Developing Countries 2014*. 10.1109/REDEC.2014.7038558

Beacham, A. M., Vickers, L. H., & Monaghan, J. M. (2019). Vertical farming: A summary of approaches to growing skywards. *The Journal of Horticultural Science & Biotechnology, 94*(3), 277–283. doi:10.1080/14620316.2019.1574214

Behera, R. K., Das, S., Jena, M., Rath, S. K., & Sahoo, B. (2017). A comparative study of distributed tools for analyzing streaming data. In *2017 International Conference on Information Technology (ICIT)* (pp. 79-84). IEEE. 10.1109/ICIT.2017.32

Behera, R. K., Rath, S. K., Misra, S., Leon, M., & Adewumi, A. (2019). Machine learning approach for reliability assessment of open source software. In Computational Science and Its Applications–ICCSA 2019: 19th International Conference. Springer International Publishing.

Belista, F. C. L., Go, M. P. C., Luceñara, L. L., Policarpio, C. J. G., Tan, X. J. M., & Baldovino, R. G. (2018). A smart aeroponic tailored for IoT vertical agriculture using network connected modular environmental chambers. *2018 IEEE 10th International Conference on Humanoid, Nanotechnology, Information Technology, Communication and Control, Environment and Management (HNICEM)*, 1–4.

Bennis, G., Karim, M., & Lagrioui, A. (2015). Optimization of the performance of a photovoltaic system with MPPT controller. *2015 3rd International Renewable and Sustainable Energy Conference (IRSEC)*. 10.1109/IRSEC.2015.7455115

Bernhardsson. E. (2014). *Recurrent neural networks for collaborative filtering*. arXiv preprint.

Bhattacharjee, K., Bhattacharya, A., & Dey, S. H. N. (2014a). Chemical reaction optimisation for different economic dispatch problems. In IET Generation, Transmission & Distribution (Vol. 8, Issue 3, pp. 530–541). doi:10.1049/iet-gtd.2013.0122

Bhattacharjee, K., Bhattacharya, A., & Dey, S. H. N. (2014b). Oppositional Real Coded Chemical Reaction Optimization for different economic dispatch problems. In International Journal of Electrical Power & Energy Systems (Vol. 55, pp. 378–391). doi:10.1016/j.ijepes.2013.09.033

Bhattacharjee, K., Bhattacharya, A., & Dey, S. H. N. (2014c). Solution of Economic Emission Load Dispatch problems of power systems by Real Coded Chemical Reaction algorithm. In International Journal of Electrical Power & Energy Systems (Vol. 59, pp. 176–187). doi:10.1016/j.ijepes.2014.02.006

Bhattacharjee, K., Shah, K., & Soni, J. (2021). Solving Economic Dispatch using Artificial Eco System-based Optimization. In Electric Power Components and Systems (Vol. 49, Issues 11-12, pp. 1034–1051). doi:10.1080/15325008.2021.2013995

Bhowmick, S., Biswas, B., Biswas, M., Dey, A., Roy, S., & Sarkar, S. K. (2019). Application of IoT-enabled smart agriculture in vertical farming. *Advances in Communication, Devices and Networking. Proceedings of ICCDN, 2018*, 521–528.

bin Ismail, M. I. H., & Thamrin, N. M. (2017). IoT implementation for indoor vertical farming watering system. *2017 International Conference on Electrical, Electronics and System Engineering (ICEESE)*, 89–94.

Bird, J. J., Barnes, C. M., Manso, L. J., Ekárt, A., & Faria, D. R. (2022, February). Fruit quality and defect image classification with conditional GAN data augmentation. *Scientia Horticulturae, 293*, 110684. doi:10.1016/j.scienta.2021.110684

Bisong, A., & Rahman, M. (2011). An overview of the security concerns in enterprise cloud computing. *arXiv preprint arXiv:1101.5613*.

Blanco, G. & Lourenço, A. (2022). Optimism and pessimism analysis using deep learning on COVID-19 related twitter conversations. *Information Processing & Management, 59*(3), 102918. . doi:10.1016/j.ipm.2022.102918

Boiral, O., Brotherton, M. C., Rivaud, L., & Guillaumie, L. (2021, January). Organizations' management of the COVID-19 pandemic: A scoping review of business articles. *Sustainability (Basel), 13*(7), 3993. doi:10.3390u13073993

Borkowski, K., & Krzyżak, A. T. (2018). Analysis and correction of errors in DTI-based tractography due to diffusion gradient inhomogeneity. *Journal of Magnetic Resonance (San Diego, Calif.), 296*, 5–11. doi:10.1016/j.jmr.2018.08.011 PMID:30195248

Börner, K., Rouse, W. B., Trunfio, P., & Stanley, H. E. (2018, December 10). Forecasting innovations in science, technology, and education. *Proceedings of the National Academy of Sciences of the United States of America, 115*(50), 12573–12581. doi:10.1073/pnas.1818750115 PMID:30530683

Bottazzi, G., Casalicchio, E., Cingolani, D., Marturana, F., & Piu, M. (2015). MP-Shield: A Framework for Phishing Detection in Mobile Devices. *IEEE International Conference on Computer and Information Technology; Ubiquitous Computing and Communications; Dependable, Autonomic and Secure Computing; Pervasive Intelligence and Computing (CIT/IUCC/DASC/PICOM)*, pp. 1977-1983. IEEE (2015) 10.1109/CIT/IUCC/DASC/PICOM.2015.293

Brafman, R. I., Heckerman, D., & Shani, G. (2000). Recommendation as a stochastic sequential decision problem. In ICAPS, 164–173.

Bricout, S. (2020). *Environmental analysis of innovative sustainable composites with potential use in aviation sector—A life cycle assessment review*. Research Gate. https://www.researchgate.net/figure/Materials-used-in-a-modern-aircraftthe-Airbus-A350-XWB-5_fig6_318923824

Calinescu, G., & Wan, P. (2003). Range assignment for high connectivity in wireless ad hoc networks. *Lecture Notes in Computer Science, 2865*, 235–246. doi:10.1007/978-3-540-39611-6_21

Carlson, H. L., Laliberté, C., Brooks, B. L., Hodge, J., Kirton, A., Bello-Espinosa, L., Hader, W., & Sherman, E. M. S. (2014). Reliability and variability of diffusion tensor imaging (DTI) tractography in pediatric epilepsy. *Epilepsy & Behavior*, *37*, 116–122. doi:10.1016/j.yebeh.2014.06.020 PMID:25014749

Castro, P., Ishakian, V., Muthusamy, V., & Slominski, A. (2019). The rise of serverless computing. *Communications of the ACM*, *62*(12), 44–54. doi:10.1145/3368454

Chalh, A., Chaibi, R., Hammoumi, A. E., Motahhir, S., Ghzizal, A. E., & Al-Dhaifallah, M. (2022). A novel MPPT design based on the seagull optimization algorithm for photovoltaic systems operating under partial shading. *Scientific Reports*, *12*(1), 21804. doi:10.103841598-022-26284-x PMID:36526663

Chao, K.-H., & Rizal, M. N. (2021). A Hybrid MPPT Controller Based on the Genetic Algorithm and Ant Colony Optimization for Photovoltaic Systems under Partially Shaded Conditions. In Energies (Vol. 14, Issue 10, p. 2902). doi:10.3390/en14102902

Chatterjee, R., Gupta, R., & Gupta, B. (2021). Depression Detection from Social Media Posts Using Multinomial Naive Theorem. *IOP Conference Series. Materials Science and Engineering*, *1022*(1), 012095. doi:10.1088/1757-899X/1022/1/012095

Chavda, A., Dsouza, J., Badgujar, S., & Damani, A. (2021). Multi-Stage CNN Architecture for Face Mask Detection. *6th International Conference for Convergence in Technology(I2CT)*, 1-8. 10.1109/I2CT51068.2021.9418207

Chen, T. (2021). Development and Implementation of Anti Phishing Wi-Fi and Information Security Protection APP based on Android. *J. Phys.*

Cheng, J., Yang, Y., Tang, X., Xiong, N., Zhang, Y., & Lei, F. (2020, December 31). Generative Adversarial Networks: A Literature Review. *KSII Transactions on Internet and Information Systems*, *14*(12), 4625–4647. doi:10.3837/tiis.2020.12.001

Chen, M., Hao, Y., Hwang, K., Wang, L., & Wang, L. (2017). Disease prediction by machine learning over big data from Healthcare Communities. *IEEE Access : Practical Innovations, Open Solutions*, *5*, 8869–8879. doi:10.1109/AC-CESS.2017.2694446

Chen, X., Liu, X., Gales, M. J., & Woodland, P. C. (2015). Recurrent neural network language model training with noise contrastive estimation for speech recognition. In ICASSP. IEEE. doi:10.1109/ICASSP.2015.7179005

Chitra, A., Indragandhi, V., & Razia Sultana, W. (2022). *Smart Grids and Green Energy Systems*. John Wiley & Sons. doi:10.1002/9781119872061

Cho, K., Merrienboer, B. V., Bahdanau, D., & Bengio, Y. (2014). On the properties of neural machine translation: Encoder-decoder approaches. In *Proceedings of SSST@EMNLP 2014, Eighth Workshop on Syntax, Semantics and Structure in Statistical Translation*. IEEE..

Choi, J., & Lee, S.-W. (2020). Improving FastText with inverse document frequency of subwords. *Pattern Recognition Letters*, *133*, 165–172. doi:10.1016/j.patrec.2020.03.003

Choi, J., Tamí-Maury, I., Cuccaro, P., Kim, S., & Markham, C. (2023). Digital Health Interventions to Improve Adolescent HPV Vaccination: A Systematic Review. *Vaccines*, *11*(2), 249. doi:10.3390/vaccines11020249 PMID:36851127

Choi, S., Park, S., Lee, M., & Choo, J. (2021, June). VITON-HD: High-Resolution Virtual Try-On via Misalignment-Aware Normalization. *2021 IEEE/CVF Conference on Computer Vision and Pattern Recognition (CVPR)*. 10.1109/CVPR46437.2021.01391

Choudhary, A. (n.d.). *Face Mask Detection using Raspberry Pi and OpenCV*. Available at: https://circuitdigest.com/microcontroller-projects/face-mask-detection-using-raspberry-pi-and-opencv.May13,2021

Chtita, S., Motahhir, S., El Hammoumi, A., Chouder, A., Benyoucef, A. S., El Ghzizal, A., Derouich, A., Abouhawwash, M., & Askar, S. S. (2022). A novel hybrid GWO-PSO-based maximum power point tracking for photovoltaic systems operating under partial shading conditions. *Scientific Reports*, *12*(1), 10637. doi:10.103841598-022-14733-6 PMID:35739302

Chulkov, A. O., Nesteruk, D. A., Vavilov, V. P., Shagdirov, B., Omar, M., Siddiqui, A. O., & Prasad, Y. L. V. D. (2021). Automated procedure for detecting and characterizing defects in gfrp composite by using thermal nondestructive testing. *Infrared Physics & Technology*, *114*, 103675. doi:10.1016/j.infrared.2021.103675

Ciałkowski, M. J., & Grysa, K. (2010). Trefftz method in solving the inverse problems. *Journal of Inverse and Ill-Posed Problems*, *18*(6), 595–616. doi:10.1515/jiip.2010.027

COCO-Common Objects in Context. (n.d.). Available at: https://cocodataset.org/#download

Coenen, V. A., & Reisert, M. (2021). DTI for brain targeting: Diffusion weighted imaging fiber tractography—Assisted deep brain stimulation. In E*Emerging Horizons in Neuromodulation: New Frontiers in Brain and Spine Stimulation* (Vol. 159, pp. 47–67). Academic Press. https://doi.org/https://doi.org/10.1016/bs.irn.2021.07.001

Convolutional Neural Networks. (n.d.). Available at: https://www.ibm.com/cloud/learn/convolutional-neural-networks

COVID-19: Physical distancing. (n.d.). Available at: https://www.who.int/westernpacific/emergencies/covid-19/information/physical-distancing

Crisnapati, P. N., Wardana, I. N. K., Aryanto, I. K. A. A., & Hermawan, A. (2017). Hommons: Hydroponic management and monitoring system for an IOT based NFT farm using web technology. *2017 5th International Conference on Cyber and IT Service Management (CITSM)*, 1–6.

Dagal, I., Akın, B., & Akboy, E. (2022). MPPT mechanism based on novel hybrid particle swarm optimization and salp swarm optimization algorithm for battery charging through simulink. *Scientific Reports*, *12*(1), 2664. doi:10.103841598-022-06609-6 PMID:35177713

Dahiwade, D., Patle, G., & Meshram, E. (2019). Designing disease prediction model using machine learning approach. *2019 3rd International Conference on Computing Methodologies and Communication (ICCMC)*. 10.1109/ICCMC.2019.8819782

Daniel. (2011). *Role of Mimics a CAD Software in 3D Reconstruction of CT Data in Oral and Maxillofacial Surgery* [Dissertation]. Tamil Nadu Dr. M. G. R. Medical University.

Darknet: Open-Source Neural Networks in C. (n.d.). Available at: https://pjreddie.com/darknet/

Dar, S. A., & Imtiaz, N. (2023). Classification of neuroimaging data in Alzheimer's disease using particle swarm optimization: A systematic review. *Applied Neuropsychology. Adult*, 1–12. doi:10.1080/23279095.2023.2169886 PMID:36719791

Dauer, F. (2022, June 29). Law Enforcement in the Era of Deepfakes. *Police Chief Magazine*. https://www.policechiefmagazine.org/law-enforcement-era-deepfakes/?ref=cdc285c5f3355599c05402cb647b0694

Deng, L., & Hu, H. (2022). Fine-Grained Urban Functional Region Identification via Mobile App Usage Data. *Mobile Information Systems*, *2022*, 1–17. Advance online publication. doi:10.1155/2022/6434598

Deshpande, P. S., Sharma, S. C., & Peddoju, S. K. (2019). *Security and Data Storage Aspect in Cloud Computing* (Vol. 52). Springer. doi:10.1007/978-981-13-6089-3

Deverall, J., Lee, J., & Ayala, M. (2017). Using Generative Adversarial Networks to Design Shoes: The Preliminary steps. *CS231n in Stanford*. http://cs231n.stanford.edu/reports/2017/pdfs/119.pdf

Dewa, C. S., Chau, N., & Dermer, S. (2010, July). Examining the comparative incidence and costs of physical and mental health-related disabilities in an employed population. *Journal of Occupational and Environmental Medicine*, *52*(7), 758–762. doi:10.1097/JOM.0b013e3181e8cfb5 PMID:20595909

Dham, S., Sharma, A., & Dhall, A. (2017). *Depression Scale Recognition from Audio*. Visual and Text Analysis.

Dhingra, S., Madda, R. B., Patan, R., Jiao, P., Barri, K., & Alavi, A. H. (2021). Internet of things-based fog and cloud computing technology for smart traffic monitoring. *Internet of Things (Netherlands)*, *14*, 100175. Advance online publication. doi:10.1016/j.iot.2020.100175

Dikaiakos, M. D., Katsaros, D., Mehra, P., Pallis, G., & Vakali, A. (2009). Cloud computing: Distributed internet computing for IT and scientific research. *IEEE Internet Computing*, *13*(5), 10–13. doi:10.1109/MIC.2009.103

Ding, S., & Zhao, K. (2018). Research on Daily Objects Detection Based on Deep Neural Network. *Materials Science and Engineering*, *322*(6).

Divya, A., Deepika, B., Durga Akhila, C. H., Tonika Devi, A., Lavanya, B., & Sravya Teja, E. (2022). Disease prediction based on symptoms given by user using machine learning. *SN Computer Science*, *3*(6), 504. doi:10.100742979-022-01399-0

Divya, S., Indumathi, V., Ishwarya, S., Priyasankari, M., & Devi, S. K. (2018). A Self-Diagnosis Medical Chatbot Using Artificial Intelligence. *Journal of Web Development and Web Designing*, *3*(1). https://core.ac.uk/download/pdf/230494941.pdf

Dong, J., & Duan, X. (2023). A Robust Control via a Fuzzy System with PID for the ROV. *Sensors (Basel)*, *23*(2), 821. Advance online publication. doi:10.339023020821 PMID:36679618

Dwivedi, Y. K., Hughes, L., Baabdullah, A. M., Ribeiro-Navarrete, S., Giannakis, M., Al-Debei, M. M., Dennehy, D., Metri, B., Buhalis, D., Cheung, C. M., Conboy, K., Doyle, R., Dubey, R., Dutot, V., Felix, R., Goyal, D., Gustafsson, A., Hinsch, C., Jebabli, I., ... Wamba, S. F. (2022, October). Metaverse beyond the hype: Multidisciplinary perspectives on emerging challenges, opportunities, and agenda for research, practice and policy. *International Journal of Information Management*, *66*, 102542. doi:10.1016/j.ijinfomgt.2022.102542

Dynamic Behavior Analysis of ANFIS Based MPPT Controller for Standalone Photovoltaic Systems. (2020). In International Journal of Renewable Energy Research (Issue v10i1). doi:10.20508/ijrer.v10i1.10244.g7897

Dziugaite, G. K., Roy, D. M., & Ghahramani, Z. (2015, May 14). *Training generative neural networks via Maximum Mean Discrepancy optimization*. arXiv.org. https://arxiv.org/abs/1505.03906v1

E., C., Ayirci, T. C, Plu, & Emiroglu. (2005). Power aware many to many routing in wireless sensor and actuator networks. In *Proceedings of the Second European Workshop on Wireless Sensor Networks* (pp. 236–245). IEEE.

Eder, M. A., Sarhadi, A., & Chen, X. (2021). A novel and robust method to quantify fatigue damage in fibre composite materials using thermal imaging analysis. *International Journal of Fatigue*, *150*, 106326. doi:10.1016/j.ijfatigue.2021.106326

Edo-Osagie, O., De La Iglesia, B., Lake, I., & Edeghere, O. (2020). A scoping review of the use of Twitter for public health research. *Computers in Biology and Medicine*, *122*, 103770. doi:10.1016/j.compbiomed.2020.103770 PMID:32502758

Edwin, B., Veemaraj, E., Parthiban, P., Devarajan, J. P., Mariadhas, V., Arumuganainar, A., & Reddy, M. (2022). Smart agriculture monitoring system for outdoor and hydroponic environments. *Indonesian Journal of Electrical Engineering and Computer Science*, *25*(3), 1679–1687. doi:10.11591/ijeecs.v25.i3.pp1679-1687

Elbagoury, B. M., Vladareanu, L., Vlădăreanu, V., Salem, A. B., Travediu, A. M., & Roushdy, M. I. (2023). A Hybrid Stacked CNN and Residual Feedback GMDH-LSTM Deep Learning Model for Stroke Prediction Applied on Mobile AI Smart Hospital Platform. *Sensors*, *23*(7), 3500. doi:10.3390/S23073500

El-Khatib, M. F., Sabry, M.-N., El-Sebah, M. I. A., & Maged, S. A. (2023). Hardware-in-the-loop testing of simple and intelligent MPPT control algorithm for an electric vehicle charging power by photovoltaic system. *ISA Transactions*, *137*, 656–669. Advance online publication. doi:10.1016/j.isatra.2023.01.025 PMID:36725414

Eltamaly, A. M., & Abdelaziz, A. Y. (2019). *Modern Maximum Power Point Tracking Techniques for Photovoltaic Energy Systems*. Springer.

Emokhare, B. & Igbape, B. (2015). Fuzzy Logic Based Approach to Early Diagnosis of Ebola Hemorrhagic Fever. *Proceedings of the World Congress on Engineering and Computer Science, 2*, 1-6.

Expand work contractions: https://pypi.org/project/pycontractions/

Explorations in Quantum Computing. (n.d.). Retrieved January 21, 2023, from https://www.amazon.com/Explorations-Quantum-Computing-Colin-Williams/dp/038794768X

Facchinetti, G., Petrucci, G., Albanesi, B., De Marinis, M. G., & Piredda, M. (2023). Can Smart Home Technologies Help Older Adults Manage Their Chronic Condition? A Systematic Literature Review. *International Journal of Environmental Research and Public Health*, *20*(2), 1205. doi:10.3390/ijerph20021205 PMID:36673957

Face Mask Detection. (n.d.). Available at: https://www.kaggle.com/andrewmvd/face-mask-detection

Fan, Z., Li, S., Cheng, H., & Liu, L. (2021). Perturb and Observe MPPT Algorithm of photovoltaic System: A Review. *2021 33rd Chinese Control and Decision Conference (CCDC)*. 10.1109/CCDC52312.2021.9602272

Fan, L., & Ma, X. (2022). Maximum power point tracking of PEMFC based on hybrid artificial bee colony algorithm with fuzzy control. *Scientific Reports*, *12*(1), 4316. doi:10.103841598-022-08327-5 PMID:35279691

Farajdadian, S., & Hassan Hosseini, S. M. (2019). Optimization of fuzzy-based MPPT controller via metaheuristic techniques for stand-alone PV systems. In International Journal of Hydrogen Energy (Vol. 44, Issue 47, pp. 25457–25472). doi:10.1016/j.ijhydene.2019.08.037

Farghally, H., Ahmed, N., & Fahmy, F. (2018). Design and optimization of standalone photovoltaic system based on MPPT FLC controller for electric bikes charging station. In *The International Conference on Electrical Engineering* (Vol. 11, Issue 11, pp. 1–24). 10.21608/iceeng.2018.30177

Farooqui, M. E., & Ahmad, D. J. (2020). Disease prediction system using support vector machine and multilinear regression. *International Journal of Innovative Research in Computer Science & Technology*, *8*(4), 331–336. doi:10.21276/ijircst.2020.8.4.15

Femia, N., Petrone, G., Spagnuolo, G., & Vitelli, M. (2017). *Power Electronics and Control Techniques for Maximum Energy Harvesting in Photovoltaic Systems*. CRC Press. doi:10.1201/b14303

Ferreira, J. A., & van Wyk, J. D. (n.d.). Transistor inverter optimization employing self-oscillation for low cost and simplicity. *Conference Record of the 1988 IEEE Industry Applications Society Annual Meeting*. 10.1109/IAS.1988.25177

FeynmanR. P.FeynmanR.SocietyA. P. (n.d.). *Gate1*. doi:10.1007/978-1-84628-887-6

Frothingham, S. (2019, April 30). *Are Left Handers Less Healthy Than Right Handers?* Healthline. https://www.healthline.com/health/left-handers-and-health-risk

Gameti, N., & Vairagi, B. D. (2021). Artificial intelligence technique based MPPT controller for standalone solar energy conversion system. In International Journal of Technical Research & Science (pp. 15–21). doi:10.30780/IJTRS.V06.I12.002

Gandam & Sidhu. (2016). Video processing & its applications. *International Research Journal of Engineering and Technology, 3*(8).

Geetha, G., Saranya, G., Chakrapani, K., Ponsam, J. G., Safa, M., & Karpagaselvi, S. (2020). Early Detection of Depression from Social Media Data Using Machine Learning Algorithms. *2020 International Conference on Power, Energy, Control and Transmission Systems (ICPECTS)*, (pp. 1-6). IEEE. 10.1109/ICPECTS49113.2020.9336974

Georgakopoulos, D., Budovsky, I., Benz, S. P., & Gubler, G. (2018). Josephson Arbitrary Waveform Synthesizer as a Reference Standard for the Measurement of the Phase of Harmonics in Distorted Signals. *2018 Conference on Precision Electromagnetic Measurements (CPEM 2018)*. 10.1109/CPEM.2018.8501223

Ghazi, A., Ghazi, G. A., Al-Ammar, E. A., Hasanien, H. M., & Turky, R. A. (2022). Transient Search Optimization Based Fuzzy-PI Controller for MPPT of Standalone PV System. *2022 23rd International Middle East Power Systems Conference (MEPCON)*. 10.1109/MEPCON55441.2022.10021781

Ghosh, S., Bhatia, S., & Bhatia, A. (2018). Quro: Facilitating User Symptom Check Using a Personalised Chatbot-Oriented Dialogue System. In E. Cummings, A. Ryan, & L. K. Schaper (Eds.), Connecting the System to Enhance the Practitioner and Consumer Experience in Healthcare (Vol. 252, Ser. pp. 51–56). IOS Press.

Gil, G. (2020, May 14). *AI to design new products using Deep Product Learning*. https://www.commerce.ai/blog/ai-to-design-new-products-using-deep-product-learning

GitHub - Strilanc/Quirk: A drag-and-drop quantum circuit simulator that runs in your browser. A toy for exploring and understanding small quantum circuits . (n.d.). Retrieved January 18, 2023, from https://github.com/Strilanc/Quirk

Gm, H., Gourisaria, M. K., Pandey, M., & Rautaray, S. S.GM. (2020, November). A comprehensive survey and analysis of generative models in machine learning. *Computer Science Review*, *38*, 100285. doi:10.1016/j.cosrev.2020.100285

Goel, D., & Jain, A. K. (2018). Mobile phishing attacks and defense mechanisms: State of the art and open research challenges. *Computers & Security*, *73*, 519–544. doi:10.1016/j.cose.2017.12.006

Golestan, S., Habibi, M. R., Mousazadeh Mousavi, S. Y., Guerrero, J. M., & Vasquez, J. C. (2023). Quantum computation in power systems: An overview of recent advances. *Energy Reports*, *9*, 584–596. doi:10.1016/j.egyr.2022.11.185

Gonal, V. S., & Sheshadri, G. S. (2016). Solar energy optimization using MPPT controller by maximum conductance method. *2016 IEEE 7th Power India International Conference (PIICON)*. 10.1109/POWERI.2016.8077445

Gong, C., Liu, J., Zhang, Q., Chen, H., & Gong, Z. (2010, September). The characteristics of cloud computing. In *2010 39th International Conference on Parallel Processing Workshops* (pp. 275-279). IEEE. 10.1109/ICPPW.2010.45

Gong, L., Hou, G., & Huang, C. (2022). A two-stage MPPT controller for PV system based on the improved artificial bee colony and simultaneous heat transfer search algorithm. *ISA Transactions*. Advance online publication. doi:10.1016/j.isatra.2022.06.005 PMID:35753811

Gorbatsevich, A. A., & Shubin, N. M. (2018). Quantum logic gates. *Physics Uspekhi*, *61*(11), 1100–1115. doi:10.3367/UFNe.2017.12.038310

Gornet, L., Wesphal, O., Burtin, C., Bailleul, J., Rozycki, P., & Stainier, L. (2013). Rapid determination of the high cycle fatigue limit curve of carbon fiber epoxy matrix composite laminates by thermography methodology: Tests and finite element simulations. *Procedia Engineering*, *66*, 697–704. doi:10.1016/j.proeng.2013.12.123

Görtz, M., Wendeborn, A., Müller, M., & Hohenfellner, M. (2023). The Mobile Patient Information Assistant (PIA) App during the Inpatient Surgical Hospital Stay: Evaluation of Usability and Patient Approval. *Healthcare (Switzerland)*, *11*(5), 682. doi:10.3390/healthcare11050682 PMID:36900686

Govindharaj, A., & Mariappan, A. (2019). Adaptive Neuralback Stepping Controller for MPPT in Photo Voltaic Systems. *2019 IEEE International Conference on Intelligent Techniques in Control, Optimization and Signal Processing (INCOS).* 10.1109/INCOS45849.2019.8951363

Graves, A., Mohamed, A. R., & Hinton, G. (2013). Speech recognition with deep recurrent neural networks. In *Acoustics, Speech and Signal Processing (ICASSP), IEEE International Conference,* (pp. 6645–6649). IEEE. 10.1109/ICASSP.2013.6638947

Greff, K., Srivastava, R. K., Koutník, J., Steunebrink, B. R., & Schmidhuber, J. (2015). LSTM: A search space odyssey. arXiv preprint arXiv:1503.04069.

Grover's Algorithm | CNOT. (n.d.). Retrieved January 17, 2023, from https://cnot.io/quantum_algorithms/grover/grovers_algorithm.html

Grover's Algorithm. (n.d.). Retrieved January 18, 2023, from https://qiskit.org/textbook/ch-algorithms/grover.html

Guanlei, X., Xiaogang, X., Xun, W., & Xiaotong, W. (2020). A novel quantum image parallel searching algorithm. *Optik, 209*(May), 164565. doi:10.1016/j.ijleo.2020.164565

Guo, X., Liu, R., Lu, J., Wu, C., Lyu, Y., Wang, Z., Xiang, J., Pan, C., & Tong, S. (2019). Alterations in Brain Structural Connectivity After Unilateral Upper-Limb Amputation. *IEEE Transactions on Neural Systems and Rehabilitation Engineering, 27*(10), 2196–2204. doi:10.1109/TNSRE.2019.2936615 PMID:31443033

Gupta & Gill. (2020). Coronamask: A Face Mask Detector for Real-Time Data. *International Journal of Advanced Trends in Computer Science and Engineering, 9*(4).

Gupta, B. B., Tewari, A., Jain, A. K., & Agrawal, D. P. (2017). Fighting against phishing attacks: State of the art and future challenges. *Neural Computing & Applications, 28*(12), 3629–3654. doi:10.100700521-016-2275-y

Gupta, L., Malhotra, S., & Kumar, A. (2022). Study of applications of Internet of Things and Machine Learning for Smart Agriculture. *2022 IEEE International Conference on Current Development in Engineering and Technology (CCET),* 1–5. 10.1109/CCET56606.2022.10080342

Gupta, S., Modgil, S., Bhatt, P. C., Chiappetta Jabbour, C. J., & Kamble, S. (2022). Quantum computing led innovation for achieving a more sustainable Covid-19 healthcare industry. *Technovation.* Advance online publication. doi:10.1016/j.technovation.2022.102544

Hai, T., Zhou, J., & Muranaka, K. (2022). An efficient fuzzy-logic based MPPT controller for grid-connected PV systems by farmland fertility optimization algorithm. In Optik (Vol. 267, p. 169636). doi:10.1016/j.ijleo.2022.169636

HamdiT.ElleuchK.AbidH.ToumiA. (n.d.). *Sliding mode controller with fuzzy supervisor for MPPT of Photovoltaic Pumping system.* doi:10.21203/rs.3.rs-2021791/v1

Haq, I. U., Khan, Q., Ullah, S., Khan, S. A., Akmeliawati, R., Khan, M. A., & Iqbal, J. (2022). Neural network-based adaptive global sliding mode MPPT controller design for stand-alone photovoltaic systems. *PLoS One, 17*(1), e0260480. doi:10.1371/journal.pone.0260480 PMID:35051183

Hasan, M. A., & Sher-E, K. M. (2010). -Alam, A.R. *Chowdhury Human Disease Diagnosis Using a Fuzzy Expert System Journal of Computing, 2,* 66–70.

Hashizume, K., Rosado, D. G., Fernández-Medina, E., & Fernandez, E. B. (2013). An analysis of security issues for cloud computing. *Journal of Internet Services and Applications, 4*(1), 1–13. doi:10.1186/1869-0238-4-5

Hassan, M., & Hasson, S. T. (2020). *A controllability algorithm to minimize the spreading chance of COVID-19 in individual networks.* In Proc. 4th Int. Conf. I-SMAC, Palladam, India. 10.1109/I-SMAC49090.2020.9243481

Hattu, E. (2019). Colling System Application In PV Module Toward Output Voltage And Current PV Module. *Proceedings of the 1st International Conference on Engineering, Science, and Commerce, ICESC 2019, 18-19 October 2019, Labuan Bajo, Nusa Tenggara Timur, Indonesia.* 10.4108/eai.18-10-2019.2289921

Hegazy, E., Saad, W., & Shokair, M. (2020). Studying the Effect of Using a Low Power PV and DC-DC Boost Converter on the Performance of the Solar Energy PV System. *2020 15th International Conference on Computer Engineering and Systems (ICCES).* 10.1109/ICCES51560.2020.9334581

Hidasi, B., Karatzoglou, A., Baltrunas, L.,& Tikk. D. (2015). *Session-based recommendations with convolutional neural networks.* CoRR.

Hinduja, S., Afrin, M., Mistry, S., & Krishna, A. (2022). Machine learning-based proactive social-sensor service for mental health monitoring using twitter data. *International Journal of Information Management Data Insights, 2*(2), 100–113. doi:10.1016/j.jjimei.2022.100113

Hochreiter, S., & Schmidhuber, J. (1997). Long short-term memory. *Neural Computation, 9*(8), 1735–1780. doi:10.1162/neco.1997.9.8.1735 PMID:9377276

Hockaday & Bühler. (2019, July 18). *GANs. Comparing machine learning techniques.* Avira Blog. Retrieved January 11, 2023, from https://www.avira.com/en/blog/gans-comparative-with-machine-learning

Hopman, H. J., Chan, S. M. S., Chu, W. C. W., Lu, H., Tse, C. Y., Chau, S. W. H., Lam, L. C. W., Mak, A. D. P., & Neggers, S. F. W. (2021). Personalized prediction of transcranial magnetic stimulation clinical response in patients with treatment-refractory depression using neuroimaging biomarkers and machine learning. *Journal of Affective Disorders, 1*(290), 261–271. https://drive.google.com/drive/u/0/folders/1bpbE4_ibxwsKhjpalzq-sJcg4MOxfGMm. doi:10.1016/j.jad.2021.04.081 PMID:34010751

Hörrmann, S., Adumitroaie, A., Viechtbauer, C., & Schagerl, M. (2016). The effect of fiber waviness on the fatigue life of CFRP materials. *International Journal of Fatigue, 90*, 139–147. doi:10.1016/j.ijfatigue.2016.04.029

Hosseini, S. H., Varesi, K., Ardashir, J. F., Gandomi, A. A., & Saeidabadi, S. (2015). An attempt to improve output voltage quality of developed multi-level inverter topology by increasing the number of levels. *2015 9th International Conference on Electrical and Electronics Engineering (ELECO).* 10.1109/ELECO.2015.7394622

Hu, Z., Norouzi, H., Jiang, M., Dadfar, S., & Kashiwagi, T. (2022). Novel hybrid modified krill herd algorithm and fuzzy controller based MPPT to optimally tune the member functions for PV system in the three-phase grid-connected mode. *ISA Transactions, 129*(Pt B), 214–229.

Hua, R., Marin-Quiros, S., Mohan, H. K., & Wang, Y. (2022). Maximum power point tracking for a multi-layered piezoelectric heel charger with a levered mechanism toward impact-based energy harvesting. *The Review of Scientific Instruments, 93*(9), 095001. doi:10.1063/5.0091254 PMID:36182488

Hucka, M. (2018). Spiral: Splitters for identifiers in source code files. *Journal of Open Source Software, 3*(24), 653. doi:10.21105/joss.00653

Hunt, D., Dighe, M., Gatenby, C., & Studholme, C. (2019). Automatic, Age Consistent Reconstruction of the Corpus Callosum Guided by Coherency From In Utero Diffusion-Weighted MRI. *IEEE Transactions on Medical Imaging, 39*(3), 601–610. doi:10.1109/TMI.2019.2932681 PMID:31395540

Huynh, K. M., Chen, G., Wu, Y., Shen, D., & Yap, P.-T. (2019). Multi-site harmonization of diffusion MRI data via method of moments. *IEEE Transactions on Medical Imaging*, *38*(7), 1599–1609. doi:10.1109/TMI.2019.2895020 PMID:30676953

IBM - India | IBM. (n.d.). Retrieved January 18, 2023, from https://www.ibm.com/in-en

IBM Quantum Computing | Tools. (n.d.). Retrieved January 18, 2023, from https://www.ibm.com/quantum/tools

IBM Quantum Computing. (n.d.). Retrieved January 17, 2023, from https://www.ibm.com/quantum

Image Processing in Python: Algorithms, Tools, and Methods You Should Know. (n.d.). Available at: https://neptune.ai/blog/image-processing-in-python-algorithms-tools-and-methods-you-should-know

ImageNet Classification. (n.d.). Available at: https://pjreddie.com/darknet/imagent/

Implementasi Perbandingan Algoritma Simple Hill Climbing Dan Algoritma Ascent Hill Climbing Pada Permainan 8-Puzzle. (2021). In *Edik Informatika* (Vol. 8, Issue 1, pp. 41–52). doi:10.22202/ei.2021.v8i1.5054

Incemehmetouglu, A. (2012). *Investigation the effects of different support medium on product with nutrient film technique*. Middle East Technical University.

Intanagonwiwat, C., Govindan, R., & Estrin, D. (2004). Directed diffusion: a scalable and robust communication paradigm for sensor networks. In *Proceedings of ACM Mobicom 2000* (pp. 56–67). ACM. 10.1145/345910.345920

Ioffe, S., & Szegedy, C. (2015, June 1). *Batch Normalization: Accelerating Deep Network Training by Reducing Internal Covariate Shift*. PMLR. https://proceedings.mlr.press/v37/ioffe15.html

Islam, M. R., Kabir, A., Ahmed, A., Kamal, A. R. M., Wang, H., & Ulhaq, A. (2018). Depression detection from social network data using machine learning techniques. *Health Information Science and Systems*, *6*(1), 8. doi:10.100713755-018-0046-0 PMID:30186594

Iyer, R., & Kleinrock, L. (2003). QoS control for sensor networks. *IEEE International Conference on Communications, ICC'03*, *1*, 517–521. 10.1109/ICC.2003.1204230

Jabalameli, S., Xu, Y., & Shetty, S. (2022). Spatial and sentiment analysis of public opinion toward COVID-19 pandemic using twitter data: At the early stage of vaccination. *International Journal of Disaster Risk Reduction*, *80*, 103204. doi:10.1016/j.ijdrr.2022.103204 PMID:35935613

Jagwani, S., & Venkatesha, L. (2019). Particle Swarm Optimization-Based MPPT Controller for Wind Turbine Systems. In *Data* (pp. 313–319). Engineering and Applications. doi:10.1007/978-981-13-6351-1_25

Jansen, W. A. (2011, January). Cloud hooks: Security and privacy issues in cloud computing. In *2011 44th Hawaii International Conference on System Sciences* (pp. 1-10). IEEE.

Jarry, J. (2021, September 17). *Are You Left-Handed? Science Still Yearns to Know Why*. Office for Science and Society. https://www.mcgill.ca/oss/article/health-general-science/are-you-left-handed-science-still-yearns-know-why

Jayakrishnan, R. (2018). Multi-Class Emotion Detection and Annotation in Malayalam Novels. *2018 International Conference on Computer Communication and Informatics (ICCCI)*, (pp. 1-5). IEEE. 10.1109/ICCCI.2018.8441492

Jiayu, Z., Junsuo, Z., Fanjiang, X., Haiying, H., & Peng, Q. (2014). Analysis and simulation of grover's search algorithm. *International Journal of Machine Learning and Computing*, *4*(1), 21.

Jin, S., Zhou, M., & Wu, A. S. (2003). Sensor network optimization using a genetic algorithm. *7th World Multiconference on Systemics, Cybernetics, and Informatics*, Orlando, FL.

Joby, K. J., & Priyanga, K. K. (2021, June). Face Mask Detection System. *International Journal of Innovative Research in Science, Engineering and Technology, 10*(6).

John, R., Sheik Mohammed, S., & Zachariah, R. (2017). Variable step size Perturb and observe MPPT algorithm for standalone solar photovoltaic system. *2017 IEEE International Conference on Intelligent Techniques in Control, Optimization and Signal Processing (INCOS)*. 10.1109/ITCOSP.2017.8303163

Jolly, M., Prabhakar, A., Sturzu, B., Hollstein, K., Singh, R., Thomas, S., Foote, P., & Shaw, A. (2015). Review of Non-destructive Testing (NDT) Techniques and their Applicability to Thick Walled Composites. *Procedia CIRP, 38*, 129–136. doi:10.1016/j.procir.2015.07.043

Jouda, A., Elyes, F., Rabhi, A., & Abdelkader, M. (2017). Optimization of Scaling Factors of Fuzzy–MPPT Controller for Stand-alone Photovoltaic System by Particle Swarm Optimization. In Energy Procedia (Vol. 111, pp. 954–963). doi:10.1016/j.egypro.2017.03.258

Józefowicz, R., Zaremba, W., & Sutzkever. I. (2015). *An empirical exploration of recurrent network*. arXiv.

K, P., & Punitha, K. (n.d.). *Horse Herd Optimization Algorithm based MPPT controller for Solar Tree Application.* doi:10.22541/au.167285877.71885740/v1

Kahng, M., Thorat, N., Chau, D. H. P., Viegas, F. B., & Wattenberg, M. (2019, January). GAN Lab: Understanding Complex Deep Generative Models using Interactive Visual Experimentation. *IEEE Transactions on Visualization and Computer Graphics, 25*(1), 310–320. doi:10.1109/TVCG.2018.2864500 PMID:30130198

Kaibi, I., Nfaoui, E. H., & Satori, H. (2019). A Comparative Evaluation of Word Embeddings Techniques for Twitter Sentiment Analysis. *2019 International Conference on Wireless Technologies, Embedded and Intelligent Systems (WITS)*, (pp. 1-4). IEEE. 10.1109/WITS.2019.8723864

Kalantari, F., & Akhyani, N. (2021). Community acceptance studies in the field of vertical farming—A critical and systematic analysis to advance the conceptualisation of community acceptance in Kuala Lumpur. *International Journal of Urban Sustainable Development, 13*(3), 569–584. doi:10.1080/19463138.2021.2013849

Kamalakannan, C., Padma Suresh, L., Dash, S. S., & Panigrahi, B. K. (2014). Power Electronics and Renewable Energy Systems*: Proceedings of ICPERES 2014*. Springer.

Kamali, A., Sherbaf, F. G., Rahmani, F., Khayat-Khoei, M., Aein, A., Gandhi, A., Shah, E. G., Sair, H. I., Riascos, R. F., Esquenazi, Y., & ... (2020). A direct visuosensory cortical connectivity of the human limbic system. Dissecting the trajectory of the parieto-occipito-hypothalamic tract in the human brain using diffusion weighted tractography. *Neuroscience Letters, 728*, 134955. doi:10.1016/j.neulet.2020.134955 PMID:32278940

Kannadasan, R., Prabakaran, N., Boominathan, P., Krishnamoorthy, A., Naresh, K., & Sivashanmugam, G. (2018). High Performance Parallel Computing with Cloud Technologies. *Procedia Computer Science, 132*, 518–524. doi:10.1016/j.procs.2018.05.004

Kannampallil, T., Dai, R., Lv, N., Xiao, L., Lu, C., Ajilore, O. A., Snowden, M. B., Venditti, E. M., Williams, L. M., Kringle, E. A., & Ma, J. (2022). Cross-trial prediction of depression remission using problem-solving therapy: A machine learning approach. *Journal of Affective Disorders, 308*, 89–97. doi:10.1016/j.jad.2022.04.015 PMID:35398399

Kapur, I., Jain, D., Jain, A., & Garg, R. (2020). Adaptive Neuro Fuzzy Inference System for MPPT in Standalone Solar Photovoltaic System. *2020 IEEE 17th India Council International Conference (INDICON)*. 10.1109/INDICON49873.2020.9342105

Karetsos, S., Costopoulou, C., Gourdomichali, N., & Ntaliani, M. (2022). A Mobile App for Supporting Citrus Fruit Growers in Greece. *Electronics, 11*(20), 3342. doi:10.3390/ELECTRONICS11203342

Karl, H. & Willig, A. (2003). *A short survey of wireless sensor networks, TKN.* Technical Report Series.

Kaur, N., Kaushal, J., Mahajan, P., & Srivastav, A. L. (2022). *Design of hydroponic system for screening of ornamental plant species for removal of synthetic dyes using phytoremediation approach.* Academic Press.

Kaur, P. J., & Kaushal, S. (2011). Security concerns in cloud computing. In *High Performance Architecture and Grid Computing: International Conference, HPAGC 2011,* (pp. 103-112). Springer Berlin Heidelberg.

Kay, J., & Frolik, J. (2004). Quality of service analysis and control for wireless sensor networks. In *2004 IEEE International Conference on Mobile Ad-hoc and Sensor Systems*, (pp. 359–368). IEEE. 10.1109/MAHSS.2004.1392175

Keller, E., & Rexford, J. (2010). The" Platform as a Service" Model for Networking. *INM/WREN, 10*, 95-108.

Kempf, M., Skrabala, O., & Altstädt, V. (2014). Acoustic emission analysis for characterisation of damage mechanisms in fibre reinforced thermosetting polyurethane and epoxy. *Composites. Part B, Engineering, 56*, 477–483. doi:10.1016/j.compositesb.2013.08.080

Keniya, R., Khakharia, A., Shah, V., Gada, V., Manjalkar, R., Thaker, T., Warang, M., & Mehendale, N. (2020). Disease prediction from various symptoms using machine learning. SSRN *Electronic Journal.* doi:10.2139/ssrn.3661426

Keras Optimizers. (n.d.). Available at: https://keras.io/api/optimizers/

Keras. (n.d.). Available at: https://keras.io/

Kettner, B., & Geisler, F. (2022). IoT Hub, Event Hub, and Streaming Data. In *Pro Serverless Data Handling with Microsoft Azure: Architecting ETL and Data-Driven Applications in the Cloud* (pp. 153–168). Apress. doi:10.1007/978-1-4842-8067-6_8

Khalil, I. M., Khreishah, A., Bouktif, S., & Ahmad, A. (2013, April). Security concerns in cloud computing. In *2013 10th International Conference on Information Technology: New Generations* (pp. 411-416). IEEE. 10.1109/ITNG.2013.127

Khan, M. Y. A. (2019). Design and Analysis of Maximum Power Point Tracking (MPPT) Controller for PV System. In Journal of Mechanics of Continua and Mathematical Sciences (Vol. 14, Issue 1). doi:10.26782/jmcms.2019.02.00019

Khan, Z. A., Khan, L., Ahmad, S., Mumtaz, S., Jafar, M., & Khan, Q. (2021). RBF neural network based backstepping terminal sliding mode MPPT control technique for PV system. *PLoS One, 16*(4), e0249705. doi:10.1371/journal.pone.0249705 PMID:33831094

Khasanah, I. (2021). Sentiment Classification Using fastText Embedding and Deep Learning Model. *Procedia Computer Science, 189*, 343–350. doi:10.1016/j.procs.2021.05.103

Kien, D. N., & Zhuang, X. (2021). A deep neural network-based algorithm for solving structural optimization. *Journal of Zhejiang University. Science A, 22*(8), 609–620. doi:10.1631/jzus.A2000380

Kim, J., & Lee, K. (2019, July). Functionbench: A suite of workloads for serverless cloud function service. In *2019 IEEE 12th International Conference on Cloud Computing (CLOUD)* (pp. 502-504). IEEE. 10.1109/CLOUD.2019.00091

Kim, M., Jeon, S., Shin, H., Choi, W., Chung, H., & Nah, Y. (2019). Movie Recommendation based on User Similarity of Consumption Pattern Change. In *IEEE Second International Conference on Artificial Intelligence and Knowledge Engineering (AIKE),* (pp. 317-319). IEEE. 10.1109/AIKE.2019.00064

Kingma. D., & Adam. J. Ba. (2014). *A method for stochastic optimization.* arXiv preprint arXiv:1412.6980.

Kiyoshi, K., Hiroshi, H., & Gouki, K. (2013). Eddy current nondestructive testing for carbon fiber-reinforced composites. *Journal of Pressure Vessel Technology – Transactions of the ASME.* 10.1115/1.4023253

Klein, S., & Klein, S. (2017). Azure data factory. *IoT Solutions in Microsoft's Azure IoT Suite: Data Acquisition and Analysis in the Real World,* (pp. 105-122). Springer.

Koenraads, Y., Porro, G. L., Braun, K. P. J., Groenendaal, F., De Vries, L. S., & Van Der Aa, N. E. (2016). Prediction of visual field defects in newborn infants with perinatal arterial ischemic stroke using early MRI and DTI-based tractography of the optic radiation. *European Journal of Paediatric Neurology, 20*(2), 309–318. doi:10.1016/j.ejpn.2015.11.010 PMID:26708504

Kohli, P. S., & Arora, S. (2019). Application of machine learning in disease prediction. *2018 4th International Conference on Computing Communication and Automation (ICCCA).* 10.1109/CCAA.2018.8777449

Koike, T., Tanaka, S., Kin, T., Suzuki, Y., Takayanagi, S., Takami, H., Kugasawa, K., Nambu, S., Omura, T., Yamazawa, E., Kushihara, Y., Furuta, Y., Niwa, R., Sato, K., Uchida, T., Takeda, Y., Kiyofuji, S., Saito, T., Oyama, H., & Saito, N. (2022). Accurate Preoperative Identification of Motor Speech Area as Termination of Arcuate Fasciculus Depicted by Q-Ball Imaging Tractography. *World Neurosurgery, 164,* e764–e771. doi:10.1016/j.wneu.2022.05.041 PMID:35595046

Kosgi, D., & Kulkarni, V. V. (2022). To Investigate the Failure in Sensor Assembly Due to Temperature Variational Loading, and to Provide Optimum Material Solution to Avert This Failure. SAE Technical Paper Series. doi:10.4271/2022-28-0369

Krishnan, S. P. T., & Gonzalez, J. L. U. (2015). *Building your next big thing with google cloud platform: A guide for developers and enterprise architects.* Apress. doi:10.1007/978-1-4842-1004-8

Krutz, R. L., Krutz, R. L., & Russell Dean Vines, R. D. V. (2010). *Cloud security a comprehensive guide to secure cloud computing.* Wiley.

Kuiper, E., Van Dam, F., Reiter, A., & Janssen, M. (2014, October). Factors influencing the adoption of and business case for Cloud computing in the public sector. In *eChallenges e-2014 Conference Proceedings* (pp. 1-10). IEEE.

Kumar, A., Malhotra, S., Kaur, D. P., & Gupta, L. (2022). Weather Monitoring and Air Quality Prediction using Machine Learning. *2022 1st International Conference on Computational Science and Technology (ICCST),* 364–368.

Kumar, A., Rizwan, M., & Nangia, U. (2021). Development of ANFIS-based algorithm for MPPT controller for stand-alone photovoltaic system. In International Journal of Advanced Intelligence Paradigms (Vol. 18, Issue 2, p. 247). doi:10.1504/IJAIP.2021.112906

Kumar, G. V., & Vinodh Kumar, G. (2012). Performance Enhancement in PV System using Intelligent Controller based MPPT Controller. In *IOSR Journal of Engineering* (Vol. 2, Issue 2, pp. 284–287). doi:10.9790/3021-0202284287

Kumar, K. S., Sai Sathya, M., Nadeem, A., & Rajesh, S. (2022). Diseases prediction based on symptoms using database and GUI. *2022 6th International Conference on Computing Methodologies and Communication (ICCMC).* 10.1109/ICCMC53470.2022.9753707

Kumar, V., & Kumar, R. (2015). Detection of a phishing attack using visual cryptography in ad hoc network. *2015 International Conference on Communications and Signal Processing (ICCSP),* (pp. 1021–1025). IEEE. 10.1109/ICCSP.2015.7322654

Kumar, G. S., & Shetty, S. D. (2021). Application Development for Mask Detection and Social Distancing Violation Detection using Convolutional Neural Networks. *Proceedings of the 23rd International Conference on Enterprise Information Systems (ICEIS 2021),* 1, 760-767. 10.5220/0010483107600767

Kumari, A., Behera, R. K., Sahoo, B., & Sahoo, S. P. (2022). Prediction of link evolution using community detection in social network. *Computing, 104*(5), 1–22. doi:10.100700607-021-01035-4

Kumari, A., Sahoo, B., Behera, R. K., Misra, S., & Sharma, M. M. (2021). Evaluation of integrated frameworks for optimizing QoS in serverless computing. In *Computational Science and Its Applications–ICCSA 2021: 21st International Conference, Cagliari, Italy, September 13–16, 2021* [Springer International Publishing.]. *Proceedings, 21*(Part VII), 277–288.

Kumar, P., Singh, S., Ali, I., & Ustun, T. S. (2018). *Handbook of Research on Power and Energy System Optimization.* IGI Global. doi:10.4018/978-1-5225-3935-3

Kuščer, K., Eichelberger, S., & Peters, M. (2022). Tourism organizations' responses to the COVID-19 pandemic: An investigation of the lockdown period. *Current Issues in Tourism, 25*(2), 247–260. doi:10.1080/13683500.2021.1928010

Lakshmi, G. V., & Reddy, K. H. (2022). Improved tunicate swarm search-based MPPT for photovoltaic on a "grid-connected" inverter system. *Environmental Science and Pollution Research International, 29*(52), 78650–78665. doi:10.100711356-022-21157-2 PMID:35691948

Lassner, C., Pons-Moll, G., & Gehler, P. V. (2017, October). A Generative Model of People in Clothing. *2017 IEEE International Conference on Computer Vision (ICCV)*. 10.1109/ICCV.2017.98

Lauraitis, R. & Maskeliūnas, R. (2018). Damaševičius ANN and Fuzzy Logic Based Model to Evaluate Huntington Disease Symptoms. *J HealthcEng, 2018*, 1–10.

Lavanya, R., et al. (2021).Comparison Study on Improved Movie Recommender Systems. *Special Issue on Computing Technology and Information management.*

Le Yang, D. J., He, L., Pei, E., Oveneke, M. C., & Sahli, H. (2016). Decision Tree Based Depression Classification from Audio Video and Language Information. In *Proceedings of the 6th International Workshop on Audio/Visual Emotion Challenge (AVEC '16).* Association for Computing Machinery. 10.1145/2988257.2988269

Lee, E.-H., & Sohn, B.-J. (2011). Recent increasing trend in dust frequency over Mongolia and Inner Mongolia regions and its association with climate and surface condition change. In Atmospheric Environment (Vol. 45, Issue 27, pp. 4611–4616). doi:10.1016/j.atmosenv.2011.05.065

Lee, H., Satyam, K., & Fox, G. (2018, July). Evaluation of production serverless computing environments. In *2018 IEEE 11th International Conference on Cloud Computing (CLOUD)* (pp. 442-450). IEEE. 10.1109/CLOUD.2018.00062

Lee, S., Gu, G., Park, S., Choi, S., & Choo, J. (2022, October 24). *High-Resolution Virtual Try-On with Misalignment and Occlusion-Handled Conditions.* doi:10.1007/978-3-031-19790-1_13

Lee, H., Lim, H. J., Skinner, T., Chattopadhyay, A., & Hall, A. (2022). Automated fatigue damage detection and classification technique for composite structures using Lamb waves and deep autoencoder. *Mechanical Systems and Signal Processing, 163*, 108148. doi:10.1016/j.ymssp.2021.108148

Lee, Y. C., & Zomaya, A. Y. (2012). Energy efficient utilization of resources in cloud computing systems. *The Journal of Supercomputing, 60*(2), 268–280. doi:10.100711227-010-0421-3

Lefebvre, J., Buffet-Bataillon, S., Henaux, P. L., Riffaud, L., Morandi, X., & Haegelen, C. (2017). Staphylococcus aureus screening and decolonization reduces the risk of surgical site infections in patients undergoing deep brain stimulation surgery. *The Journal of Hospital Infection, 95*(2), 144–147. doi:10.1016/j.jhin.2016.11.019 PMID:28081909

Li & Zhang. (n.d.). *Object Detection and Its Implementation on Android Devices.* Department of Electrical Engineering, Stanford University.

Li, Y., Swersky, K., & Zemel, R. (2015, June 1). *Generative Moment Matching Networks*. PMLR. https://proceedings.mlr.press/v37/li15.html

Li, N., Yan, F., & Hirota, K. (2022). Quantum data visualization: A quantum computing framework for enhancing visual analysis of data. *Physica A*, *599*, 127476. doi:10.1016/j.physa.2022.127476

Lipp, I., Parker, G. D., Tallantyre, E. C., Goodall, A., Grama, S., Patitucci, E., Heveron, P., Tomassini, V., & Jones, D. K. (2020). Tractography in the presence of multiple sclerosis lesions. *NeuroImage*, *209*, 116471. doi:10.1016/j.neuroimage.2019.116471 PMID:31877372

Liu, S., You, H., Liu, Y., Feng, W., & Fu, S. (2022). Research on optimal control strategy of wind-solar hybrid system based on power prediction. *ISA Transactions*, *123*, 179–187. doi:10.1016/j.isatra.2021.05.010 PMID:33994212

Liu, W., Anguelov, D., Erhan, D., Szegedy, C., Reed, S., Fu, C.-Y., & Berg, A. C. (2016). SSD: Single Shot MultiBox Detector. *Lecture Notes in Computer Science*, *9905*, 21–37. doi:10.1007/978-3-319-46448-0_2

Liu, W., & Tang, W. (2022). Effects of Age-Appropriate Mobile APP Use Behavior on Subjective Well-being of Young Elderly. *Security and Communication Networks*, *2022*, 1–12. Advance online publication. doi:10.1155/2022/3209804

Li Y. Feng Y. (n.d.). *Power Prediction Method of PV System Based on Bifacial PV Modules*. doi:10.21203/rs.3.rs-2145030/v1

Li, Y., Lin, Y., Wang, Y., Ye, K., & Xu, C. (2022). Serverless computing: State-of-the-art, challenges and opportunities. *IEEE Transactions on Services Computing*, *16*(2), 1522–1539. doi:10.1109/TSC.2022.3166553

Lotfi, M., Hamblin, M. R., & Rezaei, N. (2020). COVID-19: Transmission, prevention, and potential therapeutic opportunities. *Clinica Chimica Acta*, *508*, 254–266. doi:10.1016/j.cca.2020.05.044 PMID:32474009

Lu, N., & Shimamura, S. (2018). Protocols, issues and potential improvements of current cultivation systems. *Smart Plant Factory: The Next Generation Indoor Vertical Farms*, 31–49.

Lynn, T., Rosati, P., Lejeune, A., & Emeakaroha, V. (2017, December). A preliminary review of enterprise serverless cloud computing (function-as-a-service) platforms. In *2017 IEEE International Conference on Cloud Computing Technology and Science (CloudCom)* (pp. 162-169). IEEE. 10.1109/CloudCom.2017.15

Lythgoe, M. P., & Middleton, P. (2020, June 1). Ongoing clinical trials for the management of the COVID-19 pandemic. *Trends in Pharmacological Sciences*, *41*(6), 363–382. doi:10.1016/j.tips.2020.03.006 PMID:32291112

M, D., Dharani, M., & Usha, P. V. (2015). A Novel Topology for Controlling a Four Port DC-DC Boost Converter for a Hybrid PV/PV/Battery Power System. In *TELKOMNIKA Indonesian Journal of Electrical Engineering* (Vol. 14, Issue 3). doi:10.11591/telkomnika.v14i3.7854

Ma, L., Jia, X., Sun, Q., Schiele, B., Tuytelaars, T., & Van Gool, L. (2017). Pose Guided Person Image Generation. In *Neural Information Processing Systems* (Vol. 30, pp. 406-416). https://papers.nips.cc/paper/2017/file/34ed066df378efacc9b924ec161e7639-Paper.pdf

Mahamkali, N., & Ayyasamy, V. (2015). OpenCV for Computer Vision Applications. *Proceedings of National Conference on Big Data and Cloud Computing(NCBDC'15)*.

Mahesh, P. J., Naheem, M., Mubafar, R., Shyba, S., & Beevi, S. (2016). New aspect for organic farming practices: Controlled crop nutrition and soilless agriculture. *2016 IEEE Global Humanitarian Technology Conference (GHTC)*, 819–824. 10.1109/GHTC.2016.7857374

Mahmood, M., Ali, I., & Ahmed, O. (2020). Comparative Study of Perturb & Observe, Modified Perturb & Observe and Modified Incremental Conductance MPPT Techniques for PV Systems. In Engineering and Technology Journal (Vol. 38, Issue 4A, pp. 478–490). doi:10.30684/etj.v38i4A.329

Mahmoud, A., Fath, H., & Ahmed, M. (2018). Enhancing the performance of a solar driven hybrid solar still/humidification-cation-dehumidification desalination system integrated with solar concentrator and photovoltaic panels. In Desalination (Vol. 430, pp. 165–179). doi:10.1016/j.desal.2017.12.052

Mahmoud, Y. (2022). New Approach for Controlling PV-PV Differential Power Processing Converters. *2022 13th International Renewable Energy Congress (IREC)*. 10.1109/IREC56325.2022.10001944

Mainka, C., Mladenov, V., Schwenk, J., & Wich, T. (2017, April). SoK: single sign-on security—an evaluation of openID connect. In *2017 IEEE European Symposium on Security and Privacy (EuroS&P)* (pp. 251-266). IEEE. 10.1109/EuroSP.2017.32

Maithani, M. (2021, January 6). Hands-On Guide To Nvidia Imaginaire: Image & Video translation GAN Library. *Analytics India Magazine*. https://analyticsindiamag.com/guide-to-nvidia-imaginaire-gan-library-in-python/

Male and Female walking on street wearing face masks-An Asian couple wearing face masks walk down the street. (n.d.). Available at: https://www.videvo.net/video/male-and-female-walking-on-street-wearing-face-masks/464817/

MalletJ.DaveR.SeliyaN.VanamalaM. (2022, July 27). *Using Deep Learning to Detecting Deepfakes*. doi:10.1109/IS-CMI56532.2022.10068449

Manasa, Vikas, & Subhadra. (2019). Drowsiness detection using Eye-Blink frequency and Yawn count for Driver Alert. *International Journal of Innovative Technology and Exploring Engineering, 9*(2).

Mandviwalla, A., Ohshiro, K., & Ji, B. (2019). Implementing Grover's Algorithm on the IBM Quantum Computers. *Proceedings - 2018 IEEE International Conference on Big Data*, 2531–2537. doi:10.1109/BigData.2018.8622457

Mann, M., Wright, C. H., Jella, T., Labak, C. M., Shammassian, B., Srivatsa, S., Wright, J., Engineer, L., Sajatovic, M., & Selman, W. (2021). Cranial Surgical Site Infection Interventions and Prevention Bundles: A Systematic Review of the Literature. *World Neurosurgery, 148*, 206–219.e4. doi:10.1016/j.wneu.2020.12.137 PMID:33412319

Manvi, S. S., & Shyam, G. K. (2014). Resource management for Infrastructure as a Service (IaaS) in cloud computing: A survey. *Journal of Network and Computer Applications, 41*, 424–440. doi:10.1016/j.jnca.2013.10.004

Mao. (2020, July 10). *Minimax Game for Training Generative Adversarial Networks*. Lei Mao's Log Book. Retrieved January 13, 2023, from https://leimao.github.io/blog/Generative-Adversarial-Networks-Minmax-Game/

Marani, R., Palumbo, D., Galietti, U., & D'Orazio, T. (2021). Deep learning for defect characterization in composite laminates inspected by step-heating thermography. *Optics and Lasers in Engineering, 145*, 106679. doi:10.1016/j.optlaseng.2021.106679

Marappan, R., & Bhaskaran, S. (2022, May 6). Movie Recommendation System Modeling Using Machine Learning. *Trends Journal of Sciences Research, 1*(1), 12–16. doi:10.31586/ijmebac.2022.291

Marivate, V., & Sefara, T. (2020). Improving Short Text Classification through Global Augmentation Methods. In A. Holzinger, P. Kieseberg, A. Tjoa, & E. Weippl (Eds.), Lecture Notes in Computer Science: Vol. 12279. *Machine Learning and Knowledge Extraction. CD-MAKE 2020*. doi:10.1007/978-3-030-57321-8_21

Martinovic, I. (2007). Phishing in the Wireless: Implementation and analysis. *IFIP International Information Security Conference*. Springer. 10.1007/978-0-387-72367-9_13

Mathew, R. B., Varghese, S., Joy, S. E., & Alex, S. S. (2019). Chatbot for Disease Prediction and treatment recommendation using machine learning. *2019 3rd International Conference on Trends in Electronics and Informatics (ICOEI)*. 10.1109/ICOEI.2019.8862707

McCandless Farmer, B. (2022, July 31). The impact of deepfakes: How do you know when a video is real? *CBS News*. https://www.cbsnews.com/news/deepfakes-real-fake-videos-60-minutes-2022-07-31/

McGrath, G., & Brenner, P. R. (2017, June). Serverless computing: Design, implementation, and performance. In *2017 IEEE 37th International Conference on Distributed Computing Systems Workshops (ICDCSW)* (pp. 405-410). IEEE.

McMahon, D. (2007). *Quantum computing explained*. John Wiley & Sons. doi:10.1002/9780470181386

Mendel, J., Hagras, H., Tan, W.-W., Melek, W. W., & Ying, H. (2014). *Introduction To Type-2 Fuzzy Logic Control: Theory and Applications*. John Wiley & Sons. doi:10.1002/9781118886540

Mete, M. O., & Yomralioglu, T. (2021). Implementation of serverless cloud GIS platform for land valuation. *International Journal of Digital Earth*, *14*(7), 836–850. doi:10.1080/17538947.2021.1889056

Mikolov, T., Chen, K., Corrado, G., & Dean, J. (2013). Efficient estimation of word in vector space. arXiv preprint arXiv:1301.3781.

Mikolov, T., Karafiát, M., Burget, L., Cernock'y, J., & Khudanpur, S. (2010). Recurrent neural network-based language model. In INTERSPEECH, 2, 3.

Miloslavskaya, N., & Tolstoy, A. (2016). Big data, fast data and data lake concepts. *Procedia Computer Science*, *88*, 300–305. doi:10.1016/j.procs.2016.07.439

MirzaM.OsinderoS. (2014, November 6). *Conditional Generative Adversarial Nets*. https://arxiv.org/abs/1411.1784v1

Model Training | Runway. (n.d.). https://runwayml.com/training/

Mojtahedi, A., Hokmabady, H., Kouhi, M., & Mohammadyzadeh, S. (2022). A novel ANN-RDT approach for damage detection of a composite panel employing contact and non-contact measuring data. *Composite Structures*, *279*, 114794. doi:10.1016/j.compstruct.2021.114794

Molina, F., Barbancho, J., & Luque, J. (2003). Automated meter reading and SCADA application. *Lecture Notes in Computer Science*, *2865*, 223–234. doi:10.1007/978-3-540-39611-6_20

Mukherjee, P. (2005). Diffusion Tensor Imaging and Fiber Tractography in Acute Stroke. *Neuroimaging Clinics of North America*, *15*(3), 655–665. doi:10.1016/j.nic.2005.08.010 PMID:16360595

Mukherjee, P., Chung, S. W., Berman, J. I., Hess, C. P., & Henry, R. G. (2008). Diffusion tensor MR imaging and fiber tractography: Technical considerations. *AJNR. American Journal of Neuroradiology*, *29*(5), 843–852. doi:10.3174/ajnr.A1052 PMID:18339719

Munivel, E., & Kannammal, A. (2019). New authentication scheme to secure against phishing attacks in mobile cloud computing. *Security and Communication Networks*, 2019.

Musthyala, H., & Nagarjuna Reddy, P. (2021). Hacking wireless network credentials by performing phishing attack using Python Scripting. *2021 5th International Conference on Intelligent Computing and Control Systems (ICICCS)*. IEEE. 10.1109/ICICCS51141.2021.9432155

Mutibara, A. B., & Refianti, R. (2010). Simulation of Grover algorithm Quantum search in a Classical Computer. *International Journal of Computer Science and Information Security*, *8*(9).

Najibi, M., Samangouei, P., Chellappa, R., & Davis, L. S. (2017). Ssh: Single stage headless face detector. *Proceedings of the IEEE International Conference on Computer Vision (ICCV)*. IEEE. 10.1109/ICCV.2017.522

Nangia, U., Kumar, A., & Rizwan, M. (2021). Development of ANFIS based Algorithm for MPPT Controller for Standalone Photovoltaic System. In International Journal of Advanced Intelligence Paradigms (Vol. 18, Issue 1, p. 1). doi:10.1504/IJAIP.2021.10017382

Nanthakumar, S. S., Lahmer, T., Zhuang, X., Zi, G., & Rabczuk, T. (2016). Detection of material interfaces using a regularized level set method in piezoelectric structures. *Inverse Problems in Science and Engineering, 24*(1), 153–176. doi:10.1080/17415977.2015.1017485

Naphtali, J. H., Misra, S., Wejin, J., Agrawal, A., & Oluranti, J. (2022). An Intelligent Hydroponic Farm Monitoring System Using IoT. In *Data, Engineering and Applications: Select Proceedings of IDEA 2021* (pp. 409–420). Springer. 10.1007/978-981-19-4687-5_31

Naved, M., Sanchez, D. T., Dela Cruz, A. P., Peconcillo, L. B. Jr, Peteros, E. D., & Tenerife, J. J. L. (2022). Identifying the role of cloud computing technology in management of educational institutions. *Materials Today: Proceedings, 51*, 2309–2312. doi:10.1016/j.matpr.2021.11.414

Ndaïrou, F., Area, I., Nieto, J. J., & Torres, D. F. (2020, June 1). Mathematical modeling of COVID-19 transmission dynamics with a case study of Wuhan. *Chaos, Solitons, and Fractals, 135*, 109846. doi:10.1016/j.chaos.2020.109846 PMID:32341628

Ni, J., Liu, B., Li, J., Gao, J., Yang, H., & Han, Z. (2022, January 22). Detection of Carrot Quality Using DCGAN and Deep Network with Squeeze-and-Excitation. *Food Analytical Methods, 15*(5), 1432–1444. doi:10.100712161-021-02189-9

Ni, Q. Q., Hong, J., Xu, P., Xu, Z., Khvostunkov, K., & Xia, H. (2021). Damage detection of CFRP composites by electromagnetic wave nondestructive testing (EMW-NDT). *Composites Science and Technology, 210*, 108839. doi:10.1016/j.compscitech.2021.108839

NVIDIA. (n.d.). Available at: https://www.nvidia.com/en-in/

Odena, A., Olah, C., & Shlens, J. (2017, July 17). *Conditional Image Synthesis with Auxiliary Classifier GANs*. PMLR. https://proceedings.mlr.press/v70/odena17a.html

Oussama, M., Abdelghani, C., & Lakhdar, C. (2022). Efficiency and robustness of type-2 fractional fuzzy PID design using salps swarm algorithm for a wind turbine control under uncertainty. *ISA Transactions, 125*, 72–84. doi:10.1016/j.isatra.2021.06.016 PMID:34167819

Owen, S. L. F., Heath, J., Kringelbach, M., Green, A. L., Pereira, E. A. C., Jenkinson, N., Jegan, T., Stein, J. F., & Aziz, T. Z. (2008). Pre-operative DTI and probabilisitic tractography in four patients with deep brain stimulation for chronic pain. *Journal of Clinical Neuroscience, 15*(7), 801–805. doi:10.1016/j.jocn.2007.06.010 PMID:18495481

Owens, C. D., & Stoessel, K. (2008). Surgical site infections: Epidemiology, microbiology and prevention. *The Journal of Hospital Infection, 70*, 3–10. doi:10.1016/S0195-6701(08)60017-1 PMID:19022115

Oxford Street Dataset. (n.d.). Available at: https://www.youtube.com/watch?v=osaJ2oaOiV8

Ozols, M., & Walter, M. (2018). The *quantum quest*. www.quantumquest.nl

Padilla, R., Filho, C., & Costa, M. (2012). Evaluation of Haar Cascade Classifiers for Face Detection. *International Conference on Digital Image Processing*.

Panda, S., Gupta, M., & Malvi, C. S. (2020). Advances in perturb and observe based MPPT algorithm. In *WEENTECH Proceedings in Energy* (pp. 21–27). 10.32438/WPE.060245

Pandey, S. (2022). *MATLAB Model of an Optimized Battery Charge Controller.* SUBRATA PANDEY.

Papa, I., Lopresto, V., & Langella, A. (2021). Ultrasonic inspection of composites materials: Application to detect impact damage. *International Journal of Lightweight Materials and Manufacture, 4*(1), 37–42. doi:10.1016/j.ijlmm.2020.04.002

Parthiban, S., & Durairaj, D. (2015). Standalone photovoltaic system with MPPT techniques on single-phase eleven-level inverter for utility applications. *2015 International Conference on Electrical, Electronics, Signals, Communication and Optimization (EESCO).* 10.1109/EESCO.2015.7253884

Pascal VOC 2007. (n.d.). Available at: https://www.kaggle.com/zaraks/pascal-voc-2007

Pascal VOC 2012. (n.d.). Available at: https://www.kaggle.com/huanghanchina/pascal-voc-2012

Passos, L. A., Jodas, D., & da Costa, P. (2022, February 12). *A Review of Deep Learning-based Approaches for Deepfake Content Detection.* https://arxiv.org/abs/2202.06095v1

Patra, M. K., Patel, D., Sahoo, B., & Turuk, A. K. (2020, January). A randomized algorithm for load balancing in containerized cloud. In *2020 10th International conference on cloud computing, data science & engineering (confluence)* (pp. 410-414). IEEE. 10.1109/Confluence47617.2020.9058147

Patra, M. K., Sahoo, S., Sahoo, B., & Turuk, A. K. (2019, December). Game theoretic approach for real-time task scheduling in cloud computing environment. In *2019 International Conference on Information Technology (ICIT)* (pp. 454-459). IEEE. 10.1109/ICIT48102.2019.00086

Perillo, M., & Heinzelman, W. (2003). Sensor management policies to provide application QoS. *Ad Hoc Networks, 1*(2-3), 235–246. doi:10.1016/S1570-8705(03)00004-0

Perkowski, M. (2022). Inverse problems, constraint satisfaction, reversible logic, invertible logic and Grover quantum oracles for practical problems. *Science of Computer Programming, 218*, 102775. doi:10.1016/j.scico.2022.102775

Peyrac, C., Jollivet, T., Leray, N., Lefebvre, F., Westphal, O., & Gornet, L. (2015). Self-heating method for fatigue limit determination on thermoplastic composites. *Procedia Engineering, 133*, 129–135. doi:10.1016/j.proeng.2015.12.639

Phukan, S., Singh, J., Gogoi, R., Dhar, S., & Jana, N. D. (2022). COVID-19 Chest X-ray Image Generation Using ResNet-DCGAN Model. *Lecture Notes in Networks and Systems*, 227–234. doi:10.1007/978-981-19-0825-5_24

Pogiatzis, A., & Samakovitis, G. (2020). An event-driven serverless ETL pipeline on AWS. *Applied Sciences (Basel, Switzerland), 11*(1), 191. doi:10.3390/app11010191

Poupon, C., Clark, C. A., Frouin, V., Regis, J., Bloch, I., Le Bihan, D., & Mangin, J.-F. (2000). Regularization of diffusion-based direction maps for the tracking of brain white matter fascicles. *NeuroImage, 12*(2), 184–195. doi:10.1006/nimg.2000.0607 PMID:10913324

Prabakaran, N., Sai Kumar, S. S., Kiran, P. K., & Supriya, P. (2022, January 22). A Deep Learning Based Social Distance Analyzer with Person Detection and Tracking Using Region Based Convolutional Neural Networks for Novel Coronavirus. *Journal of Mobile Multimedia.* doi:10.13052/jmm1550-4646.1834

Prabakaran, N., & Kannan, R. J. (2016, September 14). Sustainable life-span of WSN nodes using participatory devices in pervasive environment. *Microsystem Technologies, 23*(3), 651–657. doi:10.100700542-016-3117-7

Prabakaran, N., Palaniappan, R., Kannadasan, R., Dudi, S. V., & Sasidhar, V. (2021, August 24). Forecasting the momentum using customised loss function for financial series. *International Journal of Intelligent Computing and Cybernetics*, *14*(4), 702–713. doi:10.1108/IJICC-05-2021-0098

Prajapati, S., & Shah, M. T. (2021). Novel MPPT Algorithm for Standalone Solar Photovoltaic System. *2021 International Conference on Advance Computing and Innovative Technologies in Engineering (ICACITE)*. 10.1109/ICACITE51222.2021.9404599

Precup, R.-E., Kamal, T., & Hassan, S. Z. (2019). *Advanced Control and Optimization Paradigms for Wind Energy Systems*. Springer. doi:10.1007/978-981-13-5995-8

Priya, M. A. J., Ashok Kumar, B., & Senthilrani, S. (2018). Phase Locked Loop for controlling inverter interfaced with grid connected solar PV system. *2018 National Power Engineering Conference (NPEC)*. 10.1109/NPEC.2018.8476728

Puengsungwan, S., & Jiraserccamomkul, K. (2018). IoT Based Stress Detection for Organic Lettuce Farms Using Chlorophyll Fluorescence (ChF). *2018 Global Wireless Summit (GWS)*, 354–357.

Qian, N. (1999). On the momentum term in gradient descent learning algorithms. *Neural Networks*, *12*(1), 145–151. doi:10.1016/S0893-6080(98)00116-6 PMID:12662723

Qiu, M., Zhang, J., Zhang, Y., Li, Q., Xie, B., & Wang, J. (2012). Diffusion tensor imaging-based research on human white matter anatomy. *TheScientificWorldJournal*, *2012*, 2012. doi:10.1100/2012/530432 PMID:23226983

Radford, A., Metz, L., & Chintala, S. (2016). *Unsupervised Representation Learning with Deep Convolutional Generative Adversarial Networks*. Cornell University. https://arxiv.org/pdf/1511.06434

Radhika, S., Shree, S. R., Divyadharsini, V. R., & Ranjitha, A. (2020). Symptoms Based Disease Prediction Using Decision Tree and Electronic Health Record Analysis. *European Journal of Molecular and Clinical Medicine*, *7*(4), 2060–2066. https://ejmcm.com/pdf_1944_cb7aaa34894c921618817c5c40cdaf5d.html

Raghuvir. (2020). *COVID-19: Emergence, Spread, Possible Treatments, and Global Burden* (Vol. 8). Frontiers in Public Health.

Rahim, A., Maqbool, A., & Rana, T. (2021, February 25). Monitoring social distancing under various low light conditions with deep learningand a single motionless time of flight camera. *PLoS One*, *16*(2), e0247440. Advance online publication. doi:10.1371/journal.pone.0247440 PMID:33630951

Rajdhan, A., Agarwal, A., Sai, M., Ravi, D., & Ghuli, D. P. (2020). Heart disease prediction using machine learning. [IJERT]. *International Journal of Engineering Research & Technology (Ahmedabad)*, *09*(04), 659–662. doi:10.17577/IJERTV9IS040614

Rakocevic, V., Rajarajan, M., McCalla, K., & Boumitri, C. (2004). QoS constraints in bluetooth-based wireless sensor networks. *Lecture Notes in Computer Science*, *3266*, 214–223. doi:10.1007/978-3-540-30193-6_22

Ramakrishnam Raju, S. V. S., Dappuri, B., Ravi Kiran Varma, P., Yachamaneni, M., Verghese, D. M. G., & Mishra, M. K. (2022). Design and Implementation of Smart Hydroponics Farming Using IoT-Based AI Controller with Mobile Application System. *Journal of Nanomaterials*, *2022*, 1–12. doi:10.1155/2022/4435591

Ramu, E., & Sobhana, O. (2018). Standalone PV system with Fuzzy MPPT controller. *2018 International Conference on Recent Innovations in Electrical, Electronics & Communication Engineering (ICRIEECE)*. 10.1109/ICRIEECE44171.2018.9009379

Rashid, A., & Chaturvedi, A. (2019). Cloud computing characteristics and services: A brief review. *International Journal on Computer Science and Engineering*, *7*(2), 421–426.

Reay, D. S. (2004). New Directions: Flying in the face of the climate change convention. In Atmospheric Environment (Vol. 38, Issue 5, pp. 793–794). doi:10.1016/j.atmosenv.2003.10.026

Reda, M., Suwwan, R., Alkafri, S., Rashed, Y., & Shanableh, T. (2022). AgroAId: A Mobile App System for Visual Classification of Plant Species and Diseases Using Deep Learning and TensorFlow Lite. *Informatics, 9*(3), 55. doi:10.3390/INFORMATICS9030055

Reddy, M. V., Abhijith, G. V. P. S., Nath, K. S., & Sathyanarayana, M. (2022). Disease predictor based on symptoms using machine learning. *International Journal for Research in Applied Science and Engineering Technology, 10*(6), 2549–2555. doi:10.22214/ijraset.2022.44408

Reid, L. B., Cespedes, M. I., & Pannek, K. (2020). How many streamlines are required for reliable probabilistic tractography? Solutions for microstructural measurements and neurosurgical planning. *NeuroImage, 211*, 116646. doi:10.1016/j.neuroimage.2020.116646 PMID:32084566

Rekioua, D., & Matagne, E. (2012). *Optimization of Photovoltaic Power Systems: Modelization, Simulation and Control.* Springer Science & Business Media. doi:10.1007/978-1-4471-2403-0

Rendle, S., & Freudenthaler, C., & Thieme. L. Schmidt. (2010). Factorizing personalized Markov chains for a next-basket recommendation. *In Proceedings of the 19th international conference on the world wide web*, (pp. 811–820). ACM. 10.1145/1772690.1772773

Rezaei, M., & Azarmi, M. (2020). DeepSOCIAL: Social Distancing Monitoring and Infection Risk Assessment in COVID-19 Pandemic. *Applied Sciences (Basel, Switzerland), 10*(21), 7514. doi:10.3390/app10217514

Rheault, F., St-Onge, E., Sidhu, J., Maier-Hein, K., Tzourio-Mazoyer, N., Petit, L., & Descoteaux, M. (2019). Bundle-specific tractography with incorporated anatomical and orientational priors. *NeuroImage, 186*, 382–398. doi:10.1016/j.neuroimage.2018.11.018 PMID:30453031

RobinD.HuguesB. (2017). *Collaborative Filtering with Recurrent Neural Networks.* arXiv:1608.07400 [cs.IR].

Rouabah, B., Toubakh, H., Kafi, M. R., & Sayed-Mouchaweh, M. (2022). Adaptive data-driven fault-tolerant control strategy for optimal power extraction in presence of broken rotor bars in wind turbine. *ISA Transactions, 130*, 92–103. doi:10.1016/j.isatra.2022.04.008 PMID:35450727

Royer, E., & Toh, C. K. (1999). A review of current routing protocols for ad-hoc mobile wireless networks. *IEEE Personal Communications, 4*(2), 46–55.

Ruengittinun, S., Phongsamsuan, S., & Sureeratanakorn, P. (2017). Applied internet of thing for smart hydroponic farming ecosystem (HFE). *2017 10th International Conference on Ubi-Media Computing and Workshops (Ubi-Media)*, 1–4.

Ruihui, M., Xiaoqin, Z., & Lixin, H. (2018). A Survey of Recommender Systems Based on Deep Learning. *IEEE Access : Practical Innovations, Open Solutions, 6*, 1–1. doi:10.1109/ACCESS.2018.2880197

S, N., Singh, H., & N, A. U. (2022). An extensive review on quantum computers. *Advances in Engineering Software, 174*(September), 103337. doi:10.1016/j.advengsoft.2022.103337

Sabata, B., Chatterjee, S., Davis, M., Sydir, J., & Lawrence, T. (1997). Taxonom for QoS specifications. In *Proceedings of the third International Work- shop on Object-Oriented Real-Time Dependable Systems*. IEEE.

Sabino, C. P., Ball, A. R., Baptista, M. S., Dai, T., Hamblin, M. R., Ribeiro, M. S., Santos, A. L., Sellera, F. P., Tegos, G. P., & Wainwright, M. (2020, November 1). Light-based technologies for management of COVID-19 pandemic crisis. *Journal of Photochemistry and Photobiology. B, Biology, 212*, 111999. doi:10.1016/j.jphotobiol.2020.111999 PMID:32855026

Saginbekov, S., & Korpeoglu, I. (2005). An energy efficient scatternet formation algorithm for bluetooth-based sensor networks. In *Proceedings of the Second European Workshop on Wireless Sensor Networks*. IEEE. 10.1109/EWSN.2005.1462012

Salvi, S., Jain, S. A. F., Sanjay, H. A., Harshita, T. K., Farhana, M., Jain, N., & Suhas, M. V. (2017). Cloud based data analysis and monitoring of smart multi-level irrigation system using IoT. *2017 International Conference on I-SMAC (IoT in Social, Mobile, Analytics and Cloud)(I-SMAC)*, 752–757. 10.1109/I-SMAC.2017.8058279

Samui, P., Mondal, J., & Khajanchi, S. (2020, November 1). A mathematical model for COVID-19 transmission dynamics with a case study of India. *Chaos, Solitons, and Fractals*, *140*, 110173. doi:10.1016/j.chaos.2020.110173 PMID:32834653

Sandesh, Sridhar, Rishikesh, Farheen, & Tameem. (n.d.). Smart Door Lock/Unlock Using Raspberry Pi. *International Journal of Scientific Research in Computer Science, Engineering and Information Technology*, 543-548. doi:10.32628/CSEIT2063135

Sangamnerkar, S., Srinivasan, R., Christhuraj, M. R., & Sukumaran, R. (2020). An Ensemble Technique to Detect Fabricated News Article Using Machine Learning and Natural Language Processing Techniques. *2020 International Conference for Emerging Technology (INCET)*, (pp. 1-7). IEEE. 10.1109/INCET49848.2020.9154053

Sangeeta, L., Lipika, T., Ravi, R., Verma, A., Sardana, N., & Mourya, R. (2020). Analysis and Classification of Crime Tweets. *Procedia Computer Science*, *167*, 1911–1919. doi:10.1016/j.procs.2020.03.211

Sansone, C., & Sperlí, G. (2022, May). Legal Information Retrieval systems: State-of-the-art and open issues. *Information Systems*, *106*, 101967. doi:10.1016/j.is.2021.101967

Santos de Araújo, J. V., Villanueva, J. M. M., Cordula, M. M., Cardoso, A. A., & Gomes, H. P. (2022). Fuzzy Control of Pressure in a Water Supply Network Based on Neural Network System Modeling and IoT Measurements. *Sensors (Basel)*, *22*(23), 9130. Advance online publication. doi:10.339022239130 PMID:36501831

Sardare, M. D., & Admane, S. V. (2013). A review on plant without soil-hydroponics. *International Journal of Research in Engineering and Technology*, *2*(3), 299–304. doi:10.15623/ijret.2013.0203013

Sarkar, K., Sharma, R., & Bhattacharyya, S. P. (2012). A constrained variational approach to the designing of low transport band gap materials: A multiobjective random mutation hill climbing method. In International Journal of Quantum Chemistry (Vol. 112, Issue 6, pp. 1547–1558). doi:10.1002/qua.23119

Sbarski, P., & Kroonenburg, S. (2017). *Serverless architectures on AWS: with examples using Aws Lambda*. Simon and Schuster.

Scikit-learn, Machine Learning in Python. (n.d.). Available at: https://scikit-learn.org/stable/

Searing, L. (2019, August 12). The Big Number: Lefties make up about 10 percent of the world. *Washington Post*. https://www.washingtonpost.com/health/the-big-number-lefties-make-up-about-10-percent-of-the-world/2019/08/09/69978100-b9e2-11e9-bad6-609f75bfd97f_story.html

Seegerer, S., Michaeli, T., & Romeike, R. (2021). Quantum Computing As a Topic in Computer Science Education. In *ACM International Conference Proceeding Series (Vol. 1*, Issue 1). Association for Computing Machinery. 10.1145/3481312.3481348

Sen, J. (2015). Security and privacy issues in cloud computing. In *Cloud technology: concepts, methodologies, tools, and applications* (pp. 1585–1630). IGI global. doi:10.4018/978-1-4666-6539-2.ch074

Sewak, M., & Singh, S. (2018, April). Winning in the era of serverless computing and function as a service. In *2018 3rd International Conference for Convergence in Technology (I2CT)* (pp. 1-5). IEEE. 10.1109/I2CT.2018.8529465

Shafiei, H., Khonsari, A., & Mousavi, P. (2022). Serverless computing: A survey of opportunities, challenges, and applications. *ACM Computing Surveys*, *54*(11s), 1–32. doi:10.1145/3510611

Shah, K., Soni, J., & Bhattacharjee, K. (2023). Artificial Electric Field Algorithm Applied to the Economic Load Dispatch Problem With Valve Point Loading Effect. In International Journal of Swarm Intelligence Research (Vol. 14, Issue 1, pp. 1–23). doi:10.4018/IJSIR.317136

Shah, R., & Rabaey, J. (2002). Energy aware routing for low energy ad hoc sensor networks. In *Proceedings of IEEE WCNC*, (pp. 17–21). IEEE. 10.1109/WCNC.2002.993520

Sharma, S., Shakya, H. K., & Mishra, A. (2022). Medical Data Classification in Cloud Computing Using Soft Computing With Voting Classifier: A Review. *The Internet of Medical Things (IoMT) Healthcare Transformation*, 23-44.

Shete. (n.d.). *Social Distancing and Face Mask Detection using Deep Learning and Computer Vision* [MSc. diss.]. National College of Ireland, Dublin.

Shetty, N., Muniyal, B., Anand, A., Kumar, S., & Prabhu, S. (2020). Predicting depression using deep learning and ensemble algorithms on raw twitter data. [IJECE]. *Iranian Journal of Electrical and Computer Engineering*, *10*(4), 3751. doi:10.11591/ijece.v10i4.pp3751-3756

Sheu, P., Chien, S., Hu, C., & Li, Y. (2005). An efficient genetic algorithm for the power-based qos many-to-one routing problem for wireless sensor networks. In *International Conference on Information Networking, ICOIN 2005*, (pp. 275–282). IEEE. 10.1007/978-3-540-30582-8_29

Shi, D., Lu, X., Liu, Y., Yuan, J., Pan, T., & Li, Y. (2021). Research on Depression Recognition Using Machine Learning from Speech. *2021 International Conference on Asian Language Processing (IALP)*, (pp. 52-56). IEEE. 10.1109/IALP54817.2021.9675271

Shobanadevi, N. (n.d.). Adaptive Black Widow Optimization Based MPPT Controller in High-Gain Non-Isolated DC-DC Converter for PV Applications. doi:10.21203/rs.3.rs-2473630/v1

Shukla, D. M., Sharma, K., & Gupta, S. (2020). Identifying Depression in a Person Using Speech Signals by Extracting Energy and Statistical Features. *2020 IEEE International Students' Conference on Electrical, Electronics and Computer Science (SCEECS)*, (pp. 1-4). IEEE. 10.1109/SCEECS48394.2020.60

Siless, V., Davidow, J. Y., Nielsen, J., Fan, Q., Hedden, T., Hollinshead, M., Beam, E., Bustamante, C. M. V., Garrad, M. C., Santillana, R., & ... (2020). Registration-free analysis of diffusion MRI tractography data across subjects through the human lifespan. *NeuroImage*, *214*, 116703. doi:10.1016/j.neuroimage.2020.116703 PMID:32151759

Singh, M. P., Hoque, M. A., & Tarkoma, S. (2016). A survey of systems for massive stream analytics. *arXiv preprint arXiv:1605.09021*.

Singh, B., & Shukl, P. (2021). Seamless Power Transfer of Solar PV Based Grid Interactive System. *2021 National Power Electronics Conference (NPEC)*. 10.1109/NPEC52100.2021.9672533

Singh, S., Sarje, A. K., & Misra, M. (2012). Client-side counter phishing application using adaptive neuro-fuzzy inference system. In *2012 Fourth International Conference on Computational Intelligence and Communication Networks* (pp. 788–792). IEEE

Smitha, Afshin, & Hegde. (2020). Face Recognition based Attendance Management System. *International Journal of Engineering Research & Technology (Ahmedabad)*, *9*(5). Advance online publication. doi:10.17577/IJERTV9IS050861

Smith, R. E., Tournier, J. D., Calamante, F., & Connelly, A. (2012). Anatomically-constrained tractography: Improved diffusion MRI streamlines tractography through effective use of anatomical information. *NeuroImage, 62*(3), 1924–1938. doi:10.1016/j.neuroimage.2012.06.005 PMID:22705374

Softmax Activation Function with Python. (n.d.). Available at: https://machinelearningmastery.com/softmax-activation-function-with-python/

Song, H., You, J., Chung, J., & Park, J. (2018). *Feature Attention Network: Interpretable Depression Detection from Social Media*. PACLIC.

Soni, J. M., Patel, D. V., Patel, R. V., & Modha, H. P. (2020). A Strategic Community Control-Based Power Flow Between Grid-Integrated PV Houses. In Lecture Notes in Electrical Engineering (pp. 1061–1071). doi:10.1007/978-981-15-7031-5_101

Soni, J., & Bhattacharjee, K. (2022). Sooty Tern Optimization Algorithm for Solving the Multi-Objective Dynamic Economic Emission Dispatch Problem. In International Journal of Swarm Intelligence Research (Vol. 13, Issue 1, pp. 1–15). doi:10.4018/IJSIR.308292

Soni, J., & Bhattacharjee, K. (2023). Sine-Cosine Algorithm for the Dynamic Economic Dispatch Problem With the Valve-Point Loading Effect. In International Journal of Swarm Intelligence Research (Vol. 14, Issue 1, pp. 1–15). doi:10.4018/IJSIR.316801

Soni, P., Tewari, Y., & Krishnan, D. (2022, January 1). Machine Learning Approaches in Stock Price Prediction: A Systematic Review. *Journal of Physics: Conference Series, 2161*(1), 012065. doi:10.1088/1742-6596/2161/1/012065

Soumya, S., & Pramod, K. V. (2020). Sentiment analysis of malayalam tweets using machine learning techniques. *ICT Express., 6*. doi:10.1016/j.icte.2020.04.003

Soviany & Ionescu. (2018). *Optimizing the Trade-off between Single-Stage and Two-Stage Deep Object Detectors using Image Difficulty Prediction*. doi:10.1109/SYNASC.2018.00041,2018

Sprenger, W., Wilson, H. R., & Kuhn, T. E. (2016). Electricity yield simulation for the building-integrated photovoltaic system installed in the main building roof of the Fraunhofer Institute for Solar Energy Systems ISE. In Solar Energy (Vol. 135, pp. 633–643). doi:10.1016/j.solener.2016.06.037

Srinivasan, R., & Subalalitha, C. N. (2023). Sentimental analysis from imbalanced code-mixed data using machine learning approaches. *Distributed and Parallel Databases, 41*, 37–52. doi:10.100710619-021-07331-4 PMID:33776212

Srivastav, A. L., Patel, N., Rani, L., Kumar, P., Dutt, I., Maddodi, B. S., & Chaudhary, V. K. (2023). Sustainable options for fertilizer management in agriculture to prevent water contamination: A review. *Environment, Development and Sustainability*, 1–25. doi:10.100710668-023-03117-z

Stamile, C., Cotton, F., Sappey-Marinier, D., & Van Huffel, S. (2019). Constrained Tensor Decomposition for Longitudinal Analysis of Diffusion Imaging Data. *IEEE Journal of Biomedical and Health Informatics, 24*(4), 1137–1148. doi:10.1109/JBHI.2019.2933138 PMID:31395569

Stieninger, M., & Nedbal, D. (2014). Characteristics of cloud computing in the business context: A systematic literature review. *Global Journal of Flexible Systems Managment, 15*(1), 59–68. doi:10.100740171-013-0055-4

Stosovic, M. A., Dimitrijevic, M., & Litovski, V. (2013). MPPT controller design for a standalone PV system. In *2013 11th International Conference on Telecommunications in Modern Satellite, Cable and Broadcasting Services (TELSIKS)*. 10.1109/TELSKS.2013.6704427

Stratil, H. (2005). Distributed construction of an underlay in wireless networks. In *Proceedings of the Second European Workshop on Wireless Sensor Networks*. IEEE. 10.1109/EWSN.2005.1462009

Su, S., Delbracio, M., Wang, J., Sapiro, G., Heidrich, W., & Wang, O. (2017). Deep video deblurring for hand-held cameras. *Proceedings of the IEEE Conference on Computer Vision and Pattern Recognition (CVPR)*, (pp. 1279–1288). IEEE.

Sun, W., Zhang, K., Chen, S. K., Zhang, X., & Liang, H. (2007). Software as a service: An integration perspective. In *Service-Oriented Computing–ICSOC 2007: Fifth International Conference*. Springer Berlin Heidelberg.

Sun, Y., Zeng, Y., & Zhang, T. (2021). Quantum superposition inspired spiking neural network. *iScience*, *24*(8), 102880. Advance online publication. doi:10.1016/j.isci.2021.102880 PMID:34401664

Sutskever, I., Vinyals, O., & Le, Q. V. (2014). Sequence to sequence learning with neural networks. In Advances in neural information processing systems, 3104–3112.

Syafaruddin, S., Hiyama, T., & Karatepe, E. (2010). Investigation of ANN performance for tracking the optimum points of PV module under partially shaded conditions. *2010 Conference Proceedings IPEC*. 10.1109/IPECON.2010.5697002

Taha, M. F., ElMasry, G., Gouda, M., Zhou, L., Liang, N., Abdalla, A., Rousseau, D., & Qiu, Z. (2022). Recent Advances of Smart Systems and Internet of Things (IoT) for Aquaponics Automation: A Comprehensive Overview. *Chemosensors (Basel, Switzerland)*, *10*(8), 303. doi:10.3390/chemosensors10080303

Takabi, H., Joshi, J. B., & Ahn, G. J. (2010). Security and privacy challenges in cloud computing environments. *IEEE Security and Privacy*, *8*(6), 24–31. doi:10.1109/MSP.2010.186

Talekder, A., Bhatt, R., Chandramouli, S., Ali, L., Pidva, R., & Monacos, S. (2005). Autonomous resource management and control algorithms for distributed wireless sensor networks. In *The 3rd ACS/IEEE International Conference on Computer Systems and Applications* (pp. 19–26). ACM.

Tallus, J., Mohammadian, M., Kurki, T., Roine, T., Posti, J. P., & Tenovuo, O. (2023). A comparison of diffusion tensor imaging tractography and constrained spherical deconvolution with automatic segmentation in traumatic brain injury. *NeuroImage. Clinical*, *37*, 103284. doi:10.1016/j.nicl.2022.103284 PMID:36502725

Tan, C. Y., Selvaraj, J., & Abd Rahim, N. (2014). Improvement of hill climbing method by introducing simple irradiance detection method. *3rd IET International Conference on Clean Energy and Technology (CEAT) 2014*. 10.1049/cp.2014.1493

Tao, X., Chi, O., Delaney, P. J., Li, L., & Huang, J. (2021). Detecting depression using an ensemble classifier based on Quality of Life scales. *Brain Informatics*, *8*(1), 2. doi:10.118640708-021-00125-5 PMID:33590388

Tatas, K., Al-Zoubi, A., Christofides, N., Zannettis, C., Chrysostomou, M., Panteli, S., & Antoniou, A. (2022). Reliable IoT-based monitoring and control of hydroponic systems. *Technologies*, *10*(1), 26. doi:10.3390/technologies10010026

Teferra, D. M., Ngoo, L. M. H., & Nyakoe, G. N. (2023). Fuzzy-based prediction of solar PV and wind power generation for microgrid modeling using particle swarm optimization. *Heliyon*, *9*(1), e12802. doi:10.1016/j.heliyon.2023.e12802 PMID:36704286

Thien Phung. (2022, October 27). *Predicting FIFA World Cup 2022™ using Machine Learning*. TGM Research. Retrieved January 27, 2023, from https://tgmresearch.com/predicting-fifa-world-cup-2022.html

This Sneaker Does Not Exist! (2021). https://thissneakerdoesnotexist.com/

Tian, Y., Zhang, Y., Fu, Y., & Xu, C. (2020). Tdan: Temporally-deformable alignment network for video super-resolution. *Proceedings of the IEEE/CVF Conference on Computer Vision and Pattern Recognition (CVPR)*. IEEE. 10.1109/CVPR42600.2020.00342

Transfer Learning in Keras with Computer Vision Models. (n.d.). Available at: https://machinelearningmastery.com/how-to-use-transfer-learning-when-developing-convolutional-neural-network-models/

Trotzek, M., Koitka, S., & Friedrich, C. (2018). Utilizing Neural Networks and Linguistic Metadata for Early Detection of Depression Indications in Text Sequences. *IEEE Transactions on Knowledge and Data Engineering, 32*(3), 588–601. doi:10.1109/TKDE.2018.2885515

Trupthi, M., Pabboju, S., & Narasimha, G. (2017, January). Sentiment analysis on twitter using streaming API. In *2017 IEEE 7th international advance computing conference (IACC)* (pp. 915-919). IEEE. 10.1109/IACC.2017.0186

Tzani-Tzanopoulou, P., Rozumbetov, R., Taka, S., Doudoulakakis, A., Lebessi, E., Chanishvili, N., Kakabadze, E., Bakuradze, N., Grdzelishvili, N., Goderdzishvili, M., Legaki, E., Andreakos, E., Papadaki, M., Megremis, S., Xepapadaki, P., Kaltsas, G., Akdis, C. A., & Papadopoulos, N. G. (2022). Development of an homeostasis model between airway epithelial cells, bacteria and bacteriophages: A time-lapsed observation of cell viability and inflammatory response. *The Journal of General Virology, 103*(12). Advance online publication. doi:10.1099/jgv.0.001819 PMID:36748697

Unde, M., Hans, M., & Navghare, M. (2020). Grid Tie PV Inverter Using Buck-Boost Based Converter Maximizing Power Yield in Mismatched Environmental Condition Controlling Two Solar PV Arrays. *2020 IEEE International Symposium on Sustainable Energy, Signal Processing and Cyber Security (iSSSC)*. 10.1109/iSSSC50941.2020.9358896

V.V., R., Rajasegharan, V. V., L., P., & R., R. (2018). Modelling and controlling of PV connected quasi Z-source cascaded multilevel inverter system: An HACSNN based control approach. In *Electric Power Systems Research* (Vol. 162, pp. 10–22). doi:10.1016/j.epsr.2018.04.020

Vadivel, R., Parthasarathi, R. V., Navaneethraj, A., Sridhar, P., Nafi, K. A. M., & Karan, S. (2019). Hypaponics-monitoring and controlling using Internet of Things and machine learning. *2019 1st International Conference on Innovations in Information and Communication Technology (ICIICT)*, 1–6.

van der Walt, Colbert, & Varoquaux. (2011). The NumPy Array: A Structure for Efficient Numerical Computation. *Computing in Science & Engineering, 13*, 22 - 30. . doi:10.1109/MCSE.2011.37,2011

Vasant, P., Zelinka, I., & Weber, G.-W. (2019). *Intelligent Computing and Optimization: Proceedings of the 2nd International Conference on Intelligent Computing and Optimization 2019 (ICO 2019)*. Springer Nature. 10.1007/978-3-030-00979-3

Vasant, P., Zelinka, I., & Weber, G.-W. (2022). *Intelligent Computing & Optimization: Proceedings of the 4th International Conference on Intelligent Computing and Optimization 2021 (ICO2021)*. Springer Nature. 10.1007/978-3-030-93247-3

Venkatesh, K., Dhyanesh, K., Prathyusha, M., & Teja, C. H. N. (2021). Identification of Disease Prediction Based on Symptoms Using Machine Learning. *Journal of Advanced Composition, 14*(6), 86–93. https://drive.google.com/file/d/1lunpeHjQcZUHWiZt24pMd72Y0pUEw6jI/view

Venkateshkumar, M. (2018). Fuzzy Controller-Based MPPT of PV Power System. Fuzzy Logic Based in Optimization Methods and Control Systems and its Applications. doi:10.5772/intechopen.80065

Verma, D., Soni, J., Kalathia, D., & Bhattacharjee, K. (2022). Sine Cosine Algorithm for Solving Economic Load Dispatch Problem With Penetration of Renewables. In International Journal of Swarm Intelligence Research (Vol. 13, Issue 1, pp. 1–21). doi:10.4018/IJSIR.299847

Villegas-Mier, C. G., Rodriguez-Resendiz, J., Álvarez-Alvarado, J. M., Rodriguez-Resendiz, H., Herrera-Navarro, A. M., & Rodríguez-Abreo, O. (2021). Artificial Neural Networks in MPPT Algorithms for Optimization of Photovoltaic Power Systems: A Review. *Micromachines, 12*(10), 1260. Advance online publication. doi:10.3390/mi12101260 PMID:34683311

VondrickC.PirsiavashH.TorralbaA. (2016, January 1). *Generating Videos with Scene Dynamics*. doi:10.13016/m26gih-tnyz

WackA.PaikH.Javadi-AbhariA.JurcevicP.FaroI.GambettaJ. M.JohnsonB. R. (2021). *Quality, Speed, and Scale: three key attributes to measure the performance of near-term quantum computers.* https://arxiv.org/abs/2110.14108

Waghmare-Ujgare, V., Goudar, M. D., & Kharadkar, R. D. (2022). Optimized maximum power point tracker for partially shaded PV system: adaptive duty cycle control. International Journal of Intelligent Robotics and Applications. doi:10.100741315-022-00249-9

Wahab, N. A., & Mohamed, Z. (2022). *Control, Instrumentation and Mechatronics: Theory and Practice.* Springer Nature. doi:10.1007/978-981-19-3923-5

Wang, H., Zhang, F., Wang, J., Zhao, M., Li, W., Xie, X., & Guo, M. (2018). RippleNet: Propagating User Preferences on the Knowledge Graph for Recommender Systems. *International Conference on Information and Knowledge Management,* (pp. 417-426). ACM. 10.1145/3269206.3271739

Wang, S. W., Chiou, C. C., Su, C. H., Wu, C. C., Tsai, S. C., Lin, T. K., & Hsu, C. N. (2022). Measuring Mobile Phone Application Usability for Anticoagulation from the Perspective of Patients, Caregivers, and Healthcare Professionals. *International Journal of Environmental Research and Public Health, 19*(16), 10136. doi:10.3390/IJERPH191610136

Wang, B., Fan, Y., Lu, M., Li, S., Song, Z., Peng, X., Zhang, R., Lin, Q., He, Y., Wang, J., & Huang, R. (2013). Brain anatomical networks in world class gymnasts: A DTI tractography study. *NeuroImage, 65,* 476–487. doi:10.1016/j.neuroimage.2012.10.007 PMID:23073234

Wang, C., Ma, Z., & Tong, S. (2022). Adaptive fuzzy output-feedback event-triggered control for fractional-order nonlinear system. *Mathematical Biosciences and Engineering, 19*(12), 12334–12352. doi:10.3934/mbe.2022575 PMID:36654000

Wang, T. C., Liu, M. Y., Zhu, J. Y., Tao, A., Kautz, J., & Catanzaro, B. (2018, June). High-Resolution Image Synthesis and Semantic Manipulation with Conditional GANs. *2018 IEEE/CVF Conference on Computer Vision and Pattern Recognition.* 10.1109/CVPR.2018.00917

Wang, Z. (2011, October). Security and privacy issues within the Cloud Computing. In *2011 International Conference on Computational and Information Sciences* (pp. 175-178). IEEE. 10.1109/ICCIS.2011.247

Wang, Z., Wang, C., Cheng, L., & Li, G. (2022, November). An approach for day-ahead interval forecasting of photovoltaic power: A novel DCGAN and LSTM based quantile regression modeling method. *Energy Reports, 8,* 14020–14033. doi:10.1016/j.egyr.2022.10.309

Wani, J. A. (2018). Different methods for controlling the power flow in RERs based power system. In International Journal of Trend in Scientific Research and Development (Vol. -2, Issue -3, pp. 1798–1803). doi:10.31142/ijtsrd11647

Wasserthal, J., Neher, P. F., Hirjak, D., & Maier-Hein, K. H. (2019). Combined tract segmentation and orientation mapping for bundle-specific tractography. *Medical Image Analysis, 58,* 101559. doi:10.1016/j.media.2019.101559 PMID:31542711

Watson, C. G., DeMaster, D., & Ewing-Cobbs, L. (2019). Graph theory analysis of DTI tractography in children with traumatic injury. *NeuroImage. Clinical, 21,* 101673. doi:10.1016/j.nicl.2019.101673 PMID:30660661

Waugh, J. L., Kuster, J. K., Makhlouf, M. L., Levenstein, J. M., Multhaupt-Buell, T. J., Warfield, S. K., Sharma, N., & Blood, A. J. (2019). A registration method for improving quantitative assessment in probabilistic diffusion tractography. *NeuroImage, 189,* 288–306. doi:10.1016/j.neuroimage.2018.12.057 PMID:30611874

Wiangtong, T., & Sirisuk, P. (2018). IoT-based versatile platform for precision farming. *2018 18th International Symposium on Communications and Information Technologies (ISCIT),* 438–441.

Wiggers, K. (2020, June 5). *Amazon's new AI technique lets users virtually try on outfits.* VentureBeat. https://venturebeat.com/ai/amazons-new-ai-technique-lets-users-virtually-try-on-outfits/

Wright, J., & Tseng, T. (2015). *Lecture 04: Grover's Algorithm*. Academic Press.

Wu, L., Du, X., & Wu, J. (2014, August). MobiFish: A lightweight anti-phishing scheme for mobile phones. In *Computer Communication and Networks (ICCCN), 2014 23rd International Conference on* (pp. 1-8). IEEE. 10.1109/ICCCN.2014.6911743

Wu, D., Gan, J., Zhou, J., Wang, J., & Gao, W. (2021, November 12). Fine-grained semantic ethnic costume high-resolution image colorization with conditional GAN. *International Journal of Intelligent Systems, 37*(5), 2952–2968. doi:10.1002/int.22726

Wu, J., Xu, X., Liu, C., Deng, C., & Shao, X. (2021). Lamb wave-based damage detection of composite structures using deep convolutional neural network and continuous wavelet transform. *Composite Structures, 276*, 114590. doi:10.1016/j.compstruct.2021.114590

Wu, Q., Chen, Y., & Meng, J. (2020). DCGAN-Based Data Augmentation for Tomato Leaf Disease Identification. *IEEE Access : Practical Innovations, Open Solutions, 8*, 98716–98728. doi:10.1109/ACCESS.2020.2997001

Wu, Y., Wei, D., & Feng, J. (2020). Network attacks detection methods based on deep learning techniques: A survey. *Security and Communication Networks, 2020*, 1–17. doi:10.1155/2020/8872923

Wu, Z., Jiang, Z., Li, Z., Jiao, P., Zhai, J., Liu, S., Han, X., Zhang, S., Sun, J., Gai, Z., Qiu, C., Xu, J., Liu, H., Qin, R., & Lu, R. (2023). Multi-omics analysis reveals spatiotemporal regulation and function of heteromorphic leaves in Populus. *Plant Physiology, 192*(1), 188–204. Advance online publication. doi:10.1093/plphys/kiad063 PMID:36746772

Xiao, Z., Lu, J., Wang, X., Li, N., Wang, Y., & Zhao, N. (2022, December 3). WCE-DCGAN: A data augmentation method based on wireless capsule endoscopy images for gastrointestinal disease detection. *IET Image Processing, 17*(4), 1170–1180. doi:10.1049/ipr2.12704

Xue, T., Chen, B., Wu, J., Wei, D., & Freeman, W. T. (2019). Video enhance- ment with task-oriented flow. *International Journal of Computer Vision, 127*(8), 1106–1125. doi:10.100711263-018-01144-2

Yamamoto, K., & Shinohara, K. (1996). Analysis of AC Servo Motor Driven by PWM Inverter with Switching Dead-Time and Compensation for Output Voltage Deviation. In IEEJ Transactions on Industry Applications (Vol. 116, Issue 9, pp. 924–933). doi:10.1541/ieejias.116.924

Yan, D., Li, K., Gu, S., & Yang, L. (2020). Network-Based Bag-of-Words Model for Text Classification. *IEEE Access : Practical Innovations, Open Solutions, 8*, 82641–82652. doi:10.1109/ACCESS.2020.2991074

Yang, C., Lu, X., Lin, Z., Shechtman, E., Wang, O., & Li, H. (2017). *High-Resolution Image Inpainting Using Multi-scale Neural Patch Synthesis*. doi:10.1109/CVPR.2017.434

Yang. Z., & Cheng, J. (2021). Recommendation Algorithm Based on Knowledge Graph to Propagate User Preference. *International Journal of Computational Intelligence Systems*. . doi:10.2991/ijcis.d.210503.001

Yang, H., Yuan, C., Xing, J., & Hu, W. (2017). SCNN: Sequential convolutional neural network for human action recognition in videos. *IEEE International Conference on Image Processing (ICIP)*, 355-359. 10.1109/ICIP.2017.8296302

Yeh, F.-C. (2020). Shape analysis of the human association pathways. *NeuroImage, 223*, 117329. doi:10.1016/j.neuroimage.2020.117329 PMID:32882375

Ye, L., Lu, Y., Su, Z., & Meng, G. (2005). Functionalized composite structures for new generation airframes: A review. *Composites Science and Technology, 65*(9), 1436–1446. doi:10.1016/j.compscitech.2004.12.015

YOLO: Real Time Object Detection. (n.d.). Available at: https://pjreddie.com/darknet/yolo/

Yoon, S., Kwan, Y. H., Phang, J. K., Tan, W. B., & Low, L. L. (2022). Personal Goals, Barriers to Self-Management and Desired mHealth Application Features to Improve Self-Care in Multi-Ethnic Asian Patients with Type 2 Diabetes: A Qualitative Study. *International Journal of Environmental Research and Public Health, 19*(22), 15415. doi:10.3390/ijerph192215415 PMID:36430134

Yu, J., Xue, A., Redei, E., & Bagheri, N. (2016). A support vector machine model provides an accurate transcript-level-based diagnostic for major depressive disorder. *Translational Psychiatry, 6*(10), e931. doi:10.1038/tp.2016.198 PMID:27779627

Yusof, S. S. S., Thamrin, N. M., Nordin, M. K., Yusoff, A. S. M., & Sidik, N. J. (2016). Effect of artificial lighting on typhonium flagelliforme for indoor vertical farming. *2016 IEEE International Conference on Automatic Control and Intelligent Systems (I2CACIS)*, 7–10. 10.1109/I2CACIS.2016.7885280

Zhang, Q., & Huo, Z. (2022). Effect of Continuous Nutrition Management Intervention on Nutritional Status and Development of Premature Infants Based on Mobile Medical APP. *Computational and Mathematical Methods in Medicine, 2022*, 1–8. Advance online publication. doi:10.1155/2022/8586355 PMID:35979052

Zhan, H., Zha, T., Hong, B., & Shan, L. (2023). Particle size distribution inversion using the Weibull-distribution adaptive-parameters cuckoo search algorithm. *Applied Optics, 62*(1), 235–245. doi:10.1364/AO.476741 PMID:36606870

Zhan, L., Zhou, J., Wang, Y., Jin, Y., Jahanshad, N., Prasad, G., Nir, T. M., Leonardo, C. D., Ye, J., & Thompson, P. M. (2015). Comparison of nine tractography algorithms for detecting abnormal structural brain networks in Alzheimer's disease. *Frontiers in Aging Neuroscience, 7*, 48. doi:10.3389/fnagi.2015.00048 PMID:25926791

Zhao, Z., Zheng, P., Xu, S., & Wu, X. (2019, November). Object Detection with Deep Learning: A Review. *IEEE Transactions on Neural Networks and Learning Systems, 30*(11), 3212–3232. doi:10.1109/TNNLS.2018.2876865 PMID:30703038

Zhou, J., Ho, V., & Javadi, B. (2022). New Internet of Medical Things for Home-Based Treatment of Anorectal Disorders. *Sensors, 22*(2), 625. doi:10.3390/S22020625

Zhu, J. Y., Krähenbühl, P., Shechtman, E., & Efros, A. A. (2016). Generative Visual Manipulation on the Natural Image Manifold. *Computer Vision – ECCV 2016*, 597–613. doi:10.1007/978-3-319-46454-1_36

About the Contributors

* * *

Nisha Banerjee is a Computer Science Student from St. Xavier's (Autonomous) College, Kolkata. She received her bachelor's degree from St. Xavier's (Autonomous) College, Kolkata and is currently pursuing her Masters from the same Institution. She is an organized, motivated, curious and hardworking individual who dreams of building a world around research and development.

Kuntal Bhattacharjee is working as an associate professor at the department of electrical engineering, institute of technology, Nirma University. He obtained BE degree in electrical engineering from Burdwan University, West Bengal on the year 2003. He received his MTech and Ph.D. degree in electrical engineering (power system) from NIT, Durgapur, and Jadavpur University, Kolkata in the year 2005 and 2015 respectively. He has published 12 international/national journal research papers and 10 international/national conference papers. He is a reviewer of prestigious journals of IET, Elsevier, IEEE Access, Taylor & Francis, and Springer. His areas of interest are - power system optimization, optimization techniques, power system operation and control, and hydro-thermal scheduling problems.

Rajeswari D. received her Ph.D. in Information and Communication Engineering from Anna University in 2017. Prior to joining SRM Institute of Science and Technology, Kattankulathur as an Assistant Professor at the Dept. of Computer Science and Engineering in 2018, she worked as an Assistant Professor at RMK Engineering College, Chennai from 2010 - 2018. Dr. Rajeswari is currently an Associate Professor in the Dept. of Data Science and Business Systems at SRMIST. She has an intensive research experience in the field of Cloud Computing, Big Data Analytics, Internet of Things, and Machine Learning. She holds 1 Patent and has published 30+ papers in journals and conferences. She received International Travel Support (ITS) from SERB to attend the conference in USA on may 2023.

Kswaminathan Kalyanaraman working as a teaching faculty in University College of Engineering Pattukkottai (Anna University). He has more than 10 teaching experience. The area interest is VLSI, Reconfigurable computing, networking, IoT, WSN. He published more than 15 research papers in various national and international journals. He is a member of various international technical bodies like ESRII, IFERP, Internet Society IEI, ISTE, IAENG.

Jenifer Mahilraj is working as an Associate Professor in the Department of Artificial Intelligence and Data Science at NPR college of Engineering and Technology,Natham. She received her B.Tech degree in Information Technology and M.E. degree in Computer science Engineering from Karpagam University. She has done her doctoral Studies at MAHER University, Chennai, India. She is in teaching profession more than 11 years. She has published around 24 research papers and presented many paper in various international conferences.she is holding 8 patents and published 2 books. Her main area of specialization includes Machine Learning, Data science and Artificial Intelligence.

Raajan N. R. received B.E. degree in Electronics and Communication Engineering from Bharathidasan University, Trichy, India, M.E. degree in Communication Systems from Anna University, Chennai, India, Ph. D. from SASTRA University Thanjavur, India. He joined SASTRA University, Thanjavur, Tamil Nadu, India as a Lecturer in the Department of Electronics and Communication Engineering since 2005 and is now Senior Assistant Professor, His research interests include Augmented reality (AR), Image & Video Processing, Hydrophone Communication, Signal processing and Wireless Network Security. He has authored a chapter on book titled speech enhancement, modeling and recognition algorithms and applications," Mathematical modeling of speech production and its application to noise cancellation". He has published 120+ Research articles in National & International journals and 30+ IEEE conference papers with 2 BEST paper awards. He also hold Certificate of Appreciation from TI in 2007 for Project presentation, Guiding "Automatic assistance for physically challenging people" and won the first prize. Recently He also served as TPC member & review member for 3 IEEE & Elsevier supported International Conferences apart from 3+ peer reviewed Journals.

Athish Parthiban is a senior-year student at SRM Institute of Science and Technology, Kattankulathur pursuing a B.Tech in Computer Science and Business Systems. In 2019 he was recruited as an Office Bearer by the Student Chapter of the IET at SRMIST and is currently the Chairperson of SRM IET on Campus. Athish also leads the Technical Team of The Directorate of Student Affairs at SRMIST as its Convener. He primarily writes and presents widely on Cloud Computing, Distributed Computing, Deep Learning Algorithms, and DevOps. He holds accolades from various hackathons and is a finalist in the software edition of the All-India Level Smart India Hackathon 2022.

Regan R. is working as an Assistant Professor in the department of Computer Science and Engineering at University College of Engineering Villupuram, Anna University. He has over 15 years of experience in educational institution. He has to his credit 13 publications in National/International conferences and journals and published 5 international books. His areas of interest include Mobile Ad hoc Networks, Wireless Sensor Networks, Wireless security.

Srinivasan Rajendran received a Bachelor's degree in Computer Science and Engineering from Anna University in 2010 and a Master's degree in Computer Science and Engineering from Anna University in 2012. He is currently an Assistant Professor in the Department of Computing Technologies at SRM Institute of Science and Technology, Chennai, India.

Sree Nandha S. S. is a final year student at SRM Institute of Science and Technology in Kattankulathur studying Computer Science and Business Systems. He released a study on train track crack classification using lenet -5 architecture in 2022. He mostly publishes and speaks about Data Analytics, Distributed

Computing, Statistical Modeling, including the development of machine learning and deep learning models in automotive industry. He has received awards from numerous hackathons. His contributions to crop prediction and football match prediction projects are among his most notable accomplishments.

Bibhudatta Sahoo is a Professor in the Department of Computer Science & Engineering at the National Institute of Technology Rourkela, India, where he has been a faculty member since 2000. He is a Communication and Computing Research Group member and a Professor in charge of the Cloud Computing Research Laboratory. His research interests lie in Parallel and Distributed Systems, Cloud Computing, Sensor Networks, the Internet of Things, Software-defined networks, Multicore Architecture, 5g Networks, Web Engineering and Algorithmic Engineering. Dr Sahoo is a Fellow of the Institution of Electronics and Telecommunication Engineers (IETE), the Computer Society of India (CSI), the Indian Society for Technical Education (ISTE), the Indian Science Congress Association (ISCA), and the Orissa Science Academy. Dr Sahoo is also a member of IEEE, and professional member of ACM, and the author or co-author of over 250 publications, book chapters, research monographs, and books.

Minakshi Sharma has received her Ph.D. degree in Computer Science from Banasthali University, Rajasthan India, in 2015. In 2017, she joined as an Assistant Professor in NIT Kurukshetra in the Department of Computer Engineering. She has more than 10 papers to her credit in national and international conferences and journals. Her research interests include Image Processing, Deep Learning, Artificial Intelligence, Neural Network, Fuzzy Logic Based systems.

Sunil Sharma has received his Ph.D Degree in Electronics and Communication Engineering from NIT Kurukshetra, India in 2018. Currently, he is working as an Assistant Professor in the department of Electronics and Communication Engineering in National Institute of Technology, Kurukshetra, India. His research interest includes Signal Processing and Communication Theory & Systems. He has more than 20 research papers to his credit in national and international conferences and journals.

Tripti Sharma has achieved her M.Tech. and Ph. D. degree in the field of Low Power VLSI Circuits Design. She has 21 years of teaching experience along with intense research interest. Her research interests include Digital & Analog low power VLSI circuits and Double Gate MOSFET Circuit Design & Analysis. She has more than 80 publications in International Journals and National/ International Conferences in the areas of high-performance integrated circuits and emerging semiconductor Technologies. She has also authored 07 technical books useful for research in the field of digital circuit design and also has 01 patent granted and 03 published to help the society. This all research contribution of her value for 291 Google Citation Index. She is on the editorial panel of International journal published from Kenya as well as reviewer of the SCI indexed journals such as International Journal of Electronics, Taylor & Francis Group and Journal of Circuits, Systems and Computers, World Scientific Publishing Company. She also reviewed several research papers for the IEEE conferences.

Jatin Soni has completed his B.E. in electrical engineering from BVM engineering college, Anand and M.E.. in electrical power system from L.E. college, Morbi in 2016 and 2018 respectively. He is currently pursuing PhD in Institute of technology, Nirma University. His research interest is optimization technique, artificial intelligence and Economic load dispatch.

Avudaiappan T. is working as Associate Professor in Computer Science and Engineering department since January 2017 at K. Ramakrishnan College of Technology, he completed his B.E. degree from the Department of Computer Science and Engineering, Jayaraj Annapackiam CSI college of Engineering from Anna University, Chennai in the year 2010. He has completed his M.E. Degree from the Department of Computer Science and Engineering from Karpagam University, Coimbatore in the year 2012. He completed his Ph.D., Degree from the Department of Computer Science and Engineering, Manonmaniam Sundaranar University, Tirunelveli 2016. He Published more than 15 international journals and international conferences.

Nithya V. is working as Teaching Fellow in the department of CSE in University College of Engineering, Villupuram, and Anna University, India. she has over 9 years of experience in educational institution. She has more than 8 publications in International Journals, presented papers in International conferences and published 3 international books. Her area of interest includes Web Application Security, Information Security, Artificial Intelligence and Automata Theory.

Index

Y

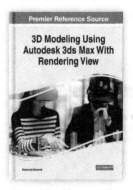

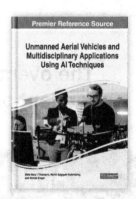

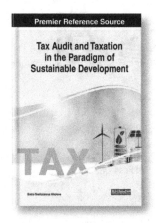

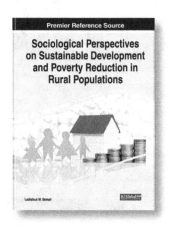

ed States
Publisher Services

Printed in the Uni
by Baker & Taylor

Printed in the United States
by Baker & Taylor Publisher Services